The Fiction of Truth

The Fiction of Truth

Structures of Meaning in Narrative and Dramatic Allegory

by CAROLYNN VAN DYKE

Cornell University Press

ITHACA AND LONDON

ITHACA AND LONDON

ITHACA AND LONDON

ITHACA AND LONDON

Cornell University Press gratefully acknowledges a grant from the Andrew W. Mellon Foundation that aided in bringing this book to publication.

First published 1985 by Cornell University Press.
Published in the United Kingdom by Cornell University Press Ltd., London.

International Standard Book Number 0-8014-1760-0
Library of Congress Catalog Card Number 84-15607

Printed in the United States of America

Librarians: Library of Congress cataloging information appears on the last page of the book.

The paper in this book is acid-free and meets the guidelines for permanence and durability of the Committee on Production Guidelines for Book Longevity of the Council on Library Resources.

For my parents

Contents

Preface

After bearing for two centuries the stigma imposed on it by the German and English Romantics, allegory has recently been embraced by various critics for various reasons. Because it predates both romanticism and realism, it attracts those who are disillusioned with those modes. Because it is said to subvert the link between sign and meaning, it interests critics who explore the problems and complexities of linguistic reference. And because it is supposed to be didactic, it is acclaimed by readers who seek in literature values beyond the narrowly aesthetic.

But renewed interest does not guarantee clarified perception. The Romantics and their successors regarded allegory as ungenuine: the allegorist, in their view, translates an abstract message into fabricated imagery or tells a story as if it were a different story. Recent writers reverse the judgment conveyed by such definitions of allegory but do not discredit the definitions themselves. Many of them agree that allegory says something other than it means; a few others reject that formulation but substitute for it an analysis that blurs the distinction between allegory and other nonmimetic modes. Neither approach sheds much light on the continuities and changes in the form that dominated European writing for over a thousand years. We need, therefore, to redefine allegory with full respect for its integrity, both semiotic and historical. This book attempts that task.

9

No project of such scope is carried out in isolation. This one has been from the beginning a conversation with previous writers. Two in particular have contributed more than my text and notes may indicate: Rosemond Tuve, whose *Allegorical Imagery* is to my mind our most perceptive and most underrated book on allegory, and E. Talbot Donaldson, whose work remains for me a model of brilliant, balanced, and loving criticism.

Several presses have permitted extended citations of copyrighted works. I am grateful to Harvard University Press for permission to use H. J. Thomson's translation of the *Psychomachia* of Prudentius; to Princeton University Press for permission to quote from Charles R. Dahlberg's translation of the *Romance of the Rose* and from Charles Singleton's edition of the *Divine Comedy;* to Houghton Mifflin Company for allowing me to reproduce passages from three plays in *Medieval Drama,* edited by David M. Bevington; to The Bodley Head Ltd. for permission to use John D. Sinclair's translation of the *Divine Comedy;* and to The Johns Hopkins University Press for allowing me to quote from *The Works of Edmund Spenser: A Variorum Edition.* A version of part of Chapter 3 appears, as "The Intangible and Its Image: Allegorical Discourse and the Cast of *Everyman,*" in *Acts of Interpretation: The Text in Its Contexts, 700–1600,* edited by Mary J. Carruthers and Elizabeth D. Kirk (Norman, Okla.: Pilgrim Books, 1982).

For a summer research grant that supported my work on the definition of allegory, I am grateful to Lafayette College. At an earlier stage of my work the outstanding collection of the Cleveland Public Library provided essential support of another kind. I appreciate the help of Roxanne Lalande of the French Department at Lafayette College in checking my translations. I also thank the staff at Lafayette's academic computer center for their expertise and patience, which helped to make the physical production of the manuscript exciting and satisfying in itself.

Whatever is valuable in *The Fiction of Truth* reflects the contributions of my students, colleagues, and friends. The book began as a graduate seminar at Case Western Reserve University in the fall of 1977; I am grateful to the students in English 507 for undertaking those first explorations with me. Roger Salomon, former head of that department, provided generous professional support—and some astute suggestions for reading in a field far from his own. Julia Dietrich of the University of Louisville offered not only her own provocative comments but also the chance to present my ideas in a conference session at the Medieval Institute. Finally, I owe a boundless and welcome debt of gratitude to Ann Carter, who was throughout this book's writing its ideal reader.

CAROLYNN VAN DYKE

Easton, Pennsylvania

The Fiction of Truth

Introduction:
Allegory as Other

In his massive and rehabilitative *Allegory: The Theory of a Symbolic Mode,* Angus Fletcher remarks that allegory has often been used as a scapegoat by critics eager "to praise some other procedure they prefer." Support for his statement leaps to the mind of anyone familiar with allusions to allegory during the past two hundred years. Goethe defended symbolism by distinguishing it sharply from allegory, which is not, he suggested, really poetic. His position was transmitted to nineteenth-century English and American Romantics by Coleridge; in the early twentieth century, C. S. Lewis' designation of symbolism as a "mode of thought" and allegory as a "mode of expression" reinforced, perhaps inadvertently, his readers' tendency to link the allegorical with the ungenuine.[1] Other writers have replaced "symbol" with some other positive term, such as "myth," "archetype," "true metaphor," or "concrete universal."[2] But what-

1. Angus Fletcher, *Allegory: The Theory of a Symbolic Mode* (Ithaca: Cornell University Press, 1964), p. 304; Johann Wolfgang von Goethe, *Maximen und Reflexionen* 749–52, in *Goethes Werke: Hamburger Ausgabe,* 14 vols. (Hamburg: Christian Wegner, 1953), XII, 470–71; C. S. Lewis, *The Allegory of Love: A Study in Medieval Tradition* (Oxford: Clarendon Press, 1936), p. 48.

2. See, for instance, Carl Jung, *The Archetypes and the Collective Unconscious,* 2d ed., trans. R. F. C. Hull, Bollingen Series XX (Princeton: Princeton University Press, 1969), pp. 6, 173; Philip Wheelwright, *The Burning Fountain: A Study in the Language of Symbolism* (Bloomington: Indiana University Press, 1954), pp. 87–88;

ever the designation of its opposite, allegory in those pairings is the
negative term. Mechanical instead of organic, fanciful and cold instead of imaginative and spontaneous, an amusement rather than a
revelation, allegory readily degenerates, we are told, into "un genre
de littérature complètement faux."[3]

Of course, beyond the literary period dominated by Romantic theory we find a reversal of that judgment. Not only was allegory highly
valued in the Middle Ages, but, as Murray Krieger points out, it has
also become a positive term for many poststructuralists.[4] But as the
evaluation changes, something more fundamental persists: an assumption that allegory is a secondary mode, logically or chronologi-
cally if not preferentially. For the Middle Ages it was a method of
exegesis operating upon a prior text or upon a "literal" story within a
present text. Because the prior text or story carries its own pre-
allegorical meaning, allegory appears as the alternative (usually the
superior alternative) to a more obvious, more common way of reading or writing. Modern writers looking back on medieval allegory
regard it as the "instrument of accommodation and compromise"
which rationalized and redirected earlier discourse. It is often said to
have originated, in fact, as a technique for demonstrating the compatibility of Homeric narrative with the ideas of later writers. Thus
Northrop Frye finds allegory the mode characteristic of the second
phase of literary history.[5] Nor is the status of allegory as a posterior
mode simply a matter of its historical position. The Romantics and

---

and Owen Barfield, *Poetic Diction: A Study in Meaning*, 3d ed. (Middletown, Conn.:
Wesleyan University Press, 1973), p. 201.

3. Samuel Taylor Coleridge, "Allegory" (Lecture III), in *Miscellaneous Criticism*,
ed. Thomas Middleton Raysor (Cambridge: Harvard University Press, 1936), p. 30;
William Butler Yeats, "Edmund Spenser" (1902) and "William Blake and His Il-
lustrations to the *Divine Comedy*" (1924), in *Essays and Introductions* (London:
Macmillan, 1961), pp. 382, 116; Gaston Paris, *Esquisse historique de la littérature
française au moyen age* (Paris: Armand Colin, 1907), p. 196.

4. Murray Krieger, "'A Waking Dream': The Symbolic Alternative to Allegory,"
in *Allegory, Myth, and Symbol*, ed. Morton W. Bloomfield (Cambridge: Harvard
University Press, 1981), pp. 1–22.

5. Fletcher, *Allegory*, p. 332; Edwin Honig, *Dark Conceit: The Making of Allegory* (1959; rpt. Cambridge: Walker-DeBerry, Boar's Head, 1960), p. 171. For the
idea that allegory began with adaptations of Homer, see, for instance, Roger Hinks,
Myth and Allegory in Ancient Art (1939; rpt. Nendeln, Liechtenstein: Kraus Reprint,
1968), pp. 62–63; and J. Tate, "On the History of Allegorism," *Classical Quarterly*
28 (1934):105–7. Northrop Frye's remarks are in "Literary History," *NLH* 12
(1981):223.

their successors, writing not about literary history but about aesthetic psychology, portray allegory as the rationalization of or the abstraction from a direct intuitive perception. What was indirect and therefore closer to recondite truth for the medieval exegete is indirect and therefore less authentic for the Kantian critic. More recent literary theorists have included in their great "deconstruction" of Romantic thought an attack on the attack on allegory, but their project preserves the role of allegory as a literary pariah. Thus they extend in a new direction a tradition as old as Western literary history: the treatment of allegory as a despised or celebrated alternative to the dominant modes of signifying. Whether or not "other-speech" is an accurate etymological definition for *allegoria,* allegory has always functioned among literary kinds as the Other.

Like most versions of the Other, allegory seems to need no definition; we feel that we recognize it intuitively. Thus the term is often used without definition, and such generalizations as are offered usually assume preliminary agreement about what does and does not fall within the category. But, as is also typical of the Other, agreement about the identity of allegory extends only to cursory definitions; beyond that, disparities proliferate. For instance, the bold distinction between symbol and allegory is oddly unstable. "Between 1800 and 1832," writes Paul de Man, "under the influence of Creuzer and Schelling, Friedrich Schlegel substitutes the word 'symbolic' for 'allegorical' in the oft-quoted passage of the 'Gespräch über die Poesie': '. . . alle Schönheit ist Allegorie.' "6 One suspects that Schlegel had changed not his ideas about beauty but his definition of "allegory." Throughout the Romantic period, certain American writers persisted in using "allegory" for the phenomena that their English counterparts were praising as allegory's antithesis, symbolism.7 That the distinction itself is unstable, not just the terminology, is attested by such

6. Paul de Man, "The Rhetoric of Temporality," in *Interpretation: Theory and Practice,* ed. Charles S. Singleton (Baltimore: Johns Hopkins University Press, 1969), pp. 175–76.

7. See Emerson's statement in "Nature" (*The Complete Works of Ralph Waldo Emerson* [Boston: Houghton Mifflin, 1903], I, 31): "A man conversing in earnest, if he watch his intellectual processes, will find that a material image more or less luminous arises in his mind, contemporaneous with every thought, which furnishes the vestment of the thought. Hence, good writing and brilliant discourse are perpetual allegories. This imagery is spontaneous. It is the blending of experience with the present action of the mind. It is proper creation."

statements as these: "We may be misled if we start the critique of the 'Mariner' and 'Kubla Khan' with the disjunction of allegory from symbol in mind. For all allegory involves symbolism. . . ."; "To some extent, myth is allegory; or, perhaps, allegory is myth; but both modes of imaginative thought are little more than one or more symbols with positive or negative value attached to some natural object and provided with a predicate."[8]

Similar reversals and coalescences confound another opposition that appears to define allegory, the opposition of "literal" and "allegorical." We are often told that certain kinds of allegory are contained in the "literal level" or that a text switches between "literal" and "allegorical." We may have difficulty distinguishing those terms even hypothetically, however, since "literal" refers sometimes to a set of explicit concretions that we are to "allegorize" and sometimes to the implicit abstract statement that the author has allegorized *into* a set of explicit concretions.[9] And if allegory's antinomies are unstable, so are its relations with potential synonyms. Personification, assumed by many to be the surest sign of allegory, is dismissed by Bernard Spivack as incidental and declared by Ellen Leyburn to be "contrary to the essential conception of concealment which is basic in allegory."[10]

Those confusions concern allegory primarily in its character as a procedure or device. As Edwin Honig and others remind us, the term may also refer to a genre, a kind of interpretation, or even a philosophy.[11] Each of those acceptances in turn looks blurry under scrutiny. Generic or "modal" definitions that are plausible in themselves turn out to provide little illumination of allegorical texts and to include forms that we intuitively regard as unallegorical: detective stories,

8. Humphry House, cited in Louis MacNeice, *Varieties of Parable* (Cambridge: Cambridge University Press, 1965), p. 67; Don Cameron Allen, *Mysteriously Meant: The Rediscovery of Pagan Symbolism and Allegorical Interpretation in the Renaissance* (Baltimore: Johns Hopkins University Press, 1970), p. vii.

9. On the coincidence of literal and allegorical, see Morton W. Bloomfield, "Allegory as Interpretation," *NLH* 3 (1972):313–17. For contradictory uses of "literal," see Owen Barfield, "The Meaning of the Word 'Literal,'" in *Metaphor and Symbol*, ed. Lionel C. Knights and Basil Cottle (London: Butterworth, 1960), pp. 48, 57; and J. A. Scott, "Dante's Allegory," *Romance Philology* 26 (1972):584.

10. Bernard Spivack, *Shakespeare and the Allegory of Evil: The History of a Metaphor in Relation to His Major Villains* (New York: Columbia University Press, 1958), p. 96; Ellen Douglass Leyburn, *Satiric Allegory: Mirror of Man* (New Haven: Yale University Press, 1956), pp. 3–4.

11. Honig, pp. 14–15, 179–80.

modern experimental fiction, the General Prologue to the *Canterbury Tales,* even psychoanalytic discourse. Sometimes, indeed, allegory is explicitly made conterminous with discourse itself, so that the category is enlarged beyond usefulness.[12] On the other hand, each of the works usually grouped under the genus "allegory" has at one time or another been called "not really allegorical" by its devotees, until the category is left virtually empty.[13] Nearly the same thing happens when one writer says first that allegory is a way of reading and then that all interpretation is allegorical, while others continue to insist that allegorical interpretation is merely a spurious way of reading.[14] Finally, when allegory is called a "conceptual framework," it sometimes names a perception of continuity in the universe and sometimes a belief in radical discontinuity.[15] "I have found 'allegorical' a splendid term to cover up one's ignorance," writes Arnold Williams, "but a useless one for communicating any valuable information."[16]

12. Allegory is taken to include detective fiction by Fletcher, experimental novels by Maureen Quilligan (*The Language of Allegory* [Ithaca: Cornell University Press, 1979]), and psychoanalysis by Joel Fineman ("The Structure of Allegorical Desire," in *Allegory and Representation,* ed. Stephen J. Greenblatt [Baltimore: Johns Hopkins University Press, 1981], pp. 26–60). Greenblatt, in the Preface to *Allegory and Representation* (p. viii), makes allegory conterminous with discourse.

13. Erich Auerbach, for instance, demonstrates that the *Divine Comedy* is figural, not allegorical; Henri Talon, following Coleridge, finds that the characters of *The Pilgrim's Progress* "have too much flesh and blood to be merely allegorical"; C. S. Lewis declares the second and major portion of the *Romance of the Rose* not allegorical but literal; and Graham Hough expresses what has come to be a consensus that *The Faerie Queene* is not continuous allegory. See Auerbach, "Figura" (1944), trans. Ralph Manheim, in *Scenes from the Drama of Western Literature* (New York: Meridian Books, 1959), pp. 60–76; Talon, *John Bunyan: The Man and His Works,* trans. Barbara Wall (Cambridge: Harvard University Press, 1951), p. 215; Lewis, *Allegory of Love,* p. 141; Hough, *A Preface to "The Faerie Queene"* (1962; rpt. New York: W. W. Norton, 1963), p. 108.

14. See Northrop Frye, "Allegory," in *Princeton Encyclopedia of Poetry and Poetics;* and, for the opposing position, E. Talbot Donaldson, "Patristic Exegesis in the Criticism of Medieval Literature: The Opposition," in *Critical Approaches to Medieval Literature,* ed. Dorothy Bethurum (New York: Columbia University Press, 1960), pp. 1–26.

15. For the first position, see Thomas P. Roche, Jr., *The Kindly Flame: A Study of the Third and Fourth Books of Spenser's "Faerie Queene"* (Princeton: Princeton University Press, 1964), pp. 7–8; for the second, see T. K. Seung, *Cultural Thematics: The Formation of the Faustian Ethos* (New Haven: Yale University Press, 1976), p. 175.

16. Arnold Williams, "The English Moral Play before 1500," *Annuale Mediaevale* 4 (1963):9.

Perhaps it is the nature of the Other to be both self-defining and undefinable. Perhaps the phenomena that function as Other do so not because of shared characteristics but because of their opposition to whatever we regard as prior or basic. But such an account of the Other is not a sufficient analysis of allegory. Most of us would still grant, as I will assume in this study, that certain texts that are almost universally called "allegories" share intrinsic features that distinguish them from other texts. Even if that were not true, and allegory were only a definitional heuristic, it would merit further investigation, for the ways in which we identify and use the Other, in literature as in any other signifying system, can tell us a great deal about the system itself.

Of the kinds of phenomenon to which "allegory" can refer—tropes, texts, ways of reading, and philosophies—this study is based in the second. That is, I will assume that allegory is a literary genre. The assumption cannot be justified until my generic definition of allegory has been explained and tested, but I derive it in a preliminary way from the long-standing habit of designating as "allegories" certain narrative and dramatic works, beginning with Prudentius' *Psychomachia* and ending with Bunyan's *Pilgrim's Progress*. But while pursuing the generic basis of those works, I will not neglect altogether the other uses of "allegory," for it seems unwise to separate absolutely that which our terminology has joined: surely there are important connections among allegory as rhetorical device, as genre, as interpretation, and as philosophy.

One methodological advantage of regarding allegory as a genre is that proposed definitions can be checked against various examples. I will first formulate my definition through a reading of the poem commonly regarded as the earliest and simplest allegory, the *Psychomachia,* and then elaborate it through the reading of several other texts. In so doing I will be rejecting the argument of certain contemporary theorists that the proper study of literary structures or "codes" does not include readings of texts. A literary genre, for my purposes, can indeed be identified by a set of conventions based on an inferable semiotic code, but the code and the conventions do not fully constitute the genre. The genre is also the texts that realize the code—or realize it to a significant degree (an admittedly and inevitably subjective qualification). To rest content with a study of the codes themselves is to falsify the objects under study, whether those objects are individual texts, genres, or literature as a whole. With regard to the first, Tzvetan Todorov is eloquent: "A work of art (or of science) . . . cannot be presented as the simple product of a pre-existing combinatorial system; it is that too, but at the same time it transforms the system of elements, it establishes a new code of which it is the first (the only) message. A work which would be the pure product of a *pre-existing* system does not exist." Stephen Greenblatt reminds us also that discourse itself "is improvisation, both an entry into and a deflection of existing strategies of representation."[17] The definition that I propose in Chapter 1 will identify both a semiotic code that distinguishes allegorical works and the ways in which Prudentius uses that code. Subsequent chapters will suggest the ways in which other writers use and therefore alter the code, until it can no longer usefully be regarded as the same code.

It should already be apparent that this study draws heavily on the work of others. In particular, it grows out of a reinvestigation of allegory which began with the publication in 1957 of Edwin Honig's *Dark Conceit: The Making of Allegory* and has continued through a number of other outstanding books. Predictably, however, I find shortcomings in the work of my predecessors. I will explain many of my reservations in the pages that follow, but they can be summarized here.

Students of allegory have always had to confront in some way the persistent identification of allegory as Other. Two obvious responses present themselves: to accept the identification or to deny it. The first option obliges the conscientious reader to approach allegory in a way quite unlike the methods used for other texts—to engage, for instance, in unremitting translation from apparent to actual meaning. Since that obligation soon becomes intolerable and unrewarding, wise readers usually shed it without notice, even at the cost of inconsistency between dogma and practice. Thus Angus Fletcher virtually ignores throughout most of his study the conventional view of allegory that he endorses in his introduction.[18] The alternative approach,

17. Tzvetan Todorov, "The Ghosts of Henry James," in *The Poetics of Prose*, trans. Richard Howard (Ithaca: Cornell University Press, 1977), p. 185; Greenblatt, Preface, p. xiii.

18. Fletcher invokes the conventional definition in several places throughout *Allegory*, but most succinctly on p. 2: "Allegory says one thing and means another." But

to disregard or repudiate the identification of allegory as Other, also
has its dangers. Assuming, quite properly, that allegories are susceptible to the same questions and techniques as are other literary works,
such commentators as Edwin Honig and Stephen Barney leave us
with valuable insights into allegories but with a weak grasp of the
distinctive qualities of allegory. They sometimes illustrate their generalizations with texts whose differences from self-denominated medieval and Renaissance allegory are more striking than their resemblances. A similar injudicious opening of allegory's borders weakens
the only study to date that has set out to redefine allegory as a genre,
Maureen Quilligan's *Language of Allegory*. Quilligan's definition—
"the generation of narrative structure out of wordplay" (p. 22)—
applies admittedly to the novels of Kafka, Hawthorne, and Pynchon
and arguably to texts as diverse as *Othello* and *Alice in Wonderland*.
If, as I will try to show in Chapter 1, Quilligan is correct in attacking
traditional assumptions about allegory, then she is also correct in
attempting an inductive redefinition. But we can legitimately expect
such a redefinition to distinguish between allegorical and non-
allegorical works more clearly than Quilligan's does.

It must be conceded at the outset that my own definition will not
fully meet that expectation, either. Literary definition is inherently an
endless task, for part of what it attempts to classify is the unfixable
perceptions of readers. This study is intended, therefore, as a contri-
bution to the uncompletable reclamation of that Other which still
defines us.

---

he incorporates that definition into his analysis in only one chapter, "Cosmic Imagery"—and only in part of that one. Elsewhere he does not distinguish between what is
said and what is meant; he offers encyclopedic and penetrating comments on what is
said *and* meant.

Part I

THE PARADIGM

1 The *Psychomachia* and the Nature of "Pure" Allegory

The Meaning of Other-Speech

If allegory has always functioned as Other among literary kinds, it has done so without explicit notice. "Otherness" has, however, long been explicitly associated with allegory in a different way—as the principle of meaning within allegory itself. The term clearly derives from *allos* and was defined by rhetoricians as *inversio* or *alieniloquium*. For Quintilian, *allegoria* is the alienation of words from meaning: "Allegory . . . presents either one thing in words and another in meaning, or even something quite opposed." That is the definition offered by rhetoricians through the Middle Ages and the Renaissance; Richard Sherry, for instance, writes, "*Allegoria,* the seconde parte of Trope is an inuersion of wordes, where it is one in wordes, and another in sentence or meanynge." And whatever confusions attend modern analyses of allegory, nearly all writers on the subject begin with Quintilian's definition. "In the simplest terms," writes Angus Fletcher, "allegory says one thing and means another."[1]

1. The definition of allegory as *inversio* is exemplified by several rhetoricians cited in Fletcher, *Allegory,* p. 2n. *Alieniloquium* is a term first used for *allegoria* by Isidore of Seville; his definition and that of Quintilian are cited by William J. Kennedy in "Irony, Allegoresis, and Allegory in Virgil, Ovid, and Dante," *Arcadia* 7 (1972):117–18. Quintilian's seminal definition is from his *Institutio Oratoria,* VIII, vi, 44. See Richard Sherry, *A Treatise of Schemes and Tropes* (1550; rpt. Gainesville, Fla.: Scholars' Facsimiles and Reprints, 1961), p. 45; Fletcher, *Allegory,* p. 2.

In serving so many generations, Quintilian's definition has of course been elaborated. Saying one thing and meaning another can easily be taken as a definition of figurative speech in general, and so students who are not content to include irony, sarcasm, antiphrasis, and even metaphor under "allegory," as some rhetoricians do, have added several *differentiae*. First, allegory is extended, usually the basis for an entire narrative; second, the words and meaning in allegory correspond not antithetically, as in irony, but on parallel planes. "We can, then, call allegory the particular method of saying one thing in terms of another in which the two levels of meaning are sustained and in which the two levels correspond in pattern of relationship among details."[2] Having said that much, the student of allegory can then go on to define the relationship between levels. The first is explicit, the second implicit; the first is always concrete but the second is often abstract; the first is a fiction, while the second is "real" or in some way more important. "An Allegory is a Fable or Story," according to an eighteenth-century writer, "in which, under imaginary Persons or Things, is shadow'd some real Action or instructive Moral."[3] There may in fact be more than two of these levels, but the first is always the "literal level" while the others are collectively termed "allegorical" and function together as secondary. The greater importance of the second level or levels—"once seen, it is [or they are] felt strongly to be the final intention behind the primary meaning"—immediately suggests the way in which allegories ought to be read.[4] Michael Murrin explains that for Renaissance scholars, "it is the critic's function to fill in the unspoken part of the analogy when he examines an allegory." Alexander Pope mocks his contemporaries' zeal in executing that function: "[The Moral and Allegory] you may extract out of the Fable afterwards, at your leisure: Be sure you *strain* them sufficiently." In our day, Northrop Frye has said that allegorical texts prescribe their own commentaries, and J. Hillis Miller calls them pictures that need legends. Fletcher provides a confident summary: "Allegories are based on parallels between two levels of being that correspond to each other, the one supposed by the reader, the other literally presented in the fable. This is well known."[5]

2. Leyburn, *Satiric Allegory*, p. 6.
3. John Hughes, cited in Fletcher, *Allegory*, p. 237n.
4. Fletcher, *Allegory*, p. 8.
5. Michael Murrin, *The Veil of Allegory: Some Notes toward a Theory of Allegorical Rhetoric in the English Renaissance* (Chicago: University of Chicago Press,

The "well-known" definition of allegory can be linked closely to the treatment of allegory as Other among modes of discourse. In saying one thing and meaning another, allegory "destroys the normal expectation we have about language, that our words 'mean what they say.' When we predicate quality x of person Y, Y really is what our predication says he is (or we assume so); but allegory would turn Y into something other (*allos*) than what the open and direct statement tells the reader."[6] Other-speech is abnormal language.

Recent literary theorists have offered what might appear to be the first widespread challenge to these received ideas about allegory. They argue that allegory's indirect signification is actually the property of all language, for no statement is open and direct; "words do not signify the presence of things but their absence."[7] Allegory bases itself frankly on the disruption of signifier and signified and therefore renounces the illusions of semantic unity and directness promoted by such modes as symbolism. "Thus generalized, allegory rapidly acquires the status of trope of tropes, representative of the figurality of all language, of the distance between signifier and signified, and, correlatively, the response to allegory becomes representative of critical activity *per se*."[8]

Examined more closely, however, the poststructuralist discussion of allegory is not a substantial reformulation. It leaves untouched the assumption that allegory operates on parallel levels, one of which is now called the "signifier" while the other, implicit level is the "signified." That assumption subverts the poststructuralists' attempt to normalize allegory as the condition of all textuality, for it sets up an unacknowledged equivoque. In language generally, for the poststructuralist, the signified is forever irrecoverable, an "absence" created by its expulsion from the signifier;[9] but that is not the kind of distance between signifier and signified established by allegorical parallelism.

1969), p. 57; Alexander Pope, *The Art of Sinking in Poetry*, ed. Edna Leake Steeves (New York: King's Crown Press, 1952), p. 82; Northrop Frye, *Anatomy of Criticism* (Princeton: Princeton University Press, 1957), p. 90; J. Hillis Miller, "The Two Allegories," in *Allegory, Myth, and Symbol*, ed. Bloomfield, p. 360; and Fletcher, *Allegory*, pp. 172, 323, 113.

6. Fletcher, *Allegory*, p. 2.

7. Todorov, "Speech According to Constant," in *Poetics of Prose*, p. 101.

8. Fineman, "Structure of Allegorical Desire," p. 27; see also Krieger, "'A Waking Dream,'" pp. 5–7.

9. Fineman, pp. 44–45.

Allegory has always been understood to separate signifier from signified merely rhetorically—that is, provisionally and reversibly.
When Dante declares that a poet must be able to disclose the implicit
true meaning of a figure of speech, he is speaking particularly of
personification, allegory's most common trope.[10] Thus other-speech
as traditionally conceived actually guarantees the eventual discovery
of genuine meaning and of congruence between signifiers and sig-
nifieds. We must remember that allegory belongs to Derrida's "epoch
of the logos," in which the distance between signifier and signified is a
function of their homology and assumes the existence of a transcen-
dental signified.[11] In simpler terms, when we hunt for second meanings we assume that they exist and can be deduced from the "literal"
signs. Moreover, language that operated on parallel levels would also
conceal any disjunction of meaning that existed within the first or
literal level, for readers would take the significance of that level for
granted when they set out to look beyond it. In short, if language in
general is now said to be characterized by an irreversible disjunction
of signifier and signified, allegory as traditionally defined will still be
Other, but for a new reason: it deconstructs or conceals that disjunction under a second-order signification. Poststructuralist critics have
not challenged our long-standing assumption that allegory is abnormal in involving a translation from one level of meaning to another.

Indirectly, however, poststructuralist ideas about language do constitute a challenge to the traditional definition of allegory. We have
seen that other-speech is the antithesis of the self-deconstructing literature celebrated by poststructuralists. A text that convinces us that its
ultimate signified is separate from its signifiers but fully recoverable
would be semiotically dishonest and naively logocentric. But perhaps
that kind of signification is posited not by allegory itself but merely by
our traditional conception of allegory. Deconstructionist critics tell us
that we habitually blind ourselves to problems of meaning, convincing ourselves through various subterfuges that language points uni-
vocally to real entities. The idea that there is some abnormal form of
discourse in which words do not mean what they say must be the

10. Dante Alighieri, *La Vita Nuova*, trans. Barbara Reynolds (Baltimore: Penguin,
1969), XXV, 81–84.
11. On the epoch of the *logos*, see Jacques Derrida, *Of Grammatology*, trans.
Gayatri Chakravorty Spivak (Baltimore: Johns Hopkins University Press, 1976), pp.
12–13, 18.

chief among those subterfuges, for it implies that words usually do mean what they say. Jonathan Culler suggests that philosophy "has always depended for its existence on . . . [setting] aside certain kinds of language as fictional or rhetorical, with an oblique and problematic relationship to truth." Those kinds of language have been termed "literary" by philosophers, according to Culler. But it seems to me that students of literature have carried out a similar strategy, and that the language we have set aside as rhetorical or oblique is what we term allegory. "Allegory" is for literature, as "literature" is for philosophy, the "derivative, problematical, nonserious" realm that constitutes by contrast a "pure, logical [or genuine] means of expression."[12] Our conception of allegory, no less than philosophy's notion of literary "feigning," is our self-validating fabrication.

"Quintilian was simply wrong," asserts Maureen Quilligan at the beginning of *The Language of Allegory* (p. 25). Her assertion sounds overweening, and so may my statement that the traditional definition of allegory is a fabrication. Is there no literature that does in fact say one thing and mean another?

That question must be answered in several ways. One is to examine in the light of Quintilian's definition a text that appears to represent allegory at its most typical. A likely candidate is the poem regarded by C. S. Lewis as the first full-scale allegory and more recently by Stephen Barney as a "pure allegory":[13] the *Psychomachia* of Prudentius.

Like allegory itself, the *Psychomachia* has enjoyed an unfortunate kind of success. Surviving in hundreds of manuscripts, many of them illustrated, and in countless medieval adaptations, it was unquestionably popular and influential in its age.[14] It is mentioned in virtually every modern work on allegory; like certain commercial products, it is so widely known that its name is now a common noun. But its currency has earned the *Psychomachia* neither careful examination nor approbation.[15] Twentieth-century critics usually dismiss the

12. Jonathan Culler, *The Pursuit of Signs: Semiotics, Literature, Deconstruction* (Ithaca: Cornell University Press, 1981), p. 222.
13. Stephen A. Barney, *Allegories of History, Allegories of Love* (Hamden, Conn.: Shoe String Press, Archon Books, 1979), p. 42.
14. See M. Lavarenne, ed. and trans., *Prudence* (Paris: Belles Lettres, 1943–48), II, 22–28; III, 25–46.
15. To my knowledge only one book has been published in English on the poem: Macklin Smith, *Prudentius' "Psychomachia": A Reexamination* (Princeton: Prince-

poem as intrinsically weak, attributing its success to a keen and un-
critical appetite for its genre:

> This work enjoyed a tremendous success in the Middle Ages, . . .
> even though it may seem quite mediocre to us today.[16]

> If, in fact, the mountains travailed and a mouse was born, [the histo-
> rian] must be content with the anticlimax. Such an anticlimax has to
> be faced when we reach the fully-fledged allegorical poem, the *Psy-
> chomachia* of Prudentius. . . . When the demand is very strong a poor
> thing in the way of supply will be greedily embraced.[17]

For such critics, the importance of the *Psychomachia* is its introduction in pure but crude form of a technique that later writers would
complicate and refine.[18]

   That technique is personification allegory, which everybody understands because it is so transparent—and dislikes for the same reason.
The poem can be summarized in a line or two: "The struggle of the
Vices and the Virtues . . . is represented as a great battle, in which
certain individual combats receive particular notice."[19] It can also be
diagrammed with geometric clarity. Each Vice (we expect that there
will be seven) is a warrior, appropriately distinguished as proud,
angry, envious, and so forth, and each fights and is slain by its opposing Virtue. The entire battle is fictional but represents, on a second
level, real moral conflict. One could reinvent the details oneself, if
there were nothing better to do, for pure personification allegory is "a
mere recreation of the fancy," "mechanically worked out like a
sleight-of-hand trick."[20] And a reader not discouraged by boredom

---

ton University Press, 1976). Although Smith is more sensitive to Prudentius' allegorical techniques than were previous commentators, he considers those techniques to
be of secondary importance; his focus is on the poem's Christian themes (see, e.g., p.
167). Several continental studies are cited by M.-R. Jung, *Etudes sur le poème allégorique en France au moyen age*, Romanica Helvetica, vol. 82 (Berne: Francke, 1971),
p. 25n.

   16. Jean Batany, *Approches du "Roman de la Rose"* (Paris: Bordas, 1973), p. 32.

   17. Lewis, *Allegory of Love*, p. 66.

   18. See Lavarenne, III, 45; Lewis, *Allegory of Love*, p. 68; and Robert Hollander,
Allegory in Dante's "Commedia" (Princeton: Princeton University Press, 1969), pp.
4–6.

   19. Batany, p. 32.

   20. John Ruskin, *The Stones of Venice*, 3 vols. (New York: John Wiley, 1872), II,
356; Honig, *Dark Conceit*, p. 46. Honig is paraphrasing Coleridge's remarks in
Miscellaneous Criticism, p. 30.

can, with minimal effort, see through the tricks to the serious meaning of the poem.

There has been some disagreement about the serious meaning. For certain early critics the poem was a veiled attack on fourth-century heresies, and to a more recent writer it "symbolizes . . . the conversion of humanity to the Christian ideal."[21] The clear consensus, however, has been that Prudentius used the form of an epic battle to represent what C. S. Lewis calls the *bellum intestinum* or, more generally, the inner life.[22] Such a reading appears to be confirmed by the poem's title, which is usually rendered as "the battle within [or 'for'] the soul." It also seems to salvage the "bizarre, verbose and grandiloquent narrative"[23] by asserting that, under the allegorical trappings, the poem's real subject is that unimpeachable modern theme, internal conflict.

Despite those advantages, reading the poem as the externalization of internal conflict is remarkably frustrating. We begin easily enough with the description of Faith, for her disordered dress, bare shoulders, untrimmed hair, and exposed arms correspond to the psychological corollaries of faith—namely, total dedication and holy recklessness.[24] Prudentius even allegorizes explicitly: "For the sudden glow of ambition, burning to enter fresh contests, takes no thought to gird on arms or armor" (ll. 24–25). We may be a bit puzzled, though, that his allegorization uses some of the same "fictional" terms—arms and armor—as the initial image; Prudentius is not keeping his levels separate. Faith is immediately challenged by "Worship-of-the-Old-Gods," appropriately described as fillet-decked and stained with sacrificial blood (pagan religion is decadent and contaminated by brutality). Because Cultura Deorum Veterum looks so much more like a public religion than an internal motion of the soul, it is difficult not to

21. Lavarenne, III, 9–10; Batany, p. 32.

22. Lewis, *Allegory of Love*, p. 68. Concurrence with Lewis can be found in Hollander, p. 6; Barney, p. 60; and Smith, p. 144. A few modern writers believe that the poem represents not just an internal battle but also the struggles of the early church (see M.-R. Jung, p. 27; Smith, p. 29). Nonetheless, they take the moral life of the individual to be the poem's primary reference.

23. Lavarenne, III, 45.

24. Prudentius (Aurelius Prudentius Clemens), *Psychomachia*, trans. H. J. Thomson, in *Prudentius*, vol. 1, Loeb Classical Library (Cambridge: Harvard University Press, 1949), ll. 22–23. Future citations are documented by line number in the text. All translations are Thomson's unless otherwise specified. They are reprinted by permission of the publishers.

conclude, with Marc-René Jung, that Prudentius has here lost his psychological focus—"and this already in the first battle."[25] We can adjust, though, by seeing the conflict between Christianity and paganism as occurring within the individual soul, as no doubt it did. Faith now kills her enemy:

> [Faith], rising higher, smites her foe's head down, with its fillet-decked brows, lays in the dust that mouth that was sated with the blood of beasts, and tramples the eyes under foot, squeezing them out in death. The throat is choked and the scant breath confined by the stopping of its passage, and long gasps make a hard and agonising death.   [Ll. 30–35]

Such a graphic passage challenges us to allegorize in detail. "Rising higher" is easy, but do the mouth, eyes, and throat of Cultura Deorum Veterum correspond to any psychological or spiritual principle? Tentative solutions—Faith is blocking the inspiration of pagan worship but the latter dies hard—betray the absurdity of the procedure. We may safely conclude that these details are "epic convention"[26] and declare that no allegorical image can correspond perfectly to thematic meanings. Still, we may wish that the image had been more appropriate or more sensitively handled.

Those are precisely the complaints of C. S. Lewis. "While it is true that the *bellum intestinum* is the root of all allegory," he writes, "it is no less true that only the crudest allegory will represent it by a pitched battle." Lewis prefers allegories based on the image of the journey, which "represents far more truly than any combat in a *champ clos* the perennial strangeness, the adventurousness, and the sinuous forward movement of the inner life." Endorsing Lewis, Jean Batany writes that the *Psychomachia* is psychologically unrealistic, untrue to inner experience, and Gay Clifford adds, "Unfortunately, Prudentius' extended metaphor of legionary combat is simply too inelastic to express the diversities of *non simplex natura*."[27]

25. M.-R. Jung, p. 27.

26. They are attributed to *Aeneid* 12.303 and 8.260 by Sister M. Clement Eagan in "The Spiritual Combat," trans. Eagan, in *The Poems of Prudentius*, vol. 2, Fathers of the Church 52 (Washington, D.C.: Catholic University of America Press, 1965), p. 82nn.

27. Lewis, *Allegory of Love*, pp. 68–69; Batany, p. 33; Gay Clifford, *The Transformations of Allegory* (London: Routledge & Kegan Paul, 1974), p. 28.

Such reasoning is circular: the writer assumes that Prudentius intends to depict the inner life, then complains that he depicts it imperfectly. It is indeed possible that the poet fell short in some ways of his general plan, but the epic-battle-equals-inner-conflict schema is increasingly unsatisfactory as the poem proceeds. The next Virtue is Pudicitia, usually Englished as "Chastity"; she is attacked by Sodomita Libido ("Lust"). When the Virtue triumphs, again in a graphically bloody fashion, she exclaims, "Hoc habet," and delivers a long, exultant speech. Such behavior and speech offend several critics, particularly Lavarenne:

> It is not without a certain shocked astonishment that we read of the murders that are carried out more or less savagely, greatly intensified by declamatory tirades, by those modest and pure maidens who the Christian Virtues ought, in our eyes, to be. We expect from them sweetness of behavior, modesty of speech: and behold, they appear as amazons, destitute of all timidity. . . . Is it essential that these daughters of the God of love and humility attack with such ardor, kill with such joy . . . ?[28]

A milder but more general protest is lodged by Clifford: "There is insuperable impropriety in involving the Virtues in armed combat."[29] Thus not only does the epic image express the internal theme inadequately; image and theme are fundamentally in conflict. Lewis points out that the problem becomes more acute as the out-of-context form of the Virtue is more passive: "How is Patience to rage in battle? How is Mercy to strike down her foes, or Humility to triumph over them when fallen?"[30]

Aside from the mismatch between image and theme, two additional difficulties recur in translating from epic battle to internal conflict. First, many long descriptive passages are like Faith's graphic triumph in that they suggest no internal translations. A good example is Deceit's inadvertent destruction of Pride by means of a camouflaged pit (ll. 257–73). To say that pride has fallen in the snare of deceit is merely to summarize the episode, not to translate it; and the reader struggles in vain toward a psychological parallel for the lengthy, cleverly realized, but stubbornly concrete narrative. Again, the behav-

28. Lavarenne, III, 11–12.
29. Clifford, p. 28.
30. Lewis, *Allegory of Love,* p. 69.

ior of Avaritia presents the kind of vivid but opaque surface that leads
commentators to call the characters of Langland and Bunyan "typical" instead of "really allegorical":

> Nor is she content to fill her roomy pockets, but delights to stuff her
> base gain in money-bags and cram swollen purses to bursting with
> her pelf, keeping them in hiding behind her left hand under cover of
> her robe on the left side, for her quick right hand is busy scraping up
> the plunder and plies nails hard as brass in gathering the booty.   [Ll.
> 458–63]

A second and complementary difficulty is that many passages cannot be allegorized because they are doctrinally explicit already. Chastity's long victory speech, for instance, straightforwardly explains the
effect of the Incarnation on lust (ll. 53–97); Hope preaches on the
elevation of the lowly and the destruction of the prideful (ll. 285–
304); Soberness expounds Christian doctrine and rebukes the Virtues
as if they were human beings: "Repent, I beseech you by the fear of
the high God, if at all it moves you, that you have desired to follow
after this pleasant sin, committing a heinous betrayal. If ye repent,
your sin is not deadly" (ll. 394–96). Does the struggle of Soberness
within the soul involve lengthy internal diatribes? "Prudentius has
not completely allegorized the action or, to speak more precisely,
personified the experience he renders," writes Stephen Barney.[31] That
is, Prudentius seems here to abandon his allegorical fiction in favor of
more direct exposition.

Together, the concrete details that cannot be allegorized and the
discourses that need no allegorization compose a substantial part of
the *Psychomachia.* If Prudentius set out to parallel his Virgilian battle
with an inner moral struggle, he was a sloppy geometrician. Furthermore, he commits an additional geometrical error that will undermine not just the epic-battle-equals-inner-struggle scheme but any
parallel structure. As has been widely recognized, the traditional definition of allegory requires that the literal level be consistent and
plausible in itself.[32] "What is said" should be independent of "what
is meant." But virtually every reader of the *Psychomachia* has pointed
to anomalies in the poem's literal fiction. For instance, the amazonian

31. Barney, p. 63.
32. For example, Fletcher, *Allegory,* p. 7, and Leyburn, p. 6.

warriors who have, we assume, been given exclusive rights to represent the virtues must share the stage with real biblical figures. "What is the actual Job doing in the train of the palpably unreal Patientia?" asks Robert Hollander.[33] Later the female personifications change without warning into a horde of nameless male soldiers (ll. 329–59, 470–82), and later still they seem to engage with actual fourth-century heretics (ll. 788–95). Apparently Prudentius could not keep straight the fictional guise of his agents. The explicit location of the action is also inconsistent, as Barney points out, and so is its implicit scale.[34] The latter is perhaps the most disturbing anomaly. The Virtues, who seem at times to be "irreducible segments of the psyche," speak at other times of their own minds and hearts and thus produce what A. D. Nuttall has termed an allegorical "regress," in which "the *homunculi* themselves are composed of even tinier *homunculi;* and so on."[35]

The indictments of Prudentius thus become so heavy that it may be wise to abandon the premises that produce them. The parallel-levels model, which is directly prescribed by the traditional definition of allegory, is an inefficient way of reading the *Psychomachia*. We might still argue for a "*sensus allegoricus* of the poem as a whole"[36] which survives the specific failures of parallelism, but such a generalized conviction is not particularly useful. Applied to this paradigmatic allegory, the traditional definition of allegory is a straitjacket that produces frustration for the reader and adverse critical judgments of the poem that it fails to fit.

The abandonment of the bilevel definition has already been urged by a handful of readers. R. W. Frank, Jr., and Morton W. Bloomfield, whose views of personification differ in other respects, both propound the paradox that "in personification-allegory the allegorical meaning (or most of it) is in the literal sense itself." More recently Maureen Quilligan has made the same assertion regarding not just personification but allegory in general. What such writers mean by

33. Hollander, p. 255.
34. Barney, p. 64.
35. Ibid.; A. D. Nuttall, *Two Concepts of Allegory: A Study of Shakespeare's "The Tempest" and the Logic of Allegorical Expression* (London: Routledge & Kegan Paul, 1967), p. 39.
36. M.-R. Jung, p. 327.

"the literal sense" is not a concrete allegorizable fiction but "the text's language—its most *literal* aspect."[37] A text's language can of course be concrete and abstract, narrative and expository, highly metaphoric and relatively plain, by turns, but it is always, for Quilligan and her predecessors, a single locus.

Although this "literalizing" runs counter to our received notions about allegory, it is such a sensible position that those who articulate it do so without extensive justification, as if simply reasserting sweet reason. "It is perhaps worth pointing out," writes Charles Williams in a discussion of Dante, "that when a poem is said to have two meanings, both are included in the poem; we have only one set of words. The meanings, that is, are united; and the poem is their union."[38] It is therefore surprising that the position has not been widely adopted. In particular, one might have expected it to be a rallying cry for the New Critics, who insisted that a poem's meanings reside "in the text" and nowhere else. For most New Critics allegory was the one form that depended on the "heresy of paraphrase."[39] Max Black's denunciation of the "substitution view of metaphor"— the idea that metaphor is "a substitute for some other literal expression . . . which would have expressed the same meaning, had it been used instead"[40]—left untouched our ideas about allegory, which we still defined as precisely that kind of trope. Perhaps the reason that the New Critics exempted allegory from their theories is that the theories themselves depended on the exemption. As I have suggested above, we can hardly conceive of texts whose meaning is unified and utterly manifest unless we contrast them with at least a hypothetical displacement of meaning. In any case, the exemption of allegory from New Critical ideas is relatively easy to undo; we simply relocate the spurious disjunction of meaning in some other literary form—or in the ideas of mistaken critics.

37. Bloomfield, "Allegory as Interpretation," p. 313; Robert Worth Frank, Jr., "The Art of Reading Medieval Personification-Allegory," *ELH* 20 (1953):237–50; Quilligan, *Language of Allegory,* p. 68.

38. Charles Williams, *The Figure of Beatrice: A Study in Dante* (London: Faber & Faber, 1943), p. 45.

39. See, for instance, Wheelwright, *Burning Fountain,* p. 88; Barfield, *Poetic Diction,* p. 201; William York Tindall, *The Literary Symbol* (New York: Columbia University Press, 1955), p. 31.

40. Max Black, "Metaphor," in *Models and Metaphors: Studies in Language and Philosophy* (Ithaca: Cornell University Press, 1962), p. 31.

But to insist that allegorical meaning resides in the text itself is a necessary but not a sufficient solution to the problem of definition. "The text itself" is something of a phantom, useful primarily for invocation against the more dangerous phantom of parallel semiotic levels. Once the exorcism is complete, we need to ask some difficult questions. What is this "text," and how does it generate meanings? Does the generation of meaning in allegory not differ, after all, from that in forms whose semiotic unity is more widely accepted? And how can a text that includes as many apparent anomalies as does the *Psychomachia* produce anything like a unified meaning?

The most useful definition of a text, it seems to me, begins with the structuralists' concept of codes. Literature is like language itself in depending on implicit "combinatory structures" that can be articulated as rules or formulae. To a certain degree the codes of literature are common to all texts, but they are subject to greater variation than are the codes of, for instance, language. A significant and widely used variation from other literary codes produces what we recognize as a genre. Each text, in turn, is constituted through less radical variations of one or more generic codes, and the process of reading consists of recognizing both certain codes and certain departures from them.

Fundamental to the texts that we commonly call allegories are the syntactic codes of narrative, or, less elegantly but more accurately, of the plot.[41] We can reduce any plot to a series of "sentences" or propositions. At their most elementary level, all of those sentences take the following form: an agent or group of agents performs some action, which may be followed by another related action. We can go on to classify the narrative sentences that that skeletal pattern subsumes, or we can formulate the rules by which the sentences are generated and are related to each other. But the student of allegory need not go beyond the fundamental form of the narrative code, because it is that fundamental form which is significantly varied by narrative allegory.

41. "Narrative" is commonly taken to exclude "dramatic," but I mean to include plays that relate sequences of events. "Narrative" is also sometimes used to refer to an individual text that tells an abstractable story, and it thereby contrasts with "plot" in the same way that *parole* opposes *langue* in Saussure's widely used distinction. That is why "plot" is more accurate for my purposes. Because it lacks an appropriate adjectival form, however, I shall refer to the "plot code" as the "narrative code." Later in this chapter I will deal briefly with allegory that does not involve plot at all.

Prudentius' variation of the narrative code is evident immediately in the names of his agents: Faith, Worship-of-the-Old-Gods, Chastity, Lust, and so forth. Sensing the anomaly of those names, we can see clearly what Todorov points out about ordinary stories: "The agents (subjects and objects) of [narrative] propositions will always be ideal proper nouns." The "ideal proper noun" is for Todorov a "blank form," paradoxically *without* properties, "which is complete[d] by different predicates."[42] In other words, the agent is pure specificity, a deictic pointer. The agents of the *Psychomachia,* in contrast, are designated not merely by common nouns but by abstract ones. If we can trust their names, Prudentius' agents are located at the opposite end of the chain of specificity from the agents of non-allegorical narrative. The syntactic code that underlies the *Psychomachia* apparently begins something like this: an abstraction or set of abstractions performs some action, which may be followed by another related action.

The extent to which Prudentius has in fact altered the narrative code might be disputed. The "sentences" of a literary code do not usually appear directly in the text, and we cannot automatically conclude from the names of Prudentius' agents that he has changed the narrative code itself. Perhaps his agents too are "ideal proper nouns" even though their names are abstract. Indeed, readers have often tried to assimilate the *Psychomachia* to the more familiar narrative model by seeking some "level" on which the poem's agents are concrete after all—amazonian warriors with abstract labels on their banners, or "components of the psyche" of a representative human being. But Prudentius tells us in his Preface that his subject is the conflict of virtue and vice. If we can take him at his word, he is not merely moralizing Virgilian warfare; nor is he simply schematizing internal experience (*psychomachia* does not designate an internal setting, contrary to a common assumption), although the soul's life is certainly at stake. He implies that his abstract nouns are the "name[s] of . . . abstract thing[s]," as Stephen Barney puts it, rather than abstractions from fundamentally deictic agents.[43]

That suggests that Prudentian allegory is modeled on philosophical realism. For the realist, universals are not merely mental constructs,

42. Todorov, "The Grammar of Narrative," in *Poetics of Prose,* p. 110.
43. Barney, p. 23.

as they are for the nominalist, but transcendent realities; that is, abstract nouns may be said to designate real entities. Barney has noted that allegory is "realistic" according to "the older definition of the real, not as the imitative and commonsensical, but as the substantial, in Platonic terms."[44] Barney's distinction between versions of the "real" is important, and I will maintain it by capitalizing the term when I use it according to the "older definition." The degree to which literary allegory actually endorses the older Realism is undecidable, for a literary text that imitates philosophical structures does not thereby affirm or deny their validity outside itself. If Prudentius' agents do act like Realistic universals, we will not therefore know that he believed them to be Realistic universals. Prudentius does imply at the end of the poem that the vices are not genuine Realities but that the virtues will indeed exist eternally—although not, of course, in their personified forms.[45] But those implications do not necessarily arise from the body of the poem, whose "realism" is not a doctrine but a certain kind of structure: a narrative whose abstract agents cannot be reduced to concrete equivalents. In that sense, the *Psychomachia* can be called Realistic narrative.

"Realistic narrative" seems to be an oxymoron, since universals in themselves cannot be said to act. Whenever an abstract noun does become the subject of a transitive verb, it thereby becomes less abstract: *faith* is static, and *faith enters the conflict* is already something of a personification. That is why many readers have assumed that a concrete equivalent accompanies each allegorical abstraction, enabling it to act by proxy. But in theory the relationship of universal to concretion cannot be equivalence or interchangeability, for universals subsume concretions. In the philosopher's realm of being, an object is compounded of substance and accident; in the semiotic system of allegory, an agent can take physical form without ceasing to be also a universal. Faith acts in its embodiments. Thus the modification of the narrative code which constitutes allegory is not exactly the introduction of abstract nouns where we expect concrete ones, but a shift of perspective to include both concrete agents and the intelligible realities in which they participate. We can think of each agent as a vertical space, dominated at the top by the abstract noun that desig-

44. Ibid., pp. 22–23.
45. See ll. 908–15 and pp. 58–61, below.

nates its essence and grounded in an embodiment that engages in the action.

The vertical space ought not to be a straight line: no single embodiment exhaustively manifests a universal. If Realistic narrative is true to its philosophical model, each agent will admit of numerous manifestations. That is in fact what happens in the *Psychomachia*. The virtues' changes from amazonian warriors to biblical figures to innumerable male soldiers and so forth—puzzling inconsistencies under the split-level definition of allegory—are in fact fulfillments of the laws of the genre. If the ordinary narrative agent is an "ideal proper noun" without properties, the Realistic agent is an ideal property that generates unlimited proper (and common) nouns. The code of Realistic narrative also prescribes shifts in temporal and spatial setting, for Faith opposes Worship-of-the-Old-Gods in the individual soul but also in biblical history and in fourth-century Spain. Like its agents, the action of Realistic narrative is simultaneously disparate and unified, a melange of temporal sequences that constitute a single timeless pattern.

It follows that allegory as exemplified by the *Psychomachia* is indeed "other-speech," but not in the sense of the rhetoricians' *alieniloquium*. "Otherness" aptly designates the relationship not between words and meaning but between elements of the poem's implicit code. Out of context, the subjects and predicates of the narrative propositions seem alien to each other—respectively timeless and timebound, Realistic and mimetic, native on the one hand to philosophical discourse and on the other to literary narrative. We imagine the *Psychomachia* as the child of Christian doctrine and Virgilian epic. I postulate that nonnarrative allegories are based on similar conjunctions of disparate elements. In descriptive allegory, intelligible subjects receive sensory descriptions; lyric becomes allegorical when ideas are apostrophized or otherwise evoked. In each case a localizing medium is opened to the timeless and the general. In short, the "pure allegory" of the *Psychomachia* is Realistic narrative, or narrative whose agents are universals, and literary allegory in general is the set of genres that are based on the synthesis of deictic and nondeictic generic codes.

The redefinitions just offered can explain away the apparent anomalies of the text on which they are based, but they are subject to the objection that that text is not representative of its class. The kind of allegory present in the *Psychomachia,* the kind assumed by my allusions to abstract nouns, is personification allegory, which is often said to be one of two major varieties of allegory and is sometimes even regarded as peripheral to the genre because it does not veil its "real meanings." Any valid definition of allegory must apply to certain texts that do not use personification—the *Divine Comedy,* for instance, and perhaps such modern parabolic narratives as George Orwell's *Animal Farm.*

Such applications will be a central concern of the rest of this study, but some preliminary comments can be offered here. Dante's great poem conforms to my general definition of allegory because it fuses first-person narrative with theological exposition. Transactions normally involving material objects—a journey, conversations, sensory observations—here involve sin, beatitude, and eventually the deity. Such intelligibles appear not as the subjects of narrative propositions but in other positions in the poem's implicit code; I will argue later that Dante's version of the allegorical code is a transformation of Prudentius'. The transformation does not seem radical enough to constitute a new genre, however. That may not be the case with such modern "allegories" as *Animal Farm,* in whose narrative codes universals do not appear at all. Such allegories are based instead on the compounding of concrete agents: each "character" in Orwell's novel is simultaneously a fictional animal and a person or group from Soviet history. But some kinship with older allegory can be detected, for in all cases a normally deictic element in the narrative code, a slot that we expect to be filled only with the name of a particular figure or object, has been widened—to include, in the older texts, an intangible Reality, and in the newer ones a historical reality. The allegorical text confounds some polarity—sensible versus intelligible or fictional versus actual—which its readers regard as fundamental.

Polarities cannot be confounded without also being implicitly asserted. If such allegories as the *Divine Comedy* and *Animal Farm* conform to my redefinition, they do not necessarily support the corollary that states that allegory does not proceed on parallel levels. Indeed, the specter of semiotic bifurcation returns here in more substantial form, for allegory that does not use personification cannot unify a compound agent under the umbrella of an abstract name. The *Divine Comedy* presents such a vivid mimetic surface that readers naturally feel that any general meanings must be implicit or even hidden—a separate level semiotically, if not ontologically. In such a work as *Animal Farm,* the case for parallelism is even clearer. Two creatures—say, a pig and Stalin—cannot be metaphysically united; the text that double-exposes them indeed seems to proceed on two levels, as an explicit fiction with implicit historical allusions. Here at least, it seems, language says one thing and means another.

But that cannot really be true, of *Animal Farm* or of any other text. If a text says one thing it also means that thing: we cannot separate speech from meaning. Thus if it says one thing and means another, it both says and means two things. And unless we are linguistic schizophrenics or are willing to ignore half of what we read, a text that says and means two things must say and mean one complex thing.

With any allegory, the notion of parallel semiotic levels is indisputably useful as an analytic tool. Readers can begin by reconstructing an implicit textual code; then, having noted that the code's components are associated by preconception with different metaphysical or literary systems, we can project the components onto separate levels of being or of discourse. In that sense the pig can be legitimately set parallel with Stalin, and such a universal as faith can even be separated from its concrete embodiments. But such an analysis of components is by no means a description of the compound. In the *Psychomachia* the text itself is neither a level with implicit parallels nor a set of parallel levels; it is a line, connecting the disparate levels that are normally associated with some of its components. The same is true, with certain variations, in such a text as *Animal Farm.* Orwell's character is a peculiar synthesis of Stalin, Napoleon, and a fictional pig, and the reader's task is not simply to identify the components but also to understand the nature of the synthesis—the common denominator, the residual incongruities, the shiftings of balance—by following the signs that constitute and develop the relationship.

The distinction I am drawing between analysis and description owes much to the work of recent literary theorists. Todorov establishes a somewhat similar distinction between "interpretation," which seeks a "second more authentic text" behind the "apparent textual fabric," and "reading," which, "instead of replacing one text by another, . . . describes the relation of the two." Michael Riffaterre insists on the difference between our discovery of a "key word or matrix" that seems to account for the poem and our "praxis of the transformation" of that matrix: the first yields "meaning," the second "significance." Jonathan Culler writes, "Any figure can be read referentially or rhetorically. 'My love is a red, red rose' tells us, referentially, of desirable qualities that the beloved possesses. Read rhetorically, in its figurality, it indicates a desire to see her as she is not: as a rose."[46] All three critics distinguish, in short, between identifying some extratextual reference, either to previous discourse or to something in the world, and recognizing the text's use of that reference. In the reading of allegorical texts the first stage takes on a peculiar form, for here we commonly identify at least two kinds of reference—concrete and abstract, or fictional and real, or literal, allegorical, tropological, and anagogical. But the lesson of modern criticism is that the identification of levels of reference is not equivalent to reading. It is a preliminary or heuristic stage, which, like the mastery of vocabulary or syntax, merely prepares a student to understand what can be said.

The confusion of the analytic and the descriptive approaches to allegory accounts for an unacknowledged disagreement about allegory's semiotic structure. Most commonly the mode is said to be disjunctive: it "recognizes the impossibility of fusing the empirical and the eternal and thus demystifies the symbolic relation by stressing the separateness of the two levels."[47] In that remark Jonathan Culler suggests, as have many others, that allegory depends on two kinds of disjunction—between the temporal and the eternal worlds to which the text refers, and between the sign and signifier in the text itself.[48] In direct contradiction, other writers describe allegory as a method of both ontological and semiotic conjunction.[49] In a certain sense both views are correct, since, as Crazy Jane told the Bishop, nothing can be

---

46. Todorov, "How to Read?" in *Poetics of Prose*, p. 238; Michael Riffaterre, *Semiotics of Poetry* (Bloomington: Indiana University Press, 1978), pp. 5–12; Culler, *Pursuit of Signs*, p. 78.

47. Jonathan Culler, *Structuralist Poetics: Structuralism, Linguistics, and the Study of Literature* (Ithaca: Cornell University Press, 1975), p. 230.

48. See also Seung, *Cultural Thematics*, p. 175, on the first, and M.-R. Jung, pp. 19–20, on the second.

49. See, e.g., Maureen Quilligan, "Allegory, Allegoresis, and the Deallegorization of Language: The *Roman de la Rose*, the *De planctu naturae*, and the *Parlement of Foules*," in *Allegory, Myth, and Symbol*, ed. Bloomfield, p. 184; Paul Zumthor, "Narrative and Anti-Narrative: *Le Roman de la Rose*," trans. Frank Yeomans, *Yale French Studies* 51 (1974):191; and Roche, *Kindly Flame*, pp. 7–8.

sole or whole that has not been rent. But the apprehension of disjunction is a less complete response to allegory, albeit an easier one, than the perception of conjunction. From the latter perspective, disjunction itself appears to be a significant kind of correlation. Even if no metaphysical hierarchy assimilates the alternative forms of an agent, even if, as in certain postallegorical works, the signifiers exist in continuous tension with their apparent referents, the disparities and tensions themselves constitute a distinctive and significant whole. What Riffaterre writes of poetry in general is no less true of allegory: "the characteristic feature of the poem is its unity"; "*the unit of significance is the text.*"[50]

Undoubtedly the reason why the allegorical text has not usually been regarded as a "unit of significance" is that one element of that text always bears disproportionate cultural weight. The universals of the *Psychomachia* are Real, particularly for a medieval Christian; the historical referents of *Animal Farm* are real and had immediate importance for Orwell's first readers. In fact, as we have seen, the nature of allegory is to integrate fictional and nonfictional discourse, and some readers in every period have understandably believed that the proper response is to extricate the nonfictional. That belief leads to *allegoresis,* the theory that the identification of a set of authentic referents is not a heuristic stage but the proper goal of reading.

Allegoresis is the most persistent form assumed by the phantom of split-level semiosis. Maureen Quilligan claims that it was identified with allegory by mistake: having arisen as a method of reinterpreting an existing text as if the agents were personifications, *allegoresis* was then assumed to be the method for composing narratives that actually did use personification. The misidentification was highly ironic, according to Quilligan, because " 'actual' allegories" are the one kind of text that does not allow the discovery of implicit ulterior meanings.[51] But that is not the only kind of *allegoresis;* indeed, I submit that it is not the practice most properly designated by that term. For the medieval exegete, *allegoresis* was not just a method of discovering implicit meanings—all criticism articulates implicit meaning—but also a declaration that certain meanings, implicit or explicit, constituted the text's intention, while other meanings, although explicit, were insig-

50. Riffaterre, pp. 2, 6.
51. Quilligan, *Language of Allegory,* pp. 29–31.

nificant. It was, in short, a method of suppressing meaning. Under that definition, *allegoresis* is applicable even to personification allegory. Quilligan's distinction is not, properly, between actual allegories and texts that permit *allegoresis* but between two methods of interpretation, *allegoresis* and holistic reading, both universally applicable. And the first of those methods is in fact particularly easy to apply to allegorical texts, because certain referents in those texts always bear greater extraliterary significance than others. Therefore, the split-level definition that I have rejected as an inaccurate description of allegorical texts can still be defended on the premise that texts are not important in allegory—that they are merely vehicles for pre-existing ideas.

Against such a premise the objections are well known. Modern criticism takes it as axiomatic that whatever truths literature conveys are essentially literary truths, inseparable from their vehicles. On a more pragmatic level, *allegoresis* quickly becomes unsatisfying for the reader; to paraphrase Maureen Quilligan, we are frustrated when we cannot find the authentic referents and bored when we can.[52] And should both of those arguments be dismissed as modern impositions on a more didactic age, we can adduce a doctrinal objection to *allegoresis,* although its full substantiation must await the readings of individual allegories in later chapters of this study. Taken out of their literary contexts, the abstract formulations of allegory often appear unorthodox or simply wrong. Can we really believe that faith has annihilated the worship of the old gods? Ought we to believe, as the extractable "moral" of *Everyman* implies, that we depend on our good deeds for our salvation?

"All telling modifies what is being told," writes Richard Howard.[53] To read an allegory properly is neither to extract a moral nor to construct a geometry of its referents but to follow what Roland Barthes calls "the very movement of meaning."[54] In allegory that movement is particularly complicated. The text operates on what may be called a vertical and a horizontal axis, and the two continually intersect: as the narrative progresses, its agents appear in various forms and at various

52. Ibid., p. 32.
53. Richard Howard, "A Note on *S/Z*," prefatory to Roland Barthes, *S/Z*, trans. Richard Miller (New York: Hill & Wang, 1974), p. xi.
54. Barthes, *S/Z*, p. 92.

levels of abstraction, and the means by which they are signified affects and even constitutes the narrative. To illustrate that kind of semiosis I return to our paradigmatic allegory, the *Psychomachia,* which looks in this light surprisingly rich and satisfyingly coherent.

The Features of Virtue

Prudentius begins by preparing us to read his poem as Realistic narrative. His Preface is an interpretive account of the life of Abraham which, read carelessly, might seem to encourage translation from a "literal" to a didactic "allegorical" level. The sacrifice of Isaac teaches us, writes Prudentius, to offer to God what is uniquely dear to our hearts (Preface, ll. 6–8); the rescue of Lot from wicked tribes delineates our liberation of our bodies, formerly "enslaved to foul desire" (Preface, ll. 53–55); and Sarah's conception signifies the soul's belated fertility (Preface, ll. 64–68). But biblical events are not an invented code, and there is no evidence that Prudentius wishes us to see them as fictional or unhistorical. The allegorical reading of Abraham's life is therefore not translation but attentive vision: "This picture has been drawn beforehand to be a model for our life to trace out again with true measure" (Preface, ll. 50–51). The "model" is essentially the pattern of the poem itself:

> The faithful patriarch who first showed the way of believing, Abram, late in life the father of a blessed progeny, . . . has counselled us to war against the ungodly tribes, himself giving us an example of his own counsel, and shown that we beget no child of wedlock pleasing to God, and whose mother is Virtue, till the spirit, battling valorously, has overcome with great slaughter the monsters in the enslaved heart.   [Preface, ll. 1–14]

By deriving the poem's abstractions from Abraham's life, the Preface teaches us to see them as widely inclusive Realities.

Prudentius then makes the transition to the poem itself with a prayer that, like the Preface, prepares us not for semiotic duplicity but for revelation:

> Say, our King, with what fighting force the soul is furnished and enabled to expel the sins from within our breast; when there is disorder

among our thoughts and rebellion arises within us, when the strife of
our evil passions vexes the spirit, say what help there is then to guard
her liberty, what array with superior force withstands the fiendish
raging in our heart.   [Ll. 5–11]

Nothing is said here, or elsewhere in the poem, about clothing ineffable
truths with beautiful lies. Instead, Prudentius paraphrases the invocation that opens the *Aeneid,* putting Christ in the place of the Muse and
asking for inspiration for a truthful account of a battle that concerns
our souls. He closes the prayer by exhorting his readers to observe
closely and accurately: "The way of victory is before our eyes if we may
mark at close quarters the very features of the Virtues [ipsas /
Virtutum facies], and the monsters that close with them in deadly struggle" (ll.
18–20). "The features of the Virtues" is of course an equivocal phrase,
equally applicable to physical faces and to intangible entities. But there
is no univocal or nonmetaphoric term to describe something that is
present equally in Abraham's actions and in Christian Reality. The
confrontation of virtues and vices which ensues will be a drama of
metamorphosis, and the various modes of representation—anthropomorphic metaphor, direct exposition, pictorial detail, mystical
symbolism, and so on—will constitute much of the story.

   The story begins with a clause that may be a nonfictional generalization, as Sister Eagan's translation makes clear: "Faith first the field of
doubtful battle seeks" ("prima petit campum dubia sub sorte duelli /
pugnatura Fides") (ll. 21–22).[55] But a full-blown personification
emerges in the adjectives that follow: "her rough dress disordered, her
shoulders bare, her hair untrimmed, her arms exposed" (ll. 22–23).
Faith is thus realized with startling vividness. She is all the more
startling because she is female: like Lavarenne, we do not expect such
obviously womanly creatures to fight. Our surprise that this one does,
and does so with great abandon, is surely part of Prudentius' intent. We
are meant to be exhilarated by the blatant courage and power of an
entity normally credited only with quiet moral strength. In lines 24
through 27, Prudentius insists that the connection between faith and
physical courage is essential, not merely rhetorical: "For the sudden
glow of ambition . . . trusting in a stout heart and unprotected limbs
challenges the hazards of furious warfare, meaning to break them

55. See Eagan.

down." The graphic account of Worship-of-the-Old-Gods' death (ll. 30–35) confirms that so far, this ideological conflict is a straightforward battle that can be won decisively. "Exultat victrix legio" (l. 36), and exultation is indeed the effect. Prudentius then extends Faith's victory into human history by placing on the battlefield the "host" of saints and martyrs (ll. 36–39). The first episode of the *Psychomachia* is the vivid and manifold embodiment of faith.

Embodiment has its perils, however. The second Vice, Sodomita Libido, attacks through the senses. She is never exactly described, but the fragmentary images of her "torch of pinewood blazing murkily with pitch and burning sulfur" (ll. 43–45), her unclean breath, and her clotted blood (ll. 50–52) are all the more powerful for being disconnected. Her adversary must restore the ordering power of principle. Pudicitia, unlike Faith, wears armor and is presented almost without images. In a long victory speech (ll. 53–97) she proclaims the dominance of Word over Flesh:

> From that day all flesh is divine, since it conceives Him and takes on the nature of God by a covenant of partnership. For the Word made flesh has not ceased to be what it was before, that is, the Word, by attaching to itself the experience of the flesh; its majesty is not lowered by the experience of the flesh, but raises wretched men to nobler things.   [Ll. 76–81]

This is one of the passages of explicit doctrine that would violate the separation of "literal" and "allegorical," if there were such a separation. But the shift into the abstract mode is in itself significant of chastity, which places reason and law in a central position in human experience. The shift in rhetorical mode is a kind of plot development.

If Fides acts and Pudicitia talks, Patientia predictably does neither, except for a short explanation of her victory. Instead, she is defined mostly by what she does not do: she stands, for forty-five lines, while Ira taunts, reviles, threatens, hits her with javelins, batters her with a sword, and finally commits suicide in frustration. This is the first of several episodes to exploit the anomaly of the nonbelligerent soldier, often cited as a sign of the weakness of Prudentius' allegorical scheme.[56] The accusation assumes that a realistic epic battle is or should be set parallel to moral conflict but that Prudentius cannot

56. See pp. 33 above.

coordinate the levels. That is, insofar as the warriors must be virtuous, they are unwarlike—Lewis sees Mens Humilis as a self-righteous governess—and insofar as the Virtues must fight, they are unlike "those modest and pure maidens who the Christian Virtues ought . . . to be."[57] If these are indeed lapses, we may wonder why Prudentius should persistently draw our attention to them by dwelling, for instance, on Patientia's unsoldierly conduct (ll. 109–12, 118). But if we give up the attempt to divorce the allegorical vehicle from its tenor, we can see the anomaly itself as significant. What Prudentius wants to say about long-suffering is not simply that it is long-suffering, but also that it sometimes appears inappropriate. More generally, these embattled Virtues are quite different from epic warriors on the one hand and Sunday-school goodness on the other. Their brutality is meant to be awesome and slightly shocking—even untypical, for these are, as the end of the poem makes clear, virtues in a crisis, responding with unexpected force to a rebellion. All of them, but especially Patientia, are defined by the anomalous conjunction of ideal stasis and engagement in time.

Lest the anomalous victory of Patientia should seem accidental, however, it is stabilized and substantiated by another allegorical technique that receives here its most extensive use in the poem. As the battle ends, Patientia is "escorted by a noble man," and we learn, somewhat to our surprise, that Job has "clung close to the side of his invincible mistress throughout the hard battle, hitherto grave of look and panting from the slaughter of many a foe, but now with a smile on his stern face . . ." (ll. 162–66). We need not try to imagine that Job has been resurrected to participate in an allegorical showdown that interests him; the allusion indicates that he has been engaged here in his own struggle against his own foes (ll. 169–71). The battle is retrospectively doubled: it has been not just the confrontation of metaphoric warriors taking place in a fictional present but also the well-known story of a biblical hero. And if it is both of those, it is also other events at other times and places. The effect of the reference to Job is stereoscopic, enabling us to see the victory of Patientia in its real—or Real—depth.

As polysemous as it is, however, Patientia's victory is not total, not the victory of *patientia* as a universal. We know that, because the

57. Lewis, *Allegory of Love*, p. 70; Lavarenne, III, 11.

outcome in our own lives is no foregone conclusion. A translation of "fictional" events into "allegorical" ideas might lead us to believe by the end of the poem that for Prudentius all the vices have been destroyed; clearly, however, they are dead only in certain manifestations. The fact that those poetic and historical manifestations can be killed does imply the ultimate destruction of the vices themselves, along with that of everything else that is bound to the material world. But at present the universal and eternal victory of *patientia* is, by a profound and famous paradox, dependent on the outcomes of the battles of *patientia*'s temporal embodiments.

Thus it is that the next Vice can challenge the Virtues' control over history and can claim that temporal existence is the sovereign Reality. Superbia boasts that human flesh and history are hopelessly unregenerate and will always be her domain (ll. 216–27). Moreover, she unbalances, in a predictable direction, the anomalous compound of physical soldier and spiritual principle which defines her opponents. Taking great care with her own appearance, she taunts the Virtues at length about their unwarlike external forms: "Is Chastity's cold stomach of any use in war, or Brotherly Love's soft work done by stress of battle? What shame it is, O God of war, O valorous heart of mine, to face such an army as this, to take the sword against such trumpery, and engage with troupes of girls . . ." (ll. 238–42). She treats this as if it were an ordinary physical battle instead of an allegorical one and is confident that she can win through a mere show of force (ll. 249–56). What follows is indeed one of the less clearly allegorical episodes in the poem, because it breaks the expected pattern. Superbia's defeat comes not through the usual conflict with an opposing Virtue but through a comic accident, narrated in considerable detail: she falls into one of the camouflaged trenches prepared by Fraus to trap the Virtues (ll. 257–73). The allegorical pattern emerges clearly enough, of course—self-deceiving pride causes its own downfall—but it emerges after a slight delay that produces irony. The allegory itself is the trap; Superbia is caught in the moral truths that do, after all, control this war.

Modern readers may sympathize with Superbia more than they would like to admit, for they sometimes complain that the war is *too* closely controlled by moral truths. The ironic delay of allegorical meaning in the defeat of Superbia shows that Prudentius is capable at least of playing significantly with the controlling pattern. And an even greater complication arises in the episode that follows. The attack of the fifth Vice, Luxuria, reveals that the pattern may not be entirely predetermined because the Virtues will not necessarily remain the virtues.

The onslaught of Luxuria earns grudging admiration even from those who dislike the *Psychomachia* as a whole, because, as Lewis notes, it is "feelingly described" and "lends the combat a faint colour of dramatic interest."[58] Luxuria is the first of the Vices to be defined in space and time: she comes from the "western bounds of the world," presumably Rome,[59] and rides into battle "languidly belching" from an all-night feast (l. 316). The vividness does not result from a sudden increase in Prudentius' imaginative powers, as Lewis implies; on the other hand, the details cannot be individually allegorized. As usual, the literalness of the narrative is itself irreplaceably meaningful. The sensory details are fascinating in themselves, aside from any ulterior significance, and that is precisely their significance. *Luxuria* is the unchecked sovereignty of the material.

The proliferation of detail is not only the means by which Luxuria is presented in the poem but also the nature of her threat. Both the Virtues and the reader are easily seduced into forgetting what, or even that, her sensual richness signifies. Moreover, she very nearly makes the Virtues forget that they are female personifications themselves. She attacks the whole group, not a single opponent, and she transforms them as a group. Her breath weakens or "unmans" their "frames," "softening their iron-clad muscles and crushing their strength" (ll. 328–31). They wish to be "governed by the loose law of the pot-house" (l. 343), to "have [their] manly hair confined by a gilded turban with its yellow band to soak up the spikenard [they] pour on" (ll. 358–59). As before, the reader who expects two separate levels will be disturbed by the implausible fiction: epic warriors should not undergo sex change on the battlefield, and Virtues should not be able to act unvirtuously.[60] In fact, though, Prudentius is again

58. Lewis, *Allegory of Love*, pp. 70–71.
59. See Thomson's note on l. 310.
60. Soon after this passage, Prudentius refers to the newly seduced soldiers as the allies of Sobrietas (l. 345), suggesting that these male warriors may be not the named Virtues but anonymous ancillary personifications, or even human followers of virtue. In the passage just cited, however, he clearly calls the "virile" fighters "the Virtues." Thus even if he later envisions them as human allies, the point of this paragraph stands

shifting his means of representing his subject, and the shift is meaningful. The subject, as always, is the confrontation of Virtues and
Vices; but the influence of this particular Vice is to entangle Virtue in
sensual reality and thus to blur its ideal nature. That is, the human
agency by which the Virtues are operative becomes far more evident
than the principles themselves.

Luxuria's onslaught, then, produces a confrontation not just between opposing moral principles but also between idealism and sen-
suality. Fittingly, the fighting method of Sobrietas is verbal and abstract. Like Pudicitia, she mostly talks, but she affects the narrative
more dramatically than Pudicitia. The speech of Sobrietas is a re-
allegorization of the vivid images that have concretized the Virtues:

> What blinding madness is vexing your disordered minds? To what
> fate are you rushing? . . . [T]o have your manly hair confined by a
> gilded turban with its yellow band to soak up the spikenard you pour
> on, and this after you have had inscribed with oil on your brows the
> signs whereby was given to you the king's annointing, his everlasting
> unction? To walk softly with a train sweeping the path you have
> trod? To wear flowing robes of silk on your enfeebled frames, after
> the immortal tunic that bountiful Faith wove with deft fingers, giving
> an impenetrable covering to cleansed hearts to which she had already
> given rebirth? And so to feasts that last into the night, where the great
> tankard spills out wasted floods of foaming wine, while the ladles
> drip on to the table, the couches are soaked with neat liquor, and
> their embossed ornaments still wet with the dew of yesterday? Have
> you forgotten, then, the thirst in the desert, the spring that was given
> to your fathers from the rock, when the mystic wand split the stone
> and brought water leaping from its top? Did not food that angels
> brought flow into your fathers' tents in early days, that food which
> now with better fortune, in the lateness of time, near the end of the
> world's day, the people eats from the body of Christ? And it is after
> tasting of *this* banquet that you let shameful debauchery carry you
> relentlessly to the drunken den of Indulgence . . . !   [Ll. 351–78]

After this reassertion of the superior reality of *invisibilia,* sustained by
Jonathan's story from 1 Samuel (ll. 397–402), Sobrietas overcomes
Luxuria in the only way possible: by the power of an ideal. She holds
up a cross, and the horses pulling Luxuria's chariot panic and flee. If

---

in modified form: the burden of the action is now being carried by mortals, not by
personifications.

we are still demanding surface plausibility, we will find this episode absurd, but the improbability of Sobrietas' victory is precisely its meaning. The frankly symbolic power of the cross, the power of the spiritual over the physical, astonishes Luxuria so that she can no longer control her chariot; she is crushed under her trappings and chokes on her teeth and blood (ll. 414–31). She is killed by her own physical nature, in revoltingly vivid detail.

The *Psychomachia* is usually regarded as a series of symmetrical, isomorphic confrontations; "variety appears in the details, but the form of battle is almost stichomythic."[61] At the highest level of abstraction the first five battles are indeed unquestionably symmetrical, but to say simply that faith, chastity, long-suffering, lowliness, and soberness triumph over the opposing vices is a most inadequate summary, neither interesting nor true. At the heart of the story is the radical complexity of the militant virtues themselves. In order to triumph over the vices, they must become embodied in time, as they do at the bold initiative of Faith. Each embodied Virtue is defined by a slightly different compound of universal with concretions; each survives because the compound remains stable, surrendering neither its immortal identity nor its force in the world. In contrast, the Vices are defeated by identification with material existence: they can be destroyed physically. In such ways, the interplay of universals and concretions—that is, the allegorical form itself—shapes and differentiates the first five episodes.

After those five episodes, which constitute slightly less than half the poem, the interplay of levels of being increasingly dominates the plot, obliterating for a time even the most general isomorphism. The first weakening of symmetry is the gradual lengthening of the battles. Lavarenne notes that the sixth is about ten times as long as the first, and he might have added that it is impossible to determine the boundaries of the seventh—if there is a seventh.[62] Along with the lengthening comes a proliferation of personnel. In the first three episodes, an individual Virtue appears and is challenged unsuccessfully by an individual Vice. But Superbia, who takes the initiative, has an ally in Fraus (albeit one who inadvertently destroys her), and Mens Humilis

61. Fletcher, *Allegory,* p. 189.
62. Lavarenne, III, 10.

is aided by Spes. Before Sobrietas appears, the Virtues have become anonymous legions, "the whole array" (l. 340). The plot becomes less regular as a result, for each episode is no longer simply a single combat. A more radical change befalls the combatants themselves, who become more human. With Luxuria, Prudentius no longer focuses on single warriors whom we identify immediately as person-ifications, largely because they are female; he presents instead a wider, less idealized, and less orderly battle among male soldiers. Luxuria's humanizing influence lingers even after the Vice is dead, for Sobrietas addresses the Virtues as "the high-born children of Ju-dah, . . . come of a long line of noble ancestors that stretches down to the mother of God" (ll. 383–85). All of those changes in the agents and the plot are not, as Lavarenne implies, Prudentius' capricious improvisations on his fundamentally dull structure, for they con-stitute a structural principle in themselves.[63] Although each Virtue has won her battle, the victories have become less decisive—Mens Humilis wins inadvertently, and Luxuria's subversion persists—and the combatants have become more complex: the domination by ideals is less and less clear.

The confusion climaxes in the attack of the final Vice, Avaritia. Avaritia does not even attack in the usual sense. She enters the poem as one of Luxuria's many camp followers—"Iocus et Petulantia," "Amor," "Pompa, ostentatrix vani splendoris," "Venusta[s]," "Dis-cordia," and "Volupta[s]" (ll. 433–44)—but as the others flee, Ava-ritia remains, gathering Luxuria's spoils and imperceptibly beginning her temptation of the Virtues (ll. 450–58). For the first time, the boundary between battles is unclear, the props and personnel of one carrying over to the next: the allegorical economy has broken down.

A further sign of its breakdown is the accelerated multiplication of abstractions, first in Luxuria's train and now in Avaritia's: "Care, Hunger, Fear, Anguish, Perjuries, Pallor, Corruption, Treachery, Falsehood, Sleeplessness, Meanness, diverse fiends, go in attendance on the monster" (ll. 464–66). Personification ordinarily individual-izes abstractions, but Prudentius here introduces so many figures so quickly that we cannot conceptualize each one separately. Greed is operating as a cancer. Another kind of disorder, equally disturbing, is the remetaphorization of the personified Avaritia as a mother of

63. Ibid.

wolves: "and all the while Crimes, the brood of their mother Greed's black milk, like ravening wolves go prowling and leaping over the field" (ll. 467–69). Anyone trying to translate the allegory will be hard put to establish a hierarchy of tropes here, for each figurative representation dissolves into another in a deliberately grotesque metamorphosis. Greed seems trebly real but frighteningly plastic.

Avaritia's climactic effects subvert the allegorical order, the social order, and the moral order simultaneously. The combats between female personifications transmute into a human civil war:

> If a soldier sees his own brother and fellow-soldier with a helmet that glances with precious stones of tawny hue, he fears not to unsheath his sword and smite the skull with a comrade's blade, purposing to snatch the gems from a kinsman's head. If a son chances to look on his father's body lying lifeless by the luck of war, he joyfully seizes the belt with its shining studs and strips off the blood-stained armor. Civil War makes plunder of his kin, the insatiable Love of Possession spares not his own dear ones, unnatural Hunger robs his own children. Such the slaughter that Greed, the conqueress of the world, was dealing among the nations, laying low myriads of men with diverse wounds.   [Ll. 470–82]

Here the Vices themselves—Civil War, Love of Possession, Hunger— are, to our horror, human beings with anonymous relatives and children, and their enemies are not Virtues in the abstract but *omne hominum, mortalia cuncta*—including the priests of the Lord (ll. 493–97). The human Vices are temporarily opposed by Christian Reason, who, like Sobrietas, reasserts immaterial values (ll. 502–28). But Avaritia has not exhausted her resources. In one final demonstration of the power of the material, she changes her appearance, reclothing herself as "the Virtue men call Thrifty" (ll. 553–54) and confounding the all-too-human Virtues:

> With such semblances she befools men and cheats their too credulous hearts. They follow the deadly monster, believing hers to be a Virtue's work. . . . The deadly creature's changing, double form makes [the Virtues'] sight unsteady and dubious, not knowing what to make of her appearance. [Ll. 564–72]

The ordering power of the virtues has apparently ended. In a rising figural cacophony, Prudentius has let personifications proliferate beyond counting, compounded metaphors, and reenvisioned his essential agents as human beings; now the very principles that formerly organized the narrative have been confounded by outward appearances. Prudentius' protean allegory has rendered a vision of moral chaos.

The virtue that saves the day is scarcely a virtue at all, in the manner of Fides, Pudicitia, and so forth, for she is not a principle of conduct. On the contrary, Operatio *is* conduct. Sister Eagan translates her name as "Mercy," and Thomson adds "Good" to "Works"; while neither translation violates Prudentius' meaning, the neutrality of the Latin name is important. I have been tracing a regression in the poem from principled order to confused concreteness, corresponding to the growing influence of the material vices. The disguise of Greed as Frugality demands that the Virtues alter their defense: virtuous principles are no longer dependable. Operatio's nature is exactly appropriate to the demand. Her name designates neither a virtuous principle nor a vicious one but a set of virtuous actions—"taking pity on the needy, whom she had cared for with kindly generosity, lavishing her patrimony with a wise prodigality" (ll. 580–81)—so that she is less abstract than the Vices or the other Virtues. On the other hand, she is not dominated by the material realm, having given up her goods to lay up wealth in heaven. She is invincible, able to slay "the cause of all our ills" (l. 607), because she is the practical fulfillment of principles, the visible implementation of invisible values.

Avaritia is immobilized by this Virtue who is immune to appearances (ll. 584–88); Operatio's victory is decisive. It literally disposes of unordered materials:

> Then from the dead body she takes the spoils. Dirty bits of unwrought gold, stuff not yet purified in the furnace, worm-eaten money-bags, coins green with rust, things long hoarded, the conqueress scatters, distributing them to the needy, giving gifts to the poor of what she has taken. [Ll. 598–603]

It dispels also the clutter of personifications: "At [Operatio's] words . . . troubles departed. Fear and Suffering and Violence, Crime and Fraud that denies accepted faith, were driven away and fled from the land" (ll. 629–31).

From now on, the allegory moves steadily, except for one interruption, away from concreteness, fragmentation, and disorder. The military imagery no longer expresses the vivid particularity of individual struggles but conveys the abstract order of squadrons, columns, and rhythmic marching (ll. 634–64). Other tropes compound the military one, but their effect is not confusion; Prudentius reinstates the allegorical economy, the coherence and coalescence of meanings. For instance, when Operatio addresses the Virtues she echoes Christ's words to his disciples: "When thou art going on a journey, carry no wallet, nor take thought, when thou goest, for another tunic to wear. And be not anxious about the morrow . . ." (ll. 613–15). Besides lending authority to Operatio's antimaterialism, the allusion superimposes biblical events on the narrative, as in the Job passage. Prudentius then introduces an "epic simile" that links his narrative with Jewish history, as did the typological Preface: the Virtues' triumphant march is like that of the Israelites through the Red Sea (ll. 650–64). Concord is now in control (ll. 644–45); the poem is increasingly harmonious both in theme and in allegorical method. The Virtues are moving toward eternal harmony and stability (ll. 640–43).

The movement is interrupted (as are similar ascents late in *Everyman* and *Piers Plowman*) by a resurgence of disorder. Like Avaritia, Discordia—alias Heresis—appears in disguise: she represents confusing variability, even bearing two names. Also like Avaritia, she returns the narrative to opaque, concrete detail (ll. 672–80). Her attack is even more radical than Avaritia's, however, for it does not simply confuse the Virtues; it denies the stability and reality of their ground of being: "The God I have is variable, now lesser, now greater, now double, now single; when I please, he is unsubstantial, a mere apparition, or again the soul within us, when I choose to make a mock of his divinity" (ll. 710–13).[64] The claims that God is "unsubstantial, a mere apparition" or "the soul within us" are like the un-Realistic

64. This is one of the many passages in which Prudentius transforms epic conventions for his own uses: the Virtues have demanded that Discordia reveal her identity, nation, and religion, as if she were an epic warrior. One of Macklin Smith's major arguments in *Prudentius' "Psychomachia"* is that Prudentius imitated Virgil not uncritically but ironically, contrasting false pagan heroism with the truly noble *psychomachia*. I would modify Smith's formulation: Prudentius writes as if the relationship between pagan and Christian warfare were not false/true but fiction/fulfillment. In evoking the conventional challenge of an opponent's identity and paternity, for instance, the speech cited above does not deny the convention's meaning but compounds it: the Virtues must discover the manifestations and origins of discord. Similarly, the boasting speech of Pride (ll. 206–52) is both conventionally appropriate to an epic challenger and particularly appropriate to pre-Christian pride.

readings of allegory—the notion, for instance, that Prudentius' personified Virtues are "shadowy abstractions" or psychological principles. Prudentius' Virtues are not God, of course, but they are of divine origin (see ll. 11–13), and their natures will endure eternally (ll. 910–15); thus Discordia/Heresis' attack denies their reality along with God's. It impugns the *Psychomachia*'s subject and the basis of allegory, for it denies the integrity of *logos*.

Concord's wound is superficial, however, and her enemy's challenge is revealed, ironically enough, to be impotent and perishable words, words with no basis in the Word. Faith destroys Discord/Heresy quite easily by stopping her speech, blocking her voice, and piercing her tongue (ll. 715–18). The Virtues then make of her what she is, a vivid image of dismemberment (ll. 719–25). The reappearance of Faith initiates the long final movement of the poem, in which the Virtues demonstrate their permanence—which is the permanence of *logos*—by exchanging their anthropomorphic form for one that is unchanging, eternal, and ineffable.

The change begins when the imagery unites the Virtues with each other and with the historical embodiments already mentioned, the victorious Israelites and Christ's disciples. Then, after the defeat of Discordia/Heresis, the Virtues are unified in a different way: spatially. Previously their battleground was by turns the biblical world, the "western shores" of Rome, and the human body—essentially an eternal present and a universal "here." Now, however, Prudentius elaborates a consistent locale that includes cities, countryside, and a military camp. For instance, the Virtues build a "platform . . . at the midmost point of the camp on an elevated ground" (ll. 730–31); Concordia says that they have defeated the "cruel savages that had beset the dwellers in the holy city round about" but warns of possible dissension "between [the nation's] citizens in field and town" (ll. 752–56).

To dismiss this as an "allegorical landscape" in the usual sense is to evade its meaning. It is, of course, morally significant—the watchtower emphasizes the need for alertness, the Virtues' tents invite lethargy, the city-field pairing implies a hierarchy of moral authority—but the significance is in the physical details, not parallel to them. Several commentators have tried to stiffen the moral significance into a full allegorical translation, partly because Prudentius does associate the tents with the body and calls the Virtues *partes Mentis* (ll. 741–

44).[65] The attempt to expand those references baffles the allegorical cartographer, though, for at other times Prudentius associates not the tents but the plain or the city with the body (ll. 752–58, 818). Clearly, many details of the landscape do not correspond consistently to human anatomy or psychology. Furthermore, it is difficult at times not to identify the "citizens" of the nation, who inhabit the tents, with the Christian community, particularly when Concord urges them in St. Paul's words to live in loving peace with their brothers (ll. 772–83) and warns them against particular fourth-century heretics (ll. 788–95). The resulting image of the early Christians living inside the human body would be another teratogeny of internal-external allegorization. It can be forestalled by a literal reading: the Virtues are not exclusively "parts of the soul" or fourth-century Christians, but the embodied virtues, and the landscape is simply the imaginatively rendered location in which they assemble and order themselves. The setting refers simultaneously to a variety of locations—the body, the soul, the Christian community, perhaps even civilization as a whole (see l. 757)—because it subsumes them all. Indeed, it does more than subsume them. The landscape's vivid details far exceed the demands of any particular reference or of all the references together; they seem clear and complete in themselves. Prudentius evokes, in fact, a setting not less but more real than its extratextual referents—more real because it projects the virtuous individual and the Christian community into one lasting, stable structure.

In the poem's climactic image, the landscape is replaced by something even more stable, an emblematic artifice; the Virtues' setting achieves a mystic finality. The temple they construct is another synthetic image, but with an important difference. Concord associates it with Solomon's temple and with the metaphor of the Christian as a temple (ll. 805–13 and 814–19); we learn also that its four sides are the four periods of human life (ll. 842–50); moreover, the inscriptions of the apostles' names above the doors confirm a natural association of the temple with the church (ll. 838–39). Finally, however, a new kind of meaning is present in the image. As numerous scholars have pointed out, the temple is virtually identical with the heavenly Jerusalem in Revelation. It thus subsumes not just biblical, psychological, and social reality, but apocalyptic reality as well.

65. See, for instance, Smith, pp. 145–46.

In fact, apocalyptic identification controls the passage, constituting the only set of detailed correspondences. If the battle and landscape were difficult to "translate" allegorically, the temple is impossible to identify consistently with anything except the New Jerusalem. An attempt to imagine it as the soul or spirit is immediately strained by the pragmatic land-surveying done by Peace (ll. 826–29). Extrapolation of the four-ages passage or of the Pauline metaphors equating "temple" and "body" soon produces a monster with twelve orifices: "On the side of the dawn stretches clear a quarter lit up by three gates; three gates open towards the south; three entrances present three doors to the west; and as many openings does the lofty house show towards the pole of the north" (ll. 830–34). And any translation whatever is sabotaged when the mechanism of the imagery literally and quite deliberately creaks: "The crane was creaking with the weight on its chains as it whirled the vast gems up to the heights" (ll. 866–67). Despite his sporadic allusions to the church, human life, and the "city of the body," Prudentius seems to call attention primarily to the visual surface of the temple-building passage. The reason is clearly not that he intends the visual surface to be without significance; rather, its significance, like that of Revelation, is visual and untranslatable. The Virtues here transform themselves from personified abstractions, whose meaning is necessarily verbal and conceptual, to twelve "virtutum gemmas" (l. 911) whose significance is symbolic and unspecified (ll. 854–65). Allegorical narrative, in which concepts interact in time, has given way to the static images of apocalyptic vision.

The *Psychomachia*'s final images compress into an allegorical tableau the metamorphoses of the entire narrative. The inner chamber of the Virtues' temple encloses a pearl "to buy which Faith had boldly sold at auction all her substance and her property, and paid for it a thousand talents" (ll. 872–74). The biblical allusion generalizes Faith—we may not immediately associate this "Faith" with the personification who defeated Cultura Deorum Veterum—and thus enhances the statement that Faith is divesting herself of substance and property. That is, Faith is disembodied as a personification and reassimilated into a familiar spiritual pattern. In the same inner chamber, the poem continues, Sapientia is enthroned, holding

a sceptre, not finished with craftsman's skill but a living rod of green wood; severed from its stock, it draws no nurture from moist earthly soil, yet puts forth perfect foliage and with blooms of blood-red roses intermingles white lilies that never droop on withering stem. This is the sceptre that was prefigured by the flowering rod that Aaron carried, which, pushing buds out of its dry bark, unfolded a tender grace with burgeoning hope, and the parched twig suddenly swelled into new fruits.   [Ll. 878–87]

Everything in that passage is multiply significant. The "living rod" is a common symbol for Christ, and, as with Faith's pearl, the symbolism is mediated through allusion to a prior, sacred text. The symbolism of the rod is further compounded by a complex typological matrix: this is the pattern for the sceptre carried by Aaron, which was itself a figure of Christ, making this rod either Christ or another figure of him. And not just images open to include sacred figures; the abstraction Sapientia also seems to be more than an abstraction. Enthroned in the inmost temple, called *domina,* bearing the blossoming sceptre and therefore serving as antitype to Aaron, Sapientia evokes Christ.

That is one of Prudentius' most striking double exposures, and it suggests to us the basis of his allegory. The representation of Christ as a personified abstraction is disturbing and even blasphemous unless we assume Christ to be the higher reality. And if *sapientia* is a name for Christ, perhaps all the virtues are ultimately versions of him. In any case, Christ provides the pattern both for their ontological metamorphoses and for their ultimate ontological stability. Nowhere is the fusion of levels of being more intense than in the image of the flowering rod cut off from the earth, an image insistently biological but unquestionably spiritual, merging the Virtues' battle with Old Testament history and with eternal truth. It leaves little doubt that the Incarnation is the model for Prudentian allegory.

That revelation does not quite end the poem. It is followed by a final anticlimax, necessitated by the distance between revealed truth and the mortal poet. Prudentius prays,

We give to Thee, O Christ, Thou tenderest of teachers, unending thanks. . . . Thou didst wish us to learn the dangers that lurk unseen within the body, and the vicissitudes of our soul's struggle. We know that in the darkness of our heart conflicting affections fight hard in successive combats and, as the fortune of battle varies, now grow strong in goodness of disposition and again, when the virtues are worsted, are dragged away to live in bondage to the worse, making

themselves the slaves of shameful sins, and content to suffer the loss
of their salvation.   [Ll. 888–98]

That prayer, more than any other passage, has led to the misunderstanding of the *Psychomachia* as an externalization of internal experience. To modern readers, Prudentius seems to be translating the fiction back to its psychological origins. Read attentively, however, his
words indicate that "conflicting affections" are not identical with the
virtues ("novimus ancipites . . . sensus / sudare alternis conflictibus,
et variato / pugnarum eventu nunc indole crescere dextra, / nunc
inclinatis virtutibus ad iuga vitae / deteriora trahi" [ll. 893–97]) and
that the mortal heart is one battlefield in a wider war: "distantesque
animat duplex substantia vires" ("and our two-fold being inspires
powers at variance with each other" [l. 909]). Prudentius is not expli-
cating his earlier narrative but withdrawing from the spectacle of
universal combat and apocalyptic victory into an anguished awareness of individual human imperfection: "Savage war rages hotly,
rages within our bones, and man's two-sided nature is in an uproar of
rebellion" (ll. 902–4). The effect of the words is less elucidative than
lyric. In the context of such deeply felt humility, Prudentius finally
reasserts the universal, eternal truth of what he has written. Individual psychic struggle will continue, but only

> until Christ our God comes to our aid, orders all the jewels of the
> virtues in a pure setting, and where sin formerly reigned builds the
> golden courts of his temple, creating for the soul, out of the trial of its
> conduct, ornaments for rich Wisdom to find delight in as she reigns
> for ever on her beauteous throne.   [Ll. 910–15]

Discussing works other than the *Psychomachia*, Angus Fletcher
writes, "Those final moments of vision which climax most major
allegorical works . . . constitute the highest function to be accorded
the allegorical mode. . . . Once allegory becomes truly apocalyptic it
ceases to be mere allegory and comes instead to share in the higher
order of mysterious language, which we may perhaps call mythical
language."[66] Aside from his perverse suggestion that allegory reaches
the highest orders of language only by self-destructing, Fletcher implies that allegorical works represent truth through a significant vari-

66. Fletcher, *Allegory*, pp. 354–55.

ety of methods, including apocalyptic vision, and that their most profound significance arises from the relationships of those methods. In the *Psychomachia,* not the apocalyptic moment itself but its climactic but penultimate position within a complex narrative exemplifies the "highest function" of allegory.

Although the *Psychomachia* has much in common with the "major allegories" to which Fletcher refers, it does not belong to the highest ranks of literature. When read sympathetically it is a powerful and well-constructed poem; but the fact that it has been read sympathetically so seldom since the Middle Ages, while such works as the *Divine Comedy* and *The Faerie Queene* have been enjoyed and admired, suggests its limitations. The *Psychomachia* lacks the greatest allegories' power to overcome the barrier between us and the mode.

Nevertheless, the unresponsiveness of modern readers is only partly the poem's fault. A mistaken theory of allegory has made us first look for a poem that Prudentius did not write and then complain when we fail to find it. Even this most basic of allegories does not respond well to the assumption that it says one thing and means another. Faith's amazon courage, Long-Suffering's awkward military posture, Indulgence's beautiful accoutrements, Greed's clutter, the familiar military camp, and the miraculous jeweled temple are as richly untranslatable as any other poetic signs. Complaints about the poem's rigid didacticism miss their mark, which ought to be our misidentification of a split-level heuristic with the text's own coherent but unchartable structure. Similarly, the objection that a pitched battle does not accurately represent the inner life is wrongheaded. The *Psychomachia* does not base itself on the inner life, and what it does say about psychological experience is said not in spite of but through the military imagery: that our moral struggles possess epic importance and intensity; that they are, or can be, of a piece with sacred and secular history; that even their accidental confusions can be absorbed into collective and permanent resolutions. Allegory, the narrative of universals, envisions human life as a continual interchange between temporal event and eternal pattern. We ought not to be surprised at the power of that vision for Prudentius' early readers.

Part II

PERSONIFICATIONS
AND PERSONAE

C. S. Lewis' widely accepted designation of the *Psychomachia* as
the first full-scale allegory should not be taken to mean that Prudentius invented the genre. We would suspect, even if we had no evidence, that allegory is nearly as old as literary discourse itself. It is
nearly inseparable from the implicit rules whose violation creates it: a
rule limiting certain predicates to animate, deictic subjects immediately invites the kind of violation represented by "nature speaks" or
"chastity kills lust," and a code that produces stories about particular
beings suggests at once the possibility of stories about generalities or
about two superimposed sets of beings. The origins of allegory are
not, therefore, to be found in history. Nonetheless, the *Psychomachia*
does inaugurate, if not generate, allegory's greatest flourishing, probably because Christianity provided Realistic narrative with a particularly strong base: the conviction that the intelligible is more authentic
than the sensible, and the equally important belief that the sensible
nonetheless participates in intelligible reality.

The first medieval narratives modeled on those convictions take
forms that seem, in retrospect, predictable. If universals are to act,

they can most naturally do so in ways that resemble the predicates normally used with abstract nouns. For the most part those predicates express either manifestation—appearing, speaking—or relationships: opposition and reconciliation, dominance and subordination. Thus we have allegorical instruction, as in Boethius' *Consolation of Philosophy;* allegorical debates, as in certain sections of Augustine's *Confessions;* allegorical quarrels and peacemaking, as in the "embryonic allegory" of the four daughters of God in Psalms; and the allegorical combats found not only in the *Psychomachia* but also in such forerunners as the *Thebaid,* which Lewis regards as a transition from the realistic to the allegorical epic.[1] In themselves, such allegorical events proceed as does the *Psychomachia*—through the interconversion of static ideas and their temporal embodiments. In their contexts, they produce another kind of interchange as well. Most of them, unlike the *Psychomachia,* are embedded within nonallegorical texts. In one way or another the allegorical Realities break through into a realistic world, somewhat as the gods intervene in the adventures of classical heroes or as Christ appears to the early disciples.

The impulse toward allegory was powerful enough and adventurous enough so that revelational and relational plots, such as dialogues and battles, did not long monopolize the allegorical tradition. The other forms that were pressed into service—romance, drama, and biography, for instance—lent themselves less easily to universal agency. Universals may reveal themselves or oppose one another, but they cannot fall in love, appear on stage, or grow older. Of course, because the universals of allegory are embodied, human experience and human actors are not ineligible for allegorical narrative. But the personae essential to romance, drama, and biography affect the structure of allegory in a different way than do, say, the personifications and the historical exemplars of the virtues. The latter may change places or double-expose each other as manifestations of a single abstraction. The former maintain their distinct concrete identities, which constitute a second semantic constant, alongside the abstractions. The difference can be imagined if we try to think of a human captain commanding the Virtues throughout their metamorphoses, or of the *Psychomachia* as a war movie. The virtues as universals might still organize the story intellectually, but at least part of our attention

1. Lewis, *Allegory of Love,* pp. 49–56.

would be directed toward intransigently human agents. Paradigmatic allegory centers on universals; allegorical romance, drama, and biography modify the paradigm by dividing our focus between universal and human agency.

If that modification produces allegory that is impure by contrast with the *Psychomachia,* it does not produce inferior allegory. On the contrary, personification allegories with personae have appealed to more readers since the Middle Ages than their more straightforward cousins. Some recent scholars even regard the persona as essential to the genre—a misunderstanding, but also a tribute.[2] One strength of the innovation is, obviously, that we can easily and continuously project ourselves into the narrative of an allegory that uses a persona or personae. Another is that such allegories incorporate the powerful effect mentioned above in connection with nonallegorical texts that become temporarily allegorical: the breakthrough of Reality into reality. In allegories that use personae, realism and Realism are maintained as alternate perspectives, one attending the human actors or the biologically based events and the other activated by the personifications. Poised between the features of virtue and human physiognomy, the allegories of mixed agency act out not only truth's intersections with time but also the gaps and oppositions. As always, however, allegorical meaning is constituted by whatever conjunction occurs, even if it should be the ironic conjunction of what cannot really be conjoined. The range of possibilities is wide, from the provisional alliances of Guillaume de Lorris through the dramatic reconciliations of the morality plays to the intense but unstable compounds of *The Pilgrim's Progress.*

2. See, for instance, Barney, *Allegories of History,* p. 37.

2 Ironic Allegory:
The Romance of the Rose

Allegory is almost as seductive a concept as reality, and for nearly the same reason: it offers confirmation of our unquestioned assumptions. If an allegory is a disposable fictional covering, what lies under it must be something that we assume to be real—that is, fundamental, nonproblematic, and irreducible. The search for such a hidden reality can distort a narrative to buttress a culture's preoccupations. Thus medieval exegetes could reclaim pagan or even scriptural texts for their own philosophic ends. "Where the Bible did not obviously mean what he thought it ought to mean," Richard Hanson writes, "or even where it obviously did not mean what he thought it ought to mean, [Origen] had only to turn the magic ring of allegory, and—Hey Presto!—the desired meaning appeared."[1] Thus, too, the twentieth century consistently interprets allegories as "profound and far-reaching exploration[s] of the human psyche."[2]

C. S. Lewis' psychological interpretation of the *Romance of the Rose,* in particular, proposes that an apparently alien mode of writing really confirms modern ideas. "Do not let us be deceived by the allegorical form," he urges. "That, as we have seen, does not mean

1. R. P. C. Hanson, *Allegory and Event: A Study of the Sources and Significance of Origen's Interpretation of Scripture* (London: SCM Press, 1959), p. 371.
2. Paul Piehler, *The Visionary Landscape: A Study in Medieval Allegory* (Montreal: McGill/Queen's University Press, 1971), p. 5.

69

that the author is talking about non-entities, but that he is talking about the inner world. . . ." Guillaume de Lorris might be called "the founder of the sentimental novel. A love story of considerable subtlety and truth is hidden in the *Romance*."[3] Lewis' approach has found nearly universal acceptance, persisting through most of the critical debates over the poem. Alan M. F. Gunn, for instance, writes, "For the allegorical story is only a thin disguise for a story of the inner life—and to a less degree of the outer fortunes—of a medieval lover. It is, as we would say today, a psychological novel in verse."[4]

As I argued in Chapter 1, the notion that allegories are psychological novels in code has produced unsuccessful and damaging readings of the *Psychomachia*. It can be shown to have distorted the *Romance of the Rose* as well. In Guillaume de Lorris' portion of the poem, for instance, psychological reading has generated sterile and unresolvable debates over the referent of Jealousy (a husband's possessiveness? the suspicions of other relatives? the beloved's own jealousy?)—debates that entail embarrassing speculation over the age and marital status of the "heroine."[5] And Jean de Meun's massive continuation can be referred to internal experience only if we posit a psyche that sustains long philosophical disquisitions with itself. Once again, the attempt to read allegory by translation yields predictably unsatisfactory results.

Indeed, allegory is unsuited to the presentation of psychological experience, because it cannot easily incorporate the experiencing consciousness. Allegorical events are categorical, "stripped," as Paul Zumthor puts it, "of whatever was unique, individual, and thus relatively unreal."[6] The persona, vehicle of individuality and subjectivity, does not appear in the *Psychomachia;* Prudentius' narrator is unob-

3. Lewis, *Allegory of Love,* pp. 115, 135.

4. Alan M. F. Gunn, *The Mirror of Love: A Reinterpretation of "The Romance of the Rose"* (Lubbock: Texas Tech Press, 1952), p. 175.

5. For attempts to attribute Jealousy and thus to specify the situation of the "heroine," see, for instance, Lewis, *Allegory of Love,* p. 134; René Louis, *Le Roman de la Rose* (Paris: Champion, 1974), p. 13; Donald Stone, Jr., "C. S. Lewis and Lorris' Lady," *Romance Notes* 6 (1965):196–99; George D. Economou, "The Two Venuses and Courtly Love," in *In Pursuit of Perfection: Courtly Love in Medieval Literature,* ed. Economou and Joan M. Ferrante (Port Washington, N.Y.: Kennikat Press, 1975), p. 29.

6. Paul Zumthor, "Narrative and Anti-Narrative: *Le Roman de la Rose,*" trans. Frank Yeomans, *Yale French Studies* 51 (1974):192.

trusive and impersonal, like the voices that narrate sacred texts, myths, and prophecies.[7] A persona is essential to a second seminal allegory, Boethius' *Consolation of Philosophy*, but Boethius' "I" is a medium rather than a protagonist; indeed, his primary task is to transcend his personal point of view. The same is true in the later allegorical pilgrimages that do, in a sense, center in a persona's experience. Those personae enact universal patterns, not the timebound experiences of particular individuals. As Rosemond Tuve points out, when Guillaume de Deguileville's persona meets the sacraments, he is not being married or ordained.[8] In all such first-person allegories, a clear boundary separates the persona's individual experience from his universal vision. From Boethius through Alan of Lille, the function of the allegorical persona is primarily to convey us beyond subjectivity.

But subjectivity is precisely the realm of romance, "the genre of the individual," as W. T. H. Jackson has called it.[9] The psychologizers of the *Romance of the Rose* stand on firmer ground than do those who would assemble Prudentius' abstractions into one superpsyche. Surely romantic love is an internal experience. Indeed, the reader of the *Romance* can notice immediately a more clearly subjective orientation than that of classical allegory. Guillaume de Lorris' narrator does not set out to impart sacred or hidden truth, but appeals to his audience, in a conversational tone, to understand and accept his story. He wishes not to enlighten us but "the more to make your hearts rejoice."[10] He presents his vision as an extension of a common experience, the onset of love's domination (ll. 21–25), preparing us less

7. The connection of allegorical revelation with priestly and prophetic utterance is explored by Honig in *Dark Conceit*, pp. 19–27.

8. Rosemond Tuve, *Allegorical Imagery: Some Mediaeval Books and Their Posterity* (Princeton: Princeton University Press, 1966), p. 159.

9. W. T. H. Jackson, "The Nature of Romance," *Yale French Studies* 51 (1974):25.

10. *Le Roman de la Rose par Guillaume de Lorris et Jean de Meun*, ed. Ernest Langlois, Société des anciens textes français (Paris: Didot [vols. 1–2], Champion [vols. 3–5], 1914–24), II, 32; translation from Charles Dahlberg, *The Romance of the Rose by Guillaume de Lorris and Jean de Meun* (Princeton: Princeton University Press, 1971), p. 31. Copyright © 1971 by Princeton University Press. I have cited Langlois rather than the newer edition by Felix Lecoy because Lecoy's decision to follow a single base manuscript produces substantial discrepancies between his text and the synthetic one still familiar to English-speaking scholars. Future references to Langlois's edition of the *Romance of the Rose* will be documented by line number in the text. English translations followed by parenthetical page numbers are from Dahlberg.

for a cosmic revelation than for a fictional experience like our own lives.

That universals do, nonetheless, enact the fictional experience constitutes the radical innovation of this first vernacular allegory. The conjunction of romance and allegory explains the poem's unsurpassed popularity in manuscript. Probably some early readers unbalanced the mixture, either dismissing the allegory as a barrier between themselves and vicarious eroticism or subordinating the romantic biography to a Real Christian allegory.[11] But the poem's art is its balancing, its interinanimation, of disparate genres. The narrative agents appear to be, alternatively and sometimes simultaneously, impersonal abstractions and human individuals. The mode of the poem is thus genuine irony, "the existence of a second perspective on a statement or action"—in this case, on all of the agents—"of which the reader is made aware."[12] Evident equally in the "dainty equivalences" of Guillaume de Lorris and the "huge, dishevelled, violent poem" of his continuator,[13] the interplay of generic perspectives is the most important shaping principle of the *Romance of the Rose*.

Guillaume's version of generic dissonance is subtle enough to charm rather than startle. Announcing his intention to recite a romance, Guillaume's narrator provides what must be literature's most courteous introduction to the visionary world, for he leads the reader not across a threshold but, in H. R. Jauss's words, "by almost imperceptible stages from that which [is] familiar to him, the courtly world, to that which [has] a dreamlike quality, the world of allegory."[14] Like

11. In our own times, the first kind of reader is likely to see the poem as thinly veiled romantic autobiography—a view that, as I have argued, we accept uncritically and unwisely. Readers of the second type are represented by D. W. Robertson, Jr., who regards the poem as a confrontation of charity (advocated by Reason) and cupidity (embodied by the God of Love and embraced by the Lover). Robertson, and following him Charles Dahlberg, see the *Romance* as ironic in a sense quite different from mine: for them the irony is unbalanced, because one point of view, the Christian, contradicts and inevitably outweighs the other. See p. 77, below.

12. M. M. Liberman and Edward E. Foster, *A Modern Lexicon of Literary Terms* (Glenview, Ill.: Scott, Foresman, 1968), p. 63.

13. Lewis, *Allegory of Love*, p. 137.

14. Hans Robert Jauss, "La Transformation de la forme allégorique entre 1180 et 1240: D'Alain de Lille à Guillaume de Lorris," *L'humanisme médiéval dans les littératures romanes du XIIe au XIVe siècle*, ed. Anthime Fourrier (Paris: Klincksieck, 1964), p. 108.

the somnolent and visionary personae before him, he has had a dream, "but in this dream was nothing which did not happen almost as the dream told it" (p. 31; ll. 1–5). The border between the visionary and the waking world seems, in fact, deliberately confounded. The careful reader cannot be sure where the dream begins:

> I became aware that it was May, five years or more ago; I dreamed that I was filled with joy in May, the amorous month. . . . [P. 31; ll. 45–48]

> In that delicious season in which everything is stirred by love, I dreamed one night that I was. [Ll. 84–86; my translation]

Did the dream occur in May, or was it May in the dream, or both? We cannot say, and the dream itself does not enlighten us. Waking to a conventional May morning, the dreamer carries out his morning routines and walks toward a river "but little smaller than the Seine" (l. 112), a river with which he seems familiar before he sees it. The landscape through which he strolls can easily be allegorized as, for instance, "the river of life, in early youth,"[15] but the text presents it only as a conventionally beautiful place seen by a particular young man. This is a vision of what might just as well be ordinary experience.

An equivocation between visionary and ordinary experience continues in the narrator's encounter with the allegorical figures on the garden wall. The figures bear abstract labels—Felony, Villainy, Hatred, and so forth—but they are objects, painted sculptures with inscriptions (ll. 129–33); the verbal description of them signifies at two removes. The narrator continually reminds us that he is describing depictions:

> I looked back to the right and saw another image named Villainy. . . .
> He who could produce an image of such a truly contemptible creature knew how to paint and portray. . . .

> This image had hands that were clawlike and hooked, appropriate to Covetousness, who is always in a fever to get the possessions of another. [P. 33; ll. 156–65, 188–91]

15. Lewis, *Allegory of Love*, p. 119.

He seems less to be encountering felony, villainy, and so on than to be admiring the decorations outside an elaborate public garden.

As the catalogue proceeds, we become aware not only that an artificer has created the figures, but also that some particular consciousness has selected them. As Lewis suggests, the catalogue sets up an expectation that it then violates: we expect something like the Seven Deadly Sins or the Prudential Vices, but "vices (such as Avarice and Envy) are mingled with misfortunes like Poverty, Age, or Sadness." Lewis' astute interpretation—that the wall presents the mixture of moral, social, and economic qualities excluded by courtly life—should not cause us to forget that the catalogue is indeed a "curious collection."[16] The established patterns of allegorical organization have been altered by a particular sensibility, with a particular point of view.

Even more strikingly, a particular sensibility also transmits the personifications. The narrator frequently extends his account of the images into an exposition of the principles themselves, as when he shifts from past to present tense to explain that Covetousness "understands nothing else, but esteems most highly what belongs to another" (p. 33; ll. 192–94). Such extrapolation from what can be seen is common in allegorical ecphrasis and can serve, as in Chaucer's *Knight's Tale*, to blend a verbal with a pictorial description and thus to redirect our gaze through all representations to the idea itself. Here, however, the extrapolations are less like alternative representations than like editorial commentary. They are heavily judgmental— Envy must pay for her malice (ll. 260–61); Papelardie and her kind will not go to heaven (ll. 434–37)—and the judgments seem personal, not those of an authoritative seer. Indeed, some of them are not moral verities but somewhat narrow-minded reactions to individuals. One comment on Old Age, for instance, is a callous dismissal of its embodiment: "If she had died, it would have been neither a great loss nor a great wrong, for age had already dried up her body and reduced it to nothing" (p. 35; ll. 348–51). Another reveals that the narrator assumes an audience as naively young as himself: "She was dressed warmly, for otherwise she would have been cold. These old people, you understand, are very cold by nature" (p. 36; ll. 403–06). And the ecphrasis of Poverty is a far cry from Augustine's encomium: the

16. Ibid., p. 126.

narrator marvels at this young woman's misery and concludes that the hour of conception of a poor person can well be cursed (ll. 441–62). The narrative claims universal validity through its allegorical form, but it conveys the subjective responses of a limited narrator.[17]

When the narrator meets his first unsculpted personification, he still does not behave as if confronting another ontological realm. Far from being overwhelmed by a majestic guardian of the threshold, he walks to the door of his allegorical locus, insists on being admitted, and meets the gatekeeper as coolly as if she were a woman of his own social class. And so she appears to be—a lovely but decidedly material figure, describable in the courtly youth's habitual vocabulary: "She had hair as blond as a copper basin, flesh more tender than that of a baby chick. . . . Her neck was of good proportion, thick enough and reasonably long, without pimples or sores. . . . She wore a coat of rich green from Ghent, cord-stitched all around" (pp. 37–38; ll. 527–28, 539–41, 564–65). The information that she is called Oiseuse by those who know her (ll. 581–82) provides a second perspective on the lady. If we now generalize, as we are probably meant to do, that leisure controls access to the walled garden, we do so only after responding to the deictic image of Oiseuse as a peer of the narrator.

Oiseuse marks the entrance to the hybrid realm of allegorical romance. Walled into a perfect square, filled with stylized sequences of objects and agents whose abstract names determine much of their behavior and appearance, the garden is clearly an order of ideas. Yet numerous other details reshape it into a picture of courtly society. The dancers called Beauty, Joy, Youth, and so forth, who act in some ways as timeless abstractions, also appear in a particular cultural context, listening to a song from Lorraine and watching two manifestly unabstract girls dressed only in kirtles (ll. 749–71). The narrator repeatedly calls them "genz" and concludes, "All together they were warm, open people, well instructed and beautifully trained" (p. 48; ll. 1282–84). In the carol, moreover, the two perspectives literally go hand in hand, for the personifications are partnered by anonymous individuals: "a young man . . . who took delight in living in fine mansions," "a knight who was easy to know and pleasant of

17. A similar point is made by Jean Batany in *Approches du "Roman de la Rose,"* p. 42.

speech," and so on (pp. 45–47; ll. 1110–13, 1245–46).[18] The garden itself wavers between the ideal realm of allegory and the more earth-bound one of the courtly persona. It seems paradisal, "esperitables" (l. 638), the creation of the idea Delight and therefore an idea itself; on the other hand, it is full of familiar plants and animals, and Delight himself is apparently a skilled landscape architect with a great deal of money (ll. 589–602).

Depending on which aspect of this intermediary garden we emphasize, we can see it as either transcendent or hyperbolic. That is, we can conclude that a genuine allegorical paradise has materialized in the twelfth-century French court, or that in regarding its creation as a paradise the court suffers from allegorical megalomania. The garden's chief inhabitant substantiates both readings. The God of Love is on the one hand a divinity, elevated above the other carolers by supernatural costuming (ll. 878–80, 895–98) and by his name. "It seemed that he was an angel come straight from heaven" (p. 43; ll. 902–3), and he rules over lords and ladies as if he were indeed divine (ll. 868–72). On the other hand, a broader perspective reveals him as a tinsel angel, for his dress and behavior are courtly clichés. When compared with a genuinely superhuman figure such as Alan of Lille's Natura, whose robe can be said without hyperbole to be made of plants and animals, he is almost parodic.

The turning point of the plot is the persona's vision of the allegorical realm that the God of Love dominates as both genuine and illusory. Two crystals at the bottom of Narcissus' well reveal, "without deceiving, the whole nature of the garden" (ll. 1560–61). In the crystals' perfect reflection, the God of Love's domain appears clear and complete. But the narrowness of the reflection constitutes falsehood, so that the narrator can add without contradiction, "That mirror deceived me" (l. 1609). Beauty is indeed here, but it has also a

18. The nameless carolers do not coalesce with their abstract partners as Job does with Patientia in the *Psychomachia*, for the compatibility of Job and Patientia depended on the latter's obvious abstractness. Patientia was a mythic figure, clearly transhuman, whereas the courtly personifications are described in the same terms as their anonymous partners. Moreover, the battle of Patientia takes place in a poetic present that can easily subsume Job's story, but the actions of Guillaume's personifications do not differ, in tense or fictionality, from those of his anonymous people. In short, Guillaume makes his two sets of characters appear ontologically equal even as he gives one of them abstract names.

wider existence; the Poverty that the narrator has described is Poverty as reflected truly—but truly in his limited vision; the God of Love reigns over mortals but does not inhabit the wider heaven. The claim that the agents are genuine universals, that the crystals reflect perfectly, teeters on the fulcrum of irony.

The balance of irony can seldom be precisely calibrated. Knowing that Christian orthodoxy would reject any subjective definition of truth, some readers accept the assessment of D. W. Robertson, Jr., that Guillaume's irony is heavily weighted toward the wider perspective normally associated with allegory. For Robertson, the garden has no legitimate claim to be an allegorical paradise; it is indeed an allegorical realm, but in terms quite unlike the ones with which it labels itself: the crystals are not magic mirrors but the purblind eyes of the flesh, the rose is sensuous beauty, and the God of Love is really Satan.[19] In making those identifications, however, Robertson shortcircuits reading by seeking referents instead of signs. With his ambivalent imagery, Guillaume directs us to, but not beyond, the tension between an objective and a subjective evaluation of the allegory. If the God of Love is not fully a god, neither is he Satan, or even a mere fantasy. As the narrator tells us, the mirror's image of perfection is both true and false; were its truth mere illusion, the Fall would never have occurred.

The center of the mirror's ironic revelation is of course the rose. The image is usually taken to be straightforward, if bilevel: literally a rosebud, allegorically a young woman. Inevitable as it seems, however, that reading is untenable. In the first place, even the literal image is patently something more than a flower. The narrator's inordinate desire to pluck the rosebud—a desire that has also seized many other men (ll. 1619–25)—can never have seemed, even to the most naively medieval of minds, even for a moment, a thicker veil than the gauze in which Chaucer saw Venus. Indeed, Venus herself will presently discard the veil altogether, when in urging Fair Welcoming to surrender the rosebud she uses terms that have nothing to do with flowers:

> "There is no lady, no châtelaine whom I should not consider base if she were to make any resistance to him. His heart will not change if

19. D. W. Robertson, Jr., "The Doctrine of Charity in Mediaeval Literary Gardens: A Topical Approach through Symbolism and Allegory," *Speculum* 26 (1951):24–49.

you grant him the kiss. A kiss would be very well used on him, since, believe it, he has very sweet breath; his mouth is not ugly but seems to be made on purpose for solace and diversion, for the lips are red and the teeth white and so clean that there is neither tartar nor filth on them." [P. 80; ll. 3455–67]

In the second place, if the rose is not really a rose, neither is it a very satisfactory symbol for a woman. Certain descriptions associate it with female genitals, but that identification, if pressed, produces marked anomalies in the plot.[20] A modest retreat to "the Lady's love"—C. S. Lewis' identification[21]—merely evades the essential question: In what sense can a flower represent someone's love? The question can be answered only by being accepted. The rose is that universal but spurious phenomenon, the *object* of love. As a representation of a human being who might feel love, it is both deficient and excessive, shimmering between vegetation and deity; yet it blocks its referent absolutely. Its multivalence is more radical than the subjective distortions of Poverty, Beauty, and the God of Love; it is the magic mirror's complete, permanent destabilization of perspective.

Unsettled by his inseparably true-and-false vision of the rose, the persona enters an allegorical episode that seems predominantly false—not merely subjectively inconsistent and implausible. His wounding by love's arrows is, of course, literally absurd. It is hardly necessary to remark that at no time does he act like a man with five arrowheads in his heart. But if we hasten to translate the fiction into its underlying psychological truth, we find the two inseparable. The arrowhead called "Simplece" is also explicitly *simplece,* which has made many young people fall in love (ll. 1737–39). Additionally, anyone who sought to translate such obviously incoherent metaphors as the arrows would seem simpleminded, because translation is gratuitous; concealment of one kind of meaning under another can hardly have been Guillaume's purpose. The episode's meaning is, in fact, inseparable from its use of conventional but specious imagery, along with clear signs of that imagery's speciousness. Guillaume represents

20. To begin with the most obvious anomaly, the roses are openly displayed in the courtly garden. Moreover, such gestures as plucking a leaf to wear and kissing the rose, where they occur later, clearly do not sustain the specifically genital identifications proffered in, for instance, ll. 1659–67. The genital symbolism is tentative and intermittent.

21. Lewis, *Allegory of Love,* p. 129.

here not an internal experience but the inhabitation of an ·invented world that is known by its inhabitants to be invented.

We presently see the persona accept the terms of the invented world both explicitly and implicitly. First, he overtly swears homage to the God of Love. Then, when the latter asks for guarantees of his loyalty, he replies, "This heart is yours, not mine. . . . You have placed within it a garrison that will guard and rule it well. Beyond all that, if you fear anything, make a key for it and carry it with you. The key will serve in place of a pledge" (p. 58; ll. 1985–93). The God of Love is delighted at this idea—as well he should be, for the narrator has demonstrated his collusion in the invented world of love, like a child elaborating his playmates' fantasy game with new invisible props.

What makes the game real is not only the lover's acceptance of it but the reader's or hearer's as well. Immediately after using the admittedly metaphoric key—"Then he touched my side and locked my heart so softly that I hardly felt the key" (p. 58; ll. 2008–10)—the God of Love issues "commandments" probably familiar to the audience from other contexts. His long lecture is not metaphoric at all: he refers not to roses, personifications, and the garden, but to streets, houses, and the lover's *amie* (e.g., ll. 2352, 2379, 2381, 2441). Accordingly, he speaks to the narrator's own hearers directly. The narrator cautions, "Let him who wishes to love give his attention to it, for the romance improves from this point on" (p. 59; ll. 2061–62). The absurd fiction is a way of conveying what we already accept as true.

Indeed, the absurd fiction is itself true. Before continuing with the plot, the narrator propounds a paradox much like that of the honest/deceptive mirror: the dream contains no lying word, but its truth is hidden (ll. 2076, 2070–75). As a preface to the ensuing action, the paradox is usually taken to mean that the literal narrative encodes psychological realities, that the confrontations that the dreamer sees among Fair Welcoming, Jealousy, Shame, Dangier, and so forth represent the real struggles of his waking courtship. Once again, however, the relationship between text and truth is not so simple. Attempts to decode the plot have hit snags, such as the difficulty of attributing Jealousy. Jealousy is in fact unattributable, and thus untranslatable; like Dangier, who is the guardian not of one rose but of roses in general, she is an attitude in the abstract. At the same time, however, she is not an entirely convincing abstraction. Although Guillaume's

allegorical confrontation is as untranslatable as Prudentius', its meaning is quite different: it is not always coherent as a conflict among
ideas. Fair Welcoming in the abstract excludes fear and anger, but
this Fair Welcoming shows both emotions (ll. 2907–19). Dangier
becomes at one point so inappropriately compliant that Shame must
remind him, "It doesn't agree with your name for you to do anything
but make trouble" (p. 83; ll. 3695–96). The allegory is, in fact, both
genuinely untranslatable and amusingly incoherent.

The paradox is the familiar one of objective and subjective perspectives. Objectively, Fair Welcoming, Shame, and Dangier are not universal Ideas, but they appear to be Realities to the committed lover, and
thus the allegory is genuine as a subjective vision. The incompleteness
of both perspectives places irony at the center of Guillaume's meaning.
When Jealousy builds a full-scale castle around the rose—four turrets,
four gates, and a central tower, defended by catapults, mangonels, and
arbolests (ll. 3797–866)—the comic hyperbole renders precisely the
disproportionate machinations and frustrations that define desire's
conflict with possessiveness. Similarly accurate is the hyperbole whereby attitudes sometimes called "internal" become life-sized personifications. "There is no key for reading the allegory of the *Romance of the
Rose*," writes Marc-René Jung. Shortly afterwards, Jung suggests one
reason for its untranslatability: "Guillaume de Lorris realizes perfectly
well that this love is a game."[22] That is, it is a serious game. Both the
genuineness and the speciousness of Guillaume's allegory are accurate
reflections of love.

Thus it is difficult to imagine how the dream could have been
explained in other terms, as Guillaume leads us to expect (ll. 2070–
75). That expectation is itself a product of his irony. The promised
"exposition" of the dream's meaning (ll. 2071–72) turns out to be
not an explanation but an incorporation of the dream into un-
dreamed romance. As the dreamer took the God of Love's inventions
for his reality, the narrator, at the conclusion of Guillaume's poem,
assimilates the dream's inventions into his waking life.

It has traditionally been assumed that Guillaume did not live to
finish his poem. The assumption rests, first, on the "prophecies" of
Jean de Meun's God of Love: Guillaume will write the story up
through Fair Welcoming's imprisonment and then will cease; "May

22. M.-R. Jung, *Etudes*, p. 310.

his tomb be full of balm . . ." (p. 187; ll. 10526–64). It rests also on readers' (and other continuators') expectations that the rose must be achieved and the dreamer must awaken. But the poem may be complete even if the love story is not. Jean de Meun does not say that Guillaume left his poem unfinished; he says that Guillaume as lover did not achieve his goal—and Jean had his own reasons for continuing the plot to its projected goal.

Paul Strohm suggests that the poem is in a sense complete: it culminates in a lament in which narrator and lover merge.[23] The clearest support for Strohm's astute suggestion is the narrator's switch in the closing lines to present tense and imperative mood.[24] After describing Jealousy's imprisonment of the rose and Fair Welcoming, the narrator explains that he was miserable at Love's disfavor. Love, he concludes, is as changeable as Fortune, whose wheel always turns (ll. 3948–90). At that point he adds, "E je *sui* cil qui *est* versez!" ("And I am the one who is turned" [l. 3991; emphasis added]). Even more surprising is his present-tense lament on the results of Jealousy's actions: "It was an evil time when I saw the walls and the moat that I neither dare nor can pass. Since Fair Welcoming has been put in prison, I have no blessings or joy whatever, for my joy and my remedy lies wholly in him and in the rose that is enclosed within the walls . . ." (p. 87; ll. 3992–98). Then, as if he were within the dream itself, the narrator addresses Fair Welcoming: "Ah, Fair Welcoming, fair sweet friend, even if you have been put into prison, keep me at least in your heart! Do not, at any price, allow Jealousy the Savage to put your heart in servitude as she has done your body" (p. 87; ll. 4003–9). He protests that he has not wronged Fair Welcoming, particularly not by saying "anything . . . that should have been hidden" (ll. 4032–33), but he fears that slanderers and traitors have lost him Fair Welcoming's good will, without which "there will never be any comfort for me" (p. 88; l. 4056).

At least one translator puts the entire speech back into the dream by changing some of the tenses, using quotation marks, and assuming a lacuna in the text.[25] Jean de Meun, at the beginning of his continua-

---

23. Paul Strohm, "Guillaume as Narrator and Lover in the *Roman de la Rose*," *Romanic Review* 59 (1968):3–9.

24. Strohm points out (pp. 6–7) that this is in fact the second monologue in the present tense, the first having occurred at ll. 3762–66.

25. Harry W. Robbins, *The Romance of the Rose*, ed. and introd. Charles W. Dunn (New York: E. P. Dutton Paperbacks, 1962), pp. 86–88.

tion, also recasts Guillaume's present-tense remarks as a speech within the dream, having, as I have suggested, other ends in view than faithfulness to his predecessor. But short of the translator's freedom or the continuator's license, we must acknowledge with Strohm that the narrator here speaks directly to his audience and "explains" the dream by merging it with his present, waking experience. As Strohm points out, we cannot simply reread the poem as an encoded version of the narrator's particular love affair; it was too impersonal and too didactic.[26] Instead, the narrator's love affair and his allegorical dream coalesce, as at the beginning of the narrative.

Where the *Psychomachia* concludes with the resolution of its abstractions into a timeless pattern, Guillaume's *Romance of the Rose* ends by merging its allegory with a particular timebound life. The merger is necessarily incomplete and thus ironic. Addressed by a waking narrator, Fair Welcoming and Jealousy are clearly exaggerated projections from a particular love affair. C. S. Lewis is right, in a sense, to see them as "confessedly less real" than the narrator and his lady.[27] Guillaume's allegory is bogus, the reification, exaggeration, and sublimation of sexual experience. At the same time, however, the allegory makes a legitimate claim to be more general and lasting, and therefore more real, than the individual. The narrator's final statement seeks our acceptance of that claim to subjective validity: "If I lose your good will, there will never be any comfort for me, since I have no ties of faith elsewhere" (p. 88; ll. 4056–58). The plea ostensibly addresses Fair Welcoming, but in so doing it appeals to our own experience of Fair Welcoming as imaginatively real. The poet himself suspends final judgment; his fictional "I" reflects back to us the simultaneous absurdity and truth of an allegorical vision of the individual life.

"Why, forty years after Guillaume de Lorris, did Jean de Meun undertake to pursue his work?" asks Paul Zumthor. The question has been asked often, partly out of a conviction that the continuator and his predecessor had very different interests. In particular, Jean de Meun is thought not to have respected Guillaume's allegory. "He utterly lacks, perhaps despises, Guillaume's architectonics and sense of proportion," according to C. S. Lewis. W. T. H. Jackson writes,

26. Strohm, pp. 7–8.
27. Lewis, *Allegory of Love,* p. 45.

"Jean de Meung's 'continuation' . . . does not really continue Guillaume's poem, because he either did not grasp the necessary connection between romance and Allegory, or, more likely, because he chose to disregard it."[28] What Jean did value, according to most critics, was certain philosophical issues, which he imposed on Guillaume's allegory.[29] Since he wanted simply a framework for those issues, his choice of an allegorical romance was somewhat arbitrary.

Granted that Jean was indeed a philosophical or intellectual poet, however, he may have understood Guillaume's allegorical romance in a different way than we do. For instance, he may have seen in his predecessor's work a playful exploration of the relationship between sensual images and universals. Personification allegory always invites speculation about the status of abstractions. When Dante explains in section 25 of the *Vita Nuova* that he knows quite well that Love is not a substance but an accident in a substance, he betrays a philosophical discomfort about allegory—a well-founded discomfort, for while he can explain his use of personification, he cannot eliminate the implication that Love is a substance without undoing his sonnets completely. Personification does not, in fact, make accidents substantial; we can avoid misunderstanding by remembering that Faith is not equatable with the armed woman but is manifested in her, as in the host of saints, in Abraham, and in many other forms. But misunderstanding is possible, for the "is" of literary representation equivocates with the "is" of philosophic equation. The opacity of Guillaume's imagery encourages such equivocation: his courtly woman seems to *be* Beauty in the same way that the human persona *is* himself—though we know that she cannot be. Moreover, in conjoining a subjective point of view with allegory, Guillaume suggests that what is experienced through the senses corresponds directly to certain concepts and abstractions. Much of his poem's charming naiveté lies in its implication that abstractions are as substantial to the intellect, even to the senses, as are courtly hostesses. At the same time, however, Guillaume undercuts those suggestions by indicating that his "ideas" are not coherent, self-sufficient Platonic essences. His consciously ironic identification of familiar images with abstractions can be seen as a parody of Boethius' claim to have conversed with a lady

28. Zumthor, p. 198; Lewis, *Allegory of Love*, p. 137; W. T. H. Jackson, "Allegory and Allegorization," *Research Studies* 32 (1964):172.
29. Lewis, *Allegory of Love*, pp. 142–43; Batany, pp. 44–45.

named Philosophy. In that ironic interplay between imagery and ideas is much to intrigue a philosophical poet.

Guillaume's allegory might interest a philosopher in another way as well. Insofar as allegory concerns abstractions and principles, it might be expected to preserve their relationships as established outside literature; indeed, allegory often expounds the relative potencies and values of Wisdom, Nature, Mind, and so forth. But insofar as allegory is narrative, it may disrupt established relationships and introduce contingency. Though Poverty is the most respectable quality on the garden wall, the narrator may dislike it as much as he does Avarice. Guillaume's clearest disruption of objective relationships is the brief episode with Reason, who should, philosophically, carry greater authority than any other figure in the garden, but who is quickly dismissed by the persona. She is replaced by Friend, a character who ought not even to confront her ontologically, much less to exceed her power. Reason's high philosophic value conflicts with her status in the narrative.

In short, Guillaume realizes at least two kinds of complexity always latent in allegory: an equivocation about the ontological status of abstractions and an ambivalence between absolute and contingent values. He uses those complexities in delineating the invented reality and the subjective morality of *fin amour*. Jean de Meun reverses Guillaume's priorities, evidently regarding *fin amour* as less important than the issues it raises; but the issues themselves interest both poets. Furthermore, Jean broadens the issues by the same means through which Guillaume suggests them: an ironic use of allegory.

In claiming that Jean uses allegory ironically, I mean to go beyond the fairly widespread recognition that he uses allegory to present an ironic ideology. "Each system of values in Jean de Meun's work is passionately and precisely conceived and sharply and unmistakably opposed to its rival systems," according to Alan Gunn; and although Gunn discerns a winner in the "great *conflictus*," more recent writers do not. In Vladimir R. Rossman's words, "Nobody can say for sure who wins the argument, but no one can deny that [the] adversaries put up a good fight." Rosemond Tuve finds that Jean "identifies no one with the right side," and Zumthor calls the entire set of discourses a "play of open interrogations."[30] Such open-ended irony

---

30. Gunn, p. 437; Vladimir R. Rossman, *Perspectives of Irony in Medieval French Literature* (The Hague: Mouton, 1975), p. 157 (Rossman actually writes "both ad-

would be present even if each of Jean's six monologuists were simply a speaker in a new *Symposium*. But because they are instead allegorical agents, not only their words but also their actions—even their existences—exert and receive ironic pressures. The focus of the irony is the ontological and ethical validity, both individual and collective, of certain ways of ordering reality.

The first blow in the ironic *conflictus* is Reason's attack on the allegorical romance. In Guillaume's narrative, both Reason's philosophical status and her tower place her as far as possible from the persona's perspective; that is probably why Jean immediately reintroduces her. She returns with a devastatingly authoritative sermon. Her demonstration that erotic love is foolish, her association of it with Fortune, and her claim to be the persona's true beloved are all drawn from unimpeachable sources.[31] Reason is, of course, no mere psychological projection or fabricated deity, but God's daughter (ll. 5813–17). As the "only unexceptionable voice" in the poem, she seems to have forestalled all possible opposition.[32]

And she appears to destroy not only the allegory's values, but also the allegory itself. In sheer length—3,000 lines, or three-fourths the length of Guillaume's entire poem—her monologue outflanks the story of the rose; in predominant mode, exposition solid with historical anecdotes, it impugns the fictional dream. Moreover, Reason occasionally employs a rival kind of figurative language that is actually antifigurative, a succession of conceits whose triteness and inconsistency direct us away from imagery and toward principles. For instance, in place of the personification named Wealth who danced in Guillaume's garden, Reason mentions unfigurative *richeces* (ll. 5183–84), then gives those riches the power to stab their "hosts" with three metaphoric blades (ll. 5190–204), then combines them into a single figure, "'a free lady and a queen'" named Wealth (ll. 5205–6), and

---

versaries," because he reduces the dispute to a debate between "courtly and religious views on love" [p. 157]); Tuve, p. 241; Zumthor, p. 195.

31. Winthrop Wetherbee points out Reason's antecedents in Bernardus Silvestris and Alan of Lille, and he cites D. W. Robertson's attribution to her of the "voice of patristic authority." See Wetherbee, *Platonism and Poetry in the Twelfth Century: The Literary Influence of the School of Chartres* (Princeton: Princeton University Press, 1972), pp. 258 and 258–59n.

32. Dahlberg, Introduction to *Romance of the Rose*, p. 6. Dahlberg qualifies that statement by noting that even Reason exists primarily as an allegorical character, but he argues that the poets endorse her viewpoint.

finally declares that she can be bestridden and made to gallop (ll. 5221–25). To Reason, such metaphoric inconsistency is unimportant, since she uses narrative and metaphor merely to embellish truths that may be discursively expressed. She needs neither narrative nor imagery to define love, "'a sickness of thought that takes place between two persons of different sex when they are in close proximity and open to each other'" (pp. 95–96; ll. 4378–80). The kind of love she offers the dreamer is free of images and of plot; in fact, he complains that it does not exist (ll. 5378–87). Reason's reply, conveyed in various ways throughout her speech, is that his allegory and its values are not real, either.

She may be right, but she is in an odd position to say so. Reason almost succeeds in making us forget that she herself is part of the allegory that she sublimely dismisses. But her apparently interminable discourse is a digression here, however correct it is in itself. The more her speech outbulks its context, the stronger the pull of the context on it. Within that context, Reason is long-winded and pompous, wasting time on such arguments as the sophistical demonstration that evil does not exist (ll. 6291–342). She is also, of course, inhumanly rational. The narrator's protest over her blunt sexual terms (ll. 5700–24) reveals primarily his own naiveté, but he does raise a cogent objection: to Reason, sexuality is simply an animal fact, as unremarkable as eating (ll. 5763–94). And Reason is callous about human feeling generally. She is even more pleased about the martyrdom of Virginia than is Chaucer's cold-blooded Physician: Virginius "'exchanged shame for injury, in a marvelous process of reasoning'" (p. 114; ll. 5632–33). Wetherbee argues that Reason has certain theological limitations: unable to understand the "full implications of human depravity," she is falsely confident in her own powers; though God's daughter, she must remain ignorant of grace.[33] Those limitations are indicated in Reason's allegorical form. As Tuve astutely notes, "Off our guard, we think Jean careless not to make her wooing of the Lover such a thing as might charm and find assent; but it dawns upon us that he means that irony too. She does not understand her subject. Few of her best defenders have ever claimed that she could."[34] Granted that inhuman rationality belongs to reason by

33. Wetherbee, pp. 258–59.
34. Tuve, p. 261.

definition, and that to call it a limitation may seem absurd, Jean's Reason is not reason-by-definition. As an anthropomorphic Reason in a story of human love, she is liable to indictments that the pure concept may escape.

The ironic presentation of Reason extends Guillaume's irony: where Guillaume revealed the subjective basis of certain abstractions, Jean presents Reason as objectively universal but limited by her subjective context. Reason is absolutely authoritative, but her authority here is not absolute. The irony is radical.

The standoff between Reason and her context provides the model for the ensuing appearances of Friend, False Seeming, La Vieille, Nature, and Genius. As Alan Gunn writes, Jean "causes all his 'masters' to speak with the voice of *auctoritas*." Various readers have identified most of the speakers with Jean de Meun himself, writing either sincerely or ironically, and have seen in each the central meaning of the poem. Lionel Friedman correctly warns that such readings ignore the monologues' context. Jean encourages such out-of-context readings by allowing each apparently interminable discourse to stretch the context perilously thin, but he eventually continues the narrative more vigorously—indeed, more effectively—than did Guillaume, and the monologuists find themselves reabsorbed into a story that somehow remains primary. Zumthor speaks of "the disaggregation of the pre-text" by the monologues, but the pre-text remains context and disaggregates in turn the perspectives of the speakers.[35]

The second "master" seems initially more an ally of the lover and the allegory than a challenger. Friend offers encouragement in the pursuit of the rose and an endorsement of the values attacked by Reason, drawing on his own experience in love: " 'You are in no way hindered if Fair Welcoming has been captured. After he has conceded so much that you were given the kiss, prison will never hold him' " (p. 138; ll. 7249–53). But the terms of Friend's encouragement are also subversive. That a prisoner has allowed a flower to be kissed ought not to mean that he is now impossible to imprison: Friend's logic is based on the sexual dynamics that the rose allegory has generally suppressed. As he continues, Friend draws more and more heavily on the terms of sensory and sensual experience. He advises the lover to

---

35. Gunn, p. 437; Lionel Friedman, " 'Jean de Meung,' Antifeminism, and 'Bourgeois Realism,' " *Modern Philology* 57 (1959–60):13–17; Zumthor, p. 203.

manipulate Dangier, Shame, Fear, and Foul Mouth as if they were not abstractions at all—to flatter them with purses and ornaments and to deceive them with onion juice (ll. 7431–86). Presently he sets the personified guardians in apposition to a woman: " 'If you waited too long, the gatekeepers would suddenly have turned elsewhere. . . . I advise that no man wait until a woman asks him for his love' " (p. 144; ll. 7645–50). Fair Welcoming is similarly compromised by appearing in apposition with a "dame a cuer vaillant": " 'Pay attention to the way Fair Welcoming looks at you. . . . Do you think that a lady with a worthy heart loves a foolish and flighty boy . . . ?' " (p. 145; ll. 7719–38). Guillaume's delicate irony about the status of his personifications is broadened into sly skepticism.

Of course, Friend himself is not a personification. We feel that he ought to be Friend*ship*, but he is not; as Jean realized, even Guillaume had his ironist's reasons for making him Friend instead. For Jean, Friend's particularity is his meaning: having lived in the world of experience, he cannot believe that the allegorical agents are as stable and impersonal as they pretend to be. Fear, Shame, and Dangier "only pretend to get angry," he says (p. 144; l. 7682). Nor does he see stability in the lover himself. Much of Friend's monologue is a speech-within-a-speech delivered by a "lover" altered by experience. Le Jaloux, like Friend, clashes with the rose allegory both ideologically and rhetorically. He is a typical individual speaking of particular events, and his scenes with his wife are not allegory but fabliau. He even presents the allegory itself as bogus rhetoric, offering a sarcastic version of Jealousy's castle: " 'and they all will surround her, beg her, try to get her favor, covet her, and carry on until in the end they will have her, for a tower besieged on all sides can hardly escape being taken' " (pp. 157–58; ll. 8592–96). Friend extends that piece of cynical allegorizing at the end of his own speech. After lengthy advice about manipulating women, he implies that the hyperbolic rose allegory, including the God of Love and his commands, have constituted a deliberate Machiavellian scheme:

> "In short, a man who wants to keep the love of any girl, whatever she may be, ugly or beautiful, must observe this commandment of mine, and he should remember it always and consider it very precious: let him give any girl to understand that he cannot protect himself against her, so dumbfounded and amazed is he by her beauty and worth. . . ." [P. 177; ll. 9935–44]

If Reason's attack on the allegory is pure idealism, Friend's is disillusioned experience.

As Guillaume has shown us, illusions are real for those who accept them. Friend's concluding advice is that the lover should watch over his rose when he attains it, and " 'then you will enjoy the little love with which no other compares; you will not find its equal in perhaps fourteen cities' " (p. 178; ll. 9996–99). That romantic sentiment immediately follows the generalization that all women, including "your rose," are as incorrigible as cats (ll. 9969–87), but the lover appears to miss the irony. He enthusiastically seconds Friend's praise of his rose, and the narrator tells us that the speech as a whole "agreed strongly with me" and brought back Sweet Thought and Sweet Talk (ll. 10007–11). We may remember that the God of Love promised those two comforters to the lover and then told him to seek a "wise and discreet companion" (l. 2687). Perhaps Friend is not the successful debunker of the God of Love, but a part of the god's own scheme, a mere intermediary for Sweet Thought and Sweet Talk. If that is true, then the mirror of Jean's allegory shrinks Friend, like Reason, into an episode in a drama of personifications.

But Friend leaves behind him a new complication: the mirror itself begins to look distorted. Between Friend's speech and the next "master" are some nine hundred lines in which Jean continues Guillaume's story with significant changes. He begins with the lover walking through a landscape that, though "bright with grass and flowers" (ll. 10018), is a meadow, not a garden. The setting has somehow broadened. And the ensuing action diverges from Guillaume's plan. Beside a beautiful fountain, the lover encounters Wealth and asks permission to enter a path called Mad Largesse, which she guards. Perhaps he did understand Friend's speech, after all, for he now attempts to bribe the guardians of the rose. If Friend was reabsorbed into the previous personification allegory as an intermediary for Sweet Thought and Sweet Talk, the allegory now reshapes itself around Friend's pragmatic program.

Pragmatic action might not damage the allegory's integrity if the narrator maintained his idealism, but his attitude becomes ambiguous. With Friend's cynicism ringing in our ears, we cannot be sure that the narrator's "his argument . . . strongly agreed with me" is simply a naive response to Friend's encouragement. Perhaps it partakes of Friend's irony; perhaps the narrator's enthusiasm for roses is a feeling somewhat more postlapsarian than it pretends to be. When he vows to continue the quest, the narrator sounds decidedly unromantic: "As soon as I saw the castle weaker than a toasted cake, and the gate open, no one would stop me; indeed I would certainly have the devil in my stomach if I did not capture it and enter therein" (p. 179; ll. 10039–44). Presently the lover meets the God of Love, who questions him about his behavior, and the narrator interjects, "He knew very well, of course, all that I had done, for God knows the whole of whatever man does" (p. 183; ll. 10317–18). Thus parodying the god's divinity, the narrator undercuts the allegory's idealism. He now speaks with two incompatible voices—a naive lover's voice, which idealizes the rose, and the more sophisticated voice of Friend's friend—and the naive one is a mere verbal mask: the narrator confesses that he is now obliged to act with an "intencion double" (l. 10301). This is not irony but duplicitousness.

With its sincerity impugned, the allegorical vision of love becomes a target for parody. The God of Love summons his troops to assault the castle, but he also launches a verbal attack on certain premises of the allegory. First, he identifies the lover as one Guillaume de Lorris, a loyal vassal whose service will consist not only of his current pursuit of the rose but also of writing the " 'romance in which all my commandments will be set down' "(p. 187; ll. 10549–50). We are to understand that the *Romance* is not yet begun—a logical extension of the premise that the vision is prophetic and the God of Love omniscient and eternal. The god then explains that unfortunately, Guillaume will complete the *romaunt* only up to a certain point, a point that the god foretells by quoting the last six lines of Guillaume's poem. Then, he continues, forty years later will come Jean Chopinel from Meun, a man so devoted to Love and so fond of the *Romance* that he will, barring misfortune, portray the attainment of the rose (ll. 10565–604). The God of Love continues to demonstrate his omniscience by praising the unborn Jean, ending with a promise of divine protection (ll. 10617–54). The extension *ad absurdum* of the pretense that the God of Love precedes and determines Jean's authorship achieves, of course, its own reversal: we become newly aware that the god, the allegory, and the lover are Jean's fabrications.

Having exposed the allegory to such parody, Jean might be expected to abandon it. That he does not indicates that his parody is no simple attack. Like many later writers who make similar sport with their creations, Jean is exposing the inevitable basis of the genre in which he writes. When Prudentius prays for divine enlightenment concerning the Virtues and Vices, he becomes as much as possible the seer instead of the maker; still, no allegorist can escape the latter role. Not only the God of Love, not only romantic allegory, but all allegorical agents must be to some extent invented in order to be revealed. We have seen that even Reason depends on the imagination. Just as the narrator embraces duplicity not by choice but by necessity (ll. 10302–6), so the poet must feign in order to communicate. Thus the allegory continues; but its subject is now, principally, allegory itself—the paradoxical status of the fiction of truth.

The next "master" brings the allegorical agents to a state of uneasy reflection on their duplicitousness. False Seeming does not seem closely connected with the allegory of love; like Reason, he delivers an apparently digressive monologue. In particular, he spends so much time discussing his activities among the secular clergy that many readers regard him merely as a channel for Jean's antimendicant satire. But False Seeming clearly is not irrelevant to the pursuit of the rose. When the God of Love suggests that he is, asking incredulously how such an ally joined his ranks, he is told that False Seeming always accompanies Constrained Abstinence, whom Love recognizes as an ally (ll. 10475–93). The narrator's confession to doing one thing while thinking another in order to achieve his goal (ll. 10297–306) demonstrates that false seeming has been present for some time, and the personified False Seeming will eventually prove indispensable to Love's barons by destroying Foul Mouth and thus breaking the stalemate that has existed since Guillaume's conclusion. Conceding his usefulness, the God of Love acknowledges him "'a mei tout'" (l. 10932). The alliance is an uneasy one, for the God of Love continues to malign and scold False Seeming; but the honesty that prompts those complaints is contradicted by Love's complicity with the culprit.

That contradiction defines False Seeming himself, and it involves something more than simple hypocrisy. As Charles Muscatine points out, False Seeming spends nearly as much time exposing and denouncing hypocrisy as he does demonstrating and advocating it.[36] He

36. Charles Muscatine, *Chaucer and the French Tradition: A Study in Style and Meaning* (Berkeley: University of California Press, 1957), p. 92.

warns the church against such "wolves" as himself (ll. 11133–58); he explains, at great length, why the self-indulgence and mendicancy that he practices are wrong (ll. 11269–508); he denounces eloquently the heretical doctrines that his companions preach (ll. 11787–844). His peroration switches at bewildering speed between self-condemnation and self-congratulation:

> "But he who fears my brothers more than God places himself under God's wrath. . . ."
>
> "What men should be honored except us . . . ?"
>
> "Certainly we shall . . . love [only] . . . Beguines with large coifs. . . . Princes should give over to them the job of governing them and their lands, in peace or war; a prince should cleave to those who want to come to great honor."
>
> "[B]ut God doesn't value him at two straws if he says that he has left the world and then abounds in worldly glory and wants to use its delights. Who can excuse such Beguines?"   [Pp. 207–8; ll. 11909–10, 11923–24, 11937–46, 11958–62]

Muscatine finds in False Seeming's contradictions a "simple inconsistency": "Jean either forgets from time to time, or doesn't care, that the promulgation of truth is not the direct concern of the hypocrite, but only an accident of his self-revelation. When Faus-Semblant turns from an indirect warning to a direct one, he is no longer False-Seeming."[37] On the contrary, he is then most essentially and ominously False Seeming—not fraud or hypocrisy, but their descendant (see ll. 10982–83). Voicing the most straightforward correctives to his dishonesty without seeming any less dishonest, False Seeming casts doubt on the efficacy of truth. Insincere in his virtue but sincere about his insincerity, he baffles our ability to distinguish truth from falsehood.

False Seeming magnifies the ambivalence introduced by Reason, whose directives were true but invalid in context. He forces the other characters to suspend considerations of truth. For instance, he presents the God of Love with a version of the all-Cretans-are-liars dilemma: " 'But to you I dare not lie. However, if I could feel that you would not recognize it, you would have a lie in hand' " (p. 208; ll.

37. Ibid.

11969–72). When the God of Love understandably demands proof that False Seeming is not lying in declaring his loyalty, loyalty being admittedly against his nature, False Seeming invites the god to take his chances, since he will never be any more certain than he is at present (ll. 11981–94). In the event, False Seeming will be both loyal and disloyal, for his loyalty is disloyalty. He does advance the battle for the rose, but in the process he asserts his own sovereignty (ll. 12340–42). Serving both love and false seeming, many of the personifications now lose their meanings; Generosity and Openness, for instance, join False Seeming in some decidedly ungenerous, uncandid behavior (ll. 12381–408). And when Love's barons triumph, much later, the ideological and doctrinal meaning of their victory will be spectacularly unclear. Under False Seeming the allegory becomes moral and intellectual anarchy.

The first two monologuists went away after speaking; False Seeming does not. He introduces—releases, in fact—the next "master," who is his logical successor. As the closest guardian of Fair Welcoming and the rose, La Vieille is supposed to be one of the enemy, and she does in fact protest her capture by Love's barons. But upon hearing of Foul Mouth's death, she redefines her capture as liberation and enthusiastically switches sides (ll. 12381–483). She is clearly without principle, but she is also entirely willing to adopt whatever principles suit her self-interest. If False Seeming introduces moral and intellectual anarchy, La Vieille manifests moral and intellectual opportunism.

That La Vieille is without principle appears in her name: she is not a quality but a woman whom "experience . . . has made wise" (l. 12805). She is thus very much like Friend. Like him, she devotes most of her speech to particularities, and she constructs dramatic scenarios much like those between Le Jaloux and his wife (ll. 13708–822, 14203–380). She also tacitly concretizes the allegory itself, making the "castle" a town house with stairways and secret passages (ll. 14706–11) and the "garden" one of many countries she has visited, comparable to England (ll. 12949, 14513–39). C. S. Lewis regards La Vieille's "introduction in her proper person" as "a complete breakdown of allegory" and thus as "a serious, though not a fatal, defect in the poem."[38] Such a breakdown is entirely consistent with Jean's

---

38. Lewis, *Allegory of Love*, p. 119.

irony, however. Like Friend, La Vieille is an alien, a jester in the allegorical realm. She is not Disillusionment or Experience or Age personified, but a living attack on the validity of personification itself.

She differs from Friend in attacking the allegory from an even more crucial position—within Jealousy's castle, where she addresses not the persona but one of the chief allegorical agents, Fair Welcoming. She teaches disillusionment to one of the illusions. In fact, she concludes her monologue with a devastating physiological identification of the allegory's central symbol: " 'Act so wisely that it may be better with you because of my instruction. For when your rose is withered and white hairs assail you, gifts will certainly fail' " (p. 248; ll. 14541–46). The worm is now within the rose.

La Vieille differs from Friend also in her opportunism, which dictates her redefinition of the allegory. She sustains the abstract and symbolic machinery, the garden and rose and personifications, even as she speaks also of houses and people. Jean has no reason to keep "the two stories—the psychological and the symbolical—distinct and parallel before his mind," as Lewis would have him do, for his subject is an unsymbolic character's version of symbolism. Lewis complains particularly about La Vieille's addresses to Fair Welcoming on feminine deportment and the management of husbands and lovers.[39] In fact, Jean does not forget, as Lewis claims, that Fair Welcoming is a young bachelor; La Vieille consistently addresses her hearer as "fair son" even in the passages most clearly appropriate to a woman (e.g., ll. 13037–44 and 14441–44). She sees Fair Welcoming as both male and female—female in irrefragable fact, but male in a fiction that cannot be trusted but ought not to be dropped. For " 'Fair Welcoming may know whomever he wishes' " (p. 227; l. 13108): a courteous young bachelor in charge of a suggestive rose may command greater liberties, more respect, and ultimately a higher price than a frank and open young woman (see ll. 13109–22).[40] The allegory of the rose is a sham, but a useful and profitable sham. As Friend hinted that the pose of subjugation by a God of Love might serve a lover's purpose,

39. Ibid., p. 140.

40. Dahlberg claims that Bel Acueil's masculinity is "chiefly grammatical, since the word *acueil* was masculine" (note to l. 2792). But in La Vieille's speech we discover that if Bel Acueil's gender was an accident, it was a functional one: it allowed for the sexlessness of the courtship. La Vieille's insistence on both his masculinity and his femininity perpetuates the fiction of sexlessness even while exposing it.

La Vieille advises that the allegorical fictions be manipulated by the beloved. She particularly recommends the bow-and-arrow routine: " 'Next, about the bow and the five arrows which are very full of good qualities and which wound so readily, know how to fire them so wisely that Love, the good archer, never drew a better bow, fair son, than do you, who have many times launched your arrows' " (p. 226; ll. 13061–68).

Fair Welcoming himself seems untouched by such allegorical cynicism, replying that loving is " 'a very strange subject to me' " (l. 14613). But he adds that he would gladly receive the lover if Jealousy's absence could only be arranged (ll. 14644–47), echoing La Vieille's ideas in an ostensibly naive tone. Like the narrator after Friend's speech, Fair Welcoming now sounds different to us. He protests, presently, that he wants to be nothing but Fair Welcoming— " 'I want to put all my attention on having a lovely, gentle manner' " (p. 249; ll. 14619–20)—but the protest subverts itself by admitting tacitly that being Fair Welcoming is a deliberate pose. And when he defends his fondness for the lover as nothing but the common friendship of a woman and a man (ll. 14630–35), Fair Welcoming casts the relationship in a heterosexual mold and thus belies his own maleness. The effect is the insidious suggestion that he knows himself to be a fiction.

La Vieille's speech has no overt effect on the ensuing "psychomachia," but even more clearly than Friend's, her disillusioned discourse leaves its traces on the allegory. Particularly potent is her suggestion that the entire opposition between the "guardians" and "Love's barons" is contrived in the interest of erotic suspense:

> "Now when she hears a lover's request, she should be reluctant to grant all her love, nor should she refuse everything, but try to keep him in a state of balance between fear and hope. . . . [S]he must arrange things, through her strength and craft, so that hope constantly grows little by little as fear diminishes until peace and concord bring the two together." [P. 235; ll. 13663–77]

As the narrative proceeds, Fair Welcoming's inaccessibility does indeed appear feigned. We are informed that Love's barons overcome the castle gate (l. 14747), but what we see is La Vieille quietly unlocking a back door (ll. 14718, 14724). After the lover enters, Fair Welcoming is attacked by Fear, Shame, and Dangier, who threaten terrible punishments—but they cannot execute them just now, being, inexplicably, in a hurry to do something else (ll. 14933–42). Although they promise to return and finish the job, "they did not hold to it" (l. 14943). And if their existence as implacable forces is an open pretense, so is their battle with Love's troops. It proceeds with Prudentian panoply, but only after a vigorously reductive prologue: "From now on we will come to the battle. . . . Here in this wood you may hear, if you listen to me, the dogs barking in chase of the rabbit that you [lovers] are after and the ferret that must surely make him leap into the nets" (pp. 257–58; ll. 15133–42). Each of the battle's properties is compounded of a military image and a reference to courtship—the shield of supplication, the sword of pleasant life, the "wattles of denials" that reinforce the castle (ll. 15331–33, 15474, 15807)—and thanks to La Vieille and the cynical narrator, we see the first term in each case as a manifest artifice. When Skillful Concealment appears with a silent sword, "like a tongue cut out," and a shield "made of a hidden place where no chicken ever laid an egg" (p. 263; ll. 15490–96), the personification as well as the military imagery is a joke. Jean's psychomachia is mock allegory, a narrative that pretends to be about abstractions.

Unlike the seven sins or the cardinal virtues, mock-allegorical agents can multiply indefinitely. Each abstraction elicits its appropriate opponent; "I never saw such coupling in battle" (p. 265; l. 15614). The God of Love wisely asks for a truce (ll. 15619–38), then employs one sure method of breaking an allegorical stalemate: he redefines the battle. His mother, Venus, whom he summons as an ally, is not a personification or even a projection, but a figure from myth and astrology who will shift the narrative from artifice to Nature and will conquer not with a powerful idea but with an elemental force. Venus immediately penetrates the allegorical fabric to its biological basis: " 'May I perish in a miserable death,' she said, 'that may take me straightway, if I ever let Chastity dwell in any woman alive . . . !' " (p. 268; ll. 15830–33). She speaks to her son not about personifications but about " 'all the men' " (l. 15836), and he exclaims, in a burst of frankness, " 'Where can one seek a better life than being in the arms of his sweetheart?' " (p. 268; ll. 15875–76).

Clearly the art of love gives place here to natural sexuality; but we cannot quite conclude with Gunn that the poem is moving toward a serious "gospel of fertility."[41] It should come as no surprise by now that Venus and Nature are both presented ironically. Jean's references to Venus have been far from reverent throughout the poem, particularly in La Vieille's allusions to Vulcan's trap (ll. 13835–74 and 14157–86). Here the God of Love's messengers find Venus lecturing Adonis on the perils of boar hunting—an odd lecture, if a sexually suggestive one, from which Jean draws the farcical moral that men had better believe their sweethearts even against the testimony of Reason and the crucifix (ll. 15751–64). Then, summoned to help her son, Venus orders her chariot prepared "since she did not want to walk through the mud" (p. 267; l. 15781). She is less a goddess than an oversized version of the human *amie;* her power is simply that of sexuality at its most mundane.

The irony concerning Nature, the fifth monologuist, is more complex and far-reaching. On the one hand, Nature is like Reason in being a genuinely universal principle; indeed, her claim to that status is unchallengeable. She exists at a higher level of abstraction than the garden, working in her forge far from the allegorical turmoil and thinking "on the things that are enclosed beneath the heavens" (p. 270; ll. 15893–94). She also subjects the allegory to an objective reordering. In her speech the only allegorical agents are Nature herself, Reason, Fortune, and the like; insofar as Love's barons are real to her, they are not personifications but the "'valiant ones . . . who try to multiply their lineages'" (ll. 19381–86). As for Jealousy, Foul Mouth, and the rest, they are the dreams of the preoccupied, who "'make many different images appear inside themselves. . . . And it seems to them then that all these images are in reality outside them'" (p. 304; ll. 18350–56). Being clearly authoritative and objective, Nature's point of view has been frequently identified with Jean's, as if the *Romance* had, after a protracted autobiographical introduction, turned into a *Complaint of Nature.*

On the other hand, recent writers have seen her as limited. George Economou points out that she is less specifically Christian than Alan of Lille's Nature, whose ideas are voiced by Jean's Reason. Moreover, Nature's speech is somewhat disturbing in form. Initially well ordered, it becomes increasingly dilatory and digressive, and most of the

41. Gunn, p. 255.

digressions concern disorder, catastrophe, and distortion. Tuve
points out the irony whereby "the pictures of reasonless chaos, of
floods, storms, destroyed streets and towers, followed by calms and
rainbows, are an 'order' supposed to contrast with man's willed dis-
orders but instead resembling them." Because of that irony, Wetherbee sees Jean's Nature as a "devastating elaboration on Alain's critique of the Chartrian faith in Nature as source and standard of moral
law."[42] If Nature presents objective order, she also presents disorder
and lawlessness: her very comprehensiveness renders her useless as a
principle.

The irony of Nature's monologue is compounded by her characterization. A number of recent critics have understood that Jean's
personification of Nature is no mere convention, but a significant
metaphor to which he loudly calls attention. Shortly after the narrator avows that "no human sense would show her" (p. 274; l.
16168), setting Nature beyond human mensuration, her own priest,
Genius, pulls her rudely back:

> "In any case, lady," he said, "I advise you to wish to abandon this
> weeping, if you indeed want to confess. . . . But it is also true, with-
> out fail, that a woman is easily inflamed with wrath. Virgil himself
> bears witness—and he knew a great deal about their difficulties—
> that no woman was ever so stable that she might not be varied and
> changeable. And thus she remains a very irritable animal." [P. 276;
> ll. 16314–29]

Thus begins a 377-line antifeminist tirade, culminating in a command
to "fair lords" to mistrust women (ll. 16323–700). Genius appends a
disclaimer that he has not been referring to Nature, but the damage
has been done; the indescribable goddess has been linked in our
minds with an "ireuse beste." And when Nature presently acknowledges her prolixity and indiscretion, she attributes those qualities to
her femininity (ll. 18296–303, 19218–21).

Some writers see in Nature's rather comic personality a further
indication that she does not really transcend the human world, but
merely generalizes it.[43] The point is well taken, but Jean's irony cuts

---

42. George D. Economou, *The Goddess Natura in Medieval Literature*
(Cambridge: Harvard University Press, 1972), pp. 118–24; Tuve, p. 274; Wetherbee,
p. 263.
43. See, for instance, Tuve, pp. 273–74; Wetherbee, pp. 258–63.

even deeper. Its object is not nature itself, or even a naive view of nature, but Nature—the literary depiction of a universal principle. By exaggerating Nature's femininity and associating her with the condescending clichés of literary antifeminism, Jean parodies the conventional allegorization of Nature as a woman, the assimilation of the cosmos into manmade molds. A further reflection on Nature's philological ontogeny is her bookishness: she borrows at length from Aristotle, Boethius, and Alan of Lille, among others, and she defers to the clerks for fuller treatments of her subjects (ll. 17727–36). The absurdity is apt, since those clerks have in fact created her. The inexpressibility topos with which Jean introduces her is no hyperbole, but it has been contradicted in nearly every text that advances it.

Nature ostensibly intervenes in the psychomachia, but as the deconstructor of her own allegorization, she can act only ironically. The message that she sends through Genius to the God of Love is simply encouragement to keep on doing what he is doing already:

> "Go, my friend, to the God of Love, carrying my complaints and outcries, not so that he may do me justice but so that he may take comfort and solace when he hears this news, which should be very pleasing to him and harmful to our enemies, and so that he may cease to be troubled by the worry that I see him occupied with." [P. 319; ll. 19369–77]

As Tuve points out, Nature's response to the human faults that she has described has been to work all the harder at perpetuating humankind, and that policy of persistence is what she passes on to the God of Love.[44] Though she seems to transcend the projections and manipulations of Love's psychomachia, she serves in the end primarily to legitimate them on their own terms, for she is the status quo elevated by the human imagination into a moral principle.

The imagination that reifies her becomes, in turn, Jean's sixth and most brilliantly ironic "master." Genius is one of the lasting puzzles of the *Romance,* particularly to those who try to read allegory by translating it. His name itself is singularly ambiguous. E. C. Knowlton informs us that "in classical Latin the world *genius* applied to a higher self, a protective spirit who enforces moral conduct"; but in making Genius Nature's priest, Alan of Lille and Jean de Meun draw

44. Tuve, p. 268.

also on the word's connection with *generare*. Furthermore, as Knowlton points out elsewhere, the bawdy zest with which Jean's Genius advocates procreation makes him a virtual parody of the "spirit who enforces moral conduct."[45] We cannot simply conclude that Genius represents the sexual urge, however, for his ironic "sermon" includes a long and orthodox repudiation of the garden of love as an inferior image of Paradise (ll. 19931–20626): in some ways he does enforce moral conduct.

Genius' unresolvable moral ambivalence becomes more meaningful in connection with another kind of inconsistency, that of his rhetoric. The sexual message that he transmits from Nature to Love's barons is diffracted through an impressive array of metaphors: " 'It was an evil hour when Nature, in accordance with her laws and customs, gave to those false ones of whom I have been speaking their styluses and tablets, hammers and anvils, the plowshares with good sharp points for the use of their plows . . .' " (p. 322; ll. 19543–52). Genius juggles all three images—stylus and tablet, hammer and anvil, plow and field—for some two hundred lines, then works in Cadmus and the serpents' teeth, Atropos and the spindle, Cerberus, and the Furies (ll. 19553–864). Equally rich in figurative language is his Christian sermon, a detailed remetaphorization of the garden of love: earthly gardens invariably fade, but there is a Fair Park whose flowers and herbs provide continual nourishment for the flocks of the Good Shepherd; the lover's fountain was actually cloudy, but there is another fountain, the fountain of life, which is clear, life-giving, and self-generating; and so forth (ll. 19931–20000). Out of context, the remetaphorization would constitute an exhortation to abandon love for paradise, but, as Paul Piehler points out, "Genius assists very actively in the assault on the Castle of the Rose, just after comparing the Rose Garden so slightingly to the Good Park."[46] Moreover, he promises that those who procreate vigorously will enter the Shepherd's Park.[47] Genius does not distinguish between fecundity and salvation, since the impulse to fecundity—rhetorical as well as sexual—is his essence.

Genius may inherit his unscrupulous rhetorical virtuosity from his

45. E. C. Knowlton, "Genius as an Allegorical Figure," *MLN* 39 (1924):89; Knowlton, "The Allegorical Figure Genius," *Classical Philology* 15 (1920):384.
46. Piehler, p. 109.
47. On the "ludicrous assumption by Nature's priest Genius that entrance into the Heavenly Jerusalem is in *his* gift," see Tuve, pp. 275–78.

predecessor in the *Complaint of Nature,* who drew with his right hand "images" that passed "from the shadow of a sketch to the truth of very being," and with his left "false and limping imagery, . . . figures of things, or rather the shadowy ghosts of figures, with incomplete depiction."[48] But where Alan's Genius was an agent of a rational Nature, Jean's stands in an ambiguous relationship to a Nature who is presented ironically. He is her worshipful servant but also her confessor, judge, and sardonic critic; she evidently cannot express herself even in soliloquy without "Genius the well-spoken" (l. 19335). Genius virtually invents his mistress. Speaking and acting without the moral control that the *Complaint of Nature* carefully establishes, Genius lends great impetus to the allegory of love but overruns its coherence. Not only does he mix exegetical and erotic discourse, but even within the latter category, his several vehicles collide and collapse under their load of double entendre: " 'The tablets have a very cruel future, since they will become all rusty if they are kept idle. Now that they let the anvils perish without striking a blow with the hammer, the rust can bring them down, and no one will hear them hammered or beaten' " (pp. 322–23; ll. 19566–72). The vehicles' collective incoherence should deter us from seeking some abstract proposition here.[49] Genius' imagery reveals primarily his own boundless energy; concomitantly, it vitalizes his referent more powerfully than direct exposition could have done, for the incoherence opens gaps through which certain referents look unmistakably real. Genius uses imagery not for allegorical revelation but for rhetorical and sexual excitement.

From here, allegory degenerates into striptease. After Venus ignites the castle, frequent references to women and men (ll. 20673–82) assure us that the refraction of human beings into personifications has all but ended. One forlorn vestige is Shame, whose protest provokes the full force of Venus' deallegorizing rage: " 'I will set fire to the whole enclosure and raze the towers and turrets. I'll warm up your rump; I'll burn the pillars, walls, and posts' " (p. 339; ll. 20729–

48. *The Complaint of Nature by Alain de Lille,* trans. Douglas M. Moffat, Yale Studies in English 36 (New York: Holt, 1908), Prose IX, ll. 105–28.

49. Many critics have claimed to see some such proposition; Stephen Barney, for instance, writes, "The humor of these sexual enigmas should not keep us from seeing that the instruments in the metaphors are both maintainers of civilization and procreators, which is Genius's point" (*Allegories of History,* p. 190). That may be Genius' point, but it is not exactly Jean's. If these vehicles are the instruments of civilization, civilization is out of control.

32). As Venus goes on, her references to enclosures that will be opened and passages that will be widened are as absurd and therefore as suggestive as Genius' plows, styluses, and anvils. Indeed, Venus no longer needs to destroy the castle, for it has already been destroyed. Once a metaphoric synthesis of the intangible social, cultural, and psychological defensework of Jealousy, it is now a weak facade for a work of Nature: "Venus . . . aimed, like a good archer, at a tiny narrow aperture which she saw hidden in the tower. This opening was not at the side, but in front, where Nature, by her great cunning, had placed it between two pillars" (p. 340; ll. 20791–96). Venus finds as the target for her arrow "an image . . . constructed, in measure, of arms, shoulders, and hands that erred in neither excess nor defect" (p. 340; ll. 20799–804). All of the poem's allegorical and symbolic imagery now appears to be elaboration on this final, irreducibly concrete image.

Immediately after describing Venus' target, Jean tells at some length the story of Pygmalion. The story should be taken not as a didactic digression but as a correlative to the vitalization of imagery in which Jean himself is now engaged. Jean compares the image at which Venus has aimed with Pygmalion's statue, which was so beautiful and lifelike that its maker was enmeshed by love (ll. 20811–40). The analogue can easily be extended. Determined to vitalize the statue by acting as if it were alive, Pygmalion adorns it with clothing and jewels (ll. 20931–21013), much as Guillaume and Jean have adorned their personifications and metaphors with lifelike detail for some twenty thousand lines. Just as Jean's narrator will do, Pygmalion kneels and prays before his creation (ll. 20907–30; cf. 21589–94). But Jean is finally able to enliven his image through the means that fail Pygmalion—the resources of art. Working in words instead of ivory, he can give the image life in the reader's mind. He will presently do so by appearing to denude it of art.

The story of Pygmalion opens the final monologue, delivered by the narrator himself. Jean has gradually transformed Guillaume's passive, dreaming narrator into a determining agent first of the plot and then of the poem. Friend's cynicism suggested that the narrator's innocent passivity is a role useful to the scheming rose plucker; then the God of Love exaggerated to absurdity the notion that the narrator is a mere experiencer and recorder of the *Romance*. And although Jean's narrator acts the pupil throughout the allegorical monologues, his appearance in that role is increasingly suspect, for the persona has no business hearing the speeches of La Vieille and Nature: La Vieille addresses Fair Welcoming in the castle while the lover waits outside, and Nature speaks in her "forge," attended only by Genius.[50] The narrator can report those speeches only by inventing them as an omniscient author. The narrator's role in the latter part of the poem thus accords fully with the speech of Genius: the narrative now proceeds more or less openly by invention, not by revelation.

To his role as the final allegorical master the narrator brings all of Genius' enthusiasm for generation, both sexual and metaphoric. He creates one of the longest double entendres in literature, impressive no less for its virtuosity than for its detailed, merciless allusiveness:

> It was my wish that, if I could bring my entire harness, just as I carried it, up to the harbor, I might touch it to the relics. . . . And I had done so much and wandered so far, my staff entirely unprotected by ferrule, that, vigorous and agile, I knelt without delay between the two fair pillars. . . . I attacked so much that I discovered a narrow passage by which I thought I might pass beyond, but to do so I had to break the paling. . . . [Pp. 351–52; ll. 21583–636]

Obviously, Jean is not seriously evoking the love-as-religion theme with his references to relics, staff, and so forth. The "pilgrimage" that he here adds to the poem's metaphoric apparatus is, in itself, implausible and incoherent, while the sexual references are only too coherent. In concocting imagery in order that we see through it, Jean may be responding with parody to the theory that allegory is a disposable covering over the truth. At any rate, he is bringing the striptease to its profoundly unallegorical climax.

It may seem imperceptive to call that climax unsatisfying. Unsatisfying it is, however, because the great goal has not been just to pluck the rose. As Gunn writes, "Every student of medieval or Renaissance letters knows that in an allegorical tale the underlying *sententia* is the important thing."[51] I have argued that the *sententia* in allegory is not underlying but central; but at the end of the *Romance*

---

50. The explanation that Bel Acueil repeated the whole of La Vieille's discourse later (ll. 12987–13000) is a mock explanation. Besides being unlikely on the grounds of the speech's length, it is contradicted in that the narrator reports actions that La Vieille takes when she is not with Bel Acueil (e.g., ll. 12541–54).

51. Gunn, p. 69.

of the Rose, despite Gunn's efforts and those of others, the *sententia* is nowhere in sight. Jean has failed, in Piehler's words, "to make a clear statement concerning the hierarchical relationships of his *potentiae.*"[52] We are left with a completed action but without a coherent meaning. Indeed, the closing instructions of the final allegorical master concern not truth but successful praxis: "You, my young lords, shall know both the deed and the manner, so that if, when the sweet season returns, the need arises for you to go gathering roses, either opened or closed, you may go so discreetly that you will not fail in your collecting. Do as you hear that I did . . ." (p. 353; ll. 21677–83). Furthermore, the spectacularly ironic imagery that closes the narrative questions the very possibility that a sustained metaphor will convey truth, beyond the so-called facts of life.

Paul Zumthor finds a radical skepticism about allegorical truth not only in the *Romance* but also in other narratives from the thirteenth through the fifteenth centuries:

> Narrative discourse, eroded by reasoning, by glossing, by the growing pressure of referential exigencies which weigh down upon it, collapses at the same time as the optimistic synthesis of the great philosophical *summae,* drawing along in their catastrophe the confidence, of which they had been testimony, in our possibilities of knowledge and understanding, and in our competence to make a coherent world exist by means of language.[53]

But that is an incomplete and an excessively pessimistic conclusion. Shortly after the *Romance* was completed, Dante acknowledged in his allegory the difficulty of attaining certain knowledge but magnificently affirmed the value of language in overcoming that difficulty. And Jean de Meun, too, in his own way, leaves us with a kind of faith in allegorical possibility. It is true that each of Jean's allegorical masters undermines in one way or another the validity of the kind of categorical idea in which certain medieval thinkers located reality. On the other hand, in shifting those categories to a new basis in human experience and invention, Jean does not simply cause them to collapse. At the end of the *Complaint of Nature,* the dreamer falls back into sleep, his revelation over. At the end of the *Romance of the Rose,*

52. Piehler, p. 109.
53. Zumthor, p. 204.

the dreamer, to our considerable surprise, wakes up, for "then it was day" (l. 21780). That the extended discourses of Reason, Friend, Nature, and the rest—particularly the brazen monologue of the narrator—can be dismissed as parts of a Maytime dream almost exceeds belief. But if the dismissal suggests that all our allegorical ideas may be no more substantial than erotic dreams, it allows them also the inexhaustible vitality of Genius. Jean denudes the rose but leaves it pregnant, able to generate more dreams—some of which may indeed be as true as "the vision that came to King Scipio" (ll. 7–8).

3 Allegorical Spectacle: Medieval Morality Drama

The genial undercurrents of psychological realism and "human interest" that carry modern readers through the allegory of love are seldom felt in medieval allegorical drama. Our term for the most clearly allegorical plays records a conviction that they are essentially abstract, fundamentally didactic, and probably dull. "Moralities. The very word is like a yawn," wrote Katherine Lee Bates in 1893, and the disarming concession has lost little of its force. What Bates calls the morality plays' "cardinal sin," "the forsaking of the concrete for the abstract," is particularly repellant to us when committed in the theater.[1] Modern dictionaries treat "dramatic" as synonymous with "vivid"; modern theatergoers usually demand some kind of lifelike representation; modern acting students are often encouraged to prepare for their roles by speculating about the characters' biographies and motives. It is not surprising, therefore, that the plays whose *dramatis personae* are personifications have seldom been produced since the Renaissance.

To be sure, allegorical drama has not been neglected altogether. Indeed, the first post-Renaissance production of a morality play, William Poel's of *Everyman* in 1901, inspired a modest but recurrent revival. Fundamental to the revival is the premise that the characters

---

1. Katherine Lee Bates, *The English Religious Drama* (New York: Macmillan, 1893), pp. 201–2.

of morality drama are not really abstract after all—at least, not on stage. Robert Potter describes the surprise of Poel's audience when "the 'lifeless abstractions' of the medieval text turned out to be . . . not walking categories, but realized figures, parts in a play." Convinced that skillful acting can transform personifications into personalities, enterprising directors have given us Fellowship with a North Country accent, Everyman in jeans and a reefer jacket, and Death as a "Marine Commando."[2]

Regardless of their success, however, such realistic productions do not challenge the modern assumption that allegory is inherently undramatic. Indeed, the revisionist approach reinforces that assumption, for it sets out to produce good drama by deallegorizing the allegorical. It is therefore vulnerable, as its participants well know, to the charge of distorting or obscuring an "original doctrinal purpose."[3] Therein may lie the reason that the revival has been limited to a single play, Everyman: its participants suspect that they are engaged in an exciting but somewhat illegitimate experiment. Occasionally modern writers try to legitimize the experiment by claiming that the plays proceed simultaneously on two levels, realistic and didactic, but the attempt at double reading meets no greater success here than in narrative allegory. For the most part, modern critics and directors have chosen either the didactic pill or the realistic sugar coating.

The persistence of the assumption that drama and allegory are incompatible says a great deal about the power of received ideas, for the assumption is contradicted by the opening scene of Everyman. On the one hand, if Everyman were reducible to a didactic message, the Messenger's prologue would render the play superfluous:

> Here shall you se how Falawship and Jolité,
> Bothe Strengthe, Pleasure, and Beauté,
> Will fade from the[e] as floure in Maye;
> For ye shall here how our heven Kinge
> Calleth Everyman to a generall rekeninge.[4]

2. Robert Potter, The English Morality Play: Origins, History, and Influence of a Dramatic Tradition (London: Routledge & Kegan Paul, 1975), p. 2; Glynne Wickham, Shakespeare's Dramatic Heritage: Collected Studies in Mediaeval, Tudor, and Shakespearean Drama (New York: Barnes & Noble, 1969), p. 33.

3. Lawrence V. Ryan, "Doctrine and Dramatic Structure in Everyman," Speculum 32 (1957):722–23.

4. Everyman, in Medieval Drama, ed. David M. Bevington (Boston: Houghton Mifflin, 1975), ll. 16–20. Copyright © 1975 by Houghton Mifflin Company. Future citations of this edition of Everyman will be documented by line number in the text.

On the other hand, by the time the human protagonist enters, the dialogue of God and Death has raised the play far beyond ordinary realism. And more important, neither doctrine nor dramatic realism alone can account for the effect produced by Everyman's entrance, for the concrete character seems to materialize out of the didactic speeches. When the Messenger first uses "everyman" he names a category; the pronoun is only technically singular, as many a freshman composition student can attest. V. A. Kolve points out that in God's subsequent speeches, "Everyman is spoken of as both singular and plural in number":[5] "Every man liveth so after his owne pleasure, / And yet of their life they be nothinge sure" (ll. 40–41). The shifts in number become significant when we see the collective pronoun take the form of a single man. As Everyman enters, walking "gaily" toward some destination of his own (ll. 85–86), we realize that he is happily unaware of having been categorized so authoritatively. The first direct address to him, Death's electrifying "Everyman, stande still!" (l. 85), produces for the audience a particular kind of shock of recognition on behalf of the protagonist. We recognize that the condition of every man is about to come home to Everyman.

That effect demands that we redefine "dramatic." Obviously it does not arise from an ordinary conflict of characters. Neither can it be attributed to something that the traditional idea of allegory would lead us to expect: a purely abstract confrontation, a "conflict of spiritual opposites."[6] What we have witnessed is not even a human drama on one level and a didactic tableau on another. The dramatic moment is the one at which an abstract category becomes a human character. That kind of drama, based on ontological metamorphosis, is peculiar to allegory.

Moreover, just as the scene's drama depends on allegory, its allegory is defined by drama. That is, the relationship of concretion and universal here is slightly different than in the *Psychomachia*. An obvious formulation of the difference is that Everyman is not just a universal but also a real human being, played by a living actor. Applied under scrutiny to allegorical drama as a whole, however, the obvious formulation wilts. Ritual performances and religious cere-

---

5. V. A. Kolve, "*Everyman* and the Parable of the Talents," in *The Medieval Drama*, ed. Sandro Sticca (Albany: State University of New York Press, 1972), pp. 82–83.

6. Spivack, *Shakespeare and the Allegory of Evil*, p. 72.

monies show us that theater is not inherently realistic in any simple sense; actors are signs, as are the words of a text, and what they signify may be even less verisimilar or concrete than are parts of the *Psychomachia.* The difference between theatrical and written allegory is, rather, that the play takes place: it is an event in a particular physical location. The actors and the public occasion establish not exactly verisimilitude, but a deictic perspective, the expectation that the play's referents will be the finite actions of particular agents. Of course, a second, broader perspective is established as soon as the characters receive abstract names or echo the words of sacred figures, showing themselves to be embodied universals or manifestations of divine being, as Realistically coherent as Prudentius' Virtues. But our deictic perspective on them persists, the product of an intransigently localizing medium. The actors' idiosyncrasies, the weather, diversions in the audience, or, for the solitary reader, the need to imagine how the play would look on stage, all counterpoint our apprehension of the spectacle as the interaction of ideas. Each Virtue in the allegorical narrative unfolds its embodiment from a constant center; in contrast, an allegorical *dramatis persona* vacillates in our minds between two frames of reference, the particular and the universal.

The vacillation is exploited by the skillful playwright. In particular, the categorical redefinition of Everyman exemplifies particularly clearly something that happens to virtually all of the "characters" in the morality plays: a revision in level of abstraction. When the personified deadly sins appear at the beginning of a French morality, Lucifer proudly records their natures as eternally fixed. But then a pious hermit takes pity on the sins, engaging Lucifer in a debate over their ontological status. His position is that the sins can be reformed—that they are embodiments of sin, not immutable quiddities. The hermit wins, for the sins are first revealed as human exemplars of sin and then converted into exemplars of the *remedia.*[7] Certain roles in the morality plays are less susceptible to human exemplification than the sins and the *remedia,* but even Death, God, and the Devil are not impersonated merely by theatrical convention—or rather, their impersonation is a conspicuous convention, bearing meaning. The distinction between

---

7. *Moralité des sept péchés mortel,* in *Mystères et moralités du manuscrit 617 de Chantilly,* ed. Gustave Cohen (Paris: Champion, 1920), pp. 39–77; discussed in Potter, p. 26.

the immaterial entity and its material representation is always potentially significant.

The relationship between those levels of reality is the allegorical
version of dramatic conflict and resolution. In its permutations,
which range from immanence to rupture, it shapes and distinguishes
the plays more fully than do the doctrinal messages that can be ex-
tracted. A classification and reading of the forms of ontological confrontation may explain how "the primitive drama" could, in the
words of a reviewer of Poel's *Everyman*, "have passioned our fore-
fathers—[and] is, indeed, capable of passioning us."[8]

A taxonomy of allegorical drama can begin where many of the
plays begin and end: with the alignment of the two sets of referents.
At the conclusion of *The Castle of Perseverance*, the actor who has
been speaking God's words begins without transition to address the
audience in his own person. "Thus endith oure gamys," says Pater
Sedens in Juditio; "*Te Deum laudamus!*"[9] In shifting from his role to
his unmasked self, the actor superimposes the divine message that he
has been pronouncing and the human performance that conveys it.
All of the morality plays are framed in some version of that superim-
position:

> For ye shall here how our heven Kinge
> Calleth Everyman to a generall rekeninge.
> Give audience, and here what he doth saye.
>
> > [*Everyman*, ll. 19–21]
>
> Wyrschep[f]yll sofereyns, I have do my propirté:
> Mankind is deliveryd by my faverall patrocinye.[10]
>
> Yff ye wyll wet the propyrte
> Ande the resun of my nayme imperyall,
> I am clepyde of hem that in erthe be
> Euerlastynge Wysdom, to my nobley egalle. . . . [11]

---

8. Potter, p. 4.

9. *The Castle of Perseverance*, in *Medieval Drama*, ed. Bevington, ll. 3644–49.
Future citations of this edition of *The Castle of Perseverance* will be documented by
line number in the text.

10. *Mankind*, in *Medieval Drama*, ed. Bevington, ll. 903–4. Future citations of this
edition of *Mankind* will be documented by line number in the text.

11. *Wisdom*, in *The Macro Plays*, ed. Mark Eccles, E.E.T.S. 262 (London: Oxford
University Press, 1969), ll. 1–4.

The significance of those speeches can be seen most clearly through comparison with a similar address to the audience in Shakespeare's *Henry V*. The speaker of Shakespeare's prologue also refers frankly to the theatrical performance, even while asserting that the subject represented by the performance is real. But he emphasizes the disparity between representation and subject: "Can this cockpit hold / The vasty fields of France?" (*Henry V*, Prologue, ll. 11–12). The actors of morality drama, in contrast, assert a genuine revelation, telling us that we have seen the salvation of Mankind, or that the actor's name, Wisdom, corresponds to his noble nature. The closest Shakespearean approach to such bold identification of actors with roles is parodic. But unlike Bottom and his company, the allegorical actor can claim real representational power without naiveté, for what he represents is not an absent object or creature but an ever-present truth. In the play, as elsewhere, God does call Everyman to a reckoning, mercy and wisdom are indeed evident, and "parcellys" of the Christian condition are "before [us] in syth." Thus when they draw our attention equally to a particular performance and to the doctrines behind it, the prologues and epilogues define morality drama as a point of balance between the two kinds of reality that govern our lives.

Within the plays, the alignment of those two kinds of reference is rarely so stable. The movement of the audience's perspective between them can be classified according to its directions. Two general possibilities are downward and upward. That is, we may apprehend intelligible truth as materially real, or we can recognize material reality's participation in universal truth. A third possibility is the alternation of perspective between particular and universal, a kind of allegorical conflict. Each of those kinds of movement dominates in a single play.

The Castle of Perseverance: Allegorical Materialization

The longest of the surviving English moralities takes place at a high level, in more senses than one. Much of the action occurs on five scaffolds surrounding the playing area. Moreover, we see the story from a high level of abstraction, thanks to an unusually clear and dominant moral scheme. The "cast of abstractions" is, in David Bevington's words, "balanced with majestic symmetry into opposing camps": Good Angel and Bad Angel, Virtues and Sins.[12] The moral symmetry is underscored by the scaffolds, and in that form it provides a diagrammatic superstructure for the entire plot. Of the five scaffolds, only those of Caro, Mundus, Belial, and Avaritia are used throughout most of the play; Avaritia's is placed at an odd angle to the rest, and the entrance of God on the fifth scaffold concludes the play by squaring the circle. But even at the beginning, the unusually long and elaborate banns, which clearly summarize the play in advance, elevate us above the ordinary contingencies of plot. We are assured that the play represents human life (ll. 14–15), but it does so from the lofty vantage point of doctrinal abstraction.

Of course, all of the morality plays begin at a high level of abstraction, thanks to their sermon-like prologues, and none of them can stay there permanently, because action requires embodiment. But the abstract apparatus of *The Castle of Perseverance* is unusually clear and neat, and it remains to dominate the action. The first part of the play is a series of self-expositions by Mundus, Belial, and Caro. Static on their scaffolds, costumed in "ryal aray," declaiming in end-rhymed, heavily alliterative verse with formal diction, the three enemies of man are at this point more masquelike than dramatic. What distinguishes the scene from masque is that these magnificently visible and audible forms seem to have materialized out of the doctrinal statements in the banns. Mundus' opening words echo the banns so closely in style and subject that a spectator who lacked a program might mistake him at first for another *vexillator,* talking about *mundus.* We are prepared for such confounding of exposition and performance by a bit of verbal legerdemain in the banns themselves, in which the Second Vexillator's outline of human salvation double-exposes with the First Vexillator's advertisement of the play:

SECOND VEXILLATOR.   Thus mowthys confession
  And his hertys contricion
  Schal save Man fro dampnacion,
  By Goddys mercy and grace.
FIRST VEXILLATOR.   Grace if God wil graunte us, of his mikyl myth,
  These parcell[ys] in propyrtes we purpose us to playe. . . .

                                                      [Ll. 127–32]

12. Bevington, *Medieval Drama,* p. 796, which also presents a diagram of the stage for *The Castle of Perseverance* as found in the manuscript (V.a.354).

The link between those speeches momentarily merges what it distinguishes, doctrine and theatrical performance; both arise simultaneously from God's grace. Such equivocal transitions render the ensuing spectacle transparent to abstractions.

Especially remarkable is the transparency of the play's human protagonist. We think of the "mankind figures" of the moralities as representative individuals, but the identity of Humanum Genus is at first entirely generic. "Aftyr oure forme-faderys kende, / This nyth I was of my moder born," he begins (ll. 275–76). When he goes on to explain the spiritual condition of mankind in four eloquent rhymed stanzas, he may seem to be a bizarrely precocious newborn. But what speaks here is the generic wisdom of the Christian, available through the church and the Holy Spirit as soon as the child needs it. Humanum Genus confirms that our lofty perspective on the play is the one native to the Christian, who comes into the world as the exemplar of a pattern of sin and redemption.

But if we feel that such perfect coalescence between infant and pattern is a bit unnatural, the play soon accommodates our reservations. Although Humanum Genus has clearly articulated the difficulties he can expect to encounter, including his temptation by a "bad angel" and his recourse against it, he quickly forgets what he knows when Malus Angelus actually speaks to him. "Whom to folwe, wetyn I ne may!" he cries, despite his earlier clarity on just that matter (l. 375; cf. 301–19). His difficulty arises because he must now encounter his bad angel as a particular experience rather than just as received knowledge. Malus Angelus detaches worldly enticements from the doctrinal pattern in which Humanum Genus initially saw them and represents them in the context of an individual life. Humanum Genus will be so rich that "in londe be him non lyche" (l. 344)—a nonsensical promise insofar as the antecedent of "him" is humankind itself; but that antecedent immediately obliges his seducer by redefining himself in terms of particular circumstances: he is still young, he says, and can follow the world "a lityl throwe" (ll. 423, 396–97).

Humanum Genus has here begun a descent into particularity—an exaggerated, faulty version of the materialization of doctrine which began the play. For him, the link between pattern and instance has weakened drastically, and his attempt to base himself in particularity will occupy much of the play. It has two aspects. First, he attends to the world of particularity, as embodied in Mundus, Caro, and Ava-

ritia. Second, Humanum Genus now regards himself as particular—
that is, as autonomous and unique. He will have no more truck with
good men, he decides (l. 446), and he even allows himself to be
convinced that he can "do as no Man dos" (l. 1063). Apparently he
expects to separate himself from the species that he represents.

As Humanum Genus falls into particularity, he does not take the
play and the audience with him. To some degree the action becomes
more vigorous and the dialogue earthier, but they remain predominantly ritualistic and symbolic, a series of processions among scaffolds and formal addresses by personified Vices. Watching such stylized sin, the audience can feel little empathy with Humanum Genus;
thus his fall produces a distance between his perspective and ours, a
distance that widens painfully as he embraces more and more of his
allegorical enemies. When Mundus orders that Humanum Genus be
given great wealth, Voluptas responds ingratiatingly, but adds, "In
Lickinge-and-Lust / He schal rust, / Til dethys dust / Do him to day"
(ll. 631–38). Detractio openly describes his own destructive effects
even though he is introduced to Humanum Genus simply as a messenger and guide (ll. 770–72). We must not defend Humanum Genus
by claiming that he cannot see the allegorical identifications that are
available to us. Avaritia frankly promises him to induce a desire for
"mekyl more / Thanne evere schal do the[e] goode" (ll. 839–40);
after that, Humanum Genus can praise Avaritia's benevolence (ll.
869–70) only because he has not been paying attention. Equally
obtusely, Humanum Genus greets Wrath and Envy, after their frank
self-expositions, as "hende" (ll. 1101, 1131). From our perspective,
he is willfully blind to general meanings.

The gap between his perspective and ours is all the more painful
because we cannot dissociate ourselves intellectually from his: Humanum Genus is, after all, our representative. Subtly the play has
reminded us of that. "The case of oure cominge, you to declare, /
Every man in himself forsothe he it may finde," begins one speaker of
the banns (ll. 14–15), and in their opening monologues the vice
characters claim to operate in familiar places: "Iwis, fro Carlylle into
Kent my carpinge they take!" (l. 201). Later Belial insinuates that the
protagonist's name is a universal plural (ll. 222–25), and Bonus Angelus identifies the fallen Humanum Genus with "worldly wittys" in
the audience (l. 795). We can easily ignore those reminders of our
involvement, particularly when we see Humanum Genus' folly from a
superior perspective. But in fact the playwright has not allowed us to

sustain only one perspective. We must continue to acknowledge participation in Humanum Genus' fall even as we look down on it from the vantage point of the angels.

The first crisis of *The Castle of Perseverance* is a conflict between those two perspectives—the protagonist's myopia and the enlightenment provided by the allegorical schema. The arena of conflict is the definition of *humanum genus*. When seduced by Ira and Accidia, our hero does not simply acquiesce; he declares the acquiescence of all mankind:

> [Envy's] counsel is knowyn thorwe mankinde,
> For ilke man callith other "hore" and "thefe."
>   . . .
> Cum up, Envye, my dere derlinge!
> Thou hast Mankindys love.
>
> > [Ll. 1133–43; cf. 1221–31]

Thus he generalizes his absorption in particularity, making it, paradoxically, a new categorical law. Standing on Avaritia's scaffold, he formulates the new law as a revised self-definition:

> "Mankinde" I am callyd by kinde,
> With curssydnesse in costys knet.
> In sowre swettenesse my syth I sende,
> With sevene sinnys sadde beset.
> Mekyl mirthe I move in minde,
> With melody at my mowthis met. . . .
>
> > [Ll. 1238–43]

The redefinition has strong inductive support. Humanum Genus is probably right that there is "no man but they use somme / Of these seven Dedly Sinnys" (ll. 1249–50); as he will presently say to Confessio, "We have etyn garlek everychone" (l. 1369). But inductive validity, with its basis in particularity, is not the only standard here. Humanum Genus' redefinition of himself contradicts not only his own earlier statements but also our sense of logical propriety. A certain incoherence appears in his own oxymorons—he claims to live in sour sweetness, in dangerous mirth—and in the incongruity between his boastful tone and his devastating admission that he is "sadde beset" and bound for hell. More significantly, his claim that mankind is inherently sinful forms part of a circular argument: he offers it to justify prolonging the very behavior that substantiates the claim. In short, if Humanum Genus' generalizations about himself are well supported statistically, they are emotionally and logically untenable as formal laws of his nature. The standoff between empirical and formal logic extends to a quarrel between Malus Angelus, who points to his victory "wel ny over al Mankinde" (l. 1285), and Bonus Angelus, who insists with equal validity that a sinful Mankind would violate "kinde" itself (l. 1289).

The standoff ends when one generic law intrudes into the material realm that constitutes its rival's power base. Humanum Genus has ignored the preaching of Confessio, but Paenitentia pricks him with what the reader must assume to be a real lance, provoking Humanum Genus to acknowledge the sudden onset of sorrow for sin (ll. 1377–1404). The episode is of course metaphoric, but the metaphor's vehicle is a significantly physical gesture even if no blood is drawn. The materialization of doctrine here takes its most intense form, producing the only plot development so far to be based on physical action. Through the grace of God, "Goddys lawys" intrude even on the man who has insulated himself in the spurious laws of the material world (l. 1398).

Appropriately, the response of Humanum Genus is that relocation of reality which we call conversion. He addresses two personifications that have not appeared on stage, Mercy and "sory sinne" (ll. 1408, 1410), acknowledging the power of what he cannot see. He further reformulates reality by declaring that his elevated enemies made him to "sinke sore" and that his current descent from the scaffolds is more truly an ascent (l. 1471). With the help of Confessio, Humanum Genus abjures his past perversion as a species of madness (ll. 1483, 1498–1532); he also reformulates the laws that define him:

> For, thou[gh] Mankinde have don amis,
> And he wil falle in repentaunce,
> Crist schal him bringyn to bowre of blis,
> If sorwe of hert lache him with launce.
>
> [Ll. 1416–19]

And his reformulation embraces the audience, to whom he offers himself as Christian exemplar: "Lordingys, ye se wel alle this: / Mankinde hathe ben in gret bobaunce" (ll. 1420–21). Humanum Genus has apparently rejoined the generic Reality that produced him at the beginning of the play.

He rejoins it changed, though—newly aware of his capacity for change. He knows now that mankind is susceptible of two generic definitions and that each person must reject the spurious one: "For thow[gh] *Mankinde* be wonte therto, *I* wil now al amende *me*" (ll. 1444–45; emphasis added). When Malus Angelus invites him back into particularity, reminding him of his increasing age and suggesting that he play with "Sare and Sisse" instead of with the "olde trat" who enjoins penance, Humanum Genus firmly chooses instead to be governed by the patterns of "holy writ" (ll. 1575–78, 1598–1601).[13] He has learned, in short, that the conflict between tyrannical particularity and transcendent law can be arbitrated by human will. One result is his request that Schrift show him "sum place of surete" against his enemies (l. 1543). Such a place would have to be also an internal condition, of course, but that is Humanum Genus' point. He is not naively looking for physical defense against spiritual attack; nor is he setting us up to accept a stage contraption as the token for an abstract "location." What he wants, and what he attains even by wanting it, is to live in an allegorical structure: particular reality informed by doctrinal truth, doctrine materially realized. In the castle of perseverance he can "dwelle withoutyn distaunsce" (l. 1547)— without distance between concrete signifier and abstract sign, or between flesh and spirit—because that is the nature of the castle and the meaning of Christian perseverance.

Because of a lacuna in the manuscript, we do not know how Humanum Genus' meeting with the seven virtues begins. That it should begin at this point is appropriate, however, for although he has previously been capable of practicing virtue, he is now ready to acknowledge the Virtues as realities. They materialize for him in the proper sense in which the entire play originally materialized from the abstractions in the banns. Indeed, they materialize polysemously, somewhat like the Virtues in the *Psychomachia*. One by one they locate

---

13. I here disagree with Bevington's identification, in a note to ll. 1575–77, of "Sare and Sisse" as the personified Virtues. The Virtues have not yet appeared; surely "Sare and Sisse" are typical human beings, who can be thought of as realistic embodiments of Luxuria and Accidia. The "olde trat" may be Confessio, Paenitentia, or, by slanderous feminization, Bonus Angelus; my guess is the last, since he is the speaker's particular enemy.

themselves in sacred history, in categorical opposition to the sins, and in individual human behavior; Humanum Genus, in turn, accepts them as elements in his own life (ll. 1602–92). The ceremoniousness of the scene underscores the allegorical harmony.

A spectator might be excused for thinking that the play is over, for in Humanum Genus' allegorical resolution we can see the salvation of the race, a salvation not merely prescribed but attained through experience. But as Humanum Genus has heard, our generic salvation cannot be categorical. That paradox is enacted when Humanum Genus withdraws into the castle of perseverance, for in his absence, mankind's fate is again contested.

The contest begins with a renewal of the split in allegorical perspectives, but the positions of the two perspectives are reversed. Earlier we saw the general truths to which involvement in particularity blinded Humanum Genus; now Humanum Genus has attained allegorical clarity, but we experience the confusion reintroduced by his allegorical enemies. Malus Angelus summons Detractio, who alarms Mundus, Caro, and Belial with the news of Humanum Genus' conversion. The resurgence of the evil characters is clearly not a projection of the protagonist's state of mind, as modern readers sometimes assume, for Humanum Genus is persevering in virtue (e.g., ll. 1758–61). The hostility of his opponents has its own momentum. In fact, the primary instigator of the hostility is a quintessential disruptor of allegorical harmony. Detractio's Middle English name, Bakbiter, imperfectly expresses his habitual operation, which is not only to disparage goodness but more generally to produce disparity: he reintroduces "distaunsce" and thus undermines the castle of perseverance.

Detractio's most obvious disseverance is to provoke the three "kings" and the sins against the Virtues; but that is not in itself a serious threat, since, as we will see, the Virtues are stronger. He takes greater pleasure in producing dissension among the evil characters themselves by insinuating to the three kings that their lieutenants have let Humanum Genus slip away. The resulting quarrels may seem to injure only the participants, but they also muddy the allegorical scheme: no longer is evil simply fighting good. And the bickering blurs our allegorical perceptions in another, more insidious way. It is probably the most entertaining section of the play, beginning with Detractio's ferocious energy—"I go, I go, on grounde glad, / Swifter

thanne schip with rodyr!" (ll. 1737–38)—and continuing in a great
blowing of horns and cracking of skulls. Apparently the reform of
Humanum Genus has increased the earthy vigor of his enemies:

> Whanne Mankind growith good,
> I, the Werld, am wild and wod.
> Tho bicchys [the Virtues] schul bleryn in here blood,
> With flappys felle and fele.
>
> [Ll. 1882–85]

Perhaps the most amusing issue of the Vices' liveliness is their impu-
dent overhumanizing of the personified Virtues, whom they persistently call "wenchys," "skallyd skoutys," "mamering modrys,"
and so on. When Gula boasts to "makyn swiche a powdyr, / Bothe
with smoke and with smodyr, / They schul schityn for fere" (ll.
1965–68), his scurrility overmatches Genius' irreverent reduction of
Nature to a talkative female in the *Romance of the Rose*. If we
remember that this is allegory, we can attribute such raillery to the
same particularistic vision that earlier endangered Humanum Genus:
the absorption in physical action, the focus on the Virtues' visible
forms without regard to their intelligible identities. But we are more
likely to respond to the scene as farce, in which no one looks for
serious meaning. The dissociation of emotional response from moral
judgment is another kind of *distaunsce* introduced by Detractio.

Still another kind of dissonance is the fragmentation of *humanum
genus*. Throughout the first part of the play Humanum Genus was the
exemplar of humanity, even when we felt superior to him, and even
when his categorical integrity was in doubt. But now, just when
identification with him seems most natural and desirable, Detractio
evokes an alternate vision of humanity:

> Ya! for God, this was wel goo,
> Thus to werke with Bakbitinge!
> I werke bothe wrake and woo,
> And make iche man other to dinge.
>
> [Ll. 1778–81]

He goes on to insinuate that we may in fact be versions of him, not of
Humanum Genus:

> Ye bakbiterys, loke that ye do so!
> Make debate abowtyn to springe
> Betwene sister and brother!
> If any bakbiter here be lafte,
> He may lere of me his crafte;
> Of Goddys grace he schal be rafte,
> And every man to killyn other.
>
> [Ll. 1784–90]

Detractio claims to divide the species, both ontologically and socially, separating part of it from God's grace.

For the moment, Humanum Genus is not affected by the allegorical fragmentation. Speaking from his castle after long silence, he formulates what is happening as a coherent piece of doctrine:

> Whanne Mankind drawith to goode
> Beholde what enmys he schal have.
> The Werld, the Devil, the Flesche, arn wode;
> To men they casten a careful kave.
>
> . . .
>
> Therfore iche man bewar of this!
>
> [Ll. 1997–2004]

His vision reunites mankind itself and bridges again the gap between universal and particular. And the scene that follows sustains Humanum Genus' allegorical harmony even in the midst of conflict.

The "psychomachia" of *The Castle of Perseverance* begins as a ritualistic confrontation, the materialization of a predetermined pattern. The Vices' physical weapons—stones, arrows, and concretizing insults—are of course useless against the Virtues' metaphoric ones, as Invidia and Ira lament:

> With worthy wordys and flourys swete,
> Charité makith me so meke
> I dare neither crye nore crepe—
> Not a schote of sklaundyr.
>
> [Ll. 2213–16]

> I, Wrethe, may singyn wele-a-wo!
> Paciens me gaf a sory dint.
> I am al betyn blak and blo
> With a rose that on rode was rent.
>
> [Ll. 2217–20]

Particularly potent are the words in which the Virtues testify to their multiple and divinely authorized manifestations. The "baner" of Humilitas is "[t]his meke kingc . . . / That was croisyd on Calvary" (ll. 2086–87), Abstentia can defeat Gula "[w]ith bred that browth us out of hell" (l. 2267), and Solicitudo explains that whoever shrives himself defeats Accidia (ll. 2345–46). Such shifts of locale and time establish a pattern of supremacy. Thus the first six Virtues win for the same reason as do the Virtues in the *Psychomachia:* they are more Real than their opponents.

And yet there is a crucial difference between this battle and the one in Prudentius' poem. It appears first in the Virtues themselves, whose polysemy rests on a human basis. They all speak as human beings transfigured by divine example. Humilitas alludes to the devil's entrapment of "us" in paradise (ll. 2098–99); Patientia gives thanks that Christ became a man, "[u]s paciens to techyn and lerne" (l. 2137); Castitas has learned from Our Lady to live a chaste life (ll. 2313–14). All three of them participate in transcendent Realities, but they allude persistently to the intersection of person and Reality, the point where, by the example of Christ, the Virtue emerges from the human being. These virtues are not pure universals but allegorized saints. Likewise, when Superbia exclaims, in the midst of battle, "My prowde pride a-doun is drevyn," or when Invidia becomes too meek to engage in slander (ll. 2204, 2213–16), the Sins look like dehumanized but reformable sinners. It follows that this battle is not the transumptive meta-event narrated by Prudentius but a particular realization of the meta-event, staged for Humanum Genus' benefit and ours. Therein lies the Virtues' hidden vulnerability, soon to be exploited.

At the prompting of Mundus, the seventh sin adopts a brilliant new strategy. Rather than affronting his opposing Virtue, Avaritia speaks directly, as an old friend, to Humanum Genus:

> How, Mankinde! I am a-tenyde
> For thou art there so in that holde.
> Cum and speke with thy best frende,
> Sir Coveitise! Thou knowist me of olde.
>
> [Ll. 2427–30]

Largitas immediately counters by invoking divine authority against Avaritia. "That Lord that restyd on the rode / Is maker of an ende," she proclaims, and a Latin tag hints at an apocalyptic victory (ll. 2451–52a). But Avaritia rejoins that he was not talking to her:

> What eylith the[e], Lady Largité,
> Damysel dingne upon thy des?
> And I spak ryth not to the[e],
> Therfore I prey the[e] holde thy pes.
> How, Mankinde! Cum speke with me;
> Cum ley thy love here in my les.
>
> [Ll. 2466–71]

Perhaps he cannot defeat the allegorical saint, and he certainly cannot overthrow *largitas* itself, but he can subvert a certain exemplar of virtue. He will do so in the way that has worked before: by loosening the exemplar from its defining pattern. Humanum Genus himself acknowledges that he is now old and poor; out of those contingencies, Avaritia builds a case for deviating from the "bok of kendys" and following instead the world's law (ll. 2513, 2482–530). Humanum Genus agrees that circumstances dictate an excursion out of the castle of perseverance, since, after all, a man must earn his bread sometime (ll. 2534–39). When Bonus Angelus appeals to the Virtues to stop him, they say, quite rightly, that they can do nothing if Humanum Genus decides to destroy his soul; "God hath govyn him a fre wille" (ll. 2557–60).

Accordingly, the Virtues prepare to retreat. They are not weakened, and, they assure us, Mankind will recognize their superior strength in the end (ll. 2596–621). But for now, they can only appeal to the audience to exonerate them of the downfall of Humanum Genus: "Ichon, ye knowyn he is a fole," says Abstentia (l. 2596). Their apologia is less important for what it says about the Virtues than for the position in which it puts the audience. The Virtues invite us to acknowledge their reality, to see our participation in the "Mankind" which can be either foolish or "trewe and sad" (l. 2590), and to fulfill the proper pattern ourselves—in short, to enter the castle of perseverance. They seem to have little hope that we will do so, "For no man can be war by other / Til he hathe al ful spunne" (ll. 2616–17). But their pessimism has managed to foreground the essential issue in this second fall of Humanum Genus: the free will of his various manifestations.

Once the Virtues have departed, Malus Angelus, Avaritia, and

Mundus conspire to persuade Humanum Genus that both the Virtues and free will are illusory. They renew their debunking of the Virtues:

> Ya! Go forthe, and lete the qwenys cakle!
> Ther wymmen arn, are many wordys:
> Lete hem gon hoppyn with here hakle!
> Ther ges sittyn are many tordys.
>
> [Ll. 2648–51]

They also exult in empirical logic, telling Humanum Genus, "Pardé, thou gost owt of Mankinde / But Coveitise be in thy mende!" (ll. 2657–58). Moreover, they exploit Humanum Genus' physical infirmity and his old age, powerful motives for seeking tangible comforts. In response, he now wants a real castle, not the castle of perseverance (ll. 2748–50).

Once again, Humanum Genus abandons himself to material reality without regard to the laws that it manifests. This time, his fall into particularity exerts a strong pull on the audience. His materialistic perspective seems to bring the stage itself down to earth, for the building that served as the castle of perseverance is now used pragmatically as a storage place for money (l. 2703 and staging diagram). And we are further drawn to the materialistic perspective by a rather startling development in the dialogue. Giving Humanum Genus wealth, Avaritia announces, "Thus hast thou gotyn, in sinful slo, / Of thine neig[h]borys, by extorcion" (ll. 2756–57). A bit later Humanum Genus mentions his intent to leave an estate to "mine childyr and to min[e] wife" (l. 2976). We have been watching his entire career, from birth to the point of death, and we have seen neither neighbors nor wife and children. Such people, along with parks and palaces and the means by which he has attained wealth, are not inherently incompatible with allegory, but they have been left implicit in this allegory's abstract topography. The concrete images that have appeared in the play have been materializations of sin, virtue, conscience, and perseverance. Now the more familiar facts of human life break through, with all the rhetorical power of reality, to support the definition of humanity proffered by Mundus and Avaritia.

So solid is this material framework that if it will last, says Humanum Genus, he will forsake God and heaven (ll. 2774–77). On some level, of course, he knows that it will not last—that realism is itself a dangerous illusion. His very expression of commitment to it is

Death's cue (ll. 2778–79). Mors fulfills the commitment to particularity, surpassing even the worldly vices in his appeal to real human
experience and his claim to empirical validity:

> Ye schul me drede, everychone;
> Whanne I come, ye schul grone!
>   . . .
> Riche, pore, fre and bonde—
> Whanne I come, they goo no more.
>   . . .
> In the grete pestelens,
> Thanne was I wel knowe.
>
>   [Ll. 2787–2816]

At the same time, however, Mors undoes the commitment to particularity by demonstrating the impotence of wealth and of Mundus (ll.
2819–27, 2856–2894). Thus the logic of realism appears in the end
absolutely binding but absolutely undependable. As if to underscore
the unreality of reality, Mundus summons as heir to Humanum
Genus a servant whose only name is "I wot nevere whoo" (l. 2968).
The dying man's protest that this heir is none of his kin becomes
ironic when we recognize that Garcio allies himself with Mundus and
dedicates himself to Avaritia exactly as did his generic exemplar. In
his very anonymity, Garcio mirrors the loss of identity to which
Humanum Genus' involvement in particularity has led him. At his
death Humanum Genus sees himself once again as exemplary, but
this time he exemplifies agony, failure, and mortality (ll. 2982–
3005). Uneasy that he has undergone no last-minute conversion and
uncomfortably aware that Mors is no fiction, his hearers are likely to
feel themselves also on the brink of nonbeing.

But we are to witness one more materialization of Reality, the most
impressive one in the play. Humanum Genus' cry of despair is not
quite his final act. "Min[e] hert brekith. I syhe sore," he says, and
then, "A word may I speke no more. / I putte me in Goddys mercy!"
(ll. 3005–7). His very last word is the first one spoken by Anima
when she emerges from beneath his deathbed:

> "Mercy!" This was my laste tale
> That evere my body was a-bowth.
> But Mercy helpe me in this vale,
> Of dampninge drinke sore I me doute.
>
>   [Ll. 3008–11]

Her second repetition of the word makes it almost a personification. A bit later, Bonus Angelus speaks also of a hope that "Mercy wil to [Anima] sende" (l. 3058). Mercy moves closer to personification when Anima addresses it directly, imploring it, on the authority of Scripture, actually to appear (ll. 3060–63). Finally, after Malus Angelus has borne Anima off to a place that he claims is hell, Misericordia enters and speaks (ll. 3129–30).

Misericordia is not a materialization directly from Scripture or doctrine, as were most of the earlier agents; she has doctrinal resonance, but she originates from the prayer of Humanum Genus. When she expresses a hope that the soul will receive mercy (l. 3131), she clearly does not speak as God's mercy; she is mercy as principle or potential. As such, she comes accompanied by three other principles with comparable claims to operate here. The modern reader who dismisses the ensuing scene as "the four-daughters-of-God topos" has probably mistaken its meaning. Certainly the scene arises from the verse in Psalms—"Mercy and Truth have met together; Righteousness and Peace have kissed each other" (Ps. 85:10–11)—but it has its own meaning, unequatable with that of its topos. As Mark Eccles points out, "*The Castle* changes the traditional time of the debate, before the Incarnation, to the judgment of the soul after death."[14] That change introduces a particular kind of suspense. By exercise of his free will, Humanum Genus himself has rejected Mercy, as Justitia and Veritas point out (ll. 3392–430, 3470–82). This meeting of the four daughters may accordingly depart from the pattern celebrated by the Psalmist, even though the pattern is universal.

In fact, the effect of scriptural precedent here is to deadlock the debate, not to resolve it. Throughout the play Latin quotations have supplemented the dialogue, identifying for the reader the sacred pretext that the spectator can easily infer. Here quotations from Scripture and creed appear in the dialogue itself, as rhetorical ammunition used by all four speakers. A verse from Psalms proclaims that truth condemns man to hell, but another records God's promise of mercy. Certain biblical passages attest to man's ingratitude and God's love of justice, while others promise peace between God and man (ll. 3284–86, 3374, 3400–3404, 3531–34). Those inconsistent texts produce an allegorical stalemate among equally authoritative abstractions.

14. Mark Eccles, note to l. 3129 of *The Castle of Perseverance*, in *Macro Plays*, ed. Eccles.

Even the passage about the four principles' reconciliation, finally cited by Pax, is here a debater's exhortation rather than a statement of fact (ll. 3519–21).

The allegorical stalemate underscores a paradox implicit throughout the play: the limited potency of the sovereign Realities. *The Castle of Perseverance* is an unquestionably Realistic vision of human life, a virtual string of allegorical clichés—the three enemies of man, the good and bad angels, the seven sins and their *remedia,* the prick of conscience, the soul's address to the body, the debate among the four daughters of God. But each of those topoi is, or becomes, a conflict unresolvable within the play by the conflicting forces themselves. During the life of Humanum Genus, allegorical oppositions are arbitrated by his will. Now the final stalemate can be resolved only by the will of God. Pax and Mercy appeal to Pater Sedens in Trono to recognize them as the truth of his own nature (e.g., ll. 3327–30), and he accedes: "I menge with my most myth / Alle Pes, sum Treuthe, and sum Ryth, / And most of my Mercy" (ll. 3571–73). If the materialization of God here seems almost shocking, that effect is also significant. Transcendent Reality has, throughout the play, depended on the realm of particularity for its realization; now God's participation in the human drama reiterates his astonishing entrance into time through Christ and conveys, more fully than does the substance of his judgment, his chosen involvement in the particularity of his creatures.

The play ends by reaffirming simultaneously the Reality of its conflicting patterns and the essential role of its audience in arbitrating them. Humanum Genus is brought at long last to God's scaffold, the true east for which the scaffold of Avaritia was an oblique substitute. Pater Sedens in Juditio grants him mercy and admits him to heaven. But then, with no break, still speaking in the second person, God talks as if the life of Humanum Genus were not over:

> Thou hast cause to love me
> Abovyn al thinge in land,
> And kepe my comaundement.
> If thou me love and drede,
> Hevene schal be thy mede;
> My face the[e] schal fede—
> This is min[e] jugement.

> [Ll. 3604–3610]

In his fully generic role, Humanum Genus is still to undergo this judgment. The play's human referents extrapolate the play, while its sacred ones transcend it. The same points are made when Justitia orders Malus Angelus, who is already in a stage hell, to go to hell (l. 3590), and again when Pater Sedens in Juditio concludes his speech by exhorting the audience and praising God. The stage and the actors easily abjure their claim to represent hell and God comprehensively, but by the same token they reaffirm the nonfictional nature of their *gamys*—that is, of the allegorical materialization that the audience will continue to enact.

Everyman: Allegorical Recognition

The twentieth century's favorite morality play does not seem to have been particularly popular on medieval and Renaissance stages. As Arnold Williams points out, we have no records of performances before the nineteenth century, and the surviving texts are unusual in including no stage directions.[15] Records and stage directions may have existed, of course. But the negative evidence does suggest a divergence between medieval and modern responses to *Everyman,* a divergence that could be attributed to certain features of the play itself. *Everyman*'s plot is more compact than those of the other moralities, focusing on Death's summons; the cast of characters is relatively small; the proportion of ceremonial apparatus—rich costumes, songs and processions, scaffolds and other constructions—appears much lower. Those characteristics render the play less clearly allegorical than, say, *The Castle of Perseverance,* and possibly less appealing to a medieval production company. By the same token, they render it more compatible with a psychologically based theater. Modern audiences can cherish *Everyman* as the one strand of gold inadvertently produced by those who thought their real business was to spin didactic straw.

Everyman does, nonetheless, depend on the semiotics of allegory, as we see when the protagonist materializes out of a collective pronoun. Here, as in the other morality plays, a sense of drama arises

15. Arnold Williams, *The Drama of Medieval England* (East Lansing: Michigan State University Press, 1961), p. 160.

from the interchange of levels of being. But the interchange differs from that in *The Castle of Perseverance* in a way that may have confused casual readers in the Middle Ages no less than it falsely attracts us now. The play proceeds, as it were, from the bottom up, basing itself in the world of individual experience.

Like the other moralities, *Everyman* begins with a didactic summary of the action. But the universalizing prologue is short here, and the play abandons direct address as soon as the Messenger exits. God's opening lament on the spiritual blindness of "the people" is less sermon than soliloquy; modern spectators may imagine that they are overhearing the reflections of a troubled monarch. Moreover, God speaks of "every man" in the third person, allowing us to detach ourselves from what he says—to feel that we are watching the imitation of an action rather than witnessing the materialization of doctrine. A distance between doctrine and action is in fact the initial premise of the plot. God's lament is that his creatures are blind in spiritual sight, too drowned in sin to know him for their God (ll. 25–26): ignoring the materialization of divine truth, they have relapsed into uninformed particularity.

Mankind's representative comes on stage so insulated in particularity that he does not even see Death and God until the latter addresses him. He responds to the name "Everyman" but not yet to the general truths that govern every man. Apparently he thinks he is merely an individual. He appears also to believe that the other characters are ordinary individuals, for when forced to acknowledge the presence of Death, he offers at first what John C. Webster terms an "extraordinarily non-plussed and (from our informed point of view) obtuse reply: 'Why askest thou? / Woldest thou wete?'" Death then introduces himself and announces his mission, but Everyman still responds as if to "a random encounter with an obnoxious stranger" who can perhaps be bribed. The resulting humorous irony is not incidental. Webster explains that "we are . . . previewing a major theme of the play, that the logic of literal things is not the only logic in the universe, that being saved depends on one's ability to keep seeing double, to keep both the literal and figurative possibilities of language in mind at once."[16] "Literal" and "figurative" are, as usual, unfortu-

16. John C. Webster, "The Allegory of Contradiction in *Everyman* and *The Faerie Queene*," in *Spenser and the Middle Ages (1976)*, ed. David A. Richardson (Cleveland: Cleveland State University Press, 1976), p. 362 (microfiche), citing *Everyman*, ll. 87–88.

nate terms; Everyman's "literal-mindedness" is a myopic focus on death's figurative representative. But if we substitute "concrete" and "abstract" for those terms, Webster's point becomes clear. Everyman responds to the visible agent and the particular encounter, not to the concept they embody.

The kind of naivcté that Everyman displays toward Death is usually regarded as a chronic condition of allegorical personae. C. S. Lewis writes that "to the characters participating in an allegory, nothing is allegorical," and Robert E. Wood cites "the essential condition of allegory, that the characters react to circumstances in their realistic rather than their allegorical significance."[17] That "essential condition" is violated in all of the allegories that use personae. Here the force of the scene between Everyman and Death depends on Everyman's unrealized ability to see Death allegorically. That does not mean that he must acknowledge himself to be dying; Death does not "represent" Everyman's expiration, as modern readers regularly assume. Death is, rather, simply mortality, here becoming materially present for Everyman in the same way as Conscience did for Humanum Genus. But unlike Humanum Genus, Everyman fails at first to understand what it is that he sees; the material world appears to him opaque and self-sufficient. That is why he immediately grasps at such materialistic remedies as more time, a bribe, and finally his earthly friends. The encounter with Death shows how far Everyman is from allegorical vision—that is, from the ability to recognize the particular and timebound as the universal.

His education in allegorical vision begins in earnest in the well-known scenes with Fellowship, Kindred, and Cousin. To expect those characters to accompany him on his journey to Death, as Everyman does at first, is once more to overlook the general nature of a particular agent. His earthly friends immediately expound their general natures, albeit inadvertently. "I will not forsake the[e] to my lives ende / In the waye of good company," vows Fellowship (ll. 213–14; emphasis added). His later apologies indicate that he overinterprets his own promises; but in fact he never promises anything that he cannot fulfill. The "way of good company" does not extend beyond the mortal world. Thus in disappointing Everyman, Fellowship sim-

17. C. S. Lewis, *Spenser's Images of Life,* ed. Alastair Fowler (Cambridge: Cambridge University Press, 1967), p. 29; Robert E. Wood, "Britomart at the House of Busyrane," *South Atlantic Bulletin* 43 (2) (May 1978):7.

ply reveals a categorical limitation of human friendship. Similarly, when Cousin and Kindred glibly generalize about their loyalty (ll. 319–26), their very reliance on shallow generalizations makes them, without their knowledge, not individuals but clichés. Even Cousin's claim to a particular exemption from Everyman's journey—"I have the crampe in my to[e]" (l. 356)—ironically confirms his categorical frailty.

To be fair to Everyman, he has good reason for missing the categorical implications of his friends' promises: his friends do not look much like categories. With the possible exception of Everyman himself, they are, in fact, the most easily individualized of allegorical actors, demonstrably more illustrative than symbolic. Thus modern readers and viewers imitate Everyman's error by imputing the infidelity of Fellowship, Kindred, and Cousin to personal weakness. But the individual weakness is itself categorical; the very notion that a more faithful earthly friend or kinsman might have gone with Everyman is the illusion proper to Fellowship and Kindred. Michael J. Warren writes that these characters "have a dual quality; at times they appear as Everyman's friends in their particularity, and at others in their abstract roles as representative figures and aspects of Everyman's thought. The first attendant problem, however, is that the separation is never exact."[18] That "problem" is not the playwright's lapse, but his point. Everyman must learn to see beyond the promises and evasions of his own friends and kin to the laws of the categories whose names they bear.

He moves through several stages in that process. After his initial naive trust proves mistaken, he feels personally betrayed, a sign that he still clings to the illusion of his friends' individual autonomy. Gradually he begins to see the general limitations of the kind of companionship they offer, and he is outraged at *their* naiveté. To Fellowship's blustering counteroffer—"Now, in good faith, I will not that waye. / But, and thou will murder, or ony man kill, / In that I will helpe th[e] with a good will"—Everyman exclaims impatiently, "O, that is a simple advise, indede" (ll. 280–83). Finally, abandoned, he acknowledges the ruling generalizations: "It is said, 'In prosperité men frendes may finde, / Whiche in adversité be full unkinde'" (ll.

18. Michael J. Warren, "*Everyman*: Knowledge Once More," *Dalhousie Review* 54 (1974):137.

309–10); "Lo, faire wordes maketh fooles faine; / They promise, and nothinge will do, certaine" (ll. 379–80).

A sign of the special power of this morality play is that Everyman's utterance of those platitudes provides not a didactic moment but an emotional one, both pathetic and frightening. "It comes as a bitter surprise," writes Tzvetan Todorov, "when we realize that our life is governed by the same laws we discovered in our morning paper and that we cannot change them."[19] The poignance of Everyman's allegorical enlightenment is of course one of the play's chief attractions for modern directors and audiences. But it is an inalienably allegorical effect, arising not from the playwright's subordination of doctrine to human experience but from Everyman's own myopic attachment to human experience. Everyman believes that he can arouse sympathy in Death, make Fellowship an ethical achievement, and take his family beyond the grave. In short, he expects people to be Real and personifications to behave like people.

The extreme case of the latter expectation is yet to come. Everyman rebounds from his despair over Kindred's and Cousin's desertion to the memory of another potential companion: "All my life I have loved riches. / If that my Good now helpe me might, / He wolde make my herte full light" (ll. 388–90). Against all common sense, he turns to a "friend" that is not even human. We nullify the effect of this scene if we assume, with Bernard Spivack, that personifications in morality drama were so conventional as to be used "without reference to their ultimate moral or metaphorical logic."[20] The personification of Goods is profoundly meaningful. It testifies to the all-too-powerful logic whereby what helps us appears to be reliably benevolent. That logic leads Everyman to expect Goods' continued loyalty; Goods is, however, incapable of such human values. He is quite literally Goods—anthropomorphic only in his ability to expound his nature to anyone who will listen:

> Who calleth me? Everyman? What, hast thou haste?
> I lie here in corners, trussed and piled so hye,
> And in chestes I am locked so fast,
> Also sacked in bagges. Thou mayst se with thin[e] eye

19. Todorov, "An Introduction to Verisimilitude," in *Poetics of Prose*, p. 87.
20. Spivack, p. 93.

I cannot stir[r]e; in packes lowe I lie.
What wolde ye have? Lightly me saye.

[Ll. 393–98]

Obviously this pseudopersonification can "folowe [no] man one fote" (l. 426). When Everyman curses him, Goods replies with chilling unconcern, "Mar[r]y, thou brought thyselfe in care, / Wherof I am [right] gladde; / I must nedes laugh, I cannot be sadde" (ll. 454–56). He appears inhuman, but only because he first, plausibly but falsely, seemed friendly. Again Everyman must learn to see beyond the individual agent to the categorical truths implicit in its name.

Having exhausted the logic of appearances, Everyman finally turns to the other perspective toward which each of his encounters has directed him. Actually, it was available to him from the beginning in the rather specific form of Death's command, "And loke thou be sure of thy rekeninge, / For before God thou shalte answere and shewe / Thy many badde dedes, and good but a fewe" (ll. 106–8). Now, Everyman ruefully acknowledges, "I shall never spede / Till that I go to my Good Dede" (ll. 480–81). He thereby recognizes as a force in his own life a general Christian truth that he has long known.

Everyman has also known something else: Good Deeds is too weak to be of much help. As evidence he has not only his guilty memory but also Death's pronouncement that his good deeds are few. But here occurs the first allegorical peripeteia. For recognizing doctrinal truth, Everyman is rewarded by a suspension of that piece of truth which renders his good deeds impotent. Weak at first, bound and inert like Goods, Good Deeds astonishes Everyman by understanding his problem without explanation and by telling him that his repentance will strengthen her. She thereby reverses Goods' behavior—or rather his nonbehavior. She also controverts the laws that Goods has just taught Everyman, for she begins to develop into a fully anthropomorphic agent, capable of expressing deep feeling, of initiating action, and, by the end of the play, of interceding for Everyman with God. Thus the acceptance of categorical law leads Everyman, paradoxically, toward freedom from such laws.

As in the scene with Goods, we miss the meaning here if we attribute the personification of Good Deeds to insignificant convention. Her genuine potency must be given its full weight as the dramatization of a miracle—the animation of what ought to be inanimate. An understanding of Good Deeds' personification can, in fact, dispel an apparent theological problem. That Good Deeds should save Every-man has disturbed some readers, especially Arnold Williams, who labels the resultant theology of "works" essentially unchristian.[21] Lawrence Ryan supplies a partial response when he points out that Good Deeds is strong enough to save Everyman only after Everyman attains a state of grace.[22] Not only is Good Deeds' strength a gift of grace; her very existence as a personification is literally gratuitous. Everyman's good deeds are initially represented in the book of ac-counts to which Death refers and which now lies, according to Good Deeds, under her feet (ll. 503–5). In that form they are indeed what we might call "works," the objective record of Everyman's praiseworthy deeds. Their second form, the personified Good Deeds, emphasizes her own redundance in saying to Everyman, "Than go you with your rekeninge and your Good Dedes togyder / For to make you joyfull at herte / Before the blessyd Trinité" (ll. 529–31). The gratuitous Good Deeds reveals to Everyman the unmerited benev-olence of that Reality whose harsher force intruded upon him in the opening scene.

His recognition of Good Deeds as an agent begins a conversion that is formalized when he encounters a second materialized abstraction. Good Deeds introduces Everyman to Knowledge, probably the most troublesome personification in the play for modern critics. So far the agents have been categories as well as abstractions—classes of peo-ple, objects, or actions. Knowledge breaks that pattern, and thus many readers have tried to pin her down to some class of knowledge-ables—one's sins, Christian doctrine, or penitential procedures. As Warren says, however, "there is no sound reason why Knowledge should not be accepted simply as Knowledge since that is the name of the character."[23] Such acceptance will be easier if we see the char-acter in context. Throughout the play, Everyman has behaved as though ignorant of anything but empirical reality, but we know that he has never in fact been without access to more general, doctrinal truth. Death's opening question to him is "Hast thou thy Maker

21. A. Williams, *Drama of Medieval England*, pp. 161–62. Williams attributes the "theology of works" to *Everyman's* Buddhist source, the Faithful Friend tale recorded in *Barlaam and Josaphat*.

22. Ryan, pp. 727–29.

23. Warren, p. 137. Warren reviews identifications of Knowledge on p. 136.

forgete?" (l. 86; emphasis added). His apparent ignorance was therefore the spurious dissociation of general truth from his particular life.
The first half of the play forces him to acknowledge what he knows;
now, in meeting Knowledge, he is not so much learning as accepting
knowledge for his companion and guide.

His recognition transforms the play. No longer dependent on empirical reality, the dialogue evokes a figurative landscape that does
not correspond to the stage:

KNOWLEDGE.   Now go we togyder lovingly
                To Confession, that clensinge rivere.
EVERYMAN.   For joy I wepe; I wolde we were there!
                But, I pray you, give me cognicion
                Where dwelleth that holy man, Confession?
KNOWLEDGE.   In the hous of salvacion.
                We shall find him in that place. . . .
                                   .   .   .
EVERYMAN.   O glorious fountaine, that all unclennes doth clarify . . .

                                                        [Ll. 535–45]

Figurative renomination is not limited to the setting. After being
called a river and a holy man, Confession is addressed as "moder of
salvacion" (l. 552); Penance is called a gem and a scourge (ll. 557,
561). Such inconsistent appositives have troubled at least one edi-
tor,[24] but in each case the images can be reconciled with each other as
variant manifestations of a transcendent Reality. Knowledge finally
directs Everyman's sight toward that which can be metaphorized
infinitely because it can never finally be named:

            O eternall God, O hevenly figure,
            O way of rightwisnes, O goodly vision, . . .
            O ghostly treasure, O raunsomer and redemer,
            Of all the worlde hope and conduiter,
            Mirrour of joye, foundatour of mercy,
            Whiche enlumineth heven and erth therby:
            Here my clamorous complaint, though it late be;
            Receive my prayers, of thy benignitye!

                                                        [Ll. 581–94]

24. A. C. Cawley, ed., *Everyman* (Manchester: Manchester University Press,
1961), note to l. 552.

In direct contrast to his stubborn materialism when Death first appeared, Everyman now recognizes Death's imminence while the personification is absent (l. 600). He has achieved "ghostly sight"—the
direct cognition of what governs appearances.

His recognition also embraces material reality itself. At the behest
of Knowledge and Good Deeds, Everyman now summons Beauty,
Strength, Discretion, and Five Wits. He is clearly not attaining beauty, strength, and so forth, as personal attributes; indeed, Death long
ago reminded him quite pointedly that he possessed at least one of
those qualities: "Everyman, thou arte mad! Thou hast thy wyttes five,
/ And here on erthe will not amende thy live" (ll. 168–69). The
present episode constitutes, therefore, Everyman's reacquaintance
with beauty, strength, discretion, and the five senses in the new context established by his allegorical conversion, the context governed by
Knowledge and Good Deeds. Earlier he mistakenly expected things to
determine his spiritual destiny; now he reperceives material reality as
the adjunct of spiritual knowledge and rightly directed will.

But even in extending Everyman's allegorical enlightenment, these
"persones of grete might" delay what he had expected to be an
immediate climax. Before their entrance he was ready to present his
"rekeninge" immediately (ll. 649–52). Like Everyman, audiences and
readers are often surprised that the action does not end with the
hero's conversion; at least one director regards lines 657 to 853 as an
expendable interpolation.[25] To students of *The Castle of Perseverance,* however, the anticlimax is familiar and proper. Neither play
ends when the protagonist first attains allegorical harmony: both give
more than passing acknowledgment to the recurrent claims of material existence. *Everyman's* anticlimax differs somewhat from that of
The Castle, for it does not culminate in the protagonist's relapse into
sin. But the introduction of Beauty, Strength, Discretion, and Five
Wits—earthly qualities directed by Christian principle—corresponds
closely to the entrance of Humanum Genus into the castle of perseverance. The sequel to allegorical epiphany in both plays is an
accommodation with temporal exigency.

As a further concession to temporal existence, Everyman's spiritual
guides advise him to seek out Priesthood, the spiritual guide through

25. John Wasson, "Interpolation in the Text of *Everyman*," *Theatre Notebook* 27
(1972):14–20.

"this transitory life" (l. 721). During Everyman's absence from the stage, Knowledge and Five Wits discuss the possibility that Priesthood may be corrupt. Their conversation digresses not only from the main plot but also from the dominant allegorical mode, for the speeches bear no clear relevance to the personifications that deliver them—or to any personifications, for that matter. Indeed, when Knowledge says that Christ did not sell the sacraments to us and Five Wits expresses trust that we will encounter no sinful priests (ll. 750–63), both speak as human beings. The Priesthood they discuss is even more clearly humanized. That, in fact, is the problem under discussion. Although Five Wits affirms Priesthood's spiritual identity and power, Knowledge is painfully aware that we do not encounter Priesthood without a priest and that the pattern may be sabotaged by its exemplars, with their "unclene life, as lustes of lechery" (l. 762). When Everyman comes back from Priesthood in a state of contentment and presumably of grace, we can assume that in his case the faith of Five Wits applies more fully than the skepticism of Knowledge. But the debate itself ends inconclusively—as it must, given the free will of Priesthood's innumerable avatars, as well as their unknowable effects on individual souls. The episode concerning Priesthood both examines and exemplifies the divergences from allegorical integrity to which particular creatures are vulnerable.

Those who call the last part of *Everyman* anticlimactic and extraneous are half right: extraneousness and anticlimax here produce the allegorical drama. Having arisen from the protagonist's experience, the play's allegorical vision is now blurred and attenuated by the prolonging of that experience. A visit to Priesthood to receive the sacraments is superfluous for a man who has already encountered Confession and Penance directly; on the other hand, Everyman's unmediated encounter with Confession was merely a respite from temporal existence. "What we call time," writes Paul de Man, "is precisely truth's inability to coincide with itself."[26]

That can explain the more obvious redundancy that follows: the second set of desertions. As he approaches the grave, confident that he and his new friends will survive the reckoning, Everyman is abandoned by Beauty, Strength, Discretion, and Five Wits—and to some

26. Paul de Man, *Allegories of Reading: Figural Language in Rousseau, Nietzsche, Rilke, and Proust* (New Haven: Yale University Press, 1979), p. 78.

degree even by Knowledge—in the same way as by Fellowship, Kindred, and Cousin much earlier. Again he is severely disappointed, even though his new friends, like his earlier ones, do nothing for which they have not implicitly prepared him: Strength promised aid "in distres, / Though thou wolde in bataile fight on the grounde," and Five Wits vowed to be loyal "though it were thrugh the worlde rounde" (ll. 684–86). But in behaving just like Fellowship *et alia,* the second group of friends frightens Everyman and puzzles audiences. He seems not to need a renewal of the lesson he learned earlier, not having relapsed into error. Indeed, his present disappointment is a consequence of his enlightenment, for the original betrayals led him to spiritual guides who recommended without qualification the perpetrators of this second set of betrayals. Thus the lesson's repetition undermines the earlier epiphany: truth reiterated turns false.

Apparently the only stable truth produced by Everyman's experience is instability, the pattern of desertion and disappointment which now looms through the entire play. Desertion is in fact the natural theme of an allegory based in individual experience. With the obvious exception of God and Death and the possible exception of Confession, *Everyman*'s agents are categories or faculties that cannot endure eternally as can the Mercy figures, the angels, and the Virtues of other morality plays. The second set of friends deliver colloquial curtain lines, amusing but pathetic, as if to remind us of their fundamental earthiness (ll. 800–850). That does not make them evil or inessential, nor does it mean that Knowledge and Good Deeds were wrong to recommend them. Everyman could have avoided neither trusting them nor being disappointed by his trust, for the allegorical agents of *Everyman* share in—indeed, they enact—the protagonist's own mortality. Having learned that lesson at last, Everyman understandably expects to be deserted also by Good Deeds, a finite category of mortal actions. "O, all thinge faileth, save God alone," he cries; "O Jesu, helpe! All hath forsaken me" (ll. 841, 851).

Against reason, he is wrong. The play's second and conclusive peripety undoes the pattern of failure as soon as Everyman has recognized it. Abandoned by Strength, Discretion, and Five Wits, feeling faint, Everyman continues for a while to stand and speak, as if exempted from dependence on physical faculties. Moreover, Good Deeds announces that she will survive her material basis, as if she were an eternal principle like Veritas or Caritas. Her survival is the more miraculous because, unlike Veritas or Caritas, Good Deeds retains a particular identification with the protagonist. To the end Everyman calls her "my Good Dedes," and she prays as his alter ego: "Shorte our ende, and minisshe our paine; / Let us go and never come againe" (ll. 869, 878–79). Only after the playwright has thus linked both Everyman and Good Deeds to mortal limitations does Knowledge report—on surmise, but with angelic confirmation offstage— that both have attained eternal life (ll. 889–901). Whereas the first peripety was Everyman's recognition of divine truth, the second is his and Good Deeds' apotheosis: the immortalization of finite and mortal agency.

The apotheosis of Everyman and Good Deeds completes a series of transmutations in the play's dramatis personae. From the beginning the personae have presented an unstable synthesis of particular forms with generic identities, of bodies with names. Everyman initially saw only the bodies, then learned to apprehend the generic identities, and later recognized, in despair, that the generic identities were all forms of transience and that the only immutable agent is God. But when Everyman and Good Deeds ascend to heaven, they enact a charade in which their bodies signify something immaterial. Thus we see them attain at last, by divine gift, identities that transcend physical limitations.

The recognition of that final transformation is the audience's. It comes also to include the audience as objects, for the last act of the allegorical drama is an invitation to us to join the cast. Shortly before his death, Everyman does for the first time what Humanum Genus did repeatedly: he addresses the audience directly. "Take example, all ye that this do here or se," he begins (l. 867). Good Deeds continues his direct address, and Knowledge then speaks not only to us but as one of us: "Now hath he suffred that we all shall endure" (l. 888). In those statements Everyman and Knowledge underline the implications of the protagonist's name, dissolving our separate identities and extending to us the promise of participation in Everyman's immortalization. At the same time, however, even in referring to Everyman as a model for us all, those statements preserve some distance between his identity and ours. We both are and are not identical with him.

A similar equivocal extrapolation occurs in the closing speech of the Doctour. He asks us to attend to the play's moral,

And forsake Pride, for he deceiveth you in the ende.
And remembre Beauté, Five Wittes, Strength, and Di[s]crecion,
They all at the last do every man forsake,
Save his Good Dedes there dothe he take.
But beware; [for], and they be small,
Before God he hath no helpe at all.
None excuse may be there for every man.
Alas, how shall he do than?

[Ll. 904–11]

The speech recasts the plot in the conditional and the future; and the reference to Pride, a character absent from *Everyman,* aligns *Everyman* with its innumerable variants. Thus the "moral" is not so much a doctrinal generalization as a projection of possibilities and a plea that we realize them. In the last line, "Amen, saye ye, for saint Charité," we are asked to consent not just to the Doctour's prayer but also to the vision that it summarizes: an allegorical pattern realized by individual experience, in the hope of Realization by grace.

Mankind: Allegorical Conflict

If the accidents of transmission and taste have benefited *Everyman,* they have done undeserved injury to *Mankind.* The relatively difficult language and the damaged manuscript have discouraged most readers, and even with those obstacles minimized by the editions of Mark Eccles and David Bevington, the play remains for the most part in obscurity. One reason for its neglect may be that *Mankind* suffers in a particular way from our misunderstandings about allegory. Readers have long recognized that it is unusually lively and entertaining but have rejected those potentially appealing elements as corruptions— commercially motivated encroachments on a properly serious didactic form.[27] The attitude closely resembles the uneasiness of Victorian and Edwardian scholars at Shakespearean and Chaucerian ribaldry, except that it seems to us, now, more defensible. We no longer attribute a narrowly didactic purpose to Chaucer or expect consistent

27. For instance, A. Williams, *Drama of Medieval England,* p. 156; E. K. Chambers, *English Literature at the Close of the Middle Ages* (Oxford: Clarendon Press, 1957), p. 62.

elevation of tone from Shakespeare, but those features are, we feel, essential to Christian allegory. Accordingly, *Mankind* must have been prostituted to suit a successful but irresponsible acting troupe.

Undeniably, didactic seriousness does play a role in morality drama. *Mankind,* for instance, opens with a direct address to the audience concerning our need to "rectifye" our conditions. Perhaps that little sermon epitomizes the play's true purpose; perhaps the comic scenes that follow provide only a cheap form of audience bait or at best an exercise in pious inattention. But the close relationship between sermon and comedy suggests that the latter is not mere distraction. "I besech yow hertily," Mercy concludes his sermon, "have this [in] premeditacion"; Mischeffe then begins, "I beseche yow hertily, leve yowr calc[ul]acion!" (ll. 44–45). The latter part of Mercy's speech uses the familiar religious metaphor of wheat and chaff; Mischeffe's first two speeches play mercilessly with the same images, in a much coarser vein. If such two-tone parallels are typical of the play—and I hope to demonstrate that they are—perhaps the low comedy in *Mankind* works like that in Shakespeare, mirroring the more serious episodes to constitute a balanced structure essential to the meaning of the play. "Comic relief" underestimates the function of such parallelism.

Even "parallelism" falls short of the relationship in *Mankind,* because the serious and comic speeches here interact directly. In particular, they compete for the audience's perceptions. Mercy urges us to think and act in the same way as Mankind will be told to do: to revere Christ's sacrifice and to accept Mercy himself as the "very mene" for our "restitucion" (l. 17). He also sets the terms in which we should see the play—the redemption of "mankinde" and the onslaught of our "gostly enemy"; "Have this [in] premeditacion," he admonishes (l. 44). In short, he invites us to see our lives and the play in the familiar Christian pattern of sin and redemption. But then, in a few deft strokes, Mischeffe establishes a far less abstract perspective. He mocks Mercy's typological explanations:

> But, ser, I prey [you] this question to clarifye:
> Misse-masche, driff-draff,
> Sume was corn and sume was chaffe,
> My dame seyde my name was Raffe;
> On-schett yowr lokke and take an halpenye.
>
> [Ll. 48–52]

If corn is to be saved and chaff burned, says Mischeffe, he himself is a thresher who knows better than Mercy what to do with such things: "*'Corn servit bredibus, chaffe horsibus, straw firybusque'*" (l. 57). The aptness of the parody appeals to us as directly as does Mercy's sermon and perhaps more successfully. The point is not mere self-ingratiation, but also the deflation of Mercy's allegorical vision: Mercy, according to Mischeffe, has a large head but not much common sense (l. 47). Because the abstractions of allegorical drama always share the stage with the particular and the concrete, we can say that Mischeffe both attacks allegory and fulfills it. From the beginning, *Mankind* exploits conspicuously the conflict proper to allegorical drama: the conflict of perspectives.

The conflict is unusually dramatic here because it is played out between opposing sets of characters. When Mischeffe leaves, as he apparently does in a missing section of the manuscript, he is replaced by three masterful allegorical detractors named New-Guise, Nowa-days, and Nought. Their very names dislocate the allegory. They are not ethical principles or categories, as we have come to expect in morality drama; exactly what they denominate is unclear, in fact, and so is the distinction among them. And their actions further blur distinctions and judgments. Although Mercy must be their proper opponent, they quarrel more energetically with each other than with him; moreover, their quarreling is good-natured enough to subvert our censure. "I beschrew ye all! Her[e] is a schrewde sorte," cries Nought, but he adds, "Have theratt, then, with a mery chere!"; then, the stage directions tell us, they dance (ll. 80–81). All here is game and sport (ll. 69, 78). Of course, that in itself is a stronger attack on Mercy's vision than outright evil would be. Like the vice characters' horseplay in *The Castle of Perseverance,* but even more effectively, it undermines intellectual and moral response altogether.

Not content with such broad subversion, the "three Ns" also carry out more pointed attacks. Like Mischeffe, they recast the play in an earthier mode, characterizing themselves as simple fellows who steal mutton and fight with their wives (ll. 126–38) and regarding Mercy as a "goode Adam," a "jentyll Jaffrey" (ll. 83, 160), who ought to relax and enjoy himself more. More audaciously, they remind us that such personifications as Mercy inhabit bodies as capable as ours of the most spectacular indignities (ll. 131–32, 143–45). Their most effective weapon, however, is not detraction but parody. Their colloquialism and scurrility usually employ exegetical terms, as did Mis-cheffe's earlier request for a "clarification" of nonsense; they are often polysyllabic, sometimes Latin or Latinate, and usually uncom-fortably close to Mercy's own speech:

> NOWADAYS. I prey yow hertily, worschipp[f]ull clerke,
> To have this Englisch mad in Laten:
> "I have etun a disch-full of curdys,
> Ande I have schetun yowr mowth full of turdys."
>   . . .
>
> [To NOUGHT.]   Go and do that longith to thin[e] office:
> *Osculare fundamentum!*
>   . . .
>
> NEW-GUISE.   Gode bringe yow, master, and blissyde Mary,
> To the number of the demonicall frairy!
>
> [Ll. 129–53]

In an important recent article, Paula Neuss points out that the parody of Mercy's style is part of *Mankind*'s pervasive concern with language. Language is in turn central to the allegorical conflict. When Mercy complains that the three Ns reject his "communicacion," they rejoin, mockingly but with serious implications, that he is "irke of [their] eloquence" (ll. 123, 150). Again, Mercy warns that their "con-dicion of leving" is dangerous because "for every idyll worde we must yelde a reson" (ll. 170–73); but if he finds their language empty, they find his unnatural and inflated: "Ey, ey, yowr body is full of Englisch Laten! / I am aferde it will brest" (ll. 124–25). Neuss sees in the reference to "Englisch Laten" a parody of the grammarians' argu-ment that classical languages cannot be used for ordinary conversa-tion.[28] Whether she is right or not, her insight suggests why language is a central theme in *Mankind*. Mercy's Latinate eloquence is the traditional vehicle for intangible truth; to his detractors, concepts conveyed in abstract language and associated particularly with Latin have no place in the transactions of every day. In a word, Mercy's language is unrealistic. Real English bodies are full of *curdys* and *turdys*, for which Mercy has no *Laten wordys*.

Mercy gets a chance for rebuttal only when the glib realists leave the stage for a time. He seeks to open to us a kind of reality to which

28. Paula Neuss, "Active and Idle Language: Dramatic Images in *Mankind*," in *Medieval Drama*, ed. Neville Denny (London: Edward Arnold, 1973), p. 51.

they are blind themselves and have attempted to blind us. First, he tells us that the three Ns "know full lityll what is ther ordinance" (l. 164)—that is, their place in the allegorical order. They do not really represent the natural as opposed to the artificial, says Mercy, but are in fact "wers then bestys," because instead of following "naturall institucion," they find pleasure in derision (ll. 165–69). With that statement Mercy places the three Ns in a moral opposition whose valences are unmistakable. The "new g[u]ise nowadays" can be either good or vicious, he concedes, but our unaided reason will tell us the difference (ll. 182–85). Mercy also clarifies his own identity by aligning himself with the exemplar of any embodiment of Mercy: in deriding him, the three Ns deride Christ. When Mercy speaks as one of us but also as God's intermediary (cf. ll. 173 and 178), we hear the echo of the Word made flesh.

Necessarily, Mercy ends his self-defense by offering us a choice: "Take that is to be takyn, and leve that is to be refusyde" (l. 185). And at this point our allegiance may well be divided. Considered carefully, Mercy's words are theologically compelling, but in the theater the chance for such careful consideration can easily slide by unused. Far more obtrusive is Mercy's style, so rarefied and artful that the character inevitably strikes us as affected; even as our consciences consent to him, the laughter aroused by his detractors lingers in our throats. And if the choice between moral substance and attractive style holds no urgency for the audience, its posing is the first cue for Mankind.

Mankind does not appear as a newborn innocent, like Humanum Genus, or as a man engrossed in particularity, like Everyman; he is an adult fully informed by experience and by doctrine. He knows his generic identity well enough to speak interchangeably of "we" and "I." Apparently he has already taken sides in the conflict of perspectives, for he first describes the division between his "flesch, that stinking dungehill," and his soul, "so sotyll in . . . substance" (ll. 204, 202), and then resolves immediately to seek Mercy. In contrast to Everyman, Mankind immediately recognizes the intangible Realities manifested by the other characters and can address Mercy as mercy: "[God] hat[h] institut you above all his werkys" (l. 224). At the same time, he imitates the character Mercy in his own speech, a sign that he is "participatt" of the "very wisdam" of which Mercy has "participacion" (ll. 190, 210). Understanding both himself and

Mercy as embodiments of general laws, clearly anticipating the
largest outlines of his own story, Mankind begins in a state of allegorical grace.

Mercy reinforces Mankind's condition with a long, duly Latinate,
highly metaphoric formulation of Mankind's upcoming trials. He
thereby charts an allegorical path through the mundane complica-
tions that dominate the latter sections of *The Castle of Perseverance*
and *Everyman*. But he ends with an earthy metaphor, something of a
concession to worldly hearers:

> If a man have an hors, and kepe him not to[o] hye,
> He may then reull him at his own dysiere;
> If he be fede over-well he will disobey
> Ande, in happe, cast his master in the mire.
>
> [Ll. 241–44]

That provides an opening for his opponents. In hiding, New-Guise
speaks like a parodic echo:

> Ye sey trew, ser; ye are no faitour:
> I have fed[d]e my wiff so well till sche is my master!
>
> · · ·
>
> Ye fede yowr hors in mesure; ye are a wise man!
> I trow, and ye were the kingys palfrey-man
> A goode horse shulde be gesunne [i.e., scarce].
>
> [Ll. 245–52]

We may recall the earlier encounter in which Mercy's metaphoric
wheat and chaff became hay for these same real horses. Here, as they
concretize the metaphor, the three Ns also attack Mercy with a persuasive practicality: horses actually should be well fed, and Mercy's
"potage" may grow "for-colde" during his long farewell to Mankind. Stalwartly ignoring such exigencies, Mercy begs Mankind to
preserve his allegorical nature—"yowr name is 'Mankinde'; / Be not
unkinde to Gode" (ll. 279–80)—and refers him to Job, who was "of
yowr nature" (l. 289) and in whose story Mankind can see his own
foreshadowed. But such allegorical perceptions now face heavy inter-
ference. Paula Neuss, who traces the correspondence between the
book of Job and *Mankind*, wisely refrains from calling the latter a
version of the former;[29] the parallel is significant largely in appearing

29. Ibid., pp. 49, 53–54.

only sporadically. After suggesting it, Mercy withdraws—not as Reality, for Mankind can always ask mercy (l. 305), but as palpable presence. He thereby leaves Mankind to those who will drown out the allegorical reverberations of his story.

New-Guise, Nowadays, and Nought bring the present forcefully back to Mankind's notice. New-Guise enters with a remarkably prosaic observation about the weather (l. 323). Seeing Mankind engaged in farming, Nowadays and Nought comment sympathetically on the smallness of his field—which probably *is* small, given the limited playing area—and on the difficulty of his labor, prompting New-Guise to make an apparently serious offer to help at harvesttime (ll. 351–67). With such innocuous comments the three Ns seek to entangle Mankind in their own temporal preoccupations.

More boldly, they challenge his conviction that he is an essentially spiritual creature. Their most notable weapon, once again, is parody. Immediately after Mercy's departure, Mankind sits down to "tityll in this papyr / The incomparable astat of my promicion / . . . [and] [t]he glori[o]use remembrance of my nobyll condicion" (ll. 315–18). To fend off "superstici[o]us charmys," he also writes a verse from Job: "*Memento, homo, quod cinis es, et in cinerem reverteris*" (ll. 319–21). Finally, he reminds us that he bears on his breast "the bagge of min[e] armys"—presumably a cross.[30] But New-Guise caps the quotation from Job with a Latin rhyme that inverts the biblical line while echoing it: "*Cum sancto sanctus eris, et cum perverso perverteris*" (l. 324). And then New-Guise, Nowadays, and Nought offer their memorable version of the writing and the "badge" that define the human condition:

> It is wretyn with a coll, it is wretyn with a coll,
>
> · · ·
>
> He that schitith with his hoyll, he that schitith with his hoyll,
>
> · · ·
>
> But he wippe his ars clen, but he [wippe his ars clen],
>
> · · ·
>
> On his breche it shall be sen, on his breche [it shall be sen].
>
> [Ll. 335–42]

The scatological motif continues when Nought makes certain suggestions to Mankind about providing "rain" and "compost" for his

---

30. The "badge" is identified as a cross by W. K. Smart, "Some Notes on 'Mankind,'" *MP* 14 (1916):295, as cited in Eccles, *Macro Plays*, note to l. 322 of *Mankind*.

small field (ll. 372–75). This is the section of the play most easily—but least justifiably—condemned as wanton slapstick. In fact, the song and the jokes are not only brilliant parody but also a serious contention about the play's central issue. Being lewd, they reinforce the three Ns' claim that Mankind is essentially a creature of earth, that the signs that truly define him are those he leaves on his breeches. Being parodic, the dialogue substantiates the three Ns' claim that human life is essentially mutable: if sacred language can be so easily transmuted, perhaps the stability that Mercy has recommended to Mankind is merely a pedant's illusion. And being witty, the three Ns' antics earn the unthinking assent of laughter.

But if we laugh, Mankind does not. Whatever assent we were offering to the reductive vision of humanity is cut short by humanity's own exemplar, who sees through the three Ns' humor to its meaning:

> It was seyde beforn, al the menys shuld be sought
> To perverte my condicions and bringe me to nought.
> Hens, thevys! Ye have made many a lesinge.

> [Ll. 385–87]

Mankind understands his enemies' jests to be statements, and therefore lies. He tries to confute the rascals with his own words, and when that attempt fails, he beats them away with his spade. Such a physical means of defense might play into their hands if he did not know that the confrontation is not really a material one. But he carefully states that his strength represents God's grace (ll. 395–96, 406–8) and that no important victory attends a material weapon: "Yit this instrument, soverens, is not made to defende. / Davide seyth, 'Nec in hasta, nec in gladio, salvat Dominus'" (ll. 396–97). Nought sticks to a humbler view of the fight's ontological status: "No, mary, I beschrew yow, it is in spadibus! / Therfor Cristys curse cum on yowr hedibus, / To sende yow lesse might!" (ll. 398–400). He does not see that Mankind's triumph is his firm grasp of the intangible truths that shape his material existence.

Immediately after his triumph, Mankind goes to fetch seed, leaving the stage to his enemies. That is clever dramaturgy, for the regrouping of the vice characters must be more interesting than any demonstration of Mankind's continued stability. In addition, however, the shift in focus begins the vices' counterattack. Seeing them make sport of their injuries and plan exuberantly for revenge, we cannot imagine that their defeat was absolute. Indeed, we will collaborate in their comeback.

From the beginning, *Mankind* has involved the audience continuously: the conflict of perspectives occurs primarily in our minds. Even when Mankind is on stage to represent us, Mercy includes "all thes[e] worschipp[f]ull men" in his instructions (l. 309), and Mankind explicitly notifies the "worschipfull soverence" of his (and our) "nobyll condicion" (ll. 317–18). The three Ns engage us still more directly. They enter, apparently, by elbowing through the audience, crying, "Make rom, sers, for we have be longe! / We will cum gif yow a Cristemes songe" (ll. 331–32). And that "Cristemes songe"—the startlingly crude "It is wretyn with a coll"—is actually a community sing, for New-Guise and Nowadays lead "all the yemandry that is here" (l. 333) in repeating each line that Nought sings. Encouraged to participate by theatrical convention, and probably unaware at first of the song's lewdness, the audience find themselves echoing vice.

The vices' drawing in of the audience may be yet another form of parody, mimicking the pious addresses and collective prayers so common in the morality plays. In any case, it escalates in Mankind's absence. After some comic byplay concerning their wounds, the three Ns and Mischeffe decide to summon Titivillus. They do so with music—and with monetary contributions from the audience. "Gif us rede reyallys, if ye will se his abhominabull presens," commands Nowadays (l. 465), and New-Guise courteously adds that those who cannot afford royals may offer groats and pence. The strategy whereby we must pay to see the devil is brilliant. Of course, this actor is not really the devil, and the players must be paid; but that is part of the strategy. The solicitation sets a spectator's response to present circumstances at odds with his intimations of wider meaning. That is, on the one hand we are encouraged to forget the characters' roles, to accept the comfortable and necessary illusion that this is just a play; on the other hand we are subtly reminded that the devil is always the biggest draw. The effect is repeated when Titivillus lets us in on his trick to expose the three Ns' dishonesty (ll. 476–91) and again when the whole group gloats over their roll call of potential victims from among the local gentry (ll. 503–17). To be drawn into complicity with such rascals is amusing, and while we laugh from behind the protection of their fictionality, we also suspect that we should not be finding them funny at all. Perhaps Titivillus is spreading his net to catch not only the Master Huntingtons and the William Thurlays but the rest of us as well.

Having subverted the audience's judgment through humor, Titivillus attacks Mankind's through frustration. He threatens Mankind more seriously than did the three Ns, because he "goth invisibull" (l. 302)—that is, he hoodwinks his victims, both offstage and on. By urging us to keep his presence secret from Mankind—an allegorical impossibility, if we stop to think about it—he insinuates that we are exempt from his attack and thus achieves his impossible request after all (ll. 539, 589). Meanwhile, he fools Mankind, as well, by producing effects that seem to have nothing to do with good and evil. The board under the ground and the stolen grain seem to Mankind to be natural setbacks: his field is simply hard and the seed is lost. He gives up farming as a bad job (l. 547). And even after renouncing bodily labor "for now and forever," Mankind kneels to hear evensong, apparently unaware that his decision concerns his relationship to God. Therein the damage is done: Mankind's conception of his earthly life has been divorced from his spiritual convictions. Thus he does not recognize Titivillus as the source of the messages whispered in his ear:

> A schorte preyere thirlith hevyn. Of thy preyere blin.
> Thou art holier then ever was ony of thy kin.
> Arise and avent the[e]! Nature compellys.
>
> [Ll. 558–60]

Mankind accepts the insinuation that nature compels without noticing its unnatural origin. When he declares upon his return from relieving himself that evensong is too long and that he will sleep in spite of Mercy, his mistake is not in obeying physical exigency—he presumably did that when he was in a state of grace—but in seeing it as an alternative to God's and Mercy's commands. To Titivillus himself the ontological status of such "natural" compulsion is clear enough: he has sent Mankind forth, he says, to "schit[t]e lesinges" (l. 568).

Titivillus does not stop with obscuring the truth; he goes on to persuade Mankind that truth is untrue to itself. "Qw[h]ist! Pesse!" he commands us. "The dev[i]ll is dede, I shall goo rounde in his ere" (l. 593). "The devil" turns out to be Mercy, by a casual antiphrasis that exemplifies Titivillus' strategy. He whispers to Mankind that Mercy has stolen a horse and an ox, run away from his master, and been hanged for his crimes (ll. 594–99). In short, he insinuates that Mercy is no stable principle, but a mere "marryde man" (l. 600), fallible and untrustworthy as Mankind himself. If David Bevington is correct that a single actor played both Mercy and Titivillus,[31] the claim that Mercy is mutable carries even greater force for the audience, and the playwright has turned to excellent advantage the practical limitations of his company. In any case, the charge against Mercy recalls the concern of *Everyman*'s Five Wits and Knowledge that priesthood could be subverted by its exemplars. Here, moreover, no one even considers the relationship between the exemplar, corrupt or not, and mercy itself. Mankind has committed himself so fully to the particularistic perspective that he does not dispute or lament the news of Mercy's death, as he would if he understood its full import, but responds as if freed from a strict chaperon. Joyfully he decides to go to the alehouse, make friends with the three champions of things present, and find a "lemman with a smattringe face" (ll. 609–11). Titivillus exits, his work done, and Mischeffe and the three Ns reassert control.

Once again the vices' antics look on one level innocent of allegorical meaning. But the effect is somewhat different here, for we are clearly offered a second perspective. Although Titivillus blinded us to our inclusion in his attacks, he was impudently candid about his assault on our exemplar. We saw the net that he cast over Mankind's eyes, and we heard the admission that Mercy is not in fact dead; we cannot now doubt that Mankind is falling into sin. The difference between our point of view and his provides an opportunity for irony which the playwright uses to the full.

Again and again, the scene that follows suggests a meaning to which the participants are blind. First New-Guise comes running in with a noose around his neck, telling us that he and Mischeffe narrowly escaped hanging for stealing a horse—precisely the offense for which Mercy was allegedly hanged (ll. 622–33). We can easily see, as Mankind does not, that the accusation leveled at Mercy was more appropriate to Mischeffe and his cohort all along: the vices have

31. Bevington, *From Mankind to Marlowe: Growth of Structure in the Popular Drama of Tudor England* (Cambridge: Harvard University Press, 1962), p. 87.

attempted to make Mercy over in their own image. Additional ironic appropriateness appears to those who know that the "neck-verse" that Mischeffe recited to escape hanging is the opening of Psalm 51, "Have mercy upon me, O Lord. . . ."[32] Mercy lives, providing even Mischeffe with the means to save himself—for the present. Then Nowadays enters, carrying what Bevington's stage direction specifies as "stolen church furnishings, including the sacrament" (l. 630 s.d.). "A chirche her[e]-beside shall pay for ale, brede, and win[e]," he announces (l. 633). In attempting to convert sacramental objects into food for immediate consumption, Nowadays unwittingly enacts his own nature—a form of dramatic irony peculiar to allegory. Next to enter is Nought, whose outrage at discovering that he "kannot geet" (l. 637) is unreasonable, considering his name. Finally, Mischeffe arrives with food and wine plundered from the jailer whom he has murdered, a meal we may recognize as a grimly suitable perversion of the one that Nowadays has presumed to pawn.

If we have missed the scene's other ironies, we can scarcely avoid the terrible resonance of the petition that Mankind now makes to the assembled rascals: "I aske mercy of New-G[u]ise, Nowadays, and Nought" (l. 650). He, too, continues to believe in mercy, but he seeks it from its enemies. The irony increases if we realize that he is asking mercy of nought; and in the scene that follows, the nothingness of the three Ns comes more and more conspicuously into play. New-Guise suggests that Mankind's name be recorded in Mischeffe's book, but Mischeffe decides instead to hold a mock court with Nought as recorder. The document that Nought produces begins as formalized illegibility—"*Blottibus in blottis, / Blottorum blottibus istis*" (ll. 680–81)—and becomes, when read by Mischeffe, virtually empty parody:

> *Carici tenta generalis,*
> In a place ther goode ale is,
> *Anno regni regitalis*
> *Edwardi nullateni,*
> On yestern day, in Feverere, the yere passith fully;
> As Nought hath writyn—here is owr Tully—
> *Anno regni regis nulli.*[33]

[Ll. 687–93]

32. I am indebted to Neuss (p. 63) for the identification.
33. I decline Bevington's emendation of "Carici" to "Curia" (l. 687), since it makes better sense of deliberate nonsense.

Like the three Ns' speeches throughout the play, the proclamation mocks formal language by rhyming it with English cakes and ale. But the *nothing*s used here for dates and names inadvertently expose the inanity of the perspective that accepts the evanescent as real. Since the rhetoric of particularity throughout the play has been parody, which is in itself essentially reductive, nought is indeed the vice characters' Tully. A similar point arises from the line of action that accompanies the mock court: New-Guise initiates a "restyling" of Mankind's coat which is actually a drastic trimming, completed by, of course, Nought.

The percentage of such innuendoes which a spectator understands is not very important, because they contribute to a broader effect. The vice characters here reveal themselves in a light that they have previously blocked and that all of them but Titivillus may be unable to see, and they do so in several ways in addition to irony. While Nought hacks away at Mankind's jacket offstage, Mischeffe induces Mankind to swear to commit lechery, gluttony, sloth, theft, and murder on a regular basis. The allegorical topos is embarrassingly explicit. The vices' self-revelation is equally obvious in its emotional effects: the trimming of Mankind's coat must disturb the audience somewhat, if only because cloth is expensive; and when the vices decide to provoke Mankind to commit suicide lest he encounter Mercy, they look for the first time clearly malicious. Ruefully we acknowledge their eponymous taunts: "A mischeff go with!" cries Mischeffe, and New-Guise says as he hands Mankind a noose, "Lo, Mankinde, do as I do: this is thy new g[u]ise" (ll. 730, 805).

As if to drive home the point that vice is vicious, the playwright provides one more parodic exchange with Mercy, and this one is not funny. When Mercy returns, crying, "Mankinde, *ubi es?*" New-Guise and Nowadays respond,

> Hic, hic, hic, hic, hic, hic, hic, hic!
> That is to sey, here, here, here, ny dede in the cryke!
>
> .   .   .
>
> If ye will have Mankinde—how, *Domine, Domine, Dominus!*—
> Ye must speke to the schrive for a *cape corpus,*
> Ellys ye must be fain to retorn with *non est inventus.*
>
> [Ll. 771–81]

Here the ridicule of Mercy's Latin conveys hostility toward both him and Mankind. The three Ns then engage in a final scatological interlude that passes the bounds of humor—especially if Nought actually defecates on his comrades' shoes, as they say he is doing (ll. 782–86).[34] What looked earlier like good-natured impudence now exposes itself, in the absence of opposition, as inanely crude malice.

The vices have therefore lost the conflict of perspectives on several fronts. Their particularistic appeal is bankrupt, having been based on illusion; ontologically, they are exposed as the champions of nullity. Our minds and perhaps Mankind's revert to what we know to be the genuine reality: Mercy rematerializes. Unfortunately, the supremacy of Mercy's Reality implies the annihilation of Mankind, who has voluntarily committed himself to illusion. In allowing himself to become one of the three Ns' "sett" (l. 379), he has negated his own nature so thoroughly that Mercy can now call him "Man on-kinde" (l. 742). Although he does not at first hear Mercy's rebuke, Mankind knows that he is "not worthy," and he anticipates New-Guise's invitation to suicide by calling for the rope himself (l. 800). Perhaps we can see in his impulse to hang himself a tacit admission that he renounced his own existence by accepting Titivillus' slander of Mercy. In any case, Mankind and his enemies know that death is now his proper state. The vices continue to gloat: if they are nothing, they have brought Mankind to nothingness as well. Even in losing the ontological war, they have captured the opposition's temporal agent.

A captured agent can be ransomed, however. In concluding that his abandonment of Reality dooms him to nonbeing, Mankind forgets that Reality is represented here by Mercy, an incurably lenient law enforcer. Mercy does declare that Mankind should be destroyed— "*Lex et natura, Cristus et omnia jura / Damnant ingratum; lugent eum fore natum*" (ll. 754–55)—but in the next line he prays for the ingrate's salvation. Moreover, he realizes Mankind's salvation, even as he desires it. He does so partly by presenting in his own person an image of humanity free from vice. In the play's most moving scene, he grieves for the lost Mankind like a father or a lover, his faith and love lifting him above the common human condition: "Wepinge, sythinge, and sobbinge were my sufficiens; / All naturall nutriment to me as caren is odibull" (ll. 738–39). In addition, Mercy's sincere and elaborate courtesy toward the audience redeems mankind by exempting us

34. See also ll. 795 and 796, which must refer to the same episode, despite Bevington's more decorous speculations. Neuss remarks that Nought's onstage defecation "outdo[es] in 'realism' anything that has yet occurred (so far as I know) on our contemporary stage" (p. 63).

from the generic degradation we have witnessed. "The terys shuld trekyll down by my chekys, were not yowr reverrence," he explains; "Without rude behaver, I kan[not] expresse this inconveniens" (ll. 735, 737). Such respect for the kin of Mankind, expressed at this point by such a speaker, is itself a form of allegorical mercy. And Mercy refers us to the great exemplar both of redeemed humanity and of unmerited courtesy:

> For, all this world was not aprehensible
> To discharge thin[e] originall offence, thraldam, and captivité,
> Till Godys own welbelovyde son was obedient and passible.
>
> [Ll. 742–44]

The Reality rejected by Mankind has already entered the world of time to ransom him from annihilation. Thus Mercy's first words to him now are "Arise, my preciose redempt son" (l. 811).

That the morality plays all concern free will, as several writers point out, inevitably follows from their conjunction of sovereign intelligibles with human agents.[35] Here, even after the truth has triumphed, and even after it has sought out and transformed mankind, Mankind must still assent to it by asking mercy of Mercy. He is delayed in doing so by his lingering particularistic myopia: Mercy stands before him, but he does not believe that he is eligible for mercy. But at Mercy's prompting, he accepts truth as the basis of his individual existence and agrees to be once again "associat" to Mercy (ll. 827, 835).

Thus begins a distinctly allegorical resolution: a harmonization of perspectives. One of its forms is the typological coalescence of Mercy with Christ, underlined in Mercy's words: "Yowr criminose compleynt wo[u]ndith my hert as a lance!" (l. 815); "O pirssid Jhesu . . ." (l. 825). Mercy identifies the present scene also with Christ's meeting with the woman taken in adultery (ll. 848–53). At the same time, he implicitly harmonizes some of the preceding action with doctrine; for instance, he warns against sinning in hope of mercy and against "veyn confidens of mercy" (ll. 845, 853), recalling Mankind's request for

35. See E. N. Thompson, "The English Moral Plays," in *Transactions of the Connecticut Academy* 14 (1910):358 (cited in Eccles, p. 185n); Merle Fifield, *The Rhetoric of Free Will: The Five-Action Structure of the English Morality Play*, Leeds Texts and Monographs, n.s. 5 (Ilkley, Yorkshire: Scolar Press, 1974), pp. 10–11.

mercy from its enemies. Finally, Mercy reconciles the play's conflicting perspectives by assimilating the anomalous agents of particularity into a doctrinal pattern. Mankind has just three enemies, he explains. Titivillus is of course the devil; New-Guise, Nowadays, and Nought together constitute the world; Mankind's own body, with its misleading "nedys," is a "gostly enmy" called the flesh (ll. 880–88). Withheld to this point, the familiar schema orders the play's exuberant materials with compelling clarity.

Mercy now pronounces a Latin benediction over Mankind which turns into a valedictory address to the audience. The doctrinal explicitness of the speech achieves something more than instruction. Discussing the liturgical drama that preceded the morality plays, Mary H. Marshall suggests that a form so "deeply rooted in belief" cannot be "a didactic drama in any overt sense."[36] Her remark can legitimately be extended to all allegory, and in particular to Mercy's concluding speech, which could not be simply didactic without being pathetically redundant. Summarizing doctrine that the play has presented in other ways and that the audience must have heard in countless sermons, the speech is significant not simply referentially but as a shift in mode: the final act in the allegorical drama. "Wyrschep[f]yll sofereyns," Mercy begins, "I have do my propirté: / Mankind is deliveryd by my faverall patrocinye" (ll. 903–4). "Propirté" is a pun, meaning both the role of an actor and the characteristic function of a quality—what is proper to Mercy and to mercy. Mercy thus joins, in his expository language, the perspectives that Mankind's enemies have persistently divided. He does the same thing when he mixes plot summary with didactic generalizations, and again when he deduces a statement about "yow all" from a third-person-singular premise about Mankind (ll. 911–14). Moreover, throughout his speech Mercy incorporates Latin scriptural quotations in English sentences, as if to answer the vice characters' parody of such mergers. The viability of "Englisch Laten" is the play's final affirmation.

Mankind deserves recognition as a masterpiece of allegorical drama. Its author's control over language appears not only in the deft

---

36. Mary H. Marshall, "Aesthetic Values of the Liturgical Drama," in *Medieval English Drama: Essays Critical and Contextual,* ed. Jerome Taylor and Alan H. Nelson (Chicago: University of Chicago Press, 1972), p. 30.

modulations of diction and the resonant linguistic parody but also in unobtrusive verbal patterning. A repetition of *tityll,* for instance, links Mankind's self-reminder about his noble condition ("Her[e] will I sitt, and tityll in this papyr") with Titivillus' antithetical message ("I shall go to his ere and tityll therin. . . . / Thou art holier then ever was ony of thy kin" [ll. 315, 557–59]), as well as with Titivillus himself.[37] That network in turn contributes to the rich central motif of language, equivocal sign of our divided nature. But verbal control is only one aspect of the playwright's masterful use of his medium. The tension among ontological perspectives, basic to the morality drama, here becomes a sustained conflict that provides both dramatic excitement and conceptual unity. Shifts of perspective unify the play in other ways as well; for instance, New-Guise, Nowadays, and Nought are spectacularly human initially but revert later to doctrinal types, while Mercy sounds like personified piety on his first entrance but turns appealingly human at last. All of those changes proceed through the direct involvement of the audience, which is here, even more clearly than in other moralities, not only an extension of the cast but also the arena of the allegorical action. And it is by no violation of its genre that that action depends on profane responses as strongly as on pious ones; such divided reactions necessarily attend the impersonation of truth. Indeed, *Mankind*'s fruitful coalition between the great disparities that seek to attract us is a kind of achievement not to be expected from even the greatest of those plays whose actors are merely creatures.

37. The uses of *tityll* in ll. 315 and 557 may represent two different words; the *OED* lists them separately but provides no etymology for the colloquial sense "to whisper." But the use of *tityll* meaning "write" or "list" was becoming rare by the time of *Mankind* and would probably have been regarded as a variant of its homonym. In any case, two homonyms meaning respectively "to whisper" and "to write" can scarcely be regarded by the untrained user as distinct words.

Neuss points out the relevance of Titivillus to the motif of language. She writes that he "appears to have been invented by medieval preachers especially to deal with those who used 'idle language' in church," and she quotes a verse from the Townley Last Judgment play: "*fragmina verborum Tutivillus colligit horum*" (pp. 55–56). Again, the historically unrelated *tittle* attaches itself naturally to Titivillus' name, and the playwright's use of the words validates the coincidence.

4 Allegory and Experience: *The Pilgrim's Progress*

The Shape of the Way

The scholar who needs to exemplify allegory for someone who has not read any cannot do better than to mention *The Pilgrim's Progress*. Whether or not they have read Bunyan's work, most people carry a kind of template for it in their heads: physical journey on one "level" and spiritual progression on the other. Even among literary critics, *The Pilgrim's Progress* serves as a touchstone for allegory without, apparently, being widely read. Roger Sharrock ought not to have been surprised to find in 1976 that "the number of articles and books on Marvell and Rochester exceeds that on Bunyan," because twenty years earlier Sharrock himself had called *The Pilgrim's Progress* a "crude popular survival, devoid of the imaginative complexity of the old allegoric mood." That is, "Piers the Plowman carries a number of meanings . . . [but] Bunyan sees only one thing at a time"—and that one thing is often explicitly allegorized.[1] Familiar and obvious as a public monument, *The Pilgrim's Progress* seems neither to merit nor to need interpretation.

1. Roger Sharrock, Introduction, *Bunyan: "The Pilgrim's Progress": A Casebook,* ed. Sharrock (London: Macmillan, 1976), p. 22; Sharrock, *John Bunyan* (London: Hutchinson's University Press, 1954), p. 93; see also Herbert Greene, "The Allegory as Employed by Spenser, Bunyan, and Swift," *PMLA* 4 (1889):159–61.

Bunyan does much to support that attitude. His disarmingly modest "Author's Apology" explains that the book virtually wrote itself, "until it came at last to be / For length and breadth the bigness which you see."[2] He dismisses charges that the result is "feigned" or "dark" by assuring us that his meaning is accessible: "Put by the Curtains, look within my Vail; . . . throw away [the dross], but yet preserve the Gold" (p. 164). Anyone can see through the "Fable" to the "Truth," which is "Nothing but sound and honest Gospel-strains" (p. 7). In short, Bunyan offers us the simplest paradigm of allegory: universal meaning transparently covered with particular images.

His text even looks like a manifestation of that paradigm, for the main narrative carries marginal glosses that Bunyan elsewhere calls "windows" onto the truth behind the fable.[3] And as he has led us to expect, the glosses often recast a fictional object or event in abstract doctrinal terms. When the narrator dreams of a man clothed in rags and carrying a burden, marginal notes refer us to biblical verses comparing righteousness to filthy rags and iniquities to a burden (p. 8). His family scolds and mocks the man for his attacks of conscience; a gloss identifies the ill treatment as "Carnal Physick for a Sick Soul" (p. 9). The parchment roll that someone named Evangelist gives to the man is glossed as "Conviction of the necessity of flying" (p. 10). Here at last is a translatable—indeed, a self-translating—allegory.

We need read no farther to substantiate the popular idea of Bunyan's allegory. And since that idea may be more important than the text itself—certainly it has been more influential—we may not need to read Bunyan at all. Let us suppose, however, that a reader stubbornly interested in the text decides to use the idea as a model for a more extensive reading. For such a reader, the way does not remain as clear as Bunyan's initial map.

The first complication concerns the glosses, not all of which translate story into lesson. In fact, the "lamentable cry" that Christian utters at the end of the first paragraph—"what shall I do?"—is glossed simply as "His Out-cry" (p. 8). That is disturbing, because

2. John Bunyan, *The Pilgrim's Progress from This World to That Which Is to Come,* ed. James Blanton Wharey; 2d ed., ed. Roger Sharrock (Oxford: Clarendon Press, 1960), p. 2. Future citations of the text of this edition will be documented by page number in the text.
3. Bunyan, "To the Reader," prefatory to *The Holy War,* in *"Life and Death of Mr. Badman" and "The Holy War,"* ed. John Brown (Cambridge: Cambridge University Press, 1905), p. 187.

the space in which we expected to find abstract interpretation is occupied instead by simple summary. Many of the glosses that follow are on the same order: "*Obstinate* and *Pliable* follow him," "*Pliable* concented to go with *Christian*," "Talk between *Christian* and *Pliable*," and so forth. Others refer to biblical passages that similarly echo the text rather than explain it. Altogether, the glosses continually invite but often frustrate the expectation of a second level of meaning.

Conversely, the text itself incorporates most of what we would expect to find in the margins. The long stretches of doctrinal discourse late in the story are notoriously direct and explicit, provoking complaints from critics that the "allegory"—that is, the fiction/doctrine separation—has been violated.[4] Besides those long sermons, innumerable bits of religious instruction punctuate the text. U. Milo Kaufmann writes of one of those short passages, "If one were defending *The Pilgrim's Progress* as simple allegory, he would have difficulty indeed explaining this hiatus, where one of the characters is tutored in the covert meanings of those characters with whom he is sharing the arena of the action."[5] In fact, interpretation intrudes into the action more regularly than Kaufmann acknowledges, for what he calls the "covert meanings" are not covert at all. The places Christian visits and the characters he meets bear their spiritual meanings quite openly, beginning with their names. The Slough of Despond, for instance, turns out to be unrepairable because it is not simply a slough but "the *Slow of Dispond* still" (p. 16). And in exclaiming, "What shall I do to be saved?" as in quoting the Bible and in admitting that he travels toward heaven (pp. 9–11), Christian characterizes himself not just fictionally, as a man on a journey, but also doctrinally, as a Christian in search of salvation.

The Pilgrim's Progress thus provides additional evidence for the thesis I proposed in Chapter 1, that doctrine and fiction cannot be separated in allegory. But it also contradicts that thesis by distinguish-

4. See, for example, Thomas Macaulay's review of Robert Southey's edition of *The Pilgrim's Progress,* reprinted (from *Edinburgh Review,* 1830) in *Bunyan,* ed. Sharrock, p. 70; John Kelman, *The Road of Life: A Study of John Bunyan's "Pilgrim's Progress"* (New York: Hodder & Stoughton, n.d.), II, 165–66, 221, 252, 271; C. S. Lewis, "The Vision of John Bunyan," in *Selected Literary Essays,* ed. Walter Hooper (Cambridge: Cambridge University Press, 1969), p. 146.

5. U. Milo Kaufmann, *"The Pilgrim's Progress" and Traditions in Puritan Meditation* (New Haven: Yale University Press, 1966), p. 19.

ing text from gloss and fiction from truth. Bunyan in fact equivocates
about the nature of his "Fable." On the one hand he presents it, and
occasionally writes it, as something apart from its doctrine; on the
other hand he insists that it can reveal truth, and, like other allegorists, he bases much of his story explicitly on spiritual principles.

A similar equivocation appears in his justly celebrated characters.
Insofar as they are, as Coleridge put it, "real persons . . . [allegorically]
nicknamed by their neighbours"—that is, particular creatures with
separable abstract designations—the characters and their names echo
the division between story and gloss.[6] That is particularly true of those
whose names are not nouns but adjectives—Pliable, Talkative,
Faithful, and so forth: as old Father Honest candidly explains, such
names must be earned (p. 247). Even the substantive names do not
determine the bearers' behavior: initially Mercie knows too little of
divine mercy to be an agent of mercy (pp. 235–36), and Bunyan
implies, until the end of Part I, that Ignorance may learn (p. 124). We
may suspect such abstractions to be merely prophetic given names; and
in fact, Charles W. Bardsley documents almost all of the favorable ones
in historical records of Bunyan's time.[7] In short, these are concrete
agents, separated from their abstract names by an ontological barrier.
Like the text/gloss division, however, the barrier between character
and abstraction is both defined and confounded. Certain agents, such
as Help, Good Will, and Despair, appear supernaturally and act only in
accord with their abstract names, like genuine universals. The Flatterer
and Vain Confidence can be seen as externalized spiritual conditions
rather than people, and even such humanized agents as Worldly-
Wiseman and Talkative seem to many readers to embody the invisible
forces and ideas of Bunyan's spiritual autobiography.[8] The con-

6. Samuel Taylor Coleridge, "Allegory," in *Miscellaneous Criticism*, p. 31.

7. Charles W. Bardsley, *Curiosities of Puritan Nomenclature* (London: Chatto &
Windus, 1897), pp. 138–201.

8. James F. Forrest, "Bunyan's Ignorance and the Flatterer: A Study in the Literary Art of Damnation," *Studies in Philology* 60 (1963):15–17; Stanley E. Fish, "Prog-
ress in *The Pilgrim's Progress*," in *Self-Consuming Artifacts: The Experience of
Seventeenth-Century Literature* (Berkeley: University of California Press, 1972), p.
254. For the idea that the agents of *The Pilgrim's Progress* personify forces in *Grace
Abounding*, see Sharrock's Introduction to *Bunyan*, ed. Sharrock, pp. 13–14;
Maurice Hussey, "The Humanism of John Bunyan," in *The Pelican Guide to English
Literature*, rev. ed. (Baltimore: Penguin, 1960), III, 225.

crete/abstract dichotomy is confounded from the opposite direction by
the agents who bear biblical names but seem in no way abstract—for
instance, Matthew, Samuel, Joseph, and James, Christiana's sons.

In itself, the mixture of concretely and abstractly named agents
would be neither an innovation nor a source of confusion. Job appears in the *Psychomachia,* and Prudentius' personifications change
temporarily into real soldiers; Everyman finds Fellowship, Cousin,
and Kindred seductively concrete. What differentiates those allegories
from Bunyan's is that in them, abstract causation is continuous. Job
fights as part of Patientia's battle; the male soldiers manifest the
Virtues, although corruptly; only temporary imperception obscures
the allegorical identities of Everyman's friends. Here, when Hopeful
despairs, he is neither Hope nor Despair. In other words, the "real
people" of *The Pilgrim's Progress* act autonomously, alongside the
abstractions. The result is equivocation about the source of causation
and uncertainty about the ontological status of a given agent. When
Simple, Sloth, and Presumption can travel together, Prudence and
Piety may be seen as dowdily named young women, while the
Jameses, Phebes, and Marthas may swell to quasi-allegorical size.

Rather than neatly paralleling explicit concretions with implicit
abstractions, *The Pilgrim's Progress* vacillates between Realistic narrative and the unallegorical fiction whose agents are concrete. That is
true not only of its agents; its setting works the same way. The
continuous focus on a human protagonist within the fable implies a
realistic treatment of time and space, a respect for the empirical continuities; indeed, Sharrock asserts that "the most ordinary chronolog-
ical links of the narrative offer . . . the very image of living on the
human scale."[9] But just as causation can shift from particular to
universal, the setting often "transcends the pragmatic distinction between 'here' and 'there.' "[10] Christian leaves his village to pass under
Mount Sinai; on the way to a town fair, Faithful recounts his meeting
with Adam and Moses (pp. 19–20, 69–71). A man leaves home,
travels for several days, and then meets another traveler who explains
what has happened in the years since they both set out.[11] A young

9. Sharrock, Introduction to *Bunyan,* p. 19.
10. Henri Talon, "Space and the Hero in *The Pilgrim's Progress:* A Study of the
Meaning of the Allegorical Universe," *Etudes anglaises* 14 (1961):126.
11. Pointed out by F. R. Leavis in Afterword to *The Pilgrim's Progress,* ed. Catharine Stimpson (New York: Signet, New American Library, 1964), p. 296.

woman marries a man whom she has catechized as a boy.[12] Such dislocations signal not the transumptive time and place of allegorical action, as in the *Psychomachia,* but a "hopeless tangle" of universal and specific settings.[13]

Narrative point of view constitutes another tangle. Bunyan establishes three speakers: an annotator, omniscient and absolutely authoritative; an empirically limited protagonist; and a dreamer, also empirically limited but with a broader perspective than the protagonist's.[14] But the dreamer immediately begins to report both empirical observations and allegorical identifications ("I looked then, and saw a man named *Evangelist* coming to him" [p. 9]), and he later alternates between naively interrogating the characters and making omniscient pronouncements on them.[15] Similarly, an odd mixture of narrative and dramatic speech assignments makes the narrator's presence equivocal: "*Good Will.* Then said *Good Will,* . . ." Sometimes a protagonist impersonates the narrator by speaking of himself in the third person (p. 253), and, at the other extreme, the godlike annotator can comment on the action as if he were a mere spectator: "O brave *Talkative*" (p. 77); "A good riddance" (p. 85). In short, any of the three voices can speak from the point of view of another, and they all fluctuate between superhuman omniscience and empirical observation.

At this point the reader has several choices. One is to reaffirm the received idea of *The Pilgrim's Progress*—it is a fiction that veils a congruent set of spiritual truths—but to add that Bunyan executed the idea imperfectly. Bunyan's humble social status and that of his admirers, his vaunted freedom from intellectual sophistication, his scorn for worldly learning, and his homely style are all traditionally associated with artlessness; thus the text's inconsistencies may be simply the slips of an unpolished genius. Alternatively, we can decide that Bunyan cared so much about his message that he neglected con-

12. Pointed out in Talon, *John Bunyan,* p. 165.
13. Kelman, II, 166.
14. For the vital distinction between annotator and dreamer, I am indebted to Elizabeth Bruss, "John Bunyan: The Patriarch and the Way," in *Autobiographical Acts: The Changing Situation of a Literary Genre* (Baltimore: Johns Hopkins University Press, 1976), pp. 55–56.
15. Pointed out in Charles W. Baird, *John Bunyan: A Study in Narrative Technique* (Port Washington, N.Y.: Kennikat Press, National University Publications, 1977), pp. 35–36.

sistency in his medium. If the first explanation is unduly condescending, the second may come close to Bunyan's own intentions. Neither, however, comes close to explaining the power of the work for many readers who care little about the message.

Taking a view both more charitable and more nearly comprehensive, we might decide that the received idea about *The Pilgrim's Progress* is only half true, because the work is half naive allegory and half something else—such as "realism." The "Bunyan of the conventicle" conflicts with the "Bunyan of Parnassus," as Coleridge puts it.[16] The Romantic or modern reader may see the latter as Bunyan's more interesting self, even his more genuine one, but in any case the two are incompatible. Some writers ascribe the split to Bunyan's uneasy relationship with his culture. U. Milo Kaufmann, for instance, notes "a conspicuous tension in Bunyan's practice between the didactic and literalist methods widespread in Puritanism and the imaginative methods native to the grand tradition in literature."[17] Jacques Blondel sees not simply tension but conflict:

> The goal that Bunyan has set for himself is located at the point of intersection of two lines which he has forced to meet. One, that of free creation, excludes utilitarianism and didactic art. The other, that of moral reflection, represents here and now the expectation of the believer, tracing, or rather sketching, the image of the converted man. A conflict arises immediately between the two directions thus indicated.[18]

For Elizabeth Adeney, the increasingly severe judgments endorsed by Christian contradict the larger, more humane responses inferable from the work as a whole.[19] All three writers find *The Pilgrim's Progress* to be interesting even though—or perhaps because—it is radically disunified.

Recent literary theorists suggest that all texts are disunified, that semiotic unity is a chimera. Whether or not that is true, the claims

---

16. Coleridge, "Allegory," in *Miscellaneous Criticism,* p. 31.

17. Kaufmann, p. 5. Kaufmann later locates the tension within certain traditions of Puritanism itself.

18. Jacques Blondel, "Allégorie et réalisme dans *The Pilgrim's Progress* de John Bunyan," *Archives des lettres modernes* 28 (1959):40.

19. Elizabeth Adeney, "Bunyan: A Unified Vision?" *Critical Review* 17 (1974):97–109.

that Bunyan's aesthetic is divided seem to me untenable. They rest on the shortsighted assumption that certain overt or inferable generalizations constitute the nonnegotiable meanings of allegory and that incompatible meanings must therefore be inadvertent or subversive. Moreover, they do not do justice to Bunyan's particular kind of inconsistencies, which are, as we have seen, not so much conflicts as equivocations.

One option remains for Bunyan's reader: to assume that the equivocations all serve some kind of semiotic unity. That may be a naive strategy, but it may also be a productive one. The unity would have to be paradoxical, given the pervasive shifts in mode, narrative point of view, setting, and so forth. But some of Bunyan's own statements about his text validate a search for paradoxical unity. Although he asserts at times the univocal supremacy of Truth over Fable, at other times he uses metaphors that confound the relationship. For instance, "None throws away the Apple for the Core" (p. 164) suggests that the external element—presumably the fiction—is nourishing and valuable.[20] And when Bunyan multiplies pairs of such metaphors, their alignment with Fable and Truth, and their relationships with each other, begin to blur:

> Would'st thou be in a Dream, and yet not sleep?
> Or would'st thou in a moment Laugh and Weep?
> Wouldest thou loose thy self, and catch no harm?
> And find thy self again without a charm?
> Would'st read thy self, and read thou know'st not what
> And yet know whether thou art blest or not,
> By reading the same lines? O then come hither,
> And lay my Book, thy Head and Heart together.

[P. 7]

The cumulative effect is of distinctions intermittently grasped and paradoxes not permanently resolved.

The end of the Apology prepares us, in fact, to find at the center of *The Pilgrim's Progress* not a nugget of truth but an experience of loss and recovery, of clarity followed by confusion and then by reclarifica-

---

20. The reversal of the usual kernel/husk distinction here is pointed out in John R. Knott, Jr., "Bunyan's Gospel Day: A Reading of *The Pilgrim's Progress*," *English Literary Renaissance* 3 (1973):444.

tion. That is indeed the experience that the text's equivocations provide when they are approached sympathetically. If "His Out-cry" seems out of place in the didacticizing margin, we soon realize that the commentator is reiterating here, not glossing, and we can then see that the dislocation fulfills a positive function: Christian's cry of anguish, cited in the space reserved for didactic translation, assumes the weight of an abstract signified. Similarly, the incursions of abstract terms into the story unify the fable with its meaning, producing a shift in perspective but also a resolution. Even the inconsistencies of place and time, clumsy as they are, convey the energy of a perceptual realignment that takes us from focused sight to universal vision and back again. And the equivocation between concrete and ideal agency can be seen as enlarging the meaning of personality. Mr. Brisk's abortive courtship of Mercie, which to Sir Charles Firth is not allegory but "simply an incident in the life of a fair Puritan described with absolute fidelity to nature,"[21] suddenly regains the allegorical perspective because of a gloss: "*Mercie* in the practice of *Mercie* rejected; While *Mercie* in the Name of *Mercie* is liked" (p. 227). Now the fair Puritan appears as an idea, one that receives lip service but to which nobody will make a serious commitment. The passage's effect depends on the shift in perspective. Normally a rather sentimentalized woman, Bunyan's Mercie here radiates, by virtue of her steadfastness in sewing for the poor, the full force of her allegorical name.

I submit that such moments, in which the perspective of empirical fiction interchanges with the allegorical perspective from which it has previously been divorced, account for the popularity of *The Pilgrim's Progress* more fully than does either its celebrated realism or its doctrinal richness. Christian's heroics with Apollyon would seem rather thin if tremendous meanings did not lurk behind every gesture, only to break through occasionally into the story itself. Conversely, Bunyan's spiritual lessons, too pervasive to be skipped over entirely, might have antagonized the young Sabbath-bound reader if they did not take on flesh and affront Christian directly. The narrative resembles a Mobius strip, a progression of images leading us improbably onto the plane of ideas that was originally its other side. Indeed, it is more complex than a single Mobius strip, since the interconversion of

21. Sir Charles Firth, Introduction to *Pilgrim's Progress*, 1848; rpt. in *Bunyan*, ed. Sharrock, p. 102.

idea and image also concatenates images that ought not to coexist in a single protagonist's experience. Distinct times and places are accessible to each other and to timelessness.

The Pilgrim's Progress is not radically disunified but radically complex, both separating and merging orders of being whose distinctions form our primary conceptual boundaries. As Blondel notes, the work is "realistic" in the scholastic sense, locating reality in universals and ideas;[22] it is also undeniably realistic in our modern sense—faithful to the empirical world of the timebound individual. All allegories with personae evoke both of those realities, but nearly all of them rest in one or the other. Thus the subjective basis of the *Romance of the Rose* discredits to varying degrees the ostensibly ideal agents, and the apparently autonomous creatures of *Everyman* are gradually absorbed into ideal categories. No such one-sided resolution occurs in *The Pilgrim's Progress*. I will argue later that eternity itself is for Bunyan an alloy of ideal and empirical realities. And throughout *The Pilgrim's Progress,* if we see through empirical experience to "a single structure of doctrine," what we see "is fully significant only because it is an experience."[23] In Bunyan's work, the impersonal, universal vision of allegory opposes, balances, and yet somehow joins "the new Protestant emphasis upon the application of Scripture to the self."[24]

The link between disjoined perspectives, the agent of paradoxical unity in *The Pilgrim's Progress,* is of course language. The importance of the Word to Bunyan and to Puritanism has been pointed out.[25] It may be true, as Kaufmann argues, that Puritans regarded the Word primarily as rational or "literal-didactic," abstracting experience into doctrine; but Kaufmann also points out the complementary awareness of words as the basis for sensual imagery and concrete narrative.[26] It does not seem to me that Bunyan emphasizes either function of language at the expense of the other, or that he is, as

22. Blondel, p. 9.

23. Kaufmann, p. 114; Blondel, p. 33.

24. Barbara Kiefer Lewalski, "Typological Symbolism and the 'Progress of the Soul' in Seventeenth-Century Literature," in *Literary Uses of Typology from the Late Middle Ages to the Present,* ed. Earl Miner (Princeton: Princeton University Press, 1977), p. 81.

25. James Sutherland, *English Literature of the Late Seventeenth Century* (Oxford: Clarendon Press, 1969), pp. 314–16; Kaufmann, p. 34.

26. Kaufmann, pp. 25–41.

Kaufmann suggests, simply divided between them. Instead, he moves from one to the other on the bridge of allegorical metaphor.

We initially see Christian with a burden on his back. The gloss refers us to a biblical simile, also involving a burden: "For mine iniquities are gone over mine head: as an heavy burden they are too heavy for me" (Ps. 38:4). Earlier I said that the gloss suggests a second "level," which most readers call a metaphoric version of the burden; we could also say, however, that the biblical verse reveals the burden's literal meaning.[27] In fact, the Psalmist and Bunyan are using the same metaphor, synthesizing the same sensual image and the same explicit reference to sin (see p. 38). What shifts with the gloss is our perspective on that metaphor. With the Psalmist we assume an abstracted perspective somewhat like an allegorist's, from which the burden looks like a mental image of the intangible reality, sin. We (and Christian) see it that way in *The Pilgrim's Progress*, too, but we also see it as if from inside—as an object with the same fundamentally empirical status that Christian has for himself. Bunyan's Slough of Despond appears, similarly, as *a* slough before being recognized as *the* slough of despond. The paradigm for the double perspective on metaphor is Christian and Hopeful's experience with the Flatterer. Only after spending some time entangled in a net do they recognize that the anonymous stranger who led them there possessed an allegorical identity and has landed them in a universal principle: "Did not the Shepherds bid us beware of the flatterers? As is the saying of the Wise man, so we have found it this day: *A man that flattereth his Neighbour, spreadeth a Net for his feet*" (p. 133). The movement toward the allegorical perspective can also be reversed, however, as when "the promises" materialize as a key, to match the empirical immediacy of Despair's prison (p. 118).

All of Bunyan's places and agents are metaphors compounded of image and concept, and all of them pivot between realities. We have seen that the characters' names are simultaneously abstract terms and personal names. Places and objects can be more explicitly duplex,

---

27. That reversal occurs, without confusion, in Bruss's *Autobiographical Acts*. She finds in *Grace Abounding*, as compared to *The Pilgrim's Progress*, a "literal quality" (pp. 38–39), but she also says, "What were figurative values in *Grace Abounding* are in a way quite literal in *Pilgrim's Progress*" (p. 51). The interchange of "literal" and "metaphoric" is the same phenomenon as the reversals in the literal/allegorical opposition which I mentioned in Chapter 1.

combining one abstract and one concrete term: the Hill Difficulty, Vanity Fair, Giant Despair. Other names are compounded with *of*— City of Destruction, Slough of Despond, Valley of Humiliation, rags of our iniquities, River of the Water of Life—in a pattern that is one of Bunyan's hallmarks. Based no doubt on biblical phrasing, those *of* compounds defy definition. The *Oxford English Dictionary*'s entry for *of* suggests a dizzying range of relationships between the concrete term and the abstract one, including "an *x* made of *y*" (a slough composed of despond); "the *x, y*" (the slough Despond; the city Destruction); "the *x* which is to undergo an action, *y*" (the city to be destroyed); "*x* in the form of *y*" or "*y* in the form of *x*" (rags in the form of iniquities, or vice versa); "an *x* characterized by *y*" (the humiliating valley); and "*x*, the object or result of *y*" (the valley created by humiliation). Context can realize and transform those possible relationships successively or concurrently.

The most essentially metaphoric of Bunyan's terms are what Sharrock calls the "archetypal figures of the pilgrim, the burden, the monsters, the road with its sloughs and by-paths, the guides true and false, the gentle hospitality at the places of resort, and the final bourne of the heavenly city across the river."[28] And of those archetypal images, the greatest is of course the channel through which Bunyan's allegory originated. According to the Apology, Bunyan began *The Pilgrim's Progress* inadvertently, while writing another kind of book:

> And thus it was: I writing of the Way
> And Race of Saints in this our Gospel-Day,
> Fell suddenly into an Allegory
> About their Journey, and the way to Glory. . . .
>
> [P. 1]

That passage at once posits and confounds a distinction between the other book and the allegory: the other book explained the saints' way and race; the new one concerns their journey and way.[29] The journey metaphor links discursive works such as *The Heavenly Footman* with fictional ones such as *The Pilgrim's Progress* and remains within the

28. Sharrock, *John Bunyan*, p. 155.
29. The identification of the other book is likely to remain conjectural. Sharrock argues at length, and I think persuasively, that the most likely candidate is *The Heavenly Footman* (Introduction to *Pilgrim's Progress*, pp. xxi–xxxv).

latter work as a major bridge between fiction and expository discourse. It can be a "dead" metaphor or a "live" one, but there is no nonmetaphoric term for it. Like Bunyan's other metaphors but more clearly, it constitutes both a double and a single reality.

An understanding of that paradox can remove a major obstacle to reading *The Pilgrim's Progress*. Coleridge, evidently the first to locate the "sort of pun" on *way* which I have been discussing, found it disturbing. Concerning the claim of Formal and Hypocrisy to be on the same road as Christian without having gone through the wicket gate, Coleridge protests, "The allegory is clearly defective. . . . But it would be very difficult to mend it." The difficulty is that Christian ought to deny that Formal and Hypocrisy are on the true spiritual "way," but he cannot do so "without contradicting the allegoric image"—the representation of the spiritual way as the physical road that Formal and Hypocrisy are in fact traveling.[30] Coleridge here adumbrates a contemporary dilemma about Christian's "progress." Stanley Fish points out that a full acceptance of the "outward" meaning of the way would constitute spiritual and aesthetic blindness. On the other hand, if the "visible and rational" meaning of the way is really "self-consuming," as Fish claims—if Formal and Hypocrisy are not in fact on the way—then Christian does not really travel, either, and the narrative is simply a series of epiphanies.[31]

That conclusion is aesthetically discomforting, since it requires us to discount Bunyan's indispensable metaphor and thus to understand the work in entirely negative terms. Fish's conclusion is also theologically questionable: David Alpaugh reminds us that Bunyan denounces the neglect of outward, experiential "profession" as vigorously as he condemns the neglect of inward grace.[32] The terms of the dilemma must, then, be reconciled. And if we see the way as radically metaphoric, the pun ceases to be a defect and becomes an essential structural principle. After progressing for a while on the ordinary, "outward" road, and taking an apparently sensible detour around the Hill Difficulty, Formal and Hypocrisy suddenly find

30. Coleridge, *Literary Remains,* ed. Henry Nelson Coleridge, 4 vols. (London: William Pickering, 1836–39), III, 405.
31. Fish, pp. 232–47.
32. David J. Alpaugh, "Emblem and Interpretation in *The Pilgrim's Progress,*" *ELH* 33 (1966):299–314. Robert Shenk makes a similar point in "John Bunyan: Puritan or Pilgrim?" *Cithara* 14 (December 1974):77–94.

themselves on weirdly allegorical by-paths called Danger and Destruction, where they cannot move (pp. 41–42). They both have and have not been on the way. Periodically the way shifts from its predominantly tangible manifestation to its character as a spiritual condition, and while Christian can negotiate the transition, Formal and Hypocrisy cannot.

Several times in his journey, Christian reaches a much-desired place from which he can see the moral landscape in which he has been traveling. The most dramatic of his revelations, repeated for the Dreamer at the end of Part I, is given through a "door in the side of an Hill" (pp. 121–22, 163). In those sudden shifts from empirical perception to miraculously complete comprehension the structure of *The Pilgrim's Progress* is also revealed. The landscape's broadest configurations, determined by eternal principles, never change; even Christian's experiences conform to an abstracted Way, a kind of vector; but he must realize the pattern by traveling his own contingent, gradually developing way. He progresses, as do we, through the paradoxical relationships between the two realities which are defined in his consciousness—over real mountains with conceptual doors in them.

Metaphoric Progress

The original readers of *The Pilgrim's Progress* had a certain advantage in beginning with a much more extensive title than the one used today: "The Pilgrim's Progress from This World, to That which is to come: Delivered under the Similitude of a DREAM Wherein is Discovered, The manner of his setting out, His Dangerous Journey; And safe Arrival at the Desired Countrey." The implications of that title are not univocal. By far the most prominent word on the original title page is DREAM, but syntax takes away what typography has granted: the dream is a "similitude" for the real subject, namely, "the manner of his setting out" and so forth. We are led both to discount the story as a dream and to discount the dream as a mere vehicle for the story. That quandry is made visual in the engraving used as a frontispiece in many copies of the third and subsequent editions. At the center and occupying almost half the space is a sleeping man, apparently Bunyan. The figures of his dream—a burdened pilgrim, an earthly city, a heavenly city, a road, and a lion in a cave—comprise not a thought bubble coming from his head but the environment in which he sleeps. Again dreaming is emphasized, but again the natural corollary, that the narrative exists only hypothetically or mentally, is contradicted. I suspect that the contradiction has been experienced less as a flaw than as a source of fascination. The engraver, the printer, and Bunyan (or whoever wrote his title) are preparing us for the composite and paradoxical perspectives within the work. If the pilgrim progresses "from this world to that which is to come," his journey must be in neither— that is, in a metaphoric dream born of the incomplete conjunction of both.

The crisis that initiates the pilgrimage is, in fact, Christian's discovery of himself in two worlds at once. The intangible realities of Scripture—man's pitiful righteousness, his burdensome sin, the imminent destruction of his earthly home—have become as real to Christian as are his wife and children. Henceforth he will inhabit a landscape containing both ordinary houses and a slough of despond. He has not only read but also "felt . . . the Powers, and Terrours of what is yet unseen" (p. 12). Thus the power of the opening of *The Pilgrim's Progress,* like that of *Everyman,* depends not on a parallel between allegorical and "realistic" orders of being but on an interchange between them. And yet the two orders remain more clearly separate than they did in *Everyman.* Christian's friends and neighbors are well aware that the realities he sees are indeed "yet unseen," and they conclude, naturally enough, that he is mad.

At first Christian's own vision of the other world is fitful and terrifying, for he sees it as an utterly separate realm that can touch his earthly world only to destroy it. He is released from that paralysis when he envisions his book as an agent, Evangelist, and accepts its metaphors as personal directives from the "world which is to come" to be acted on now:

> Then said *Evangelist,* pointing with his finger over a very wide Field, Do you see yonder *Wicket-gate? [*Mat. 7.] The Man said, No. Then said the other, Do you see yonder *shining light? [*Psal. 119.105. 2 Pe. 1.19.] He said, I think I do. Then said *Evangelist,* Keep that light in your eye. . . .[33]
>
>   [P. 10]

33. Here and in subsequent passages, asterisked materials enclosed in brackets are Bunyan's marginal glosses.

Christian then blocks out the imperatives of ordinary reality by an act of will, closing his ears to the voices of his relations, and runs almost blindly "towards the middle of the Plain" (p. 10). A great deal of ground remains between him and the light, or even between him and the wicket gate—both tangible and spiritual ground.

Early in the journey, because he clings to habits of vision appropriate only to "this world," Christian twice loses himself in experience. First, he and Pliable encounter an archetypal metaphor from the inside, without understanding it: "they drew near to a very *Miry Slow* that was in the midst of the Plain, and they being heedless, did both fall suddenly into the bogg. . . . And *Christian*, because of the burden that was on his back, began to sink in the Mire" (p. 14). Christian cannot name or locate the bog. Pliable thus instinctively retreats from it, but Christian stays because he cannot return to his former home. His eventual rescue by Help (p. 15) has struck some readers as an unconvincing piece of allegorical legerdemain: in simply hypostatizing the help that Christian obviously needs, Bunyan seems to cheat. Thus Robert Bridges complains that nothing in experience corresponds to Help or to "*the steps [*The Promises]" that Help says Christian should have sought.[34] But Bunyan's point is precisely that Christian here escapes from a disabling experience into an allegorical understanding of it in terms of Christian doctrine. As in the encounter with Evangelist, an idea becomes active. In conversation with the dreamer, who is as puzzled as many readers, Help acknowledges with almost whimsical irony the stubborn duality of this metaphoric world:

> [This place] is the descent whither the *scum and filth [*What makes the Slow of Dispond] that attends conviction for sin doth continually run, and therefore is it called the *Slow of Dispond*. . . . *Here* hath been swallowed up, at least, Twenty thousand Cart Loads; yea Millions of wholesom Instructions, that have at all seasons been brought from all places of the Kings Dominions; . . . but it is the *Slow of Dispond* still; and so will be, when they have done what they can.   [Pp. 15–16]

Particular actions cannot eliminate an allegorical metaphor; only a complete comprehension of it, the gift of the mysterious Help, can release the individual from its control.

---

34. Robert Bridges, "Bunyan's *Pilgrim's Progress*," *Speaker*, April 1905; rpt. in *Bunyan*, ed. Sharrock, pp. 109–10.

Christian leaves the Slough of Despond only to be overwhelmed in an experience of a very different kind. His conversation with Mr. Worldly-Wiseman might have been written by a novelist fond of type names. In fact, Sharrock sees the character as to some degree a portrait of Bunyan's contemporary Edward Fowler.[35] The realism of Mr. Worldly-Wiseman's manner is part of his message. Christian feels no need to seek deeper understanding of this plain-spoken fellow's advice, which is that he should ask an honest man for help with his troublesome burden, send for his wife and children, and settle into a morally upright life without "meddling with things too high for [him]" (p. 18). Unlike Evangelist's, Mr. Worldly-Wiseman's geographical directions are quite clear: one must simply go past "yonder high hill" to the first house, which is Legality's. But as Christian passes the hill, it suddenly turns unrealistic on him. "[I]t seemed so high, and also that side of it that was next the way side, did hang so much over, that Christian was *afraid to venture further, lest the *Hill* should fall on his head [*Christian afraid that Mount *Sinai* would fall on his head]" (p. 20)—as if, as Kaufmann says, the hill were a several-story building.[36] We need not blame the Bedfordshireman's ignorance of mountains for this nightmarish metamorphosis: Christian is being shown that what looked like a natural landmark is also an allegorical one. More specifically, rational morality, though accessible and comprehensible, has become threateningly absolute as the inevitably sinful Christian approaches it. When the hill flashes fire, Christian's sudden reconsideration of his experience brings back Evangelist, who gradually elucidates the allegorical pattern that the pilgrim has enacted. At last the hill appears clearly as the allegorical metaphor it is: "[A]nd with that there came words and fire out of the Mountain under which poor Christian stood, that made the hair of his flesh stand. The words were thus pronounced, *As many as are of the works of the Law, are under the curse*" (p. 24).

Having learned by experience not to proceed by experience, Christian can now literally follow Evangelist's directions. Without, significantly, any further adventures, he arrives "in process of time" at the wicket gate that he could barely see earlier (p. 25). For the first time he sees what he has been told to see. Good Will, who opens the gate

35. Bunyan, *Pilgrim's Progress*, ed. Sharrock, p. 17n.
36. Kaufmann, p. 16.

for him, is identified in Part II with Christ, but since he here talks about Christ in the third person (p. 27), we should not translate his name. Good Will is another pure abstraction, like Help, appearing magically to the eyes of faith. Indeed, his appearance signals Christian's acceptance of Evangelist's promise: "*yet will the man at the Gate receive thee, for he has *good will* for men [*Evangelist* comforts him]" (p. 24).

Good Will leads Christian in a metaphoric re-vision of his pilgrimage so far (pp. 25–28) and then directs him to the house of the Interpreter, the first of two places in which Christian receives the training in metaphoric vision which he clearly needs. The Interpreter is a virtuoso in the modulations of metaphoric perspective. He leads his visitor by the hand through a series of rooms, a realistic frame that exists, as Kaufmann suggests, in order to be violated.[37] Coleridge's objection to the Patience-and-Passion tableau—that Passion somehow bankrupts himself while Christian stands in the doorway—singles out only one of the Interpreter's many anomalies of time, space, and mode of being.[38] The first several rooms contain a parlor that is (not is like) the heart of a sinful man, a blazing fire that is grace, and figures tending the fire who are the Devil and Christ. Those displays, holographs projected from the invisible world, teach not merely doctrine but also perception. Even as Christian sees them empirically they transgress empirical limits, gradually redefining sight as the imaginative apprehension of allegorical meaning. And that modulation of vision is not the end of the Interpreter's performance. His next several displays imitate Christian's own future, with a Palace Beautiful, a man admitted to Glory, and a man imprisoned by Despair: the magic film reveals personal experience, which thus becomes a form of allegorical imagery. The next emblem, the final one, is at once the most like actual experience and the most unnerving. Like the man in the cage of Despair, the man who has dreamed of death and judgment is solid enough so that Christian can talk to him—a real person caught in an emblematic frame. But he is an analogue both of Christian, who could justly have had the same prophetic dream, and of the narrator in whose dream Christian appears. The dreaming persona watches his alter ego watching a picture that could be either of them: the regres-

37. Ibid., pp. 84–85.
38. Coleridge, *Literary Remains*, III, 402.

sion violates all boundaries between one context and another, stripping the perceiving self of any solid framework except eternal judgment.

After leaving the Interpreter, Christian knows how to move in that framework. The place with "a *Cross,* and a little below in the bottom, a Sepulcher" (p. 38) is neither a tourist's Golgotha nor a mere symbol, but an idea picture like the Interpreter's displays. Christian sees it in its complete metaphoric doubleness. He immediately gives the scene a doctrinal gloss (*"He hath given me rest, by his sorrow; and life, by his death"*), then retreats into a naive surprise "that the sight of the Cross should thus ease him of his burden," and then ends the episode by restoring the images' theological interpretation: "Blest Cross! blest Sepulcher! blest rather be / The Man that there was put to shame for me" (p. 38). His burden falls off because his abstract knowledge of redemption becomes a fact of his experience even as he continues to understand it in abstract terms.

The second stage of Christian's education in metaphoric vision is less reformation than confirmation. Whereas the Interpreter displayed unsettling images, the inhabitants of the Palace Beautiful give Christian food, rest, and conversation, but in an allegorizing context. Dwelling on the bridge between this world and the one to come, they incorporate metaphoric vision into daily human life. Through the discipline of conversation, for instance, they sustain a dual awareness of Christ as the biblical figure and as "Lord of the Hill" in their own particular "Countrey" (pp. 52–53). In simplest terms the Palace is a model Christian community, and its compassionate personifications are not Discretion, Prudence, Piety, and Charity in the abstract, but "the best type of Puritan woman."[39] But there is also a benevolent irony, a grace, in these human creatures' bearing such absolute names, for they sometimes rise to the allegorical status that such apparitions as Help and Good Will possess de facto. And before Christian leaves, the residents lead him too up a kind of allegorical ladder. They begin by displaying books that record metaphoric history, then show him the armor of faith and such "engines" as Moses' rod and David's slingshot (pp. 53–54). As the sights increasingly violate ordinary realism, they stretch Christian's vision to the universal realities of Christian tradition. When he is at last given Pauline

39. Sharrock, *John Bunyan,* p. 81.

allegorical armor for his human body, he becomes, for the first time, not so much *a* Christian as *the* Christian, the full biblical archetype.

From the top of the Palace Beautiful, Christian receives the first of his panoramic vistas. He can see details of the far-off Delectable Mountains as if they were very close, because the means of sight here is the allegorical imagination. But the residents of the Palace warn Christian that he must now descend from this vantage point, and "as it was *difficult* coming up, so . . . it is *dangerous* going down" (p. 55). The opening sequence of *The Pilgrim's Progress* has traced Christian's growth in perceptiveness. From here to the second great vantage point, the Delectable Mountains, his task is less to learn than to persevere through a series of metaphoric adventures. The series is episodic, allowing *The Pilgrim's Progress* to assimilate additions easily in revision, but the episodes fall into certain types according to the structures of their metaphors. Always the resolutions depend on shifts in perspective—not always away from the "visible and rational," as Fish implies, but in whatever direction will provide complete metaphoric comprehension.[40]

Perhaps the most exciting episodes are archetypal metaphors that, as Harold Golder long ago pointed out, recall the monsters and magic landscapes of romance.[41] Christian's descent into the Valley of Humiliation is, like his entrance into the Slough of Despond, an immersion in metaphoric experience. This time, though, he has been told where he is going and knows the name of the "foul *Fiend*" that will appear. He can even outargue Apollyon because he knows more theology:

> I was born indeed in your Dominions, but your service was hard, and your wages such as a man could not live on, **for the wages of Sin is Death* [*Rom. 6.23]. . . . All this is true, and much more, which thou hast left out; but the Prince whom I serve and honour, is merciful, and ready to forgive. . . . [Pp. 57, 58]

But such doctrinal sophistication is not enough here; Apollyon is simply stronger than Christian. When the fiend loses the argument he breaks out "into a grievous rage" like a frustrated child and resorts to

---

40. Fish, p. 237.
41. Harold Golder, "Bunyan's Valley of the Shadow," *MP* 27 (1929–30):66.

brute opposition: "Then *Apollyon* strodled quite over the whole
breadth of the way" (p. 59). Apollyon's nature appears in his hideous
polymorphousness (p. 56) and in his name, a product not of the
conceptual clarifications of allegory but of the visionary demonology
of folklore and Revelation. Although he lives in the Valley of Humiliation, his sheer force as a spiritual image exceeds any abstract correlative. The same can be said of the imagery in the Valley of the
Shadow of Death, a place whose name is itself neither abstraction nor
image but a specter of both. Here imagination simply overpowers
reason: the pilgrim hears sounds *as if* of people under misery, sees
hobgoblins, and walks in "Clouds of Confusion" (p. 62). "[I]n a
word, it is every whit dreadful, being utterly without Order" (p. 62).

Such irrational forces can be defeated only by a stronger magic that
restores them to a larger order. In "Progress in *The Pilgrim's Progress*," Fish notes that an apparently subordinate clause, "As God
would have it," can be seen as actually controlling the information
that follows ("Christian nimbly reached out his hand for his Sword,
and . . . gave [Apollyon] a deadly thrust" [pp. 59–60]).[42] That syntactic realignment is followed by other shifts in perspective. Biblical
verses suddenly restore Christian's particular experience to its context
in providential history (pp. 60, 64), and when a disembodied hand
offers leaves from the Tree of Life to heal Christian's wounds (p. 60),
the eternal manifests itself magically, a counterforce to Apollyon's
onslaught. The saving shift of perspective eventually materializes in
Faithful, who spoke one of the biblical verses and who will henceforth corroborate for Christian the reality of the things of faith. The
dangers themselves were real—the narrator insists that he saw and
heard them himself—but they recede finally into a pattern already
completed by God.

At the other end of the continuum from the monsters and
hobgoblins are the "Englishmen of flesh and blood," such as Talkative, By-ends, and the citizens of Vanity Fair. As with Mr. Worldly-
Wiseman, the challenge in such encounters is to see through familiar
impressions to their metaphoric patterns. Charles Baird is partially
correct in regarding Vanity Fair as one of the "representative settings" that "preserve the illusion that the figurative journey is also a
'real' one through a tangible, contemporaneous, countryside."[43] But

42. Fish, pp. 234–35.
43. Baird, p. 100.

Baird errs slightly in his term "illusion," for Vanity Fair is indeed the tangible and contemporaneous world, containing as it does "the *Britain* Row, the *French* Row, the *Italian* Row, the *Spanish* Row, the *German* Row" (p. 89). Vanity Fair is in fact tangible and contemporaneous in two dimensions at once. If "he that will go to the [Celestial] City, and yet not go thorow this Town, must needs *go out of the World*" (p. 89), the town must be the whole world; yet it is also, vividly, a typical part of the world, a town with fair and jury trial. Vanity Fair changes size like Alice in Wonderland, its concrete elements enlarging themselves as synecdoche while such abstractions as "Vanity" and "Lord Hategood" shrink to become derogatory labels. The equivalency thus established between the world and a town fair is the work of the devil (p. 88), although vast numbers of people accept it as reality. Readers who complain of Bunyan's callousness in listing "Wives, Husbands, Children" among the "goods" sold here miss the point that human relations are here *made* commutable with things and property.[44] The challenge to Christian and Faithful is, first of all, to separate themselves quixotically from this universal town: "Let nothing that is on this side the other world get within you" (p. 87). They meet that challenge without much difficulty, perhaps because a world that behaves like a town fair will naturally convince the perceptive inhabitant that he lives elsewhere. A greater challenge is to extend the townspeople's own vision to the places and values outside their foreshortened universe. The pilgrims do that by remaining faithful—in one case, by a grim allegorical pun, "faithful unto death" (p. 87)—to the laws of their own "country." And for at least one townsman, renamed Hopeful, Vanity's "realism" does indeed become something apart from reality.

Another kind of realistic encounter surrounding the episode at Vanity Fair presents a subtler challenge to metaphoric vision. Allegorical meanings are clear enough in the participants' names—Talkative, By-ends, and so forth—and the characters' own apparent ignorance of those meanings creates an amusing allegorical irony. The difficulty for the reader is that those characters converse piously with the good pilgrims for page after page, greatly attenuating our perception of allegorical differences among the speakers. Thus one critic justly accuses Christian of becoming more talkative than Talkative.[45]

44. See, for instance, Bridges, p. 110.
45. Ibid., p. 109.

A related but larger problem is that the conversation makes explicit many of Bunyan's religious ideas, rendering the entire narrative redundant in the eyes of some readers. "Allegory frustrates itself the moment the author starts doing what could equally well be done in a straight sermon or treatise," writes C. S. Lewis.[46] I have argued in previous chapters that the allegorist can never do in one mode what could be done equally well in another, for the choice of mode is one of allegory's principal vehicles of meaning. In Bunyan's case, the significance of didactic conversation appears if we read the work as an alloy of universal doctrine with personal experience. Those elements remain separate when doctrine manifests itself only verbally, as it does for Talkative and By-ends. In contrast, Faithful's "experimental profession" matches his verbal one (p. 83), and we have seen Christian experiencing the "insufficiency of our works," the "promises . . . of the Gospel," and so forth (p. 76) not as words but as facts. In a striking reversal of the conventional spiritual/carnal hierarchy, Christian tells Talkative that "the Soul of Religion is the pracktick Part" (p. 79). That lesson complements Bunyan's better-known conversions of experience into doctrine; *the Kingdom of God is not in word, but in power*" (p. 78).

Turning away from the "mouth-professors," Christian and Hopeful must maneuver through a rapid and varied series of metaphoric transformations. First they encounter the Plain of Ease, Lucre Hill, and Demas, see By-ends' destruction, and pass Lot's wife in the form of a pillar (pp. 106–8). When Hopeful realizes with a shock that he has nearly imitated the sin of Lot's wife, the same sin that led By-ends to Demas and the fatal hill, those brief episodes and emblems come together. Piecemeal and collectively, this part of the story has represented deviation, and the reader's and pilgrims' challenge has been to penetrate its variousness to its common significance. Hopeful's speech provides retrospective order, and there follows an episode of great harmony. The *"River of the water of life"* and the surrounding "Meadow, curiously beautified with Lilies," great metafacts, conflate biblical history with sensual imagery and abstract meaning (pp. 110–11). Then, after the river and the way part (p. 111), the pilgrims lapse into an almost fatal disunification of vision. An allegorical chimera named Vain Confidence seems to them solid enough to give advice, and *a* way looks as good as *the* way. A rising of "the Waters," which

46. Lewis, "Vision of John Bunyan," p. 146.

were not previously mentioned or accounted for (p. 113), signals a sudden shift away from realism and warns the pilgrims about their shortsighted empiricism. But they now fall victim to a more serious truncation of metaphoric vision. To the perceptive reader, the Giant Despair recalls the blustering, easily defeated ogres of children's stories. That his size carries no real power is comically suggested in the curtain lectures of his domineering wife. Moreover, the Giant's dual name indicates that he might have been reduced metaphorically to "despair," with which Christian should already have learned to deal. He is, in short, a foolish bully who collapses totally when the prisoners finally escape. The mechanism of their escape, Christian's sudden recollection that he has a key called Promise in his bosom (p. 118), is significantly unrealistic: the narrow empirical perspective that allowed Despair to imprison them opens suddenly into the wider metaphoric one that was available all along. Ideas return to a proper balance with images, and the pilgrims reach a promised land, the Delectable Mountains (p. 119).

The Delectable Mountains are a disarmingly concrete region whose name refers to no event or concept but simply to sensual pleasure. At the same time, they are hardly without metaphoric meaning, for they evoke, in various specific ways, heaven, biblical earthly paradises, the contemporary church at its best, and the locus of certain desirable qualities (Knowledge, Experience, Watchful, and Sincere). As an archetypal metaphor, the Delectable Mountains synthesize anagogic, scriptural, historical, and moral realities, along with the palpable experience fundamental to *The Pilgrim's Progress*. Appropriately the pilgrims learn here to hold in mind simultaneously the various perspectives on another archetypal metaphor, the Way:

Christian.   *Is this the way to the Coelestial City?*
Shepherds.   You are just in your way.
Chr.   *How far is it thither?*
Shep.   Too far for any, but those that *shall* get thither indeed.
Chr.   *Is the way safe, or dangerous?*
Shep.   Safe for those for whom it is to be safe, *but transgressors shall fall therein.*

[P. 119]

Like the equivocations of a Buddhist master, the dialogue juggles absolute and contingent definitions of the Way.

As a further exercise in paradoxical focus, Christian and Hopeful are told to look through a "Perspective Glass" at their entire metaphoric landscape (p. 123). This second great panorama of the pilgrimage violates empirical limits in many ways, revealing successively the unburied bodies of St. Paul's contemporaries, phantoms of Christian and Hopeful themselves in Giant Despair's prison, a hole in a hillside leading to Hell, and "something like" the gate and the glory of Heaven (pp. 120–23). Through the perspective glass Christian sees that the Delectable Mountains include, surprisingly, a hill called Errour, another called Caution, and a third that seems to enclose Hell (pp. 120–21): apparently the delight of the hills comes not from the goodness of what one sees there but from the clear and comprehensive views they permit. "Come to the *Shepherds* then, if you would see / Things deep, things hid, and that mysterious be," sing the pilgrims (p. 123). The horizontal pathway and its spiritual heights and depths are superimposed in a vision of the Way as a whole.

That climactic vision is followed immediately by "So I awoke from my Dream" (p. 123). As in *Piers Plowman,* the dream seems to have fulfilled its function of revealing truth, and so it can end. But in Langland, as in the *Psychomachia* and *Everyman,* such allegorical climaxes do not end the allegorical narrative, which concerns not truth but the human journey to truth. Here too the dreamer sleeps and dreams again, to see "the same two Pilgrims going"—of course—"down the Mountains" (p. 123), albeit still toward the Celestial City. And, as James Forrest points out, we realize not long after he sees them descending that they have partially forgotten the directions given them by the Shepherds on the Delectable Mountains.[47]

The relatively short remainder of Christian's story, which readers of Langland might call Bunyan's second vision, concerns primarily the abeyance of perfect metaphoric comprehension. At one point Christian and Hopeful lose their bearings and consult a stranger who turns out to be an allegorical impostor much like Vain Confidence. This time, however, the pilgrims do have directions to remember, and

47. Forrest, pp. 14–15. I find Forrest's by far the most convincing of several scholarly explanations of the break in Bunyan's dream. For some of the others, see Sharrock, Introduction to *Pilgrim's Progress,* p. xxxi, and Manfred Weidhorn, *Dreams in Seventeenth-Century Literature* (The Hague: Mouton, 1970), pp. 86–88.

the Flatterer damages them far less than did Vain Confidence. They soon recognize that the net into which they have fallen is a metaphor, and they wait ruefully for the Shining One who comes to release them (pp. 133–34).

More typically, Christian and Hopeful follow the shepherds' directions, and they compensate in various ways for the loss of the vision from the Delectable Mountains. Seeing a man carried off by devils to yet another door in a hill, they quiet their terror by seeking his metaphoric identity (p. 125). The information that he is an apostate prompts Christian to tell the story of Little-Faith, who had difficulties at the same place in the pilgrimage. Overtly the story demonstrates that although all pilgrims may weaken, even a little faith attracts the help of Great-Grace (pp. 131–32); but the exemplum's meaning is also in Christian's narration of it. He draws on a knowledge of previous pilgrims which he either did not possess or did not use till now, and he even recalls for Hopeful experiences of his own that we have not seen (pp. 129–30). Whether those anecdotes are supposed to precede *The Pilgrim's Progress,* to have occurred offstage, or, most likely, to remetaphorize parts of it, Christian is taking a newly active role in his understanding of pilgrimage. He is acting like his author, in fact: narrating one of the book's most colorful episodes, interpreting it theologically, and turning it into a warning for all "footmen" (p. 129). The perceptive recollection of metaphoric events now supplements metaphoric experience.

The recollection of metaphoric experience is nowhere more extensive and nowhere more important than on the Enchanted Ground. Sharrock glosses the Enchanted Ground as "a period of peace and toleration for the faithful" which followed the Declaration of Indulgence; the historical correlative points toward but does not delimit the meaning of this allegorical place.[48] The appellation "Enchanted" is paradoxical, since virtually nothing happens here—nothing, that is, except lengthy pious conversations. Christian and Hopeful might as well be talking in a Bedford house as in an allegorical narrative. But that slackening of metaphoric perspective defines the Enchanted Ground, whose enchantment produces enervation and sleep (p. 136). Talk is the only means "to prevent drowsiness in this place" (p. 136). What distinguishes Christian's and Hopeful's conversation from

48. Bunyan, *Pilgrim's Progress,* ed. Sharrock, p. 336.

Talkative's mouth profession is its basis in their experience. If readers have not always found it a successful antidote to tedium, the reason is that we, like the pilgrims, must exert considerable effort to link the dead metaphors of religious discourse with the events we have witnessed.

The discourse concerns Hopeful's experiences rather than Christian's, but of course Hopeful is a Christian; we must read the new story as both the same and different. Hopeful describes the onset of pilgrimage as it looks to a nonpilgrim. First he could not see the new light (p. 138) and made merely mechanical reforms, changes in daily habits (p. 139). "[B]ut," he continues, using the same metaphoric Scriptures that induced Christian's pilgrimage, "at the last my trouble came tumbling upon me again, and that over the neck of all my Reformations. . . . There were several things brought it upon me, especially such sayings as these; *All our righteousnesses are as filthy rags . . .*" (p. 139). Acting as Evangelist, Faithful gave Hopeful a book whose "every jot and tittle . . . stood firmer then Heaven and earth" (p. 141) and told him that he must "obtain the righteousness of a man that never had sinned" (p. 140). Clearly that could be done only figuratively, but with such conviction as to create a new reality. A personal vision of Christ had to intercede between Hopeful's life and Righteousness (p. 143). Fortunately, Hopeful says, he discovered that "running out" after Christ—experiencing and acting out the need for revelation—constitutes "believing in Christ" (p. 143). He then felt himself separate from the world: in terms of Christian's pilgrimage, he had arrived at the wicket gate. Near the end of the Enchanted Ground, Christian and Hopeful complement the account of conversion by discussing apostasy, the insufficient change of mind that begins with a willful insensitivity to invisible things (pp. 152–53). The entire conversation is a scaled-down, one-dimensional version of *The Pilgrim's Progress*—a map into and out of Bunyan's metaphoric world of faith. Thus it aids progress in itself; it seems to carry Christian and Hopeful over the Enchanted Ground and into the land of Beulah, a vividly imagined metaphoric haven.

The discipline of recapitulation is not the only possible response to the attenuations of spiritual perception, and Christian's and Hopeful's are not the only pilgrimages in the last part of the story. Bunyan brackets and punctuates his "second vision" by references to an odd character named Ignorance. A "very brisk Lad" with a knack for down-to-earth repartee, Ignorance recalls Talkative and By-ends and thus counterpoints, as did they, the sincere pilgrims' use of discourse. Thus in the famous declaration of an eighteenth-century preacher that "none of the characters in *The Pilgrim's Progress* spoke sense except Ignorance," the emphasis should fall on "spoke."[49] But Ignorance is more than another mouthprofessor. He persistently shadows the pilgrims: "So they went on, and *Ignorance* followed" (p. 132); "*Hopeful* looked back and saw *Ignorance,* whom they had left behind, coming after" (p. 144); "So I saw in my Dream, that they went on a pace before, and *Ignorance* he came hobling after" (p. 149). The almost formulaic repetitions surprise the reader, who often forgets Ignorance and cannot imagine what he has been doing since he was last mentioned. Where is he when Christian and Hopeful lie in the Flatterer's net? When he converses with the other pilgrims on the Enchanted Ground, are we to believe that he has withstood its enchantments? Does he enter the Land of Beulah with Christian and Hopeful, enjoying the comforts of the "holy People" (p. 155), or does he arrive at the river by some unmentioned other route? And if Ignorance eludes us as a physical agent, we sometimes encounter his verbal ghost when he is not apparently present. *Ignorance, ignorant,* and their synonyms sometimes equivocate with the character's name:

> So they went on, and *Ignorance* followed. They went then till they came at a place where they saw a *way* put it self into their *way*, . . . and here they knew not which of the two to take. . . .
>
> [P. 132]

> *Hopeful.* It [the Revelation of Christ] . . . confounded me with the sence of mine own Ignorance. . . .
>
> [P. 144]

> [Christian.] **Now the Ignorant know not that such convictions that tend to put them in fear, are for their good, and therefore they seek to stifle them. . . .* [*Why ignorant persons stifle convictions.]
>
> . . .
>
> *Hopeful.* I know something of this my self; for before I knew my self it was so with me.
>
> [P. 151]

49. Cited in Sharrock, *John Bunyan,* pp. 92–93.

Because his physical presence is so ambiguous, and because his
name sometimes occurs as a common noun, we may see Ignorance
here less as a person than as a state of being—specifically, as the
blindness that haunts Christian from within and without and that he
finally leaves behind. Indeed, it may be Christian and Hopeful's
"sence of [their] own Ignorance"—their reconception of this state of
being as a discrete and discardable entity—that frees them from him.
A reading of Ignorance as genuinely allegorical would excuse Bunyan
from the charge of inhumanity in damning him and would explain the
agent's absence from many episodes.[50] On the other hand, Ignorance
is too lively and shows too specific a kind of ignorance—ignorance
about justifying righteousness (p. 148)—to be transparent to the abstraction itself. More important, the suggestions that Ignorance may
reform himself (pp. 124, 149) would make no sense if the agent were
an abstraction.

In fact, Ignorance exhibits in a particularly disturbing way the
intermediary status of all Bunyan's agents. Like Faithful, Christian,
and the Mercie of Part II, he coincides at times with his idea, but he
achieves thereby the opposite of transcendence. Although ontologically capable of changing to embody a good abstraction, he
refuses to do so because, ironically, he firmly believes in human goodness (pp. 145–46). Seeing no need for allegorical transformation,
committed to the illusion of human self-sufficiency, he abdicates his
autonomy as a human agent: "*Ignorance* is thy name, and as thy
name is, so art thou" (p. 148). When he is ferried over the River of
Death by the abstraction Vain-Hope (p. 162), we see that Ignorance
has refused the immersion in metaphoric experience which could
have made him a real pilgrim—has, in fact, locked himself into a
static condition. His damnation is both allegorically inevitable and
humanly horrifying.

With great emphasis, Bunyan has framed the end of Part I in a
vision of the refusal of vision. It is intriguing that the state of sin
against which he warns is embodied in his most fully allegorical
character aside from such apparitions as Help and Vain Confidence.
Of course, his condemnation of a reprehensible abstraction does not
signal a literary decision about abstractions generally. Yet the ending

50. For a summary of critical condemnation of Bunyan's judgment of Ignorance,
see Forrest, pp. 12–13.

of Part I confirms other suggestions that redeeming vision, for Bunyan, is concrete and particular. The heaven into which Christian and Hopeful ascend consists not of universals, as does Prudentius' eternity, or of mystically incarnate forms, as does Dante's, but of images so thoroughly familiar as to seem almost childish. Courteous angels conduct the pilgrims "up through the Regions of the Air, sweetly talking as they [go]" (p. 159), promising pleasant food, reunions with friends, and frequent excursions in the King of Glory's "equipage" (pp. 159–60). Heavenly music issues unmysteriously from trumpets (p. 160), and the pilgrims are thoughtfully given harps with which to do their praising (p. 162). Even God is apparently bound by physical laws like those of the human world, for he has to ask "messengers" for information about new arrivals (p. 161). Nonetheless, he does not seem like a sham God, nor does this picture-book heaven fail to move us. The imagery resonates with ancient tradition: this is the *"Marriage Supper of the Lamb"* (p. 160); Christian and Hopeful are transfigured into the *"righteous Nation . . . that keepeth Truth"* (p. 161). But the pilgrims remain somehow themselves, with bodies and senses, even after losing their *"Mortal* Garments" (pp. 158–59). Evidently heaven sanctifies and immortalizes sensory perception.

Indeed, heaven is immediately apprehensible to the dreamer, who plays a crucial role at the end of Part I.[51] Closer now to us than to Christian, he provides in his own person our only information about heaven. Before the gates were shut, he says, he caught a glimpse of the heavenly city, "which when I had seen, I wished my self among them" (p. 162). He stays outside the gates to see the damnation of Ignorance, thus giving us a final panorama of the landscape of pilgrimage: "Then I saw that there was a way to Hell, even from the Gates of Heaven, as well as from the City of *Destruction.* So I awoke, and behold it was a Dream" (p. 163). That final sentence is unnerving. It closes the story formulaically, of course, and forestalls objections that Bunyan's vision—in particular, perhaps, his anthropomorphic heaven—trespasses on sacred ineffabilities. But coming so swiftly after the descent from glory to horror, the formulaic disclaimer ends the narrative at the height of our engagement. The primal longing and fear of

51. The dreamer's role at the end of Part I is discussed by Weidhorn, pp. 86–87, and Fish, pp. 262–64.

the closing moments survive the dreamer's awakening; our reflex is to question the reality of whatever is not this dream.

The ending of Part I reminds us that Bunyan was popular largely because of his power over his readers' emotions. Put differently, that commonplace suggests Bunyan's peculiarity as an allegorist. The most powerful final authority for his narrative is not philosophical or doctrinal, regardless of the text's doctrinal basis, but personal; and the afterword does not absorb us into an allegorical pattern but asks for our personal validation and approval (p. 164). *The Pilgrim's Progress* has been based all along not on the impersonal, sovereign, multiply embodied abstractions of such allegories as the *Psychomachia* and *Everyman,* but on the interconversion of abstractions with the objects of sensory perception. Christian's task has been to maintain or restore connections between the images he experiences and the truths he knows. But the fusion of individual experience and abstract truth can occur only within a carefully balanced imaginative structure, a metaphoric world. In the final moments of the dream, the images' emotional impact overwhelms their abstract meaning, and the multiple point of view gives way to a focus on the individual observer's responses. That unbalancing and refocusing begin a movement away from allegory that will continue when the dream resumes, in Part II.

Allegorical Reprise: The Slough in the Mind

Bunyan's original sequel to Part I of *The Pilgrim's Progress* was not Part II but *The Life and Death of Mr. Badman,* a very different kind of work. Only three of its characters bear generalized names—Mr. Wiseman, Mr. Attentive, and Mr. Badman—and the context reveals those to be type and function names instead of allegorical ones. The first of those three characters tells the story to the second; no dreaming is involved. The story itself is the biography of a type, a compilation of anecdotes that "have been acted upon the stage of this World."[52] Employers are cheated, an innocent young woman is abused, and

---

52. Bunyan, "The Author to the Reader," prefatory to *The Life and Death of Mr. Badman,* in *"The Life and Death of Mr. Badman" and "The Holy War,"* ed. Brown, p. 3.

neighbors are scandalized; no abstractions act and no metaphors come to life.

Bunyan had good reasons not to continue *The Pilgrim's Progress* allegorically. To continue it at all required abandoning the hero, who could hardly be followed farther than the Celestial City. That left two obvious alternatives: to deal with another good pilgrim or to turn to some sort of sinner. The second possibility, which produced *Mr. Badman,* gave Bunyan a protagonist who could not last long in Christian's metaphoric world, if he entered it at all. The first option, sending additional Christians in Christian's footsteps, may have seemed to Bunyan not only potentially dull but also contrary to the nature of allegory. Insofar as his hero in Part I was a categorical persona undergoing universal experiences, any attempted variation of his journey ought to produce tautology.

Yet his readers' appetites, understandably unsatisfied by *Mr. Badman,* along with his imitators' impertinences and perhaps his own uneasiness about the abandoned wife and children, drove Bunyan eventually to a retelling of his universal story. It is inevitably a retelling somewhat at odds with its original. Bunyan avoids tautology by differentiating his new pilgrims from Christian and from each other as fully as possible—that is, by particularizing them in various ways. In his preface he links the particularized characters with his diverse readers, who can find in Part II not a single universal representative but an array of personalized ones: Mercie, one of the "little *Tripping Maidens*" who follow God when old sinners do not; old Honest, who "with some gray Head . . . may prevail, / With Christ to fall in Love"; Master Fearing, who "*was* a good man, though much down in Spirit, / [and] *is* a good Man, and doth Life inherit"; and so forth (pp. 172–73). Individual personality dominates the list increasingly, and some of the names designate qualities incidental to the characters' moral status. The narrow Way broadens, from allegorical metaphor into generalization.

As a result, Part II is richer than its predecessor in what is usually called human interest. Christiana first yearns to follow her husband because of natural affection (p. 177), and Mercie attends Christiana for the same reason (pp. 183–86). "Bowels," we are told, "becometh Pilgrims" (p. 186)—a dictum that turns out to be doubly apt when Christiana's son later experiences guilt as an intestinal disorder. Matthew's bowels are part of a general acknowledgement of biological

existence, evident also in numerous nonmetaphoric meals, in a series
of marriages and pregnancies, and in practical arrangements for taking care of babies while their parents are traveling (e.g., pp. 260, 269,
and 280). But Mercie's less physiological "bowels" exemplify a similar change: a new concern with the pilgrims' emotional and psychological reactions. Even when doctrine is clearly important, as at the
Interpreter's house, allegorical processes share the spotlight with psychological ones:

> When the *Interpreter* had shewed them this, he has them into the
> very best Room in the house. . . . Then they looked round and round:
> For there was nothing there to be seen but a very great *Spider* on the
> Wall: and that they overlook't.
> Mer. *Then said* Mercie, *Sir, I see nothing; but* Christiana *held her
> peace.*
> *Inter.* But said the *Interpreter,* look again: she therefore lookt again
> and said, Here is not any thing, but an *ugly Spider,* who hangs by her
> Hands upon the Wall. Then said he, Is there but one *Spider* in all this
> spacious Room? Then the water stood in *Christiana*'s Eyes, for she
> was a Woman quick of apprehension: and she said, Yes Lord, there is
> more here then one. Yea, and *Spiders* whose Venom is far more
> destructive then that which is in her. The *Interpreter* then looked
> pleasantly upon her, and said, Thou hast said the Truth. This made
> *Mercie* blush, and the Boys to cover their Faces. For they all began
> now to understand the Riddle.   [Pp. 200–201]

Despite its initial Calvinistic harshness, the Interpreter's lesson turns
out to be just as humane as Bunyan's narration of the episode. The
pilgrims learn that however "full of the Venome of Sin" they are, they
may possess the best room in the king's house; they are all moved to
tears (p. 201).

To say that Part II is thus "humanized" because it concerns women
and children is to forestall rather than to offer an explanation.[53] The
story's humanity—that is, its focus on the individual and the in-
stinctual rather than on the universal and the abstract—follows from
Bunyan's decision to rewrite his allegory: everyman had to give way
to various people. The use of women and children reflects the same
decision. Because women and children do not conventionally repre-

---

53. See especially Sharrock, "Women and Children," in *Bunyan,* ed. Sharrock, pp.
174–86; but the explanation is common.

sent humanity, they are the natural protagonists of a narrative concerning not the essential human experience but variations on that experience. Granted, Christian himself is not simply mankind in the abstract, being differentiated to some degree from Faithful and Hopeful. But he can also appear, via metaphoric transformation, as the syncretic, universal Christian. Being a variant of him, Christiana cannot.[54]

A reduction in such metaphoric potential throughout Part II necessarily accompanies the gain in human interest. The more variously Bunyan's characters represent humankind, and the richer their biological and social milieu, the more solidly empirical their experiences remain. Bunyan omits or concretizes a number of the allegorical episodes of Part I: Help, Good Will, and Vain Confidence do not appear; the wicket gate acquires a summer parlor in which pilgrims can discuss their conversions; the magical displays at the Interpreter's house give way to spiders, hens, sheep, and flowers, supplied with clever moralizations. Such changes partially justify the famous comment of Ronald Knox: "Christian goes on a pilgrimage, Christiana on a walking-tour."[55]

But of course Knox exaggerates. Part II is not a simple travelogue; in order to follow Christian, Christiana and her companions must pass through metaphoric places. Despond cannot be removed from the Slough, nor can the Way become just a road. The reader who wishes to trace Christiana's journey rather than simply to enjoy its realistic passages must ask about the function of the remaining allegorical agents and metaphoric transformations.

A partial answer is that the allegorical remainder contrasts so

54. Christiana does achieve something like archetypal status at one point. In response to a threat from Giant Grim, she declares, "Tho' the Highways have been unoccupied heretofore, and tho the Travellers have been made in time past, to walk thorough by-Paths, it must not be so now I am risen, *Now I am Risen a Mother in* Israel [Judg. 5: 6, 7.]" (p. 219; Bunyan's gloss). But the passage is anomalous, probably because the archetype here is not "pilgrim" or "Christian" but "mother" and thus is not central to Bunyan's metaphor of pilgrimage. The ability of Mercie to embody her allegorical identity has already been mentioned, but for the most part she is a peculiarly feminine and timid mercy, a far cry from the Daughter of God or from Prudentius' Operatio; thus her temporary allegorical power in the episode with Mr. Brisk is particularly impressive. Her personality exemplifies the simultaneous feminization and sentimentalization of virtue after the Renaissance.

55. Ronald Knox, *Essays in Satire* (1928), cited in Monica Furlong, *Puritan's Progress* (New York: Coward, McCann & Geoghegan, 1975), p. 117.

strongly with its context that it produces equivocations and paradoxes even more extreme than those of Part I. At times, for instance, the
naturalistic text and its allegorical gloss divide even more sharply
here. When Christian arrived at the wicket gate, Good Will warned
him about the arrows of Beelzebub, who lurked nearby to try to keep
pilgrims out of the Way (p. 25). At the corresponding point in Part II,
Christiana, Mercie, and the children are frightened away from the
gate by a large, loudly barking dog, identified in the margin as "the
Devil, an Enemy to Prayer" (p. 188). Dog and devil are joined neither
in the text nor in a biblical citation, as were Beelzebub and the arrows
and Christian's burden and his iniquity. Furthermore, the two terms
cannot coalesce in our minds, since the vehicle is so disproportionate
to the tenor. The passage substantiates a common pejorative definition of allegory as strained encoding.

The distinction between text and gloss cannot remain so extreme,
since the pilgrims must generally know the spiritual significance of
their adventures; but even when image and idea are both present in
the text, they are often as incompatible as the dog and the devil. The
classic instance is the illness of Matthew, to which I have already
referred. He falls ill near the end of a long stay at the Palace Beautiful,
which has become something like a well-run Christian hostel. When
he is "much pained in his Bowels, so that he [is] with it, at times,
pulled as 'twere both ends together" (p. 228), Christiana sends for
"an Antient, and well approved Physician" named Mr. Skill. He
pronounces the boy "sick of the Gripes" (p. 228) and asks about his
recent diet. Nothing indicates that the illness is not simply the physical malady that it feels like to Matthew, until Mr. Skill declares that
the apples that he ate were "the Fruit of *Belzebubs* Orchard" and
prescribes a medicine "made *ex Carne & Sanguine Christi*" (p. 229).
Matthew naturally declines to take the strange stuff, but his mother
tastes it herself in order to persuade him that it is "sweeter then
Hony" (p. 230). "If we had met with this passage in a Restoration
comedy satirizing the Puritans," writes James Sutherland, "we should
probably have thought it a rather obvious piece of satire."[56] Indeed,
Bunyan seems to acknowledge comedy in the overtly serious scene,
for after naming Mr. Skill's prescription, he jokes parenthetically,
"You know Physicians give strange Medicines to their Patients" (p.

56. Sutherland, p. 333.

229). The humor depends, of course, on incongruity. The scene's vigorous naturalism cannot be fully assimilated to its doctrinal meaning; both gloss and cure are administered by an allegorist *ex machina,* and Matthew remains untouched by real guilt or remorse. If he is pulled both ends together, the reason may be that he has two kinds of illness at once. Indeed, Bunyan probably does not mean for us to seek organic unity between gripes and guilt but to enjoy the partial alignment of dissimilars.

Even more incongruous than such allegorical recastings of naturalistic events are the obviously metaphoric events that intrude into naturalistic passages. After the Interpreter has moralized his garden and farmyard for the pilgrims, a damsel takes them back into the garden for an open-air bath (p. 207). If the episode pleased the Baptists, as Sharrock suggests, it is likely to bemuse the rest of us, for this baptism is not a metaphoric event in a metaphoric landscape but a peculiar variation on normal human behavior.[57] Similarly, when the pilgrims feast on "a *Heave-shoulder,* and a *Wave-breast*" from Leviticus, the oddity is not that they literally "begin their *Meal* with Prayer and Praise to God" (p. 262) but that they do so after a long series of nonmetaphoric suppers. These anomalies cannot be resolved in the same way as can the apparent violations of realism in other allegories, including Bunyan's Part I, for the allegorical and realistic perspectives are more fully separated. Instead of living on the bridge between worlds, the characters live on one side but make sudden unannounced visits to the other.

Indeed, Part II vacillates between states of being from the beginning—not merely equivocating about its mode, as did Part I, but contradicting itself. The narrator first tells us that he would have inquired earlier about Christian's wife and children if "the Multiplicity of Business" had not prevented his making his "wonted Travels into those Parts whence [Christian] went" (p. 174). It is somewhat surprising to learn that the waking narrator has access to the regions through which Christian traveled, but it is even more surprising to read that when he does return "thitherward," he lies down to sleep and then dreams about Christian's family. Why, we wonder, did he need to be in the neighborhood to dream about it? Bunyan has introduced his narrative in two incompatible ways: as a set of events in the

57. Sharrock, *John Bunyan,* p. 144.

natural world and as a dream vision. The contradiction is presently compounded. Instead of seeing Christiana and her children, the dreaming narrator meets someone who can tell him about their pilgrimage. The informant, Mr. Sagacity, is not only superfluous but also problematic: he should not be able to report the entire pilgrimage, since such metaphors as the wicket gate can hardly be seen by a waking observer who is not himself a pilgrim. But the mismatch between the dream vision and the yarn spinner's exposition merely reflects the larger incongruity between walking tour and allegorical journey—the former eminently reportable by an observer such as Mr. Sagacity, the latter accessible only to the metaphoric seer.

Oddly enough, however, the incongruities of Part II have provoked far fewer objections from readers than those of Part I. The pilgrims themselves are also strangely free from the sense of conflict that Christian felt when he began to bridge the two worlds. With apparent equanimity, Christiana and her friends accept allegorical messengers into ordinary houses (pp. 179–80) and apocalyptic tidings from the daily post (p. 304). One character proposes to his houseguests that they spend the morning hunting an allegorical giant—after breakfast, of course (p. 266). Even the children are rarely nonplussed by the supernatural adventures of pilgrimage. Somehow the incongruous allegorical elements are assimilated into the predominantly realistic narrative.

In part the assimilation is effected by tone. At the opening of Part II, the contradiction between dream vision and reporting does not confuse the reader who notices that Bunyan seems to take neither one very seriously. Within fourteen pages Mr. Sagacity unceremoniously leaves the dreamer "to Dream out my Dream by my self" (p. 188), and the dream itself has been ironically subverted in advance: "But if thou shalt cast all away as vain, / I know not but 'twill make me Dream again," writes Bunyan in his Conclusion to Part I (p. 164). In light of that wry prediction, the dream that arrives fortuitously but superfluously, as soon as the narrator resumes his "wonted Travels" to Christiana's neighborhood, looks like a joke shared with the audience. Bunyan expects us to know that he is making it all up. What renders the playfulness especially effective is that we also recognize, from the Preface to Part II, that the codes guiding his invention here will in fact be quite different from those of the dream vision. Christiana's world reflects domestic detail and mundane experience; to

convey such homely material in a dream vision (or in a foreign correspondent's report) is pleasantly ironic. The allegorical realities that
dreaming conveyed in Part I will still be taken quite seriously, of
course. But the dream itself, like Mr. Sagacity, is frankly the author's
invention—just a figure of speech.

"Just a figure of speech" would be a most peculiar label for anything in the radically metaphoric Part I, but it fits Part II quite well. It
is justified not merely by Bunyan's tone but, more tangibly, by the
lucid explanations regularly offered here for metaphoric anomalies.
We have seen Mr. Skill's neat moralization of Matthew's double
illness; more often the pilgrims' explicator is Mr. Great-heart, an
escort from the Interpreter's house who provides continuously the
kind of interpretation that Christian achieved sporadically through
imperfect memory and painful experience. The characters of Part II
also receive instruction regularly from mental, oral, and visual memorials of Christian's experience. A brass plate explains the visible
punishment of Simple, Sloth, and Presumption (p. 214); the paths
that led Formal and Hypocrisy to destruction are blocked "with
Chains, Posts, and a *Ditch.*" As Great-heart remarks, "these ways,
are made cautionary enough" (p. 215). Of course, the explanations,
cautions, and memorials do more than simply help the pilgrims: they
relocate allegorical metaphor. Because metaphoric events and their
interpretations appear simultaneously here, the events resemble the
dead metaphors of figurative thought and speech.

In other words, the metaphoric events and images of Part II seem to
be mental ones. That is especially clear when the characters themselves invent allegorical riddles, explain doctrinal ideas, and narrate
allegorical events, as they do during much of the story (pp. 203–7,
209–13, 223–26, 247–57, 258–66, 271–73, 276–79, 289–96). A
great many of the Way's events are not experienced but described or
narrated. But even the anomalous metaphoric events differ from
Christian's experiences in being so clearly dominated by their meanings. Matthew's illness, the open-air bath, and the Levitical meats
strike us as somewhat playful creations of the imagination rather than
as supernatural facts. At one point Mr. Great-heart fancifully compares religious profession to musical performance, and he apologizes,
"I make bold to talk thus Metaphorically, for the ripening of the Wits
of young Readers" (p. 253). The solecism "Readers" betrays Mr.
Great-heart here as the mouthpiece for his author, whose metaphoric

images increasingly resemble games. The allegorical world is reconciled with the realistic one by being absorbed into the thoughts,
speech, and imaginations of human beings.

The absorption occurs not only in readers' minds, as we recognize
the metaphors as inventions, but also in the minds of the characters.
To a considerable degree the story of Part II is the pilgrims' growing
control over their allegorical world. Mr. Great-heart explains that
Apollyon attacked Christian only because of the latter's own "slips";
such an attack looks like the work of a "foul Fiend, or evil Spirit"
only to the superstitious "common people," who do not understand
that whatever affronts them in the Valley of Humiliation is "for the
fruit of their doing" (p. 236). The metaphor that looked so terri-
fyingly external in Part I is recast for Christian's successors as a
psychological idea. The change in perspective continues with a series
of metaphoric reductions in the Valley of the Shadow of Death. An
"ugly thing" in the road ahead looks like a fiend but vanishes as the
pilgrims identify its scriptural basis, and a ferocious lion mysteriously
retreats into metaphor (pp. 241–42). The mist that veils horrible
pitfalls is dispelled when Mr. Great-heart reveals the landscape as a
simile:

> This is like doing business in great Waters, or like going down into
> the deep; this is like being in the heart of the Sea, and like going down
> to the Bottoms of the Mountains: Now it seems as if the Earth with
> its bars were about us for ever. *But let them that walk in darkness and
> have no light, trust in the name of the Lord, and stay upon their
> God.*   [Pp. 242–43]

If what they are doing is *like* walking through dark and deep places, it
must be fundamentally something else—namely, a spiritual reality.
Accordingly, the pilgrims pray, and then "God sent light and deliv-
erance, for there was now no lett in their way, no not there, where but
now they were stopt with a pit" (p. 243). After the dangers of the two
Valleys have dematerialized, despair's giant image is obliterated (pp.
281–82); then the personification of worldly seduction, a mere
Madame Bubble, is exorcised with prayer (pp. 301–2).

As those metaphoric images yield to human understanding, allegorical labels also submit to human will. Mr. Honest, who comes
from the Town of Stupidity and has had to earn his name, urges
Mercie and Christiana's sons to regard their names, too, as goals (pp.

247–48). The persistence of Mr. Fearing teaches all of the pilgrims that a dominant quality—the same quality, in fact, that doomed Timorous and Mrs. Timorous—does not entirely determine one's behavior on pilgrimage (pp. 249–54). Then Mr. Self-wil, who foolishly insists on being "like himself, *self-willed*" (p. 255), is rebuked for equating pilgrims' spiritual identities with the vices and virtues they practice (pp. 255–56). We have come far indeed from the regnant abstractions of the *Psychomachia*. "It happens to us, as it happeneth to way-fairing men," explains Mr. Honest. "We are seldom at a Certainty" (p. 275). Even the town of Vanity now contains numerous pious precincts and boasts a citizen named Grace: the inhabitants have fought their allegorical destiny and won.

Whereas allegory posits the intelligible as the sovereign reality, the first part of *The Pilgrim's Progress* complicates that allegorical perspective with a different sense of reality. Alpaugh writes, "Bunyan has the same distrust of abstract reasoning not grounded in experience that we see in Rochester and Dryden up through Pope, Swift, and Johnson. . . . Bunyan conceives of the mind almost in a Lockean sense—as a receptor and arranger of sense impressions."[58] Bunyan's empiricism is not a matter just of temperament or zeitgeist but also of theology. Personal experience is vital to him because it validates doctrine. In *Grace Abounding*, Bunyan reveals an agonized awareness of other dogmas than Christian ones:

> The Tempter would also much assault me with this: How can you tell but that the Turks had as good Scriptures to prove their *Mahomet* the Saviour, as we have to prove our *Jesus* is . . . ? Everyone doth think his own Religion rightest, both *Jews,* and *Moors,* and *Pagans;* and how if all our Faith, and Christ, and Scriptures, should be but a think-so too?[59]

His solution is that he has experienced the truths of Christianity. That is, he refutes the rationalistic challenge to his beliefs with a version of the rationalistic appeal to empirical evidence. Of course, the empirical evidence in turn takes shape from doctrine. The entire system of

58. Alpaugh, p. 302.
59. Bunyan, *Grace Abounding to the Chief of Sinners*, in *"Grace Abounding" and "The Pilgrim's Progress*," ed. Roger Sharrock, Oxford Standard Authors (London: Oxford University Press, 1966), p. 33.

thought depends on what Kaufmann calls a "reciprocal illumination" of "Word and experience," though it might more harshly be called an ongoing circular proof.[60]

In the first part of *The Pilgrim's Progress* the circuit is magnificently vital; the allegorical and empirical visions continually interchange via allegorical metaphor. In Part II, however, metaphor leads us back out of allegory and into another kind of experience. At one point Mr. Great-heart states that Mr. Fearing lay at the Slough of Despond for more than a month, "[b]ut when he was over, he would scarce believe it. He had, I think, a *Slow of Dispond* in his Mind, a *Slow* that he carried every where with him . . ." (p. 249). If allegorical locales always represented states of mind, as we so easily assume, Great-heart's statement would be either a tautology or a transgression of the allegorical code. But the original Slough of Despond equivocated between individual experience and universal idea. The transition to a *"Slow of Dispond* in his Mind," typical of the internalization of metaphor in Bunyan's Part II, leads from allegory toward what we now call realism.

I do not mean to suggest that Bunyan came to define doctrinal ideas as mental fabrications or to regard only empirical experience as real—notions that would probably have outraged him—but that his focus shifted away from transcendent ideas, away even from their intersection with empirical reality, to their operation in human thought and behavior. Probably nothing was more real to Bunyan than the River of Death his pilgrims must cross or the salvation they hope to reach; but in the splendid closing of Part II we do not watch Death, salvation, or even angels, but human beings passing into eternity. Their story ends just as they enter the ideal realm. Moreover, their entrance into ideal reality is not a progressive abandonment of individuality, like Everyman's death. Paradoxically, Christiana, Mr. Ready-to-Halt, Mr. Feeble-mind, Mr. Despondencie, Mr. Honest, Mr. Valiant-for-Truth, and Mr. Stand-fast are never more vividly individualized than in their grand ceremonial relinquishments of personality:

> As for my *feeble Mind,* that I leave behind me, for that I shall have no need of that in the place whither I go; nor is it worth bestowing upon

60. Kaufmann, p. 204.

the poorest Pilgrim: Wherefore when I am gon, I desire, that you Mr. *Valiant,* would bury it in a Dunghil.   [Pp. 307–8]

My Will and my Daughters is, that our *Disponds,* and slavish Fears, be by no man ever received, from the day of our Departure, for ever; For I know that after my Death they will offer themselves to others. For, to be plain with you, they are *Ghosts,* the which we entertained when we first began to be Pilgrims, and could never shake them off after.   [P. 308]

My *Sword,* I give to him that shall succeed me in my Pilgrimage, and my *Courage* and *Skill,* to him that can get it. My *Marks* and *Scarrs* I carry with me, to be a witness for me, that I have fought his Battels, who now will be my Rewarder.   [P. 309]

Those speeches lend credence to Great-heart's prediction that friends will recognize each other even in heaven (p. 292). If the heaven of Part I immortalizes sensory perception, Part II promises the apotheosis of the individual.

Bunyan's integration of allegorical vision and empirical realism is, to my knowledge, a unique achievement; Part II testifies that it is also a fragile one, able to be undone by its own success. The Way remains an allegorical metaphor, but in Part II its allegorical dimension appears less in metamorphosis than in commentary and recollection. Communal acceptance and the subsequent internalization of metaphor have made pilgrimage not a venture into a hybrid world but a trip through the familiar one with trustworthy spiritual directions. Indeed, the Way is eventually replaced by a sinless version of the static earthly setting that Christian once fled: Christiana's children establish a town in the Land of Beulah "for the Increase of the Church in that Place where they were for a time" (p. 311). The carnal world has assimilated the allegorical one entirely. If the narrator had revisited the new city, as he here thinks of doing (p. 311), he might well have found a Mr. Sagacity there, for it is the kind of place in which a reporter with a vivid memory for details would be quite at home. The narrator can simply leave his characters there; he does not wake from this vision. The fiction of truth has given way to fictional reality.

Part III

INTEGUMENTS

Anyone who accuses recent generations of misdefining a very old literary form would be gratified to discover more acceptable definitions framed by our clearer-sighted ancestors. Alas, such gratification is not to be had. Classical, medieval, and Renaissance writers do discuss allegory, but their examples probably would not now be called allegorical. Quintilian cites, among others, Lucretius' "Pierian fields I range untrod by man," Virgil's reference to himself under the name of a shepherd, and Cicero's "What I marvel at and complain of is this, that there should exist any man so set on destroying his enemy as to scuttle the ship on which he himself is sailing." Fifteen centuries later, Thomas Wilson translates some of the same examples and adds, "It is euill puttyng strong wine into weake vesselles, that is to say it is euill trustyng some women with weightie matters."[1] Early writers

---

1. *The Institutio Oratoria of Quintilian,* trans. H. E. Butler, 4 vols., Loeb Classical Library (New York: Putnam, 1922), VIII.vi.44–47; Thomas Wilson, *The Arte of Rhetorique* (1553; rpt. Gainesville, Fla.: Scholars' Facsimiles and Reprints, 1962), pp. 198–99.

include as subdivisions of *allegoria* far more than we would—not just metaphor and allusion, but also riddles, epigrams, sarcasm, and irony.[2] More tellingly, their definitions, mostly variations on Quintilian's *aliud verbis aliud sensu,* establish precisely those dichotomies between word and meaning, lying fiction and implicit truth, which this study attempts to refute. Far from encouraging the revisionist critic, they constitute an embarrassment.

Perhaps for that reason, several recent students of allegory dismiss the classical definition as irrelevant. They allege that Cicero, Quintilian, and their successors were talking about something else altogether—about "'allegorical' modes of embellishment" instead of "allegory as a form or as a central technique of signifying," according to Robert Hollander, or about "a more general figure classified under metaphor" rather than "what we recognize as 'personification,'" according to Martin Irvine, or, for Maureen Quilligan, about "*allegoresis,* that is, the literary criticism of texts," not "allegory as allegorical narrative."[3] Attempting to explain why the early scholars should have studied only local tropes or secondary techniques rather than the principles underlying the major texts that we call allegories, Quilligan points out plausibly enough that "classical definitions of allegory were made when there were no narrative allegories to describe." That the definitions persisted through the florescence of narrative allegory she attributes to poets' tendency to "do something quite different from critics." As for the more troublesome recurrence of the classical definition in remarks made by certain Renaissance allegorists on their own works, Quilligan writes that "this erroneous definition was . . . passed down to the Renaissance with all the authority of classical precedent."[4]

As laudable as they may be from a certain point of view, those arguments cannot in good conscience be fully supported. A dichotomy between two kinds of thing both called *allegory* should induce, prima facie, discomfort in readers who postulate linguistic coherence.

---

2. See, for instance, Quintilian, *Institutio Oratoria,* VIII.vi.57–58, and Richard Sherry, *A Treatise of Schemes and Tropes* (1550), pp. 45–46.

3. Hollander, *Allegory in Dante's "Commedia,"* p. 14; Martin Irvine, "Cynewulf's Use of Psychomachic Allegory: The Latin Sources of Some 'Interpolated' Passages," in *Allegory, Myth, and Symbol,* ed. Bloomfield, p. 44; Quilligan, *Language of Allegory,* p. 26.

4. Quilligan, pp. 20, 31, 29.

Moreover, the dichotomy is never neatly formulated. A "mode of embellishment" called "allegorical" in quotation marks might conceivably overlap with the "central technique of signifying" designated simply allegory; the definition of a subcategory, such as personification, surely ought not to differ sharply from that of its parent, in this case metaphor; and even if Quintilian was indeed discussing the "literary criticism of texts," as he himself does not seem to have suspected, he was thereby proposing also a theory about texts themselves. Finally, the schism between definition and practice rests in part on the highly questionable argument that the force of classical authority induced Dante and Spenser, not otherwise known as slavish imitators, to borrow a definition for their works which did not fit at all. Reason obliges us to face instead the possibility that the classical definition does intersect to a significant degree with medieval and Renaissance practice.

They intersect, in fact, in a broad but definable area. The early theorists are describing, and the allegorists are producing, a perception of semantic double exposure: expecting a single, particular referent, the reader finds a multiple or syncretic one. In some cases certain specific terms acquire alternatives (the scuttled ship is also a damaged nation); in others, universals appear where we expect particulars (Concord speaks, a gate is opened by Oiseuse, a man seen in a dream is all Christians). For both effects, since in both we recognize something as something other than it might have been, *alieniloquium* is a defensible, if ambiguous, common term.

That said, we can see more clearly the genuine distinctions. Until well into the Middle Ages, the definitions of allegory refer to texts other than those we now call allegories; Quilligan is right to point out that the seminal classical definitions antedate narrative personification allegories. Even after the latter's appearance, certain barriers separate the two for a time. Allegorists do not usually theorize about their work; for their part, medieval theorists rarely consider contemporary works, or, aside from myth and Scripture, any texts long enough to allow the ontological unfoldings and syntheses of Realistic agency. Although the texts on either side of that barrier between theory and practice refer to something other than the single particulars that we first see or expect, the alternative referents differ significantly. The Realistic agents of personification allegory cannot properly be called alternatives at all, except in violating expectations; they do not rival but incorporate various concrete, specific manifestations. In contrast, the pairs of referents in the classical and Renaissance examples—ship and state, or vessel and woman—may be joinable by analogy but cannot be ontologically merged. To the ontological disparity between meanings, many of the illustrative texts add a temporal separation: their second referents are unstated or delayed, producing a split not exactly between word and meaning—that would be impossible—but certainly between two kinds of meaning. Thus whereas the reader of personification allegory perceives primarily synthesis and transformation, the dominant effect of the definers' examples is disjunction.

But the barrier between disjunctive rhetorical theory and conjunctive narrative practice drops during the Renaissance, when theorist and practitioner often inhabit the same body. Such allegorists as Dante and Spenser, who use versions of Quintilian's definition for their own work, write a form of allegory much closer to that definition than did their predecessors. Of their innovations, which will be explored in the ensuing chapters, the most obvious is that they virtually abandon personification: very few of their agents and objects bear abstract nouns as names. That is not to say that the agents and objects are not universals or intelligibles, but that reference to those syncretic Realities becomes delayed and somewhat oblique, justifying both poets' assumption that readers will not see all the meaning immediately. What Dante implies in distinguishing "that which is conveyed by the letter" from "that which is conveyed by what the letter signifies," and what Spenser suggests in calling his allegory a dark conceit, is that in their texts semiotic disjunction rivals conjunction.[5]

Still, the classical definition of allegory will not quite serve Dante's and Spenser's readers, for it misrepresents the principles of narrative allegory in a second and more general way—in its attitude toward multiple meaning. *Aliud verbis aliud sensu* can mean either that the text says (and means) one thing while also meaning (and saying) a second, or that it appears to mean one thing but really means another.

5. Dante, Epistola X (to Can Grande della Scalla), in *Dantis Alagherii Epistolae; The Letters of Dante*, ed. and trans. Paget Toynbee, 2d ed. (Oxford: Clarendon Press, 1966), p. 199; Edmund Spenser, "A Letter of the Authors . . . to . . . Sir Walter Raleigh," in *Edmund Spenser's Poetry: Authoritative Texts and Criticism*, ed. Hugh Maclean (New York: W. W. Norton, 1968), p. 1.

The classical writers' terms, *verbis* and *sensu,* point more strongly toward the latter possibility; so do their successors' metaphors of veil and object, kernel and husk. In all such pairs the second element is more authentic and more valuable. A similar difference in authenticity emerges from the common medieval association of the immediate meaning with the illusory, sensible realm and the delayed one with everlasting spiritual reality.[6] The classical theorizers about allegory were rhetoricians who saw metaphor primarily as a pragmatic act, a means to a nonliterary end, rather than as a sign whose words cannot be separated from its meaning. Many of their medieval successors were exegetes whose religious and literary activities depended on the assumption that the implicit meanings that they brought to light were of transcendent value. In identifying real meanings, both exegetes and rhetoricians suppressed meaning. To convey a proposition about "some women" through a statement about weak vessels is to signify, besides the proposition, a particular relationship with one's audience, not to mention a peculiar vision of humanity; to recognize only the proposition is to superimpose on the disjunctions of extended metaphor a semiotic fragmentation not proper to any linguistic form. No reader of any allegory needs to practice such truncation.

Aside from that major but extractable misconception, the definition of allegory formulated by Quintilian and transmitted to medieval scholars applies well to any text in which a single syntactic slot—subject or object of a sentence, agent or object in a narrative code—is occupied by several terms that do not fully coincide. The definition has been mistakenly broadened to include personification allegory, whose compound referents are fully unifiable; paradoxically enough, the form often called naive or pure allegory is least like what the early rhetoricians called allegory.[7]

The complementary paradox holds as well: the more disjunctive allegories of Dante and Spenser approach the traditional definition of allegory as they depart from the allegorical tradition. Like personification allegories, they can be traced to metastatements whose substantives are syncretic Realities, but Dante and Spenser modify that

6. See Beryl Smalley, *The Study of the Bible in the Middle Ages* (Notre Dame, Ind.: University of Notre Dame Press, 1964), p. 1.

7. Thus Spivack, *Shakespeare and the Allegory of Evil,* and Leyburn, *Satiric Allegory,* argue that personification allegory is not really allegory; see p. 18 of my Introduction.

semiotic structure in the direction of Quintilian's *inversio* and the medieval exegetes' *integumentum*. Nonetheless, their texts do not split between real and apparent meaning. Justly celebrated as the most complex of allegories, the *Divine Comedy* and *The Faerie Queene* stretch both ontological and semiotic coherence to their limits.

5 Truth in Transformation: The *Divine Comedy*

It is symptomatic of the post-Romantic distrust of allegory that the long-acknowledged masterpiece of the genre should regularly be declared not fundamentally allegorical after all. Coleridge formulates the position:

> The Divina Commedia is a system of moral, political, and theological truths, with arbitrary personal exemplifications, which are not, in my opinion, allegorical. I do not even feel convinced that the punishments in the Inferno are strictly allegorical. I rather take them to have been in Dante's mind *quasi*-allegorical, or conceived in analogy to pure allegory.[1]

Whatever "*quasi*-allegorical" may mean, Coleridge clearly intends to lift the *Divine Comedy* above a genre that he disrespects. Later critics achieve almost the same effect by conceding that the poem contains allegorical elements but insisting that they can and should be disregarded.[2] In Michele Barbi's words, "The allegory does not turn out

1. Samuel Taylor Coleridge, "Dante" (Lecture X), in *Miscellaneous Criticism*, p. 150.
2. That judgment originated with De Sanctis and Croce, according to Natalino Sapegno in "Genesis and Structure: Two Approaches to the Poetry of the 'Comedy,'" trans. P. Boyde, in *The Mind of Dante*, ed. U. Limentani (Cambridge: Cambridge University Press, 1965), pp. 1–16.

to be as fatal to the poem as certain critics imagine. . . . [T]here is
indeed an allegory present in the primitive conception of the poem;
but it is one so general, so unobtrusive, that it has by no means
impeded or cluttered the detailed composition that followed."[3] Finally, still other writers reject such a bisection of "allegory" and "poetry" but agree with Coleridge that the former term does not accurately
classify the *Divine Comedy*. A. C. Charity finds the poem fundamentally "history," with only sporadic use of true allegory; Luigi Pirandello calls Dante's procedure "an absolute reversal of the concept of
allegory"; and Etienne Gilson proclaims, "The text of Dante has
nothing in common with any *Pèlerinage de Vie Humaine, Roman de
la Rose,* or other allegorical rubbish."[4]

To some degree, the dissociation of the *Divine Comedy* from allegory has allowed our understanding of the former to progress independently of our misconception of the latter. Indeed, several of the
most powerful readings of Dante have been offered by critics with a
confused aversion to traditional allegory. For that reason Dante
scholars may feel little need to reconsider allegory per se. The student
of allegory, on the other hand, needs to correct misjudgments of the
Divine Comedy's relationship to the genre. Moreover, even in Dante
scholarship the allegory of the *Divine Comedy* is still a vexed question. A stubborn conviction remains that the poem is allegorical in
some way, its author having said as much in his letter to Can Grande.
If, as nearly everyone agrees, it also differs from other allegories, the
nature and extent of its difference are matters of dispute, and we may
suspect that a murky view of "other allegories" has hindered a resolution. Finally, reestablishing Dante's place in the allegorical tradition
can sharpen our admittedly rich understanding of his work. Contemporary Dante scholars may recoil from the suggestion that techniques
appropriate for reading personification allegory can illuminate the
Divine Comedy, but, as I have argued, those techniques are them-

3. Michele Barbi, "The Divine Comedy," from *Life of Dante,* trans. and ed. Paul
G. Ruggiers, rpt. in *Essays in Dante,* ed. Mark Musa (Bloomington: Indiana Univer-
sity Press, 1964), p. 29.
4. A. C. Charity, *Events and Their Afterlife: The Dialectics of Christian Typology
in the Bible and Dante* (Cambridge: Cambridge University Press, 1966), p. 259; Luigi
Pirandello, "The Poetry of Dante" (1929), trans. Gian Paolo Biasin, rpt. in *Dante: A
Collection of Critical Essays,* ed. John Freccero (Englewood Cliffs, N.J.: Prentice-
Hall, 1965), p. 22; Etienne Gilson, *Dante the Philosopher,* trans. David Moore (New
York: Sheed & Ward, 1949), p. 72.

selves less simplistic than we have assumed them to be. A lifting of the quarantine on personification allegory may allow for some transfer of insight.

Thus the aim of this chapter is threefold: to illuminate the confusion in twentieth-century discussions of the allegory of the *Divine Comedy,* to advance a redefinition of that allegory, and to return the definition to its proper use—a reading, necessarily partial, of the poem.

The quarantine on personification allegory was imposed by Dante scholars largely because of infelicitous comments on the *Comedy* in the name of allegorical reading. Commentators who identify allegory with translation have tried to decode the poem, with results that deserve John Demaray's scornful summary:

> . . . [T]he critic always proceeds in the belief that the outward narrative points to fictitious events devised by a mortal poet to hide various abstract ideas. Effort is then usually centered upon the quest for the concealed abstract truth of the poem, and here the critic can indulge in a certain amount of labeling: in the first canto of the *Inferno,* the dark wood can represent Error, and Virgil, Reason; later Beatrice can represent Theology, and so on throughout the poem. As the labeling continues, the abstractions can be seen to arrange themselves into a gigantic, pyramidal hierarchy with Pure Being at the summit; and the commentator, if he has the capacity, can then dedicate himself to the task of relating and explaining the total ideology of this fascinating philosophical-theological construct.[5]

Predictably, such decoding has proven not only unsatisfying but also impossible to sustain. The beginning reader discovers quite early that Virgil does not always act like Reason.

The poem's insusceptibility to translation has substantiated the idea that it is not really allegorical. Accordingly, such readers as Demaray study it almost without regard for its semiotic strategies and certainly without reference to allegory. Others, however, pursue Coleridge's suggestion that Dante created a form of metaphoric narrative related to allegory but utterly distinct from it. Two exponents

---

5. John G. Demaray, *The Invention of Dante's "Commedia"* (New Haven: Yale University Press, 1974), p. 97. Demaray attributes this approach to Goethe, Coleridge, Horace Walpole, Theophil Spoerri, Fr. P. Mandonnet, and others.

of that position, Erich Auerbach and Charles Singleton, have enriched our understanding of Dante immeasurably, giving shape to nearly all modern commentary on—and controversy about—his allegory.

Auerbach's direction appears in the English title of his early work: *Dante: Poet of the Secular World*. Insisting that Dante's characters are not personifications, Auerbach writes, "The earthly world is encompassed in the other world of the *Comedy;* true, its historical order and form are destroyed, but in favor of a more complete and final form in which the destroyed form is included." "The content of the *Comedy* is a vision," he adds; "but what is beheld in the vision is the truth as concrete reality. . . ." In a later essay Auerbach sets forth a "solid historical grounding" for his view of Dante as poet of the earthly world: the medieval "figural interpretation" of Scripture. Unlike ordinary allegorical reading, figural interpretation connects two events or persons that it depicts as equally "real and historical."[6] Though he expresses some doubt that figuralism constituted a method of writing as well as of exegesis, Auerbach argues convincingly that Dante ought to be read figurally. The Cato of the *Purgatorio*, for instance, is a figural fulfillment of the historical Cato,

> not an allegory like the characters from the *Roman de la Rose,* but a figure that has become the truth. . . . Cato of Utica stands there as a unique individual, just as Dante saw him; but he is lifted out of the tentative earthly state . . . and transposed into a state of definitive fulfillment, concerned no longer with the earthly works of civic virtue or the law, but with the *ben dell'intelletto,* the highest good, the freedom of the immortal soul in the sight of God.[7]

Any translation of Dante's concrete characters and events into abstract terms errs in treating figural writing like ordinary allegory.

Singleton reaches similar conclusions using more polemic terms and arguments. He observes, first, that although the *Inferno* opens with frankly symbolic actions, the narrator soon moves "toward a doorway of Hell that is no metaphor and toward a journey that is likewise no metaphor." Singleton does not mean that the journey has

6. Erich Auerbach, *Dante: Poet of the Secular World,* trans. Ralph Manheim [from *Dante als Dichter der irdischen Welt* (1929)] (Chicago: University of Chicago Press, 1961), pp. 90, 159; Auerbach, "Figura," pp. 71, 29.

7. Auerbach, "Figura," p. 67.

no meaning beyond itself but that it has such meaning in addition to, not in place of, its literal depiction:

> For in this poem, the embodied, the real and literal, the irreducible journey, "his" journey beyond, will time and again recall that other journey where the prologue scene placed us, our journey here. And will do this, not by inviting us to "undo" the journey there, not by permitting us to see through the event there as if it were not there, not by washing out the literal; but by a kind of recall more common in musical structure. . . .[8]

In later essays Singleton discusses another kind of "recall": the reflection by events and characters in the *Comedy* of events and figures in Scripture. The opening of the *Inferno,* for instance, evokes, through a series of allusions, the Exodus journey, which was perhaps the chief referent in the Old Testament for figural interpretation. Later passages in the *Comedy* also evoke Exodus, but in different ways, so that the poem embodies increasingly fully the archetypal journey to redemption. Like Auerbach, Singleton insists that such scriptural echoes operate not by reducing the earlier events to "mere" metaphors but by mirroring and clarifying them. Both the Scriptural echoes and the "dual" journey produce "not an allegory of 'this for that,' but an allegory of 'this *and* that,' of this sense plus that sense."[9]

Both Singleton and Auerbach find a precedent for such allegory only in the Bible. In fact, later writers have called it not allegory but typology—"an analogy between actions," traditionally "a way of regarding [sacred] history rather than texts."[10] History can be typological because God orders it providentially; its order appears in Scripture and must be discerned by the believer. "A poet," explains Singleton, "has not God's power and may not presume to write as He can. But he may *imitate* God's way of writing. He may construct a literal historical sense, . . . to be, in the make-believe of his poem, as God's literal sense is in His book. . . ." To distinguish the imitation of God's way of writing from "this-for-that" allegory, Singleton bor-

8. Charles S. Singleton, "Allegory," in *Dante Studies 1. Commedia: Elements of Structure* (Cambridge: Harvard University Press, 1954), pp. 11, 13.

9. Singleton, "In Exitu Israel de Aegypto," *Dante Studies 78 [78th Annual Report of the Dante Society of America]* (1960):1–24; and "Two Kinds of Allegory," in *Dante Studies 1*, p. 89.

10. Charity, pp. 136, 99.

rows a pair of terms from Dante's own *Convivio:* "allegory of the poets" and "allegory of the theologians." According to Singleton, the literal sense of the former is a fable invented only to carry the *sententia,* but the literal sense of the latter must be taken as real and historical.[11]

As alternatives to simpleminded allegorical decoding, Auerbach's and Singleton's approaches are compelling; they have been highly illuminating and influential. Nonetheless, Singleton's work in particular has drawn intense opposition, primarily over the way in which he describes Dante's allegory. Some scholars protest that the "allegory of the theologians" can be written only by God, that according to Aquinas only "things" can possess the four senses discerned in figural interpretation. Others dispute Singleton's reading of Dante's remarks about the "allegory of the poets" and the "allegory of the theologians"—remarks which are indeed ambiguous, particularly as they apply to the *Comedy.* Finally, a number of writers object to Singleton's comparison of Dante's literal level only to the Bible.[12] Those closely related issues have been disputed with surprising fervor, even bitterness, even though the disputants often claim to agree with one another. Accused of describing the *Divine Comedy* in terms inapplicable to any work of imaginative literature, Singleton and his followers insist that they have amply qualified their claims: Dante's

11. Singleton, "Allegory," pp. 15–16; and "The Irreducible Dove," *Comparative Literature* 9 (1957):131.

12. Robert Hollander cites Bruno Nardi as the modern initiator of the protest based on Aquinas; see Hollander, *Allegory in Dante's "Commedia,"* p. 18. Following this line of argument, David Thompson maintains that the events on which the *Comedy* is based can be read on four levels but that the text itself cannot; see Thompson, "Figure and Allegory in the *Commedia,*" *Dante Studies* 90 (1972):1–10. J. A. Scott, on the other hand, points out ("Dante's Allegory," *Romance Philology* 26 [1972–73]:573) that fourfold exegesis was rather commonly applied to secular texts, sometimes by the authors themselves. The argument might be resolved by a distinction between continuous four-*level* meaning, borne only by divinely ordered events, and four *kinds* of meaning, evident intermittently or in combination (but not in continuous parallel) in allegorical narrative. The attempt to interpret Dante's distinction between the kinds of allegory may be traced—partially—in Joseph Anthony Mazzeo, *Structure and Thought in the "Paradiso"* (Ithaca: Cornell University Press, 1958), pp. 29–37; Hollander, p. 29; Phillip Damon, "The Two Modes of Allegory in Dante's *Convivio,*" *Philological Quarterly* 40 (1961):144–49; and Scott, pp. 571–76. The objection to biblical comparison exclusively is voiced in, for instance, R. H. Green, "Dante's 'Allegory of Poets' and the Mediaeval Theory of Poetic Fiction," *Comparative Literature* 9 (1957):123; also Scott, p. 586.

writing is of course only analogous to God's; the *Comedy* merely sustains the "fiction . . . that it is not fiction."[13] But such moderate restatements usually go unheeded, probably because they can be applied to almost every narrative, particularly every allegory. Clearly Singleton claims something more for an allegory that he regards as unique. Thus his polemics defeat his disclaimers, provoking others to remind him again that the *Divine Comedy* is neither Scripture nor fact.

If Singleton and his followers are driven toward untenable claims about the ontological status of the *Divine Comedy,* the reason may be that they wish to contrast Dante's work as sharply as possible with a kind of writing that they regard as bogus. For Singleton and Robert Hollander, for instance, "in all such works [as the *Psychomachia,* the *Romance of the Rose,* and *The Faerie Queene*] the reader is made to understand that *this* is not actually happening; it serves only to represent *that*." "The literal sense ought always to be expected to yield another sense because the literal is only a fiction."[14] To oppose all such "allegory of the poets" to the *Divine Comedy* is to imply that the literal sense of the *Comedy* is something other than fiction or fable—presumably reality or truth, like the Bible's. In attempting to designate the opposite of "fictional" while staying clear of "real," Auerbach, Singleton, and kindred critics employ many ingenious synonyms: "real or possibly-real," "historical," "existential," "immediate and demanding," "actual," "irreducible," and even—suprisingly enough, for a poem about the dead—"embodied" and "incarnate."[15] Many of those terms point toward a genuine distinction between Dante and other allegorists, a distinction I will pursue below. But because of the misleading contrast with the "fiction" of all other secular allegory, such terms also revert to the insidious "real." The natural reflex of other critics is to protest that no poem is "real," especially not in the same sense as Scripture.

13. Singleton, "The Substance of Things Seen," *Dante Studies 1,* p. 62.

14. Hollander, p. 6; Singleton, "Two Kinds of Allegory," p. 90, and "Allegory," p. 13.

15. The terms are from, respectively, H. Flanders Dunbar, *Symbolism in Medieval Thought and Its Consummation in the Divine Comedy* (New Haven: Yale University Press, 1929), p. 500; Auerbach, "Figura"; Charity, p. 199; R. H. Green, p. 128; Hollander, p. 250; Singleton, "Irreducible Dove" (and other works); and Singleton, "Allegory," p. 12.

Dante's allegory cannot be described convincingly without a less distorted and distorting account of the allegorical tradition from which it departs. The "this-for-that" model that Singleton and others deplore may inform certain clumsy allegorical readings of the *Comedy*, as well as certain allegorizations of pagan writers and of Scripture, but it does not guide the writing of personification allegory. The "literal levels" of narrative allegories—their texts—are complex and untranslatable sequences of metaphor, allusion, and plain statement. Thus the distinction between other allegories and the *Comedy* is not that the former signify by means of spurious, discardable fictions while the latter signifies through a "real" or genuine narrative. Nor, to cite related suggestions, is it that Dante introduces into allegory richly imagined concrete detail and particular people; Prudentius, Jean de Meun, and Bunyan all use similar techniques. Dante's is not even the only allegory with figural meaning or with four senses. The *Psychomachia* also uses figuralism, and its narrative refers, by turns, to historical and biblical parallels, tropological meanings, and anagogical patterns.

Certain of Dante's alleged innovations in kind do differentiate him from other allegorists in degree: his details are more vivid, his particularized agents more numerous and more fully developed, his multiple senses more continuous and much more nearly simultaneous. One would like, however, to substantiate in some way the intuition of generations of readers that the *Divine Comedy* differs not just quantitatively but also structurally from other allegories, even from those that border on realism, such as *The Pilgrim's Progress*. A genuine structural distinction can in fact be found, but only in a radical revision of the usual formulation. Rather than the first allegory to make narrative surface as real as meaning, the *Divine Comedy* is perhaps the first to separate the two.

That Dante's critics should regard traditional allegory as an integument covering an ultimate meaning is understandable, for Dante makes the same identification. His sense of allegory is highly theoretical, derived not from Prudentius or Guillaume de Lorris but from patristic exegesis and rhetorical discussions. He apparently knew two versions of exegesis: the bilevel reading of secular texts (and sometimes of Scripture) in which the true meaning is assumed to be hidden under a fictitious surface, and the more sophisticated analogical reading of Scripture in which parallels are thought to be generated not by narrative but by sacred history itself ("non in verbis . . . sed in facto").[16] In both cases, explicit meaning is allegedly distinct from the allegorical sense or senses.

Before beginning the *Divine Comedy,* Dante made a remarkable attempt to incorporate the first kind of exegesis in a literary composition. His unfinished *Convivio* consists of odes provided with "literal" and "allegorical" readings that are not only different but also occasionally incompatible. In discussing the apostrophe of one poem literally, for instance, he explains why he addresses it to a woman instead of a man. Then, in his allegorical exposition, he declares that the "gentle lady" addressed here is *any* soul "noble in intellect and free in the exercise of its own proper power. . . ."[17] A similar disparity appears in the subject of the same ode, designated "literally" as a woman whom "I assert [to be] as perfect as the human essence can supremely be," but allegorically as the nonhuman Lady Philosophy (Third Treatise, VI and XI–XV). Dante never discusses the relationship of those literal and allegorical readings, except to suggest that the first is a fiction; thus his purpose in expounding the literal meaning is unclear.

The incompatibility of the two meanings has generated a controversy concerning the odes' subject which I cannot resolve, except to suggest the reason that it may be unresolvable. The *Convivio* is apparently an exercise in the kind of allegorical exegesis that treats a text as a fictional *integumentum* over a true meaning.[18] To my knowledge it is the first such exercise performed continuously by a

16. Dante refers to the two kinds of allegorical reading in the first chapter of the second treatise of the *Convivio,* though the references are confusingly conflated. Hollander discusses the patristic theory in chap. 1 of *Allegory in Dante's "Commedia";* he cites the quotation about words and fact, from Augustine, on p. 21. My distinction between the two kinds of exegesis corresponds to Singleton's between the "allegory of the poets" and the "allegory of the theologians," but I see the former as a method of reading that suppresses meaning, not a realizable model for sustained writing.

17. Dante, *Convivio,* trans. Philip H. Wicksteed (London: J. M. Dent, 1940), Third Treatise, chaps. VII and XIV.

18. *Integumentum* is from Bernard Silvestris: "The integument is a type of exposition which wraps the apprehension of truth in a fictional narrative, and thus it is also called an *involucrum,* a cover" (*Commentary on the First Six Books of Virgil's "Aeneid,"* trans. Earl G. Schreiber and Thomas E. Maresca [Lincoln: University of Nebraska Press, 1979], p. 5).

poet on his own work—the first, and one of very few. The procedure
is a peculiar one. Unlike the expositor of a received text, the poet-
expositor must work in two directions at once, creating a plausible
but false literal sense and expounding an ulterior meaning different
enough from the first for the envelope to remain intact. Such sleight-
of-hand can produce riddles or short set pieces but probably cannot
be sustained over a full-length allegorical narrative. Nonetheless, a
poet who came to the writing of allegory through the reading of
exegetical theory might well feel called upon to perform in that
way—or to convince himself and his readers that he had done so. The
result would be a work of divided intention, like the *Convivio*.

Dante might have turned from the uncompleted *Convivio* to poetry
that dealt directly with Philosophy and other ideas, in the manner of
personification allegory. Instead he persisted, and this time suc-
ceeded, in writing integumental allegory—narrative whose syncretic
agents are not immediately apprehensible. But he departed from the
Convivio in the relationship between immediate and Real referents:
no longer do the former conceal the latter as an envelope does its
contents; instead, the immediate apprehension of concretions stretches tissue-like, isomorphically and brokenly, between us and the syncretic agents and objects. The effect is less concealment than delay.

The simplest cause of the delay is that the names of many Real
referents are withheld. Traditional allegory refers directly to ideas or
exemplars that dominate the narrative semantically and are widely
recognized as universally real outside the text. Personification allegory makes such reference with abstract nouns, but even in those
allegories that forgo abstractions, the principal objects and events
usually bear names with universal meanings well established in the
Bible, liturgy, or dogma. That is not true in Dante. The angel's arrival
at the gates of Dis (*Inferno*, IX) evokes various sacred and intelligible
analogues—the Harrowing of Hell, the arrival of grace in the sinful
Christian's heart, the confrontation of paganism and Christianity, the
destruction of Hell at the Last Judgment—but names none of them.[19]

That universals and abstractions do in some sense organize the
Divine Comedy can be demonstrated in many ways. They are named
from time to time in explanations, usually those of Beatrice and

19. That fourfold reading of the passage is from Mark Musa, *Advent at the Gates:
Dante's Comedy* (Bloomington: Indiana University Press, 1974), chap. 4.

Virgil, if not in the action itself. Furthermore, the action continuously invites universalizing interpretation, if for no other reason than its setting in a divinely ordered, supernatural world. And most of the agents approach universal status: Beatrice is the "lady of virtue, through whom alone the human kind surpasses everything within the smallest circle of the heavens";[20] the embodied shades of Purgatory are also radiations of memory, intelligence, and will (*Purg.* XXV, 79–99); and in Paradise, Dante learns that "[t]hat which dies not and that which can die are nothing but the splendour of that Idea which our Sire, in Loving, begets" (*Par.* XIII, 52–54). Thus those who affix abstract labels to as many events and characters as possible are not entirely wrong; they just overshoot the mark. The syncretic Realities that shape the *Divine Comedy* act indirectly, either remaining implicit or appearing at some distance from the story itself.

Auerbach and Singleton properly insist that the story itself is no disposable surrogate for the implicit Realities. It is, rather, a different order of being: the empirical observations and recollections of the persona. The empirical perspective is unremitting here, never giving way, as in Bunyan, to allegorical omniscience. Even in the passages sometimes called personification allegory—the Beatrician pageant, the opening of the *Inferno,* and so forth—the objects seen by the persona require interpretation, being at least partially opaque to whatever Realities they manifest. If intelligibles are named directly as agents and objects in Prudentius' narrative code, in Dante's they are intermittently visible, incompletely reconstructable antecedents from which the narrative, like the sensible world, seems to have been derived.

I do not mean that Dante encodes or obfuscates his real meaning or that his real meaning consists of implicit abstractions. Indirect reference to abstractions is commonly regarded as the allegorist's means to protect truth from the unworthy and render it more valuable to those

---

20. Dante, *Inferno* II, 76–78. All citations of the *Divine Comedy* are from Dante Alighieri, *The Divine Comedy,* translated, with a commentary by Charles Singleton, Bollingen Series LXXX. Vol. 1: *Inferno.* Copyright © 1970 by Princeton University Press. Vol. 2: *Purgatorio.* Copyright © 1973 by Princeton University Press. Vol. 3: *Paradiso.* Copyright © 1975 by Princeton University Press. Except where noted, all translations are those of John D. Sinclair, *The Divine Comedy of Dante Alighieri,* 3 vols. (New York: Oxford University Press, 1939, 1946); they are reprinted by permission of the Bodley Head Ltd.

who can reach it;21 but abstract reference in personification allegory
is in fact not indirect at all, and Dante's indirections serve, paradoxically, to reveal. The subject of the *Divine Comedy*, as Dante tells Can
Grande, is not punishment, purgation, and beatitude, but the state of
souls in punishment, purgation, and beatitude; not justice, but man as
subject to justice. Some distance between immediate and ultimate
referent is the irreplaceable representation of the human relationship
to truth. Indeed, even when they are used, such terms as "justice" and
"beatitude" are themselves provisional means of knowing, intellectually powerful but far from absolute. As Virgil explains,

> Matto è chi spera che nostra ragione
> possa trascorrer la infinita via
> che tiene una sustanza in tre persone.
> State contenti, umana gente, al *quia;*
> ché, se potuto aveste veder tutto,
> mestier non era parturir Maria.

> Foolish is he who hopes that our reason can trace the infinite ways
> taken by one Substance in three Persons. Rest content, race of men,
> with the *quia;* for if you had been able to see all there was no need for
> Mary to give birth.

> [*Purg.* III, 34–39]

To postlapsarian minds, truth appears always in transformation.

Moreover, Dante's indirection should not be taken merely as a
regrettable consequence of human imperfection: in itself it releases
great semiotic energy, producing some of the richest meanings in our
literature. Much of the tenth canto of the *Inferno* seems irrelevant to
the sin of heresy; but because we sense that it ought to manifest
heresy in some way, we look more closely. What we see is not a code
but an implicit analogy, a narrative manifesting patterns that correspond to the idea of heresy in unexpected and unlimitable ways. John
Sinclair reads the heretics' fixation in tombs as a "fulfilment" of their
denial of the soul's life, and hence as a revelation of their unbelief.22
Beyond that, the long digression in which Farinata questions Dante
about Florentine politics signifies allegorically through its very form,
dramatizing the engrossment in temporal affairs which is essential to

---

21. That position is summarized in Murrin, *Veil of Allegory,* pp. 10–20.
22. See Sinclair's comment in *Divine Comedy,* I, 130.

Epicurean heresy. We note that Farinata and Cavalcante both initiate, insistently, conversations about earthly events, as if unaware of what dominates a reader's awareness—their present circumstances. Indeed, the very discomfort that we feel at the silence about the sin and its punishment should alert us to another implication: this kind of heresy is a grandly stubborn attachment to things the heretic cannot even see, a brave but absurd obliviousness of clear spiritual facts. Such generalizations must be inferred and cannot be definitely stated. For that reason, however, they can never be exhaustively formulated. We can continue to propose and refine abstract correlatives to the action, and thus to sharpen our understanding of heresy, as long as we study the canto. In maintaining a distance between image and idea, so that the text always "flies above" our ability to interpret it (*Purg.* XXXIII, 82–90), Dante draws our vision onward.

The never-completed movement toward understanding is the primary momentum of the poem. It does not impel us simply to reconstruct the text's implicit abstract antecedents. For Dante as pilgrim, as John Freccero points out, "the purpose of the entire journey is . . . to attain the vantage point of . . . the blessed, from which to perceive the figura and the coherence in life, and to bear witness to that coherence for other men."[23] He attains such perception in the *Paradiso* when he sees not just essence, but "substances and accidents and their relations" (*Par.* XXXIII, 88–89). As readers we cannot, of course, see with the "supersense" of the blessed, but the poem approximates their fusion of sight and thought by a dialectic of sensible and rational. To neglect any dimension of the text would collapse that dialectic. As in all allegory, each of the "manners of treatment"—"poetic, fictive, descriptive, digressive, and figurative; and, further, . . . definitive, analytical, probative, refutative, and exemplificative"[24]—is meaningful in form as well as in reference. Indeed, the choice of signifier becomes more than usually important in a poem centered not in the confrontations among ideas but in the discovery of meaning. The transformations of truth—the *quia*—are themselves our truth. If the *Divine Comedy* is "a gallery of modes of vision correlated to the ever expanding consciousness and awareness

23. John Freccero, "The River of Death: *Inferno* II, 108," in *The World of Dante: Six Studies in Language and Thought,* ed. Bernard Chandler and J. A. Molinaro (Toronto: University of Toronto Press, 1966), p. 27.

24. Dante, Epistola X, in *Dantis Alagherii Epistolae,* ed. Toynbee, p. 200.

of the pilgrim," we will see most clearly by watching the ways in which we see.[25]

More than any other way of writing, allegory has been discussed apart from extensive readings of the texts that exemplify it. Such an approach is defensible when allegory is regarded as a trope within a larger work, but it can be misleading, suggesting that the *Psychomachia* uses personification consistently or that every canto of the *Divine Comedy* corresponds to the Exodus story. If allegory is also a genre—narratives with syncretic agents—its study requires that we investigate large constellations and sequences of tropes. A complete reading of the *Divine Comedy* being infeasible, I intend to apply my definition of Dante's allegory in two ways: first by suggesting how it can correct imbalances in our reading of particular episodes and then by following the strategies of signification through four cantos of the *Purgatorio*.

At a minimum, a reading of the *Divine Comedy* which centers on the ways of signifying can spare us certain frustrations. Generations of commentators have earnestly tried to identify the anonymous Florentine suicide of the last part of *Inferno* XII, despite Dante's decision to leave him nameless. John Sinclair concludes that the character is "insignificant, as if to leave no glamour of greatness about suicide itself."[26] Accepting Dante's silence as significant in itself, however, we can see the anonymity as a vivid representation of the suicides' misguided attempt to annihilate personal identity—not through transcendent fulfillment, like that of the blessed, but through betrayal of the highest human capabilities. We are intended to question the anonymous suicide's identity, and we are probably intended not to find an answer save in the questioning. Another notorious consumer of scholarly energy is Beatrice's prophecy of "a five hundred, ten and five" that will be sent from God to destroy the "thievish woman and the giant who sins with her" (*Purg.* XXXIII, 40–45). After his own persuasive identification of the prophesied redeemer, R. E. Kaske discusses what is surely as important as the object of the prophecy: its form. "It is in keeping with the finality of heaven and hell," he writes,

25. Mazzeo, "Dante's Three Communities: Mediation and Order," in *World of Dante*, ed. Chandler and Molinaro, p. 69.
26. Sinclair, I, 178.

"that the 'trinity' of the *Inferno* is beheld as a static vision of completed and unchanging evil, and the Trinity of the *Paradiso* as a static
vision of perfect and unchangeable good; the *DXV* [which Beatrice
prophesies], by contrast, is not beheld, but is announced in a prophecy to be fulfilled in time."[27] Not only is the prophecy unfulfilled; it is
also highly and deliberately enigmatic, the climax of a canticle that
abounds in symbols demanding interpretation. Indeed, almost immediately after the prophecy Dante learns why Beatrice's words "fly
above [his] sight." Each "enigma forte" (*Purg.* XXXIII, 50) is an
irreplaceable representation of the world in process of redemption,
continually given signs that it must continually strive to read. The
commentators' attempts to identify the DXV and the anonymous
Florentine suicide deserve the gratitude of other readers of Dante;
those attempts are demonstrably valid responses to Dante's enigmas;
but to regard them as readings of Dante's text is to misread.

Such semiotic shortcuts are attempted even by sophisticated readers when they take Dante to be using traditional personification allegory. Singleton argues that the four stars of the first canto of the
Purgatorio are the four infused cardinal virtues; then, because Dante
says that the stars were previously seen by none but the first people,
Singleton wonders why only the first people beheld the cardinal virtues.[28] His complex answer merely displaces the question. If, as Singleton argues, these stars represent the traditional four rivers of Eden,
which also represented the four cardinal virtues, we must still ask
why the cardinal virtues vanished after the Fall. In fact, neither symbol can be simply equated with the cardinal virtues without "washing
out the literal," to use Singleton's own monitory phrase. The stars are
the cardinal virtues in one form—an eternal, static, and visible
form—and that form of the virtues is what only the first people saw.
The habit of reading allegory by translation lands Singleton in a
similar problem regarding the four nymphs in the Purgatorial pageant. Why, he asks, if the nymphs represent the "acquired cardinal
virtues" attained by virtuous pagans, do they not continuously escort
Virgil? If the nymphs were indeed interchangeable with the acquired
virtues, they would need, one hopes, to be in a great many places at

27. R. E. Kaske, "Dante's *DXV*," in *Dante*, ed. Freccero, p. 140.
28. Singleton, "Rivers, Nymphs, and Stars," in *Dante Studies 2. Journey to Beatrice* (Cambridge: Harvard University Press, 1958), pp. 159–65.

once. But their form as nymphs—as autonomous, anthropomorphic products of both pagan and Christian art—is as much Dante's meaning as is the phrase "acquired cardinal virtues." The acquired virtues appear in that form here, and not elsewhere, because here Dante's vision is freed from the obscurity of sin but not yet transhumanized.

The focus on modes of signifying can also enrich our readings of passages that are already well understood. The opening of the *Inferno* differs in allegorical method from the rest of the poem, as many readers have noted, but not, as is sometimes assumed, in being personification allegory instead of figural allegory. Granted, the dark wood, the mountains, the beasts, and the lake resemble elements in traditional allegory in some ways. As Singleton brilliantly demonstrates, for instance, the internal "lake of the heart" is also a "perilous water" in which the entire body struggles[29]—a conflation of inner and outer space much like Prudentius' syncretic settings. Also like Prudentian allegory is the fusion of general and particular experience in the first tercet; and we sense of course that the three beasts that appear supernaturally and arouse universal feelings represent sins or vices. Indeed, all the rhetorical signs normally associated with allegorical agents are present—all, that is, except the names. The persona finds himself in a nightmare realm midway between familiar, particular experience and allegorical order, a realm where events call out for but do not receive such labels as "lust," "pride," and "covetousness." If the sunlit hill toward which he struggles prefigures Purgatory, it is a nameless prefiguration, sought by the will that has almost lost the good of intellect.

Directly opposite semiotically to the *Inferno*'s opening sequence is its eleventh canto, which Sinclair calls "little more than a verbal diagram."[30] Before leaving the first of Hell's three great divisions, Virgil and Dante pause behind a tomb to adjust to the stench of the "profound abyss." As they wait, Virgil explains to Dante the physical arrangement of Hell. That the lengthy explanation takes place here rather than at the journey's outset may manifest Dante's sophistication about narrative exposition, but it may also bear a more positive meaning. For the pilgrim, Hell thus far has been a series of powerful impressions with only brief and specific explanations. Assaulted by

29. Singleton, "Allegory," pp. 11–12.
30. Sinclair, I, 152.

cries and strange sights, drawn by familiar shades into subjective responses, he has encountered evil but has not generally understood it. Worse, he has seen his confident, rational guide temporarily impotent against the monstrous guards of Dis. In such a context, an abstract, comprehensive "verbal diagram" of evil is no mere functional digression; it shelters the traveler from the stench of the abyss far more effectively than does Anastasius' tomb. Small wonder that Dante exclaims in gratitude, "O Sun that healest all troubled sight" (XI, 91), and that the canto ends in calm resolution. In the broadest sense the plain exposition in the eleventh canto advances the poem's action—the soul's journey through Hell—as much as do the accounts of strenuous physical travel.

As might be expected, the great climactic moments of the poem are more complex semiotically. In his powerful reading of the pageant that closes the *Purgatorio,* Singleton points to a detailed figural analogy of Beatrice with Christ.[31] The figures in the pageant are indeed clearly symbolic—unnatural, sometimes grotesque, carrying emblems and attended with supernatural signs. John Sinclair alleges in fact that "most [readers] will agree that in some of [this] imagery there is more of inventiveness than imagination."[32] That is a key to the passage: meaning is borne, deliberately but opaquely, to a receptive but not transhumanized perceiver. Understandably, few readers arrive independently at a figural reading as extensive as Singleton's, but we grope toward some such reading. The pageant is a masque, not a vision, conveying both the unmistakable presence of divine meaning and its awesome distance from our grasp.

The pageantry of the third canticle, on the other hand, is neither static nor distant from the viewer, but changes form, encircles the pilgrim, interchanges dialogue with him, and eventually transforms him along with itself. In his fine analysis of the pilgrim's vision at the end of the *Paradiso,* Daniel M. Murtaugh points to a semiotic shift that startles both pilgrim and reader: in the twenty-eighth canto, the universe is inverted. Having spent his entire journey passing through concentric circles widening out from Earth, Dante sees the Empyrean as a tiny point of indescribably brilliant light surrounded by nine spheres. Murtaugh comments, "Beatrice's solution of the problem—

---

31. Singleton, "The Pattern at the Center," in *Dante Studies 1,* pp. 45–60.
32. Sinclair, II, 387.

a proportion between dimension in the 'essemplo' and velocity in the 'essemplare'—really has the effect of reducing both images to the same convertible status as signs, with their final reality not in themselves, but in what they refer to." In the earlier pageant, unnatural symbols pointed to a tremendous meaning beyond nature; here the natural universe itself bears "the validity of a significant fiction."[33]

Then, in rendering the Empyrean, all the poem's means of signifying blend and interchange as art reaches its limit (*Par.* XXX, 31–34). Light, which is love, appears as a river, which becomes flowers, and then, when drunk by the eyes, reforms as a circle and a rose, the latter in turn becoming "a garden, a city, a kingdom, an empire."[34] Abstractions and exposition merge with visual imagery, and imagery itself crosses the boundaries between inner and outer reality, as between the normally separate senses.[35] As Murtaugh writes, "The scene responds directly to the pilgrim's power to see it, shifting kaleidoscopically like a brilliant series of metaphors in the hands of a confident poet. External reality has become as plastic as language itself, even as the poet's language concedes the impossibility of recovering that reality."[36] More and more quickly the modes of signifying shift, as the pilgrim's sight is strengthened, until two of the most basic modes—symbolic abstraction and the human image—appear as one, rendering, in Singleton's words, "the flesh there in the word and the word there in the flesh, two natures in one, fused in a vision that is irreducible to either."[37] The pilgrim's effort to understand the fusion fails, so that this final means of signifying does not, in one sense, signify at all. But meaning is not conveyed here merely by the inexpressibility topos. Although Dante cannot reduce the paradox to terms other than its own, his desire to understand is resolved more fully than it could be by understanding alone. By taking on its form, he becomes one with what he seeks to know:

33. Daniel M. Murtaugh, " 'Figurando il paradiso': The Signs That Render Dante's Heaven," *PMLA* 90 (1975):281.

34. Sinclair, III, 477.

35. In "Synaesthesia in the *Divine Comedy*," *Dante Studies* 88 (1970):1–16, Glauco Cambon points out the uses of synaesthesia at the beginning of the *Inferno* and the end of the *Paradiso;* that is one of several links between the clearly correspondent but radically different passages.

36. Murtaugh, p. 282.

37. Singleton, "The Irreducible Vision," in *Illuminated Manuscripts of the Divine Comedy,* ed. Peter Brieger, Millard Meiss, and Charles S. Singleton, 2 vols. (Princeton: Princeton University Press, 1969), I, 29.

> ma già volgeva il mio disio e 'l *velle,*
> sì come rota ch'igualmente è mossa,
> l'amor che move il sole e l'altre stelle.

But now my desire and will, like a wheel that spins with even motion,
were resolved by the Love that moves the sun and the other stars.

[*Par.* XXXIII, 143–45]

The poem ends, in fact, not in vision but in a state of being, an equilibrium of individual and essence which provides a consummation for integumental allegory.

The approach to that condition occupies the rest of the *Divine Comedy,* most noticeably the second canticle. "The whole of Purgatory," writes Joseph Anthony Mazzeo, "is an attempt on the part of the pilgrims to reconstitute the *imago,* the specifically human reflection of the Deity through the continual self-confrontations and corrections of the errant will."[38] The attempt is a semiotic process: the inhabitants of Purgatory—including the pilgrim—read signs of their imperfection and transform themselves into signs of redemption. Thus the *Purgatorio* foregrounds the movement toward understanding which structures the *Divine Comedy*. A reading of four cantos from the *Purgatorio* cannot indicate the full range of Dante's allegory, but it can demonstrate that the sequence of modes of signifying generates much of the poem's meaning.

The first quarter of the *Purgatorio* appears somewhat formless. We do not enter Purgatory itself until the ninth canto; before that, we follow Dante and Virgil through regions with no named divisions, encountering shades with no fixed places (*Purg.* VII, 40). The landscape's physical features are clear, but unlike Hell or Purgatory proper, the ante-Purgatory is not divided by moral or intellectual categories. It is not even called the "ante-Purgatory," so that anyone without editorial notes and charts would have to wait until the seventh canto to learn that this unordered place is not Purgatory itself. Like the shades there, the pilgrim travels with no clear sense of location or progression.

The end of the eighth canto and the beginning of the ninth constitute one of those lyric passages that seemed to nineteenth-century

---

38. Joseph Anthony Mazzeo, *Medieval Cultural Tradition in Dante's "Comedy"* (Ithaca: Cornell University Press, 1960), p. 42.

readers gratifyingly free from allegorical superstructure. The pilgrim
is immobilized by darkness in a beautiful valley whose occupants,
once obsessed with earthly responsibilities, now await their admission into Purgatory. The mood is quiet suspense, "a gentle melancholy and longing."[39] At the beginning of the ninth canto, several
mythic allusions, designations of the time at which Dante falls asleep,
deepen the mood with beautiful but chilling images: the mistress of
old Tithonus whitens on her balcony, her forehead shining with gems
in the form of the "cold beast that strikes men with its tail" (IX, 5–6),
and dawn approaches, "the hour near morning when the swallow
begins her plaintive songs, in remembrance, perhaps, of her ancient
woes" (IX, 13–15). In the meantime, the pilgrim, "who had with me
something of Adam, lay down, overcome with sleep" (IX, 10–11).

We need not discount the haunting images to see in the passage
significance that is in part conceptual. Discussing a section of the
Inferno, Singleton calls the text a "magnetic field within which all
particles bear a charge of attraction, as it were, to the electrifying and
controlling idea."[40] His formulation suggests both the strength and
the unfixability of the abstract correlatives to Dante's text. Here the
controlling idea is suggested but not limited by "di quel d'Adamo." It
subsumes not only sin but also ancient myths, the coldly brilliant
constellations, the endless arisings of Tithonus' mistress, and the processions of the hours—the long recurrences of human time. It includes the melancholy beauty of the swallow's song and the natural
pull of sleep, and it recalls the nostalgia for an earthly home at the
beginning of Canto VIII. A brief statement of the idea is that the earth
is old and time is unredeemed, but they hold us still. Clearly, such an
idea is no formula, but something approximated, suggested, present
only dimly to pilgrim and reader. By its bittersweet lyrical vagueness,
as well as by its content, it defines the untormented discontent of the
ante-Purgatory.

A variation on the same magnetic idea shapes Dante's dream. At
the hour when the swallow seems to remember her *primi guai,* and
the spirit, "more a pilgrim from the flesh, . . . is in its visions almost
prophetic" (IX, 16–18), he dreams that he is caught up by an eagle.
Commentary has emphasized the dream's prophetic associations with

39. Sinclair, II, 117.
40. Singleton, "Irreducible Vision," p. 18.
41. See Auerbach, "Figurative Texts Illustrating Certain Passages of Dante's *Commedia,*" *Speculum* 21 (1946):475–76.

imperial power, baptismal regeneration, and Christ,[41] but equally significant is its form, which depends, as Glyn Norton points out, "upon the psychic state [of the pilgrim]—a state of tension and anxious preoccupation."[42] The eagle of the dream appears as Jove, and like Jove it prophesies Christian truth only obscurely. Thus the dream reveals the pilgrim's inability fully to see the vision to which he aspires. He associates his ascent with Ganymede's sudden removal by a mysterious bird "terrible as lightning" (IX, 29) from everything familiar to a fiery realm in which both were burned. Attached to the unredeemed earth, Dante dreams of apotheosis as violence and danger. He wakes apparently still caught in old mythic patterns, feeling the bewilderment and fear of Achilles after an ultimately futile escape (IX, 34–42).

He opens his eyes, however, not to confusion and death but to his "comfort," Virgil, to a clear present time, and to a miraculous fulfillment of his dream (IX, 43–45). Not a rapacious Jove but a benevolent St. Lucy has caught him up, into sunlight and consolation, not fiery destruction. The patterns of myth are broken by the action of grace. Moreover, the fulfillment occurs not after but during the dream, suggesting that the myths and the dream were the pilgrim's dim perception of what was happening to him. Virgil provides a much clearer version of the same reality (IX, 49–57), a reality designatable as "apotheosis" but defined only by its various manifestations in the text. The distance between the frightening dream and the lucid explanation measures the distance between unredeemed and redeemed humanity, the one rooted in mortality, the other raised in love to the possibility of purgation.

Now the indefiniteness of ante-Purgatory gives way to emphatic identifications:

> Tu se' omai al purgatorio giunto:
>   vedi là il balzo che 'l chiude dintorno;
>   vedi l'entrata là 've par digiunto.

Now thou art come to Purgatory. See there the rampart that encloses it about; see the entrance there, where it appears cleft.

[*Purg.* IX, 49–51]

---

42. Glyn P. Norton, "Retrospection and Figuration in the Dreams of *Purgatorio*," *Italica* 47 (1970):363. I have changed Norton's "psychic state of the poet" to "psychic state [of the pilgrim]," because my practice has been to reserve "poet" for Dante as author.

The experience that Dante's dream had distorted is also explained; as a result,

> A guisa d'uom che 'n dubbio si raccerta
> e che muta in conforto sua paura,
>   poi che la verità li è discoperta,
> mi cambia' io. . . .

Like one who in doubt is reassured and whose fear is turned to confidence when the truth is revealed to him, so I was changed.

[*Purg.* IX, 64–67]

The dreams of the flesh and the poet's mythic similes give way to didactic clarity, a gift of grace.

In the first part of the ninth canto the connection between themes and modes of narration has been powerful but implicit. Now the narrator calls our attention to the connection:

> Lettor, tu vedi ben com'io innalzo
> la mia matera, e però con più arte
> non ti maravigliar s'io la rincalzo.

Thou seest well, reader, that I rise to a higher theme; do not wonder, therefore, if I sustain it with greater art.

[*Purg.* IX, 70–72]

If the aside seems somewhat disruptive, we can take that as its purpose: to prepare us to see the text as having been devised to carry thematic meaning. Throughout the next several cantos the landscape, the imagery, and even the dialogue will repeatedly announce themselves as vehicles for meaning.

In place of the natural landscape and characters of the ante-Purgatory, Virgil and Dante now encounter a locked gate, a warden with a shining sword and keys, and three steps of startling colors and materials. The materials are clearly sacramental, drawn from liturgy and scriptural metaphor, but they use the imagery not of mystical vision but of human fabrication. As Singleton points out, in the *Paradiso* St. Peter himself will not appear with a pair of keys[43]—nor would we expect him to. Purgatory is in fact closer to a picture-book heaven than is Paradise. Those who praise the realistic surface of the *Comedy* cannot be thinking of such settings, or of such events as the

---

43. Singleton, Commentary on *Purg.* IX, 117, in *Divine Comedy.*

marking of seven *P*s with a sword on Dante's forehead (IX, 112–14). Francis Fergusson calls the entire last half of the ninth canto a "set-piece" that "seems to employ an arbitrary sign language"; he adds,

> This impression, of course, is wrong, for Dante's symbols refer, not to abstract concepts, but to other objective realities, and hence there is no single key to their elucidation; one discovers that as soon as one tries, with the help of the commentators, to make a complete interpretation of this passage. But the *effect* of a sign-language which, like traffic-signals, may be blankly obeyed without full understanding or assent, is certainly intended here.[44]

Fergusson captures precisely the meaning of the method of signifying here, except that he errs in seeing the passage as typical of "Dante's symbols." This imagery is peculiarly signal-like—obviously portentous, unusually cryptic, and strongly directive.

Thus the pilgrim must indeed obey without fully understanding. He cannot bear to scrutinize the warder's face and sword, but he must indicate through a ritual of submission his obedience to their power. In climbing the white, purple, and porphyry steps, he is not magically undergoing the three elements of penance, as many commentators suggest, but accepting the need for procedures whose meaning he can read only dimly.[45] Throughout the scene, details heavy with enigmatic meaning are recorded in unquestioning parataxis:

> Cenere, o terra che secca si cavi,
>   d'un color fora col suo vestimento;
>   e di sotto da quel trasse due chiavi.

44. Francis Fergusson, *Dante's Drama of the Mind: A Modern Reading of the "Purgatorio"* (Princeton: Princeton University Press, 1953), p. 38.

45. The steps are commonly identified as contrition, confession, and satisfaction. Grandgent proposes instead that they "stand for the three stages in the career of man which lead up to the founding of the church: original innocence, sin, and atonement" (C. H. Grandgent, ed., *La Divina Commedia di Dante Alighieri*, rev. ed. [Boston: D. C. Heath, 1933], p. 399). His reason for objecting to the traditional reading is that the souls who ascend here must already have undergone contrition, confession, and satisfaction, while Dante is not ready to receive the sacrament of penance. But a similar objection could be raised to Grandgent's own reading: neither Dante nor the purgatorial souls are here reenacting the preecclesiastical career of mankind. The best solution is to avoid limiting the steps to one set of correlatives and to acknowledge that whoever ascends them is not interacting directly with particular referents but enacting a ritual in which those referents are awesomely evoked.

> L'una era d'oro e l'altra era d'argento;
> pria con la bianca e poscia con la gialla
> fece a la porta sì, ch'i' fu' contento.

Ashes, or earth that is dug dry, would be of one colour with his vesture and from beneath it he drew two keys, the one of gold and the other of silver, and he applied first the white and then the yellow to the door so that I was satisfied.

[*Purg.* IX, 115–20]

Like the dual representation of the flight to Purgatory, the symbols indicate a distance between divine meaning and human perception. But unlike the miraculous ascent, the entrance requires the soul's absolute, waking submission to a spiritual order beyond its full comprehension: "'Intrate; ma facciovi accorti / che di fuor torna chi 'n dietro si guata'" ("'Enter; but I bid you know that he that looks back returns outside'" [IX, 131–32]). Also unlike the first half of the canto, this text and its referents obviously exist "for the sake of signifying"—as devices for guidance.[46] The seven *P*s traced in Dante's forehead are not simply wounds or sins but signs, God-given signs that externalize and order the potentially infinite continuum of human inadequacy. The terrible *primi guai* of the canto's opening submits to the rational categorization of the sacramental order, and it can therefore be purged.

The end of the ninth canto reconstructs the consciousness of the pilgrim preparing to enter that redeeming but still mysterious order. Two similes, one from classical literature and the other from ecclesiastical experience, render the opening of the purgatorial gates and the sounds that the pilgrim hears beyond them:

> E quando fuor ne' cardini distorti
> li spigoli di quella regge sacra,
> che di metallo son sonanti e forti,
> non rugghiò sì né si mostrò sì acra
> Tarpëa, come tolto le fu il buono
> Metello, per che poi rimase macra.

And when the pivots of that sacred portal, which were of heavy and resounding metal, turned on the hinges, the Tarpeian roared not so

---

46. The phrase is used by Aquinas in explaining why Eden still exists; it is cited by Singleton in "A Lament for Eden," in *Dante Studies* 2, p. 143.

loud nor showed itself so stubborn when the good Metellus was taken from it so that then it was left bare.

[*Purg.* IX, 133–38]

> Tale imagine a punto mi rendea
> ciò ch'io udiva, qual prender si suole
> quando a cantar con organi si stea;
> ch'or sì or no s'intendon le parole.

What I heard gave me the same impression we sometimes get when people are singing with an organ and the words are now distinguished, now lost.

[*Purg.* IX, 142–45]

That these are similes, in contrast with the metaphors that opened the canto, conveys the pilgrim's recognition that what he now witnesses cannot be fully comprehended in familiar terms. The allusions themselves make only modest claims to clarify their referents: the first denies its adequacy and the second merely defines indistinguishability. Aware that what lies ahead surpasses the terms of earthly experience, yet able at least to articulate its strangeness, the pilgrim is ready to read the complex text that will teach him a new vocabulary.

Thereupon he passes through the gates into a world charged with moral significance. When the narrator says at the beginning of Canto X that the soul's perverse love makes "the crooked way seem straight" (X, 3), he uses *via* generally and metaphorically; but the pilgrim shortly travels a path "che si moveva e d'una e d'altra parte, / sì come l'onda che fugge e s'appressa" ("which kept bending one way and the other like a wave that comes and goes" [X, 8–9]). We naturally associate his path with the metaphoric *via* and see it in converse moral terms: seeming crooked, it is the "true way." Then the narrator identifies the path he has just left with another moral metaphor from Scripture, calling it "that needle's eye" (X, 16). In such a semiotic atmosphere, other descriptions acquire moral overtones as well: "quando fummo liberi e aperti / sù"; "ïo stancato e amendue incerti / di nostra via"; "un piano / solingo più che strade per diserti" ("when we were free and out in the open above"; "I weary and both uncertain of our way"; "a level place more solitary than a desert track" [X, 17–18, 19–20, 20–21]). The setting is almost but not quite like Bunyan's literalized metaphors, the difference being that this landscape and these events generate scriptural and moral meanings pervasively but indirectly, through the mind of the traveler-cum-reader.

Implicit significance is concentrated and graduated on the terraces of Purgatory, each of them a sequence of texts that require different kinds of reading. The first sequence begins in the tenth canto with one of the most strikingly didactic sights in the *Comedy:* lifelike exemplificatory figures carved in marble on the bank of the lowest terrace. To say merely that they illustrate humility is to decline the opportunity they provide for redefining the concept. Auerbach suggests that the self-humiliation of David, the second scene on the terrace, "offered a welcome opportunity for developing the basic Christian antithesis *humilitas-sublimitas. . . .*"[47] That antithesis is, in fact, the controlling idea for all of the carvings: the angel graciously condescending to Mary, and Mary humbling herself to turn the key to "l'alto amor" (X, 42); David becoming "both more and less than king" (X, 66); the emperor Trajan submitting, in his moment of conquest, to a widow's plea, thereby embracing the highest principles (X, 76–93). And the antithesis inheres not merely in the stories that the figures tell but also in the visible conjunction of lowly bearing with monumental dignity.

Those meanings emerge from what seems to be merely a physical description of the figures, offered by a pilgrim who does not even know yet that this is the place where pride is purged. Conceptual meaning emerges naturally, almost effortlessly, from beautiful sensuous particulars. Several scholars link the *Purgatorio* with *visio spiritualis,* the sensory imagination, as opposed to Augustine's other modes of knowing heaven: *visio corporalis,* "knowledge through the senses of material objects," and *visio intellectualis,* "intuition of spiritual substances."[48] But the revelation here is rather a perfected *visio corporalis,* anticipating in its fullness the direct knowledge in Paradise but resembling also the semiosis of earth. Although these objects are marble statues, they are also historical figures that seem alive: parts of

47. Auerbach, "Figurative Texts," p. 477.
48. The distinction among *visio corporalis, visio spiritualis,* and *visio intellectualis,* formulated by Augustine, is explained by Marguerite Mills Chiarenza in "The Imageless Vision and Dante's *Paradiso,*" *Dante Studies* 90 (1972):77. For the application of the classification to Dante's three cantiche, she cites Francis X. Newman, "St. Augustine's Three Visions and the Structure of the *Commedia,*" *MLN* 82 (1967):56–78.

them move and seem to speak and to burn incense, dividing sight from hearing and again from smell in judging whether or not they actually live (X, 55–63). The controlling idea that they suggest is not just humility, not even the more precise *humilitas-sublimitas* antithesis, but the possibility that the human creature may manifest ideal virtue. Produced by the *fabbro* whose works are not normally called sculptures, the exemplificatory figures could put both Polycletus and nature to shame (X, 32–33) because they are fully natural art and fully artful nature. Their "visible speech" (X, 95) is a didactic paradigm for the revelations that might arise continuously from history if God's creatures manifested God's art.

The carvings prepare us for a more painful kind of human imagery. The canto ends with a vivid simile for the penitents of the first terrace, an image that makes them, too, into stone carvings:

> Come per sostentar solaio o tetto,
>   per mensola talvolta una figura
> si vede giugner le ginocchia al petto,
> la qual fa del non ver vera rancura
>   nascere 'n chi la vede; così fatti
> vid' io color, quando puosi ben cura.
> Vero è che più e meno eran contratti
>   secondo ch'avien più e meno a dosso;
> e qual più pazïenza avea ne li atti,
>   piangendo parea dicer: "Più non posso."

As, for corbel to support ceiling or roof, a figure is sometimes seen joining the knees to the breast which begets from its unreality real distress in him that sees it, in such a posture I saw these when I looked carefully. They were indeed bent down more and less as they had more and less on their back, and he that had most patience in his looks seemed by his weeping to say: "I can no more."
[*Purg.* X, 130–39]

Kenneth Atchity compares the simile with God's art, in that both creations bear meaning.[49] His point may be pushed one more step: the narrator's simile imitates the divine "art" not only of the carvings but also of the penitential figures here. The torments of Purgatory are

49. Kenneth J. Atchity, "Dante's *Purgatorio:* The Poem Reveals Itself," in *Italian Literature: Roots and Branches,* ed. Giose Rimanelli and Kenneth John Atchity (New Haven: Yale University Press, 1976), pp. 94–95.

commonly understood as retribution: heavy stones punish the proud by reversing their self-exaltation in life. Dante does refer to penance as the paying of a debt (X, 108, and elsewhere); but retribution and repayment are terms of earthly justice, of the Old Law instead of the New. The first purged soul whom Dante meets will suggest that the penances are not imposed but chosen and are synonymous with the sins being purged (XXI, 58–66). As a shade on the fifth terrace will explain, "What avarice does is here declared for the purging of the converted souls" (XIX, 115–16). Here, pride appears as a painful encumbrance. The penances too constitute visible speech: a language in which the sinful souls can make themselves signs of the truth about themselves.

Properly perceived, the penances thus point, like the carvings on the bank, to the great "electrifying idea" of the first terrace, the paradox of elevation and abasement. In its broadest terms—the inversions of superficial perception which characterize sound spiritual sight—the paradox is one of the most powerful controlling ideas of the *Divine Comedy*. But it can only be inferred here, and only in limited form. Like the penitents' transformations of themselves into truthful texts, the reader's comprehension of what lies on the flat plain of the first terrace requires deliberate effort.

When Virgil turns the pilgrim's gaze away from the carvings on the bank (X, 97–102), he interrupts the contemplation of perfected visible speech in favor of a less coherent vision. At that point the poet similarly fragments our apprehension. He shifts abruptly from narration to a direct warning about the effect on us of something he has not yet mentioned:

> Non vo' però, lettor, che tu ti smaghi
> di buon proponimento per udire
> come Dio vuol che 'l debito si paghi.
> Non attender la forma del martìre:
> pensa la succession; pensa ch'al peggio
> oltre la gran sentenza non può ire.

But I would not have thee, reader, fall away from good resolve for hearing how God wills that the debt be paid; do not dwell on the form of the torment, think of what follows, think that at worst it cannot go beyond the great Judgement.

[*Purg.* X, 106–11]

In advising us to balance subjective reactions with understanding, the warning anticipates tension between those responses and elicits the very horror that understanding is supposed to check. A second apostrophe fragments apprehension in a slightly different way—by equivocating about the speaker's referent and hence about our relationship with the Purgatorial souls:

> O superbi cristian, miseri lassi,
>   che, de la vista de la mente infermi,
>   fidanza avete ne' retrosi passi,
> non v'accorgete voi che noi siam vermi
>   nati a formar l'angelica farfalla,
>   che vola a la giustizia sanza schermi?
> Di che l'animo vostro in alto galla,
>   poi siete quasi antomata in difetto,
>   sì come vermo in cui formazion falla?

O vainglorious Christians, weary wretches who are sick in the mind's vision and put your trust in backward steps, do you not perceive that we are worms born to form the angelic butterfly that soars to judgment without defense? Why does your mind float so high, since you are as it were imperfect insects, like the worm that is undeveloped?

[*Purg.* X, 121–29]

"Superbi cristian" seems initially to call on the proud still living, but it must also refer to the souls of this terrace, "miseri lassi" who, if they do not walk backward, can progress only with painful slowness. In fact it is both, and the apparent shift in referent challenges us to merge the two. Like the penitents, we are not perfected in spiritual sight. We must struggle to see that they are ourselves, that their pain is beneficial, that our acceptance of their burden can raise us. So to unify this divided text is to heal the sick mental vision that mistakes *superbia* for elevation.

For both penitents and readers, the next canto seems something of a respite. Most of it consists not of supernatural signs but of observation and conversation, the relatively formless processes of mundane life. But the relaxation merely provides a new challenge to self-transforming souls. Through the familiar discourse of the shades and the pilgrim, we continue to seek, as do they, the disciplining ideas of the first terrace.

The eleventh canto opens with a slow and solemn recitation: "O

Padre nostro, che ne' cieli stai . . ." The prayer proceeds through
eight tercets before we learn that it is spoken by the penitents who
seemed merely to be groaning in agony when the tenth canto ended.
As Singleton notes, the first seven tercets correspond to the seven
clauses of the biblical prayer and to the seven terraces of Purgatory.[50]
In praying, the souls submerge their private pain in discipline and
shape their burden in conformity with sacred ritual. Thus Dante's
"scholastic and homiletic elaboration" of the "sublime simplicity of
the Lord's Prayer" is not a "singular lapse," as Sinclair suggests, but a
conspicuous channeling of deformity into order.[51] The prayer's firm
clarity, like the penitents' relentlessly regular circling of the terrace,
purges "the fog of the world" (XI, 30).

The shades whom Dante meets also order their conversations
homiletically. Omberto Aldobrandesco begins his long speech by
promising, in answer to Virgil's question, to lead the travelers to a
passage up the mountain. He spends the rest of the speech aiding their
ascent in a different way—by exposing the sin that keeps him where
he is. He makes of himself a case study, naming for the first time the
sin of the first terrace:

> "L'antico sangue e l'opere leggiadre
> d'i miei maggior mi fer sì arrogante,
> che, non pensando a la comune madre,
> ogn' uomo ebbi in despetto tanto avante,
> ch'io ne mori', come i Sanesi sanno,
> e sallo in Campagnatico ogne fante.
> Io sono Omberto; e non pur a me danno
> superbia fa, ché tutti miei consorti
> ha ella tratti seco nel malanno.
> E qui convien ch'io questo peso porti
> per lei, tanto che a Dio si sodisfaccia,
> poi ch'io nol fe' tra ' vivi, qui tra ' morti."

"The ancient blood and gallant deeds of my ancestors made me so
arrogant that, forgetful of our common mother, I carried my scorn of
every man so far that I died for it,—how, the Sienese know and every
child in Campagnatico. I am Omberto, and not on me alone has pride
wrought ill but all my kinsfolk it has dragged with it into calamity,

50. Singleton, note to *Purg.* XI, 1–21, in *Divine Comedy.*
51. Sinclair, II, 151.

and here I must bear this load for it until God be satisfied, here
among the dead since I did it not among the living."
[*Purg.* XI, 61–72]

As the torments instruct the shades, the shades instruct themselves
and others. In Purgatory the human exemplifications of sin are not
exactly concrete examples: we know them less through memorable
description or dialogue than through their discourses. They differ in
that respect from the souls in the *Inferno,* who primarily dramatize
sins, having forfeited the ability to understand them.

But Omberto's discourse is not merely a simple statement of new-
found humility. While he understands and laments his pride, he
would like also to move Dante to pity his burden. Confident that his
notoriety obviates an account of his death, he shows a rueful pride in
his family name even while conceding that the arrogance it aroused in
life was foolish and destructive (XI, 52–57). Omberto wills humility,
"but the desire consents not which the Divine Justice, against the will,
sets to the torment as it was once set to the sin" (XXI, 64–66). His
explicit statements reveal his sound will; the poet's characterization
of him betrays his still-imperfect desire; and the two modes of signifying together delineate a soul in transformation.

The second shade who converses with Dante speaks most of the
second half of the canto. Like Omberto, Oderisi da Gubbio makes of
himself an example:

> "Ben non sare' io stato sì cortese
>   mentre ch'io vissi, per lo gran disio
>   de l'eccellenza ove mio core intese.
> Di tal superbia qui si paga il fio. . . ."

"Truly, I should not have been so courteous while I lived, for the
great desire to excel on which my heart was set; for such pride we
here pay the fee. . . ."
[*Purg.* XI, 85–88]

He seems more nearly perfected in humility than does Omberto, for
he answers Dante's flattery with an immediate and apparently sincere
disclaimer (XI, 81–83) and speaks very little of himself. Mostly he
decries human pride:

"Oh vana gloria de l'umane posse!
    com' poco verde in su la cima dura,
    se non è giunta da l'etati grosse!"

"Oh empty glory of human powers, how briefly lasts the green on its
top, unless it is followed by an age of dulness!"

[*Purg.* XI, 91–93]

"Non è il mondan romore altro ch'un fiato
    di vento, ch'or vien quinci e or vien quindi,
    e muta nome perché muta lato.
Che voce avrai tu più, se vecchia scindi
    da te la carne, che se fossi morto
    anzi che tu lasciassi il 'pappo' e 'l 'dindi,'
pria che passin mill' anni? ch'è più corto
    spazio a l'etterno, ch'un muover di ciglia
    al cerchio che più tardi in cielo è torto."

"The world's noise is but a breath of wind which comes now this way
and now that and changes name because it changes quarter. What
more fame shalt thou have if thou put off thy flesh when it is old than
if thou hadst died before giving up *pappo* and *dindi,* when a thousand
years are past, which is a shorter space to eternity than the twinkling
of an eye to the slowest-turning circle in the heavens?"

[*Purg.* XI, 100–108]

"La vostra nominanza è color d'erba,
    che viene e va, e quei la discolora
    per cui ella esce de la terra acerba."

"Your repute is as the hue of grass, which comes and goes, and he
discolors it through whom it springs green from the ground."[52]

[*Purg.* XI, 115–17]

Heartfelt as they are, however, those speeches have only to be compared with the images of humility carved in the bank to reveal
Oderisi's imperfection as a signifier of virtue. He elegizes earthly fame
even as he denounces it. Deliberate intention weighs more heavily
than inadvertent motives in determining the soul's destiny, but the
latter still prevents the will from rising (cf. XXI, 58–66). Because of
the penitent souls' division between will and desire, Dante's represen-

52. Trans. Singleton.

tation of Oderisi must be disunified: homiletic content is not reinforced but complicated by mood and tone.

Despite its semiotic complexity—rather, because of it—Oderisi's
monologue is moving. It is particularly poignant because Oderisi, an
artist, recognizes the pilgrim and talks with him about contemporary
Italian poets, including an unnamed one who is probably Dante himself. Such manifestly poetic passages, resonant with Dante's own lyric
voice and his own artistic concerns, always invoke a personal and
aesthetic frame of reference that seems to override the allegorical one.
But of course it does not. We cannot forget where this discussion of
poetry occurs and what judgement has been rendered on the absolute
devotion to art, and Dante's alliance with poets who sinned in that
way must be discomforting for his fellow travelers. Moreover, he
exacerbates that discomfort here by placing in Oderisi's mouth a
prophecy that a living poet will surpass the two Guidos (XI, 94–99):
even as the pilgrim hears artistic fame denounced, the poet apparently
stakes his claim to it. The implicit boast is incongruous—and ad-
visedly so. Humbly acknowledging the proud ambitions still har-
bored by the poet, the prophecy recalls the characterization of Omberto and Oderisi as souls intermediate in virtue. At the same time it
reveals the truth about pride, as a text for the elevation of intermediate souls. The reader who has romanticized Oderisi's attack on fame
may miss also the significance of the prophesied poet's anonymity.
"La vostra nominanza" is itself anonymity—the celebration first of
one Guido, then of another, and then of someone whose name ultimately does not signify because all names are merely changes in the
direction of the wind (XI, 100–102). The text for the discussion with
Oderisi is indeed Dante's own poetry, whose proper meaning carries
us both into and beyond the urge to endure in one's own words.

Once properly heard, the theme of anonymous *nominanza* echoes
even in the unobtrusive passages of the eleventh canto. The canto
opens with an anonymous prayer; Virgil's ensuing question begins
equally abruptly and without ascription (XI, 37–45), and the attribution that follows produces additional uncertainty:

> Le lor parole, che rendero a queste
> che dette avea colui cu' io seguiva,
> non fur da cui venisser manifeste;
> ma fu detto: . . .

It was not plain from whom came their words that replied to those
spoken by him I followed, but they were: . . .

[*Purg.* XI, 46–49]

We presently infer that Virgil's respondent—or respondents, since
Dante at first uses *lor*—cannot be identified because all of the shades'
faces are bent to the ground, the forfeiting of identity being part of the
purgatorial signification of pride. Virgil's respondent eventually
names himself as Omberto Aldobrandesco, but first, he in turn wonders about the identity of "this man who still lives and who is not
named" (XI, 55). Speeches seem to come from nowhere, or from
unidentifiable sources.

At the same time, however, both speech and action identify the
unnamed souls with each other, with the pilgrim, and with those still
on earth. In reciting the Pater Noster collectively, the shades turn the
last clause into a petition not for themselves but for the living; Dante
then urges us to reciprocate by praying for them (XI, 22–24 and 31–
36). Extending the reciprocations, Virgil expresses a wish for the
shades' disburdening (XI, 37–39). Virgil also makes a subtler but
more significant equation between the souls who must be disbur-
dened before they can lift themselves and Dante, slow at climbing
because he is encumbered by Adam's flesh (XI, 37–45). Dante himself assumes the posture of the shades as he replies to the speech that
tacitly includes him in their sin:

> Ascoltando chinai in giù la faccia;
>   e un di lor, non questi che parlava,
>   si torse sotto il peso che li 'mpaccia,
> e videmi e conobbemi e chiamava,
>   tenendo li occhi con fatica fisi
>   a me che tutto chin con loro andava.

Listening, I bent down my face, and one of them, not he that was
speaking, twisted himself under the weight that cumbered him and
saw me and knew me and called, laboriously keeping his eyes fixed
on me, who went quite bent along with them.

[*Purg.* XI, 73–78]

The confusions and interchanges of identity all point to the loss of
identity which is, paradoxically, both sin's result and its remedy. On
the one hand, as Oderisi has said, the prideful attempt to immortalize
one's name ultimately destroys identity by binding it to the evanes-

cent. That loss of identity is here made legible in the confused ascriptions, the blurring of one shade with another, and the mutual reflections among penitents, pilgrim, and living souls. On the other hand, the mutual reflections turn in another direction as well: toward the perfected collective identity first of the Eagle of Justice, many souls that speak with a single voice (*Par.* XIX–XX), and ultimately of the numberless individuals eternally infoliated in the paradisal rose. Of course, the "stellate rote" of pure harmony are distant from the weary circles of the first terrace, where collective prayers and initially anonymous speeches issue from disparate speakers whom we seek to name even as we hear that their names must vanish. In this intermediate state between egocentrism and perfect love, still clouded by the world's fog, individual identities are not transcended but confounded.

If, as Mazzeo says, the process of Purgatory is an attempt to reconstitute the human *imago,* the outlines of that form appear at this point fitfully, dimly, with varying degrees of effort. But at the end of the canto the *imago* achieves sudden, brief depth. Oderisi names as an occupant of this terrace Provenzan Salvani, once famous in Tuscany (XI, 121–26). Dante is puzzled: Provenzan appears to have repented just before his death and so should not yet be in Purgatory proper (XI, 127–32). Oderisi's explanation provides a brief sketch of humility in action, reminiscent of the figures on the terrace bank:

> "Quando vivea più glorïoso," disse,
>   "liberamente nel Campo di Siena,
>   ogne vergogna diposta, s'affisse;
> e lì, per trar l'amico suo di pena,
>   ch'e' sostenea ne la prigion di Carlo,
>   si condusse a tremar per ogne vena.
>   .   .   .
> Quest' opera li tolse quei confini."

"When he was living most gloriously" he said "he freely took his stand in the market-place of Siena, putting aside all shame, and there, to deliver his friend from the pains he suffered in the prison of Charles, he brought himself to tremble in every vein. . . . This deed released him from those bounds."

> [*Purg.* XI, 133–42]

If the story surprises the pilgrim, its relationship with the rest of the canto makes it striking to us as well. For a short time, a prideful soul abases himself—and thus exalts himself—in loving humility. But the episode's impact surpasses surprise or contrast. The man suffering to deliver his friend realizes the pattern of Christ's passion, and in the last line of the canto we can see a reference to the supreme humility that releases from their eternal "confini" all pride-encumbered souls who strive to imitate it. Provenzan, the most sinful of the souls here, briefly reflects in its perfection what we have seen only in slow formation—the essential *imago* that gives purgation form and being. The same image is, in Oderisi's prophecy, a potential mirror for Dante's own future (XI, 139–41). Juxtaposed with his present encumbrance, the story of Provenzan's one Christlike action conveys the possibility of release from the conditions of the first terrace.

Like Provenzan's story, the twelfth canto indicates, illuminates, and even produces a condition that frees the soul from pride. The canto begins with the pilgrim assuming the clearest and most deliberate identification possible with the penitents: "Di pari, come buoi che vanno a giogo, / m'andava io con quell' anima carca" ("Side by side with that burdened soul, as oxen go in a yoke, I went on" [XII, 1–2]). He too is now a text signifying the purgatorial reformation of identity and the difficult submission that elevates. But Virgil sets limits to this new identification with the penitents, for it could curtail the living soul's freedom to attain other transformations (XII, 4–6). Obeying Virgil, the pilgrim walks on erect, though his thoughts remain "bowed down and shrunk" (XII, 9). That difference between bodily and mental postures begins his release from the patterns of pride.

Walking on, he sees images of pride placed not at his eye level and above, like the statues that exemplified humility, but below him. From Lucifer's fall from heaven through Troy "abased and vile" (XII, 25–27, 62), these images reverse the *humilitas-sublimitas* paradox. They are, again, visible speech, both sensually expressive and expressive of truth:

> Morti li morti e i vivi parean vivi:
>   non vide mei di me chi vide il vero,
>   quant' io calcai, fin che chinato givi.

The dead seemed dead and the living living. He saw no better than I who saw the truth of all that which I trod upon while I went stooping.
[*Purg.* XII, 67–69]

But the vividness here differs from that of the carvings. The scenes are more numerous and far briefer, isolated rather than grouped into tableaux; more important, these lifelike figures are trapped in a two-dimensional "duro pavimento" (XII, 49). Their style deepens their meaning as visible speech: here God's art distances us from pride in portraying it flatly and rigidly.

God's art is replicated by the poet's. The instances of pride are presented in strikingly regular form: one to a tercet, with three groups of four tercets, each bound by anaphora on *Vedea, O,* and *Mostrava.* A thirteenth tercet recapitulates the anaphora in its three lines. Moreover, the first letters of the anaphoric words compose an acrostic, usually read as *UOM* or "man." Commentators have condemned the acrostic as "childish," a symptom of "the taste of the period";[53] too contrived, on the one hand, for readers who expect a realistic surface, on the other it seems crudely obvious to anyone seeking to decode the allegory. In truth, however, the anaphoric acrostic is neither a lapse of verisimilitude nor an inadequate disguise but a significantly formal and blatant sign. Pride consists, in these images, of wild actions—lightning, scattered limbs, grotesque metamorphoses, careening chariots, madness, butchery, destruction. In the *duro pavimento* and in the poet's verbal devices those actions are arrested and rigidly ordered, just as the pride that caused them was forcefully curbed. The accounts of hubris spell out the unbreakable order that the proud attempted to violate; the schematic obviousness of the acrostic measures their folly.

In its clarity the pavement should, as Virgil says, *tranquillar la via* (XII, 14) for both pilgrim and reader. Surprisingly, however, the poet's ecphrasis ends with a bitter outburst:

> Or superbite, e via col viso altero,
> figliuoli d'Eva, e non chinate il volto
> sì che veggiate il vostro mal sentero!

Wax proud now and go your way with lofty looks, sons of Eve, and bend not down your face to see your evil path!
                              [*Purg.* XII, 70–72]

---

53. Dorothy Sayers, trans. and commentator, *Purgatory* (London: Penguin, 1955), p. 162. See also Sinclair, II, 164.

Although the high style of this apostrophe implies the speaker's supe-
riority to the foolish sons of Eve, in the context of failed self-exaltation the implied claim reverses itself. Momentarily there seems to be
no escape from the patterns of the *duro pavimento*. The apostrophe's
sarcasm also implies humanity's entrapment in pride: obviously
scorning our hubris, the poet assumes that we will not reform.

But once seen, the trap ceases to exist. Immediately after the narrator's bitter forecast about all children of Eve, Virgil says, "Lift up
thy head" (XII, 77), and an angel who comes to guide the travelers
contradicts directly the implication that we are destined to prideful
ruin:

> . . . "Venite: qui son presso i gradi,
>   e agevolemente omai si sale.
> A questo invito vegnon molto radi:
>   o gente umana, per volar sù nata,
>   perché a poco vento così cadi?"

"Come; the steps are at hand here and henceforth the climb is easy.
To this bidding they are very few that come. O race of men, born to
fly upward, why do you fall back so for a little wind?"

> [*Purg.* XII, 92–96]

The sudden reversal makes the earlier sarcastic outburst seem to have
been cathartic. Indeed, what the *segno* in the pavement, the acrostic,
and Dante's sarcasm have meant is not simply that the proud must
fall, as a superficial allegorization might imply, but also that pride's
futility is overwhelmingly obvious. That perception makes pride itself
impossible. The stooping of the penitent proud was not true humility,
but the reflex of an attempt to rise where rising is impossible; slowly
they learn that resistance creates their burden. To see human limitation not as a frustrating obstacle but as reality itself is to end the cycle
of self-elevation and inevitable abasement.

Outside that static cycle, gravitation is toward God. That is the
controlling idea of the last part of the twelfth canto, shaping not only
Virgil's and the angel's explicit statements but also the narrative's
setting and style. As soon as Dante has absorbed and transmitted the
lesson of the pavement, the poem's perspective widens rapidly:

> Più era già per noi del monte vòlto
>   e del cammin del sole assai più speso
>   che non stimava l'animo non sciolto,

> quando colui che sempre innanzi atteso
> andava, cominiciò: "Drizza la testa;
> non è più tempo di gir sì sospeso."

More of the mountain was now encircled by us and much more of the sun's track was sped than my mind, not being free, had reckoned, when he who was always looking ahead as he went began: "Lift up thy head! There is no more time to go thus absorbed."

[*Purg.* XII, 73–78]

Virgil reminds the pilgrim of the road ahead, and the physical journey's momentum, suspended for four cantos, resumes. In place of the contortion, misery, and strain of the first terrace, the angel brings simple beauty and clarity:

> A noi venìa la creatura bella,
> biancovestito e ne la faccia quale
> par tremolando mattutina stella.
> Le braccia aperse, e indi aperse l'ale;
> disse: "Venite. . . ."

Towards us came the fair creature, clothed in white, and in his face he seemed like a trembling star at dawn. He opened his arms, then spread his wings and said: "Come. . . ."

[*Purg.* XII, 88–92]

The change is striking. If the ascent to Purgatory required "more art" (IX, 71), we might expect a further ascent to elicit an even loftier style. Instead, the narrative becomes swifter, simpler, less encumbered with obviously symbolic description and doctrinal discourse than at any point since the ante-Purgatory. The travelers are shown where to ascend the mountain, and they do. They hear the first beatitude sung; the narrator exclaims, with artless lucidity,

> Ahi quanto son diverse quelle foci
> da l'infernali! ché quivi per canti
> s'entra, e là giù per lamenti feroci.

Ah, how different these passages from those of Hell, for here the entrance is with songs and there with fierce lamentations!

[*Purg.* XII, 112–14]

Progression here comes not through effort, either the pilgrim's effort to understand or God's to communicate, but through the pull of grace

on the newly unresisting soul. The simple narrative of a miraculous
action realizes perfectly the *humilitas-sublimitas* paradox.

The canto ends with a touchingly human scene that seems to be one
of the poem's incidental beauties. But the manner in which the pilgrim learns that the first *P* has been removed from his forehead is as
significant as the symbolic act itself. In bringing the travelers to the
foot of the steps, the angel strikes Dante's forehead with his wings
(XII, 97–99). The poet digresses briefly to compare the passageway
here with mountain steps above Florence made in an earlier and
better-ordered age, implying new hope that the order of Purgatory
may be imitated on earth (XII, 100–108). The pilgrim then finds
himself lighter, and Virgil explains that the first *P* has been removed,
presumably by the angel's wings (XII, 121–26). It happens without
the pilgrim's knowledge, to his surprise and chagrin:

> Allor fec' io come color che vanno
>   con cosa in capo non da lor saputa,
>   se non che ' cenni altrui sospecciar fanno;
> per che la mano ad accertar s'aiuta,
>   e cerca e truova e quello officio adempie
>   che non si può fornir per la veduta;
> e con le dita de la destra scempie
>   trovai pur sei le lettere che 'ncise
>   quel da le chiavi a me sovra le tempie:
> a che guardando, il mio duca sorrise.

Then I did like those going with something on their head unknown to
them but that the signs of others make them suspect, so that the hand
helps to make sure and searches and finds, doing the office that sight
cannot serve, and with the spread fingers of my right hand I found
only six of the letters that he with the keys had traced on my temples;
and observing this my Leader smiled.

                                                    [*Purg.* XII, 127–36]

The homely scene might be thought inappropriate to a theme as
momentous as the removal of the radical sin. In fact, however, the
theme is less the purgation of pride—that having been the business of
the preceding three cantos—than the notification of its purgation.
The scene's tone bears significance in that context. In our empathy
with his unguarded gesture of embarrassment, we perceive the narrator's humility intuitively at the same time that we read the symbolic

announcement of his release from pride. The passage's meaning depends on both modes of signifying: the awesome symbol of divine grace and the immediate experience of human dependence. The canto ends in a smile of reason (XII, 136)—not merely because the character who embodies reason has smiled, but because rational interpretation coincides with subjective response in a profound acceptance of the divine order.

As a vernacular allegory—vernacular in using not only the common language but also the conventions of ordinary sensual perception—which claims to render eternal truth, the *Divine Comedy* might convict its author of the hubris that his second canticle condemns. The same conviction could arise from his claim elsewhere to have been led to an experience of God through his love for a mortal woman. That Dante has generally escaped such accusations during the centuries of his fame can be attributed to the extraordinary integrity of his allegory. Continually he acknowledges the distance between his revelations and their mundane channels; continually he attempts to bridge the distance not by poetic fiat but by difficult, uneven, openly imperfect effort. Bearing the burden of our imperfect language, he achieves, like the souls on the first terrace, a gradual elevation.

But that very modesty raises a literary problem that has been wrongly attributed to all allegory: the problem of a text that declines to state its own general meanings. Most critics have felt that a text whose meaning resides outside itself probably indicates a divided intention in the writer and must certainly thwart the reader, who cannot determine meaning in the act of reading. While some recent critics celebrate such semiotic disunity, seeing therein the paradigm of linguistic duplicity, a more common response has been to repudiate allegory as perverse or insincere and to avoid reading it—except, of course, for the quasi allegories. Scholars who persist in studying allegory alternate between conceding the intractability of extratextual meaning and arguing that somehow the meaning is in the text after all.

The difficulty can be resolved if we redefine our idea of "meaning." On the one hand, the *Divine Comedy* is shaped by a preexistent doctrine that includes many of the text's referents. On the other hand, the doctrine's existence does not render the poem redundant. The modern reader's conviction that the poem means something other than its explicit and implicit doctrines does not impose an anachronistic, unchristian aesthetic on Dante. In acknowledging the need for accommodative metaphor, and in concluding the *Paradiso* not with doctrinal statement but with inexplicable experience, Dante suggests that poetry is an essential complement of doctrine. Indeed, he comes very close to the Romantic position that the truth must always be reimagined. Of course, unlike Romantic poetry, Dante's demonstrably evokes a second way of conveying truth: abstract formulation. The narrative's setting in the Christian otherworld guarantees that we will seek doctrinal correlatives to the action, and Dante's skill as a poet ensures that we will find them, more or less continuously and more or less accurately. But because they are outside the poem, we cannot safely center our reading in them; and because they shape the poem, we do not need to. If Dante's agents and objects imply universal antecedents, the poem's meaning is their multiple ways of doing so.

At the end of the twelfth canto of the *Purgatorio,* when the pilgrim is alerted to a change in himself which he cannot see, his hand searches for it, "doing the office that sight cannot serve" (XII, 132). What he finds is no more meaningful to him, or to us, than the awkward, fumbling way in which he must find it, for the latter testifies to his dependence on God for salvation. Like him, readers of the poem are led to perceive meaning in various ways, not least of which are the shifts from one mode of communication to another. For Dante, reality itself is law-governed—every element of God's creation is part of a pattern—but the pattern is seldom directly discernible, and never fully discernible through any human medium. Revelation is a never-ending education of vision. Because his allegory participates in that process, acknowledging the limitations of human language while redefining and rewarding our faith in it, his poem can be called without arrogance "divine."

6 Truth in Abeyance:
The Faerie Queene

As A. C. Hamilton has pointed out, "the only two major classics in modern literature which were conceived by their authors as allegories" share a history of reclassification by their readers.[1] If the *Divine Comedy* has been deemed to be quasi allegory, *The Faerie Queene* looks to many readers like a dish of strawberries and cream contaminated by allegorical grit, or a collection of splendid pictures among which allegory lurks like a harmless dragon.[2] Such responses tell us as much about modern allegoriphobia as about the work of Dante and Spenser, but Hamilton also infers from them a genuine peculiarity of the two poems. Although he spends little time developing the distinction, he asserts that "Dante's 'allegory of the theologians,' for which [Singleton] argues so cogently, is uniquely paralleled by *The Faerie Queene* Book I."[3] What he appears to mean, to judge by the ensuing discussion, is that in both great poems the "story" or "imagery" possesses an integrity apart from the "theme"

1. A. C. Hamilton, *The Structure of Allegory in "The Faerie Queene"* (Oxford: Clarendon Press, 1961), pp. 30–32.
2. Edward Dowden, "Spenser, the Poet and Teacher" (1882), rpt. in *Spenser: The Faerie Queene; A Casebook*, ed. Peter Bayley (New York: Macmillan, 1977), p. 41; and William Hazlitt, "Chaucer and Spenser," *Lectures on the English Poets* (1818), in *The Collected Works of William Hazlitt*, ed. A. R. Waller and Arnold Glover, 12 vols. (London: J. M. Dent, 1902), V, 38.
3. Hamilton, *Structure of Allegory*, p. 30.

or "ideas." In other words, neither of these classic allegories seems immediately and continuously allegorical.

In Spenser's case as in Dante's, that impression is not easy to substantiate. It cannot be based on the abundant sensory detail, for no mere multiplication of visibilia could have made Guillaume's Garden or Bunyan's Way as absorbing or self-contained as Faeryland. Nor can we argue that Spenser's characters and settings are more verisimilar than those of other allegorists—that we find, say, the death of Error more plausible than the attack of Apollyon. And Spenser does not even foster his illusion of sensual reality by using historical characters and avoiding agents with abstract names, as Dante does.

The "unallegorical" quality of *The Faerie Queene* has only recently been cogently defined, and the definition sheds light on the work of both Spenser and Dante. Using E. H. Gombrich's work on the psychology of visual perception, John Bender demonstrates that Spenser's innovation is his imitation not of sensory reality but of perceptual experience. Previous narratives depend on an omniscient point of view—for instance, Ariosto describes Alcina's gown before the robe that covers it has been removed—and such details "lead us directly to the ideas [the poet] has in mind."[4] By way of contrast, Bender cites the stanza in which Guyon and the Palmer come upon Acrasia:

> Vpon a bed of Roses she was layd,
>   As faint through heat, or dight to pleasant sin,
>   And was arayd, or rather disarayd,
>   All in a vele of silke and siluer thin,
>   That hid no whit her alablaster skin,
>   But rather shewd more white, if more might bee:
>   More subtile web *Arachne* can not spin,
>   Nor the fine nets, which oft we wouen see
> Of scorched deaw, do not in th'aire more lightly flee.[5]

As Bender demonstrates, Spenser here "provokes and directs the imagination." Taking the observer's point of view, he gradually re-

---

4. John B. Bender, *Spenser and Literary Pictorialism* (Princeton: Princeton University Press, 1972), p. 46.

5. Edmund Spenser, *The Faerie Queene*, vols. 1–6 of *The Works of Edmund Spenser: A Variorum Edition*, ed. Edwin Greenlaw et al. (Baltimore: Johns Hopkins University Press, 1932–39), bk. II, canto xii, stanza 77. Future references to this edition will be documented in the text by book, canto, and stanza.

defines his rendering both of Acrasia's gown and of what it discloses, so that "the lines focus our attention on the sensuous experience of the moment."[6] We see with Guyon.

Spenser also imitates perception in a second way, according to Bender: he provides successive interpretations of an object. Various elements of the passage just cited are defined tentatively, then re-defined: Acrasia's posture suggests either recent exertion or antici-pated pleasure; she is arrayed, "or rather disarayd"; her skin shows more whitely through the thin gown, "if more might be"; the gown itself is first a cloth veil, then a web, then a net of dew. Bender concedes that the three metaphors bear more than a sensual burden, for they introduce "ominous and magical connotations" that define Acrasia intellectually and morally. But "the visual and intellectual aspects of the verse are fused"; that is, we are not simply given the conceptual meaning but must grasp it in stages, as we do the gradu-ally clarified image. Here and elsewhere the poet provides "shifting metaphorical definitions of visionary experience [which] are closely analogous to our attempts to perceive visual phenomena by categoriz-ing them within a range of familiar schemata." Thus the events and objects of Spenser's poem seem sensual and concrete because we apprehend them as we apprehend the tangible world. "*The Faerie Queene* attempts the delicate task of interpreting the ideal as height-ened, even surreal, human experience."[7]

It is in imitating sensual perception that Spenser most closely re-sembles Dante. The much-praised "plasticity" and "realism" of the *Divine Comedy* might profitably be defined in Bender's terms as the use of successive physical and metaphoric schemata to evoke a per-ceived world. In the second canto of the *Purgatorio,* the pilgrim is watching the sun set when something appears to him "qual, sorpreso dal mattino, / per li grossi vapor Marte rosseggia / giù nel ponente sovra 'l suol marino" ("as when, suffused by dawn, Mars glows ruddy through the thick vapors low in the west over the ocean floor").[8] Students of aesthetic psychology might say that the pilgrim's

6. Bender, p. 42.

7. Bender, pp. 43, 65–66. Bender borrows the term "schemata" from E. H. Gombrich, *Art and Illusion: A Study in the Psychology of Pictorial Representation,* Bollingen Series XXXV, 5 (Princeton: Princeton University Press, 1969).

8. Dante, *Purgatorio* II, 13–15; from *The Divine Comedy,* ed. and trans. Singleton.

first "schema" for what he sees is, naturally enough, an astrological one. But it is only provisional, no sooner offered than withdrawn in favor of a more general designation of the object simply as a light (*Purg.* II, 17). Then the pilgrim gradually achieves more precise definition. When he looks back after a questioning glance at Virgil, the light has grown brighter and larger (II, 19–21); he notices something white on either side of it and below (II, 22–24); both travelers see the three whitenesses appear as two wings and a pilot; then Virgil supplies simultaneously an identification and a directive: "'Fa, fa che le ginocchia cali. / Ecco l'angel di Dio" ("'Bend, bend your knees! Behold the angel of God!'" [II, 28–29]). Prompted by his more perceptive guide, the pilgrim at last sees the "divine bird" as a boat with a winged steersman (II, 31–45). Because the *Divine Comedy* as a whole concerns the pilgrim's growth in vision, Dante's "pictorialism" gradually encompasses intellectual and spiritual objects as well as physical ones; but the pilgrim always approaches and apprehends those objects—beholds them—through a process that resembles visual perception. That they can be so apprehended is the miracle that Dante celebrates.

The pictorialism of Dante and Spenser contrasts sharply with even the most vivid imagery of the other allegorists:

> So he went on, and *Apollyon* met him; now the Monster was hidious to behold, he was cloathed with scales like a Fish (and they are his pride) he had Wings like a Dragon, feet like a Bear, and out of his belly came Fire and Smoak, and his mouth was as the mouth of a Lion.[9]

Undeniably lurid, Bunyan's description nonetheless eludes visualization. The belly that emits fire and smoke is patently improbable; we get nothing of the head besides the mouth, whose resemblance to a lion's is left unspecified. But more important, we have no real need to visualize the monster. Not only was he ethically identified ten lines earlier as "a foul *Fiend*" named Apollyon; in addition, the powerful rhetoric of the passage itself—the capitalizations, the biblical cadence, the hodgepodge of animal terms—achieves the visceral effects usually produced by imagery. Throughout *The Pilgrim's Progress*, sensory perception interchanges with direct spiritual intuition of agents and objects that seem correspondingly to shift between sensi-

9. Bunyan, *Pilgrim's Progress*, ed. Sharrock, p. 56.

ble and intelligible. Thus the tangible Slow of Dispond contains metaphoric "scum and filth" arising from the intangible "conviction for
sin" (pp. 14–15). Spenser's monster Error, in contrast, vomits only
books and papers—peculiar food, to be sure, but edible without
metaphoric conversion. Spenser's pictorialism, like Dante's, separates
sensible objects and events from the intangibles of allegory, relegating
the latter for most of the poem to the characters', the narrator's, or
the reader's interpretation.

Because Spenser resembles Dante in this way, it ought to be possible to extend to *The Faerie Queene* some of my conclusions about the
Divine Comedy. Perhaps Spenser also explores the attainment of
allegorical vision—not through a single pilgrim-narrator, of course,
but through the questing knights. We can assume that his poem, too,
reveals its great organizing ideas obliquely. In Spenser's case those
ideas will be the virtues for which the various books are "legends"—
that is, texts for allegorical reading. Like Dante's pilgrim and reader,
sojourners in Faeryland must learn to apprehend the intelligible
through their senses.

That line of thought apparently led to Hamilton's comparison of
Spenser and Dante. It may also explain why the conclusions of several
Spenserians resemble those of Auerbach and Singleton about the
Comedy:

> The allegory is contained by the narrative in the same way and to the
> degree that universals are contained by particulars.[10]

> Each episode of knight errantry adds its material substance to the
> accumulated argument of a higher truth, the revelation of a providen-
> tial will.[11]

> We end by seeing into the general, the principle, the quiddity "in its
> universall consideration" as Sidney phrases it, and feel that we see it
> in essence, whole. But . . . we see . . . universals in their this-world
> shape, i.e., bodied in particulars. . . .[12]

Also like students of Dante, many Spenserians attribute their poet's
allegorical method to a world view—specifically, a hierarchical and
analogical one that assumes that "the relationship of any two things

---

10. Roche, *Kindly Flame*, p. 4.
11. Angus Fletcher, *The Prophetic Moment: An Essay on Spenser* (Chicago: University of Chicago Press, 1971), p. 44.
12. Tuve, *Allegorical Imagery*, p. 127.

in the same world or sphere may adumbrate the relationship of two other things in another world or sphere."[13]

To a considerable degree, Spenser's allegory can indeed be read like Dante's. The opening account of the Red Cross Knight's armor, for instance, points toward certain abstract ideas that remain implicit in sensory description. The Knight has inherited an ancient, well-used defense, mysteriously potent but demanding a skill in management that he does not yet possess; the relevance of that pattern to holiness can be inferred, in the same way as can the relevance to heresy of various details in Canto X of the *Inferno*. At the same time, again as in Dante, the reader who simply equates each detail with the regnant Reality loses most of the meaning—here, that the armor's significance appears only to an interpreter versed in Christian tradition, and that possession of the armor distinguishes the Knight only by way of portent. Red Cross "is" holiness only putatively and potentially. Similarly, if Una's lamb represents innocence, it means also that such univocal, emblematic innocence appears here temporarily and anomalously, its whereabouts to be henceforth problematic. Spenserians seem to concur that the poem's abstractions do not provide the meaning of the text, but vice versa.[14] In other words, shortcuts to meaning are no more legitimate in *The Faerie Queene* than in the *Divine Comedy*. The classic allusion that introduces the storm in the first canto—"angry *Ioue* an hideous storme of raine / Did poure into his Lemans lap" (I.i.6)—should not be dismissed as learned decoration, but read as an intrusion into the quest for holiness by the amoral natural world known to the pagans. If achieved for the entire poem, such a reading should unify Hamilton's "fable or image" with the "allegory or idea" and fully clarify the dark conceit.

The first difficulty with that enterprise would be its difficulty. Modern Spenserians often allude to the strenuous effort required to understand how "every gesture, every attitude, every turn of phrase contributes toward significant meaning."[15] "Disarmed by their schemes," writes Richard Pindell, "critics invading Faery often suffer

13. Roche, p. 8.

14. See, for instance, Kathleen Williams, *Spenser's World of Glass: A Reading of "The Faerie Queene"* (Berkeley: University of California Press, 1966), p. xix; Tuve, p. 126.

15. William J. Kennedy, "Rhetoric, Allegory, and Dramatic Modality in Spenser's Fradubio Episode," *ELR* 3 (1973):367.

the fate of Napoleon in Russia. They are simply overwhelmed by the
relentless flood of events. . . ."[16] The six Virtues govern their sprawl-
ing legends much more remotely than Dante's principles control his
cantos. The general relevance to holiness of Duessa's descent into
Hades may be apparent, but what of her lengthy conversation with
Aesculapius, or the story of his healing of Hyppolytus? The narrative's length and intricacy reveal one great difference between
Spenser's world and Dante's: a limitless forest cannot bear its allegorical meaning as clearly as can a hierarchic cosmos.

In themselves, the vastness and intricacy of Faeryland might constitute no more than a salutary challenge to the truly heroic reader.
They are compounded, however, by a more stubborn obstacle to
allegorical reading: the text's structure of meaning. Initially meaning
seems more accessible in *The Faerie Queene* than in the *Divine Comedy*. There we followed the pilgrim's transitions from his sensory perspective to allegorical enlightenment; here we are immediately given
the general significance of the first canto in a neat allegorical précis:

> The Patron of true Holinesse,
> Foule Errour doth defeate:
> Hypocrisie him to entrape,
> Doth to his home entreate.

> [I.i.Argument]

The very neatness of the quatrain may be puzzling, however, for it
seems to spoil the allegorical suspense, to rend the veil prematurely.
And Maureen Quilligan has pointed out another problem: the précis
is not quite accurate. The Red Cross Knight does not really defeat
error itself; his entrapment by hypocrisy is not really separate from
his encounter with Error; and the quatrain's "flat-handed statements" violate the message of the canto, which concerns the danger
of facile generalizations. After noting other, more flagrant inac-
curacies in later allegorical rubrics, Quilligan suggests that Spenser
added the quatrains in order to satisfy "editorial as opposed to poetic
demands."[17] Be that as it may, the rubrics certainly do not accurately

16. Richard Pindell, "The Mutable Image: Man-in-Creation," in *Eterne in Mutabilitie: The Unity of "The Faerie Queene,"* ed. Kenneth John Atchity (Hamden,
Conn.: Shoe String Press, Archon Books, 1972), p. 163.
17. Quilligan, *Language of Allegory*, pp. 231–32.

epitomize the poem, and I suspect that many readers end by ignoring them altogether. Still, Quilligan is wrong to dismiss them as unimportant: in promising neat allegorical correlatives that they fail to provide, they both encourage and baffle our search for universal meanings.

Nor are the rubrics the only element of the poem to offer allegorical pronouncements that turn out to be unreliable. *The Faerie Queene* abounds in explicit generalizations, most of them didactic: in the first three cantos the narrator exclaims, "God helpe the man so wrapt in *Errours* endlesse traine" (I.i.18), declares that nothing arouses more pity than does afflicted beauty (I.iii.1), and asks rhetorically, "O how can beautie maister the most strong, / And simple truth subdue auenging wrong?" (I.iii.6). But several critics have shown that such formulations are not fully authoritative. Red Cross soon escapes from the "endless traine" of the monster, but, contrary to the narrator's implication, he is not disentangled from error; and at least one commentator has been puzzled at Spenser's identification of Una as "beauty" after his previous statements that she is Truth.[18] Sometimes inconsistent and "frequently oversimplified, contradictory, or misleading," the narrator's comments are the reactions of a fallible observer.[19] Spenser's narrator thus differs radically from the persona of the *Divine Comedy,* who, though fallible, has been enlightened by his journey and thus offers no untrustworthy generalizations. And since Spenser's narrator is the most authoritative speaker we hear— avowedly the poet himself—his unreliability produces genuine uncertainty about the poem's meaning.

If Spenser does not articulate authoritative allegorical patterns, neither does he give us univocal signs for inferring them. The first major episode in Book III is a case in point. Arthur and Guyon encounter a third knight, whom the narrator calls "he" and "him" even though

    18. Hamilton, note to I.iii.1, in Hamilton, ed., *The Faerie Queene* (London: Longmans, 1977), p. 55.

    19. Jerome S. Dees, "The Narrator of *The Faerie Queene:* Patterns of Response," *TSLL* 12 (1970–71):537; see also Harry Berger, Jr., *The Allegorical Temper: Vision and Reality in Book II of Spenser's "Faerie Queene"* (New Haven: Yale University Press, 1957), pp. 164–65; Stan Hinton, "The Poet and His Narrator: Spenser's Epic Voice," *ELH* 41 (1974):165–81; Isabel G. MacCaffrey, *Spenser's Allegory: The Anatomy of Imagination* (Princeton: Princeton University Press, 1976), pp. 51–52; Jonathan Goldberg, *Endlesse Worke: Spenser and the Structures of Discourse* (Baltimore: Johns Hopkins University Press, 1981), pp. 45, 67.

the knight turns out to be Britomart. Guyon obtains from Arthur the privilege of jousting with the stranger but is promptly unhorsed. Filled with "disdaineful wrath," he is mollified only when Arthur suggests blaming his horse or his page instead of himself (III.i.9–11). Hugh Maclean asserts that "allegorically, this encounter emphasizes the power of chastity, which has strength beyond that even of temperance or continence."[20] That formulation seems to follow logically from the defeat by a knight of Chastity of a knight of Temperance, but it raises more problems than it resolves. Chastity is presumably a form of temperance; why should they conflict? Perhaps Britomart vanquishes Guyon not as chastity but as the chaste and beautiful woman, so that the episode evokes the Petrarchan topos of love as man's mysteriously invincible enemy; but that reading gives Britomart an erotic force almost opposed to her nominal virtue.

In fact, no allegorical reading fits the episode well. The suspense concerning Britomart's gender and the amusing dialogue between Arthur and Guyon distract us to some degree from general meanings. Moreover, the agents seem to betray human motives that resist abstract labels. In offering excuses for Guyon, Arthur shows a benevolent dishonesty familiar to the inhabitants of a fallen world but not clearly typical of Magnificence. Guyon's petulance is even less congruent with his virtue, Temperance; but he cannot justly be accused of surrendering his temperance to a love that he does not feel. As for Britomart, her unannounced attack may manifest either chivalric conventions or her own combativeness, but not, surely, Chastity or Love. Initially, therefore, we do not see chastity and temperance conflict; we see Britomart unhorse Guyon. And that Britomart and Guyon are not manifesting their nominal virtues is confirmed later, when they settle their dispute through an access of "goodly temperance, and affection chaste" (III.i.12). Until that reconciliation, which is ontological as well as personal, allegorical meaning is not so much latent in the episode as obscured by it.

Later in the same canto, allegorical meaning is obscured in another way. The narrator interrupts his story to praise the joust between Britomart and Guyon as an example of bygone chivalry:

> O goodly vsage of those antique times,
>   In which the sword was seruant vnto right;

20. Maclean, ed., *Edmund Spenser's Poetry*, p. 199n.

> When not for malice and contentious crimes,
> But all for praise, and proofe of manly might,
> The martiall brood accustomed to fight. . . .

[III.i.13.]

His outburst diverts us from the abstractions of allegory to their romantic and chivalric vehicle. If the episode is intended to adumbrate chastity and temperance, or any syncretic Realities at all, the narrator's praise for past behavior seems at least disingenuous and at most misleading. But generalizing commentary that falls short of the poem's major abstractions is a hallmark of Spenser's narration. At the end of Book III's first canto, he responds to Chastity's victory over the *gradus amori* by lamenting that the military prowess of the women of old has been forgotten. In Book IV, when Arthur and Amoret travel alone together and arrive at the house of Slander, the narrator ignores the clear allegorical pattern and explains prosaically that need forced the couple to accept unattractive lodgings (IV.viii.27). Oliver Steele, to whom I owe the last example, comments, "The author has made an allegorical episode; the narrator wants his audience to take the episode as mimetic."[21] And Steele amply and astutely demonstrates that throughout *The Faerie Queene,* Spenser frequently uses his narrative voice to involve us in the empirical "surface" of the story. In such cases the narrator is not simply an unreliable explicator but an obstacle to allegorical perception.

Steele's distinction between narrator and author should not be taken to mean that the former acts as an allegorical naif, ironically blind to the latter's implications. As Jerome Dees points out, the narrator "impresses us by his moral authority"; his judgments are as good as anyone's.[22] In fact, no voice or viewpoint in *The Faerie Queene* provides consistently reliable allegorical information, though many pretend to do so. If the allegorical ideas of the *Divine Comedy* exist ultimately in the mind of God, those of *The Faerie Queene* exist only in the fallible minds of the narrator, characters, author, and readers.

A context for Spenser's allegorical relativism can be found in literary history. Like Dante, Spenser knew well the theory that allegory's

---

21. Oliver Steele, Jr., "The Rhetorical Functions of the Narrator in *The Faerie Queene,*" Ph.D. diss., University of Virginia, 1965, p. 137.
22. Dees, pp. 540, 545.

explicit meanings differ from its ultimate, universal meanings, but he knew also a tradition in which those universal meanings appeared to be not merely detachable but also endlessly restatable. The narratives of Ariosto and Tasso, Spenser's models, underwent repeated speculative allegorizations: "From the fifteen-forties on almost every edition . . . [of *Orlando Furioso*] appears 'con le allegorie,' 'con le nuove allegorie,' 'con l'allegorie a ciascun canto di Thomaso Poracchi. . . .'"23 The resulting attitude toward the relationship between narrative and meaning sometimes influenced the authors of allegory. Tasso adds an allegorization to an edition of the *Gerusalemme Liberata,* for instance, and although such self-allegorizations are closely associated with the narratives, the authors subtly acknowledge what is clear to a modern reader: many of them are strained reinterpretations or "*ex post facto* rationalizations."24 Spenser incorporates such imperfectly congruent allegorizations into the narrative which they reinterpret, avowedly producing a "darke conceit," a poem which strains against many of its own meanings. Thus *The Faerie Queene* is the first great poem to realize the theory that an allegory is a duplicitous text.

Spenser's duplicity has long been the central problem faced by his readers. A few have evaded the difficulty by ignoring some of Spenser's contradictory signals, usually the signals that point toward abstractions. Justly the best known of such readers is William Hazlitt, who assured us in 1818 that "if [we] do not meddle with the allegory, the allegory will not meddle with [us]."25 Hazlitt is still sometimes taken at his word by a Spenserian who wishes to focus on "the imagery" instead of "the allegory" or "the idea."26 But most readers

23. Hough, *Preface to "The Faerie Queene,"* p. 118.

24. The quotation, which refers to Tasso's and Graziani's allegorizations, is from John Steadman, "The Arming of an Archetype: Heroic Virtue and the Conventions of Literary Epic," in *Concepts of the Hero in the Middle Ages and the Renaissance,* ed. Norman T. Burns and Christopher J. Reagan (Albany: State University of New York Press, 1975), p. 156. On John Harington's acknowledgment of strain in his allegorization of Ariosto, see Robert McNulty's Introduction to Lodovico Ariosto's *Orlando Furioso as Translated into English Heroical Verse by Sir John Harington* (Oxford: Clarendon Press, 1972), p. xxxviii.

25. Hazlitt, V, 38.

26. See, for instance, Northrop Frye, "The Structure of Imagery in *The Faerie Queene,"* UTQ 30 (1960–61):111; Hamilton, *Structure of Allegory,* p. 12.

acknowledge the need to respond in some way to the text's amphibology.

Some responses are essentially protests. John Livingston Lowes concludes in exasperation that the good characters as well as the bad ones "behav[e] as they do because at one moment they are thought of as a lovely lady and a monster and a sorcerer, and at another as Holiness and Error and Hypocrisy. . . . Is anybody in the allegory at any given moment, what he *is,* or what he *seems?* And which in Heaven's name, we ask, is which?" More recently G. Wilson Knight has declared that "the nature of [Spenser's] creation changes indecisively" from abstract didacticism to "luxuriant impressionism," and Yvor Winters has complained of an arbitrary relationship between concrete figures and abstract meanings.[27] The animus of such remarks can be explained in Hamilton's words: "Unless the poem means what it says, that is unless it is what it appears to be, it is like Duessa whose borrowed beauty disguises her reality."[28] Indeed, many readers simply repudiate *The Faerie Queene.*

A more positive approach is to celebrate the discontinuities and contradictions—proclaiming a "ballet" of meanings instead of a "maddening play of telescoping personalities," or, rather than lamenting Spenser's indecisive changes, praising his "continual flux from one to another semantic relation."[29] But although acceptance of Spenser is probably better than rejection, a simple revaluation of previously discredited traits is not particularly enlightening. As if aware that he has applauded the ballet of meanings without analyzing its choreography, Thomas Greene assures us that the poem possesses a "principle of continuity"—but one that is "scarcely to be articulated."[30] That sounds a bit like Proteus assuring Florimell of his integrity.

27. John Livingston Lowes, "The Pilgrim's Progress," in *Essays in Appreciation* (Boston: Houghton Mifflin, 1936), pp. 59–60; G. Wilson Knight, "The Spenserian Fluidity," in *The Burning Oracle: Studies in the Poetry of Action* (London: Oxford University Press, 1939), p. 12; Yvor Winters, *The Function of Criticism: Problems and Exercises* (Denver: Alan Swallow, 1957), p. 44.

28. Hamilton, *Structure of Allegory,* p. 7.

29. The laudatory quotations are from Thomas Greene, *The Descent from Heaven: A Study in Epic Continuity* (New Haven: Yale University Press, 1963), p. 332; and Harry Berger, Jr., Introduction to *Spenser: A Collection of Critical Essays,* ed. Berger (Englewood Cliffs, N.J.: Prentice-Hall, 1968), p. 5. The reference to the "play of telescoping personalities" is from Lowes, p. 60.

30. Greene, p. 334.

The poem's capacity to embrace Protean flux is unquestionably one source of its power, but those who simply celebrate the shifts of meaning overlook the tension, even the anxiety, which those shifts engender in the reader. The movements "from one to another semantic relation" are not clearly signaled, nor are they orderly. At any point various kinds of meaning and various particular meanings may hover and compete. The excuse that Arthur offers the unhorsed Guyon can be regarded—has been regarded—as the ominous lapse of Magnificence into deviousness, as an exemplary restoration of concord, or as allegorically meaningless social byplay.[31] Britomart's attack on Marinell, in the fourth canto of Book III, might be chaste love's assault on unhealthy self-containment, the random violence of eros, or the comic aggression of a headstrong youth. The most skilled readers dispute whether or not Guyon's faint at II.vii.66 bears allegorical significance, and of course what significance it bears.[32] Such questions might be less urgent if Spenser did not imply, with his allegorizing rubrics, his occasional explications, and his prefatory letter, that allegorical meaning can usually be found and is vitally important. His concession that there are "by-accidents" intermeddled with the "intendments" only increases our uncertainty, leaving us to ask with Lowes which in Heaven's name is which.[33]

The most promising approach to Spenserian duplicity comes from those who neither deplore nor embrace it, but analyze it. Generally the analysis begins with the premise that the text's duplicity reflects the human condition. Faeryland is "a world of tentative movement in the half-dark of sublunary life, becoming more confident as events slowly take shape," writes Kathleen Williams. It is therefore "very close to what it feels like to be living in a world whose significance is only dimly and occasionally discernible." Isabel MacCaffrey places more emphasis on the reader's experience: "Spenserian narrative, like Spenserian rhetoric, mimes the epistemological experience of fallen man, and in forcing the reader to participate in this mimesis, observing its darkness and its distracted incompleteness, the allegory makes its self-regarding didactic point." Both Williams and MacCaffrey achieve a change of focus that solves many problems at once. Ac-

---

31. See, for instance, Lesley W. Brill, "Battles That Need Not Be Fought: *The Faerie Queene*, III.i," *ELR* 5 (1975):202; Barney, *Allegories of History*, p. 220.
32. The dispute is summarized by Berger in *Allegorical Temper*, chap. 1.
33. Spenser, "Letter of the Authors," in Maclean, ed., pp. 1, 4.

knowledging our anxiety about Spenser's duplicity, they reveal it as part of his meaning rather than a threat to reading; as Auerbach and Singleton did for Dante, they demonstrate that Spenser's integumental allegory is no mere rhetorical exercise, but the irreplaceable rendering of a comprehensive vision of the world.[34]

Of course, a refocusing can raise new questions about the significance of its objects. In particular, the reader who sees Spenser's duplicity as mimetic may ask whether or not it can be penetrated, whether or not the text and the world that it imitates can be understood. In the work of Williams and MacCaffrey, two opposing answers emerge, neither of them very satisfactory. First, the poem may be a tissue of "clues, simple, complex, obvious, subtle, and above all, diverse, for penetrating [an enigmatic] surface." Certain passages analyzed by Williams or MacCaffrey do seem to work that way. For instance, the Red Cross Knight is initially beguiled by the forest of particulars in which he wanders; so are we, thanks to Spenser's detailed catalogue of trees. It is with a shock of recognition that we read Una's identification of the place: "This is the wandring wood, this Errours den." Again, when two bizarre figures in Book II are finally called Furor and Occasion, confirming various iconographical and circumstantial clues, "the continued metaphor emerges from darkness into the light of analysis and explicitness." But such allegorical epiphanies are rare, especially after the first two books. Elsewhere, allegorical patterns remain hypotheses, never confirmed; sometimes we cannot tell the veil from what it covers, the false leads from the genuine clues. Thence follows MacCaffrey's alternative suggestion, that Spenser's mimetic duplicity is to be not unraveled but simply acknowledged. The allegory's "self-regarding didactic point" is simply that both the universe of discourse and the wider world remain for the most part obscure and equivocal, and the demonstration "exposes and disinfects its natural fallen duplicity."[35] That seems to me a

34. K. Williams, p. xiii; MacCaffrey, p. 47. Other writers make similar claims about Spenser's allegory; Roche, for instance, writes that it reflects an analogical vision of the universe (p. 8). But they fail to recognize the severe tensions and uncertainties of Spenser's "analogy," seeing his allegory in virtually the same terms in which Singleton and Auerbach see Dante's. Williams and MacCaffrey honor the distinction by defining Spenser's subject not as the hierarchical, analogical vision granted by divine grace but as "the zodiac of [human] wit" (Williams, xii)—that is, reality as fallen humanity perceives and imagines it.

35. MacCaffrey, pp. 40, 42–45, 47, 53. The episode from bk. I is discussed in K. Williams, pp. 1–3.

true but not a sufficient conclusion, however. Aside from the anomaly whereby a text exposes the duplicity of signs and then goes on signifying, the exposure is only a negative revelation, incapable of development. To continue reading *The Faerie Queene,* we must somehow go beyond the recognition that it often cannot be read.

Williams and MacCaffrey do continue reading, greatly to the benefit of their own readers. But the two dead ends to which their central insight leads illustrate a fallacy that haunts Spenser's readers. The unsatisfactory alternatives I have outlined—either we can decipher Spenser's Real referents after all or, if we cannot, the text merely signifies its own incoherence and the world's—rest on an equation between coherent meaning and reference to allegorical Realities. As Rosemond Tuve points out, a text's meaning is never equivalent to its allegorical ideas.[36]

The false equation persists partly because Spenser himself seems to encourage it. "[T]ruth is one in all," declares Artegall (V.xi.56), and the text usually seems to point toward some great unifying allegorical pattern. That the pointing is usually obscure and frequently counteracted does not make it any less urgent. But the object of the pointing is important in its absence, not in its presence. Spenser accepts as conditions for his poem both the indecipherability of intelligibles in the fallen world and the human need to read them; "truth is one in all" constitutes neither empirical observation nor dogma but Artegall's credo. The poem both signifies allegorical ideas and signifies in opposition to them because its largest referent is allegorical meaning in abeyance—dimly sensed, aspired toward, postulated, misconceived, reformulated. The "clues" of the poem, misleading or inadequate with regard to allegorical ideas, are fully readable as signifiers of allegory in abeyance. That is not to say that they signify only the abeyance of meaning, as Jonathan Goldberg has suggested.[37] The

36. Tuve, pp. 28–29.
37. Goldberg sees in the "features which have always disturbed and provoked [Spenser's] readers" a central principle of Spenserian narration (p. xi), and he characterizes *The Faerie Queene* as "an 'endlesse worke' of substitution, sequences of names in place of other names, structures of difference, deferred identities" (p. 11). Such statements anticipate some of mine. It seems to me that Goldberg misses the allegorical dimension of the poem, however. He regards allegory as a mode that offers "explanatory principles" (p. xiii) and that invites us to "[leave] behind the narration and its actors for the sake of meaning" (p. 76n), not as a narrative principle in its own right. Thus he overlooks, for instance, the ontological metamorphoses of Timias and Florimell in bk. IV. He also sees (and deconstructs) the poem as essentially self-referential in both senses—putatively referring both to itself and to the characters'

opaque passages, the equivocations, the tentative formulations, and the occasional authoritative generalizations all define, in significantly varied ways, the ever-changing parameters of our uncertainty.

Spenser's duplicity with regard to his Real referents is neither duplicitous nor cynical with regard to our moral and intellectual condition. Duessa betrays only those who expect perceptible signs to lead directly to Truth and who then recoil, as does the Red Cross Knight, into despair about finding Truth at all. Avoiding both overcredulity and despair, the successful reader in Faeryland finds meaning in the forms of Truth's absence.

Perhaps a better exemplar of Spenser's duplicity than Duessa is Britomart, who disguises herself not to delude the credulous but to pursue a vision. Britomart's legend offers a particularly rich example of allegory in abeyance. Its concern with human love locates it "in the middest," as close to material flux as to timeless ideas. Britomart herself strikes many readers as an "extremely unallegorical" hero, and the Legend of Chastity has been called "a book of perplexities" whose "allegorical significance is fluctuating and uninsistent."[38] If its conceptual meaning is indeed especially uncertain, Book III demonstrates particularly clearly Spenser's differences from other allegorists. Focusing on the book's first six cantos, I will explore the meaning of Spenser's elusive meaning.

Book III opens with the withdrawal of an allegorical identification. The previous book's "allegorical core," to use C. S. Lewis' term, was Guyon's visit to Alma at the House of Temperance. With its two frontal beacons, its plumbing system, and its three upper chambers occupied by a sage, a historian, and a visionary (II.ix), Alma's House was a composite of building and body—a vision of the human being as a rational fabrication, a protection for virtue. At the beginning of Book III Guyon and Arthur return to Alma's dwelling to recuperate from recent adventures. The narrator tells us that after allowing their wounds to heal, they

> Of the faire *Alma* greatly were procured,
> To make there lenger soiourne and abode;

---

psyches—to the exclusion of the Real domain of allegorical reference. In this respect he resembles Angus Fletcher, whose analysis of the "daemonic agency" of allegory rests on the premise that narrative agency must normally be human (see below, n. 44).

38. Hough, p. 169; K. Williams, p. 80; Hough, p. 168.

> But when thereto they might not be allured,
> From seeking praise, and deeds of armes abrode,
> They courteous conge tooke, and forth together yode.
>
> [III.i.1]

Clearly the knights are not leaving the temperate soul and the well-ordered body; they are turning away from a climactic allegorical vision, as all questing knights eventually must do. But the treatment of Alma and her castle as ordinary chivalric props signals that allegorical vision has already left the knights—and the reader. The double perspective has flattened; most of the syncretic meaning so carefully established in Book II has quietly drained away. The knights have also lost some of their own universal meaning, for Guyon now wanders outside his own legend and Arthur is not playing his usual role as rescuer. Their adventures remain for a time the anonymous encounters of ordinary knights errant (III.i.3). Characters and reader alike await a new dispensation.

A new allegorical order does appear when Guyon and Britomart joust, but, as we have already seen, it does not fully transfigure the text. Appearing in retrospect and tentatively, it hovers above a narrative that does not completely embody it. So do all the general meanings of the first canto. We may regard the magic power of Britomart's spear as the force of love, of chastity, or of love tempered by chastity, but the identification is neither overt nor univocal; moreover, the narrator will later undermine it by telling us that the spear was enchanted by the ancient pagan magician Bladud, for his own purposes (III.iii.60). Spenser offers with one hand allegorical meanings that he retracts with the other. Similarly, when Britomart abstains from "beauties chace"—the pursuit of Florimell—and the narrator praises her "constant mind" (III.i.19), we easily infer that Chastity has resisted the allure of Sensual Beauty. But of course we are also reminded that Britomart does not care for "Ladies Loue": perhaps Chastity deserves less credit for her steadfastness than does her gender.

The same can be said of her coolness toward the lascivious Malecasta. Having defeated Malecasta's knights, Britomart enters the Castle Joyous with no passion stronger than scorn; through her visored eyes the sweet violence of the Venus-and-Adonis tapestry looks comfortably cautionary (III.i.34–40) and Malecasta's own erotic rages seem comic (III.i.41 and 48–53). But Britomart's aloofness depends partly on her disguised sex. Conversely, Malecasta's unchastity is extenuated by her understandable and presumably blameless assumption that her guest is male. The bedroom farce that closes the canto further muddles the putative confrontation between Chastity and Unchastity; finally, when Britomart is wounded by Malecasta's servant Gardante, we wonder if she has been implicated in her opponent's vice. We might subsume the entire canto under an allegorical pattern to which, we feel, it ought to conform—chastity allies itself with temperance, ignores sensual beauty, defeats lasciviousness, and finally flees unchastity—but the events coincide with those patterns only partially and, as it were, by accident.

Spenser's opening cantos typically establish simple allegorical mottoes based on two opposing terms—holiness defeats error, temperance redeems blood guilt, justice ends inequity—but set at some distance from the narrative's pictorial surface. The reader who ignores that distance, identifying narrative and motto, will be confused by later cantos. We soon discover that the Red Cross Knight has defeated not universal Error but only one metaphoric monster and that Guyon has not rescued all mankind from original sin. Here Britomart's subsequent adventures show that she has not conquered lasciviousness itself. The allegorical patterns suggested by her early encounters signify less in themselves than in their tentative, equivocal relationship with the rest of the text.

That relationship reveals the position of the patrons of virtue, intermediate between eternal formulations and contingency. After blundering and temporizing, Guyon, Arthur, and Britomart enact a *discordia concors* between temperance and chastity, but they do so as well-meaning but fallible knights. The narrator's shortsighted praise of their chivalry suggests that they are not turned into personifications by their moment of allegorical grace. Britomart's spear bears Bladud's ancient and amoral enchantment; only with luck and good will can the enchantment take form as the sacred power of virtuous love. Conversely, Britomart herself has acted out most of the operations of ideal chastity by the end of the first canto—but without full consciousness or control. Her gestures have yet to be tested and given integrity through her own erotic experience. The first canto's events both are and are not the actions of chastity, temperance, and so forth; the elimination of the ambivalence, the permanent unification of act and ideal, will be the virtuous knights' great, ultimately uncompletable quest.

After the first canto, even the mirage of allegorical certainty re-
cedes. Several critics have noted that personifications and other abstractions are rare in most of Book III.[39] So, surprisingly enough, are
episodes involving clearly chaste or lustful behavior. That does not
mean that we ignore allegorical meaning and simply enjoy the intermeddled adventures. Because Spenser's allegory is always to some
degree hypothetical, always present as a possibility, we are impelled
continuously to seek in the pictorially presented narrative the kind of
philosophical and moral coherence that we saw in the first canto's
abstractions. We cannot often find it, of course; indeed, the terms of
our failure express Spenser's vision of chastity.

The most urgent kind of pressure toward allegorical reading is the
impulse to make moral judgments. Allegory always encourages such
judgments, less because allegorists wish to preach than because good
and evil tend to subsume all other intelligibles in our culture. Book
III's summary rubrics and psychomachic opening canto, not to mention the scheme set forth in Spenser's letter to Raleigh, induce us to
assign to any narrative detail a positive or negative valence with
regard to Chastity. But the expectation is immediately frustrated in
the second canto.

Riding away from Malecasta's castle, Britomart engages in a rather
puzzling conversation with the Red Cross Knight (or with Guyon;
Spenser's slip at III.ii.4 indicates the instability of the connection
between knight and idea).[40] She asks where she can find Artegall and
explains that she wishes to avenge a great dishonor that he has done
her. In fact, of course, she seeks Artegall because she has fallen in love
with a vision of him. Her disingenuousness, which must bear partial
responsibility for certain paternalistic readings of Britomart as a
"proud girl" in love,[41] presents a genuine problem to anyone trying
to assess the wider and more serious implications of her actions. On
the one hand, reluctance to admit one's love does indicate modesty,
and thus perhaps chastity. On the other hand, Britomart could meet

39. See Foster Provost, "Treatments of Theme and Allegory in Twentieth-Century
Criticism of *The Faerie Queene*," in *Contemporary Thought on Edmund Spenser*, ed.
Richard C. Frushnell and Bernard J. Vondersmith (Carbondale: Southern Illinois
University Press, 1975), p. 13; Frederick M. Padelford, "The Allegory of Chastity in
The Faerie Queene," *SP* 21 (1924):367.

40. Goldberg makes a complementary point about this "shuffling of names": "retrospectively," he says, it "may undermine the stability of the identities of the heroes in
the first two books of the poem" (p. 5).

41. See, for instance, Hough, pp. 114–15, 169.

modesty's demands more easily by telling her companion nothing about her motives, and when she reiterates her fabrication, the praise of Artegall which she elicits from the Red Cross Knight gives her a secret and quite a sensual pleasure (III.ii.11–12, 15). We can safely conclude that Britomart's motives are mixed.[42]

A more serious ambivalence appears in the behavior of the moral exemplar of the entire poem, the Knight of Magnificence. I have noted that when Arthur, Timias, and Guyon ride after Florimell in the first canto, the narrator seems to praise Britomart for shunning "beauties chace." He thereby implicitly dispraises the male knights, though not very strongly—after all, Florimell is being threatened by a "foule foster," and virtuous knights can only wish to rescue her. But later the poem becomes markedly equivocal about Arthur's pursuit, beginning in a serpentine sentence that reports that he has found Florimell's track: "But fairest fortune to the Prince befell, / Whose chaunce it was, that soone he did repent, / To take that way, in which that Damozell / Was fled afore, affraid of him, as feend of hell" (III.iv.47). Arthur's immediate reason for regretting his good fortune is merely that it disappoints him: he does not overtake Florimell before nightfall. But he curses night and fortune in an uncharacteristically ill-tempered way (III.iv.52, 55–61), and we may wonder at his zeal in pursuing the maiden—especially since Timias has long since diverted the forester. The narrator describes Arthur as a ship "whose Lodestarre suddenly / Couered with cloudes, her Pilot hath dismayd" (III.iv.53); when the prince wishes presently that Florimell were "[h]is Faery Queene" or that Gloriana were more like Florimell (III.iv.54), he demonstrates that he has indeed lost his steady orientation toward the loadstar of his quest.

Referring to this episode, Kathleen Williams eloquently summarizes the ethical ambivalence of Book III's early cantos:

> For this is what is typical of the Faeryland of Book III, that one's own intentions and those of others, and the meaning of situations and

---

42. The reader who knows what will follow may see that Britomart's pretended antagonism to Artegall ironically anticipates their disguised combat in bk. IV and therefore inaugurates a thematic concern with love as a form of strife. But that thematic pattern is beyond Britomart's knowledge, and it is too broad and distant to carry clear ethical signals into the present episode. The action here bears an uncertain relationship with the Virtue.

actions, constitute a net of enigmatic possibilities. To ride after a distressed lady would seem to be the knightly thing, but in this area of experience its motives may turn out to be dubious enough. The obviously chivalric thing may not do, may serve only to conceal from one's self a trace of the predatory.[43]

It is true that the book's ambivalences recall the mixed motives familiar in ordinary experience, but to see them simply as psychological realism would limit our understanding of the poem. The "net of enigmatic possibilities" is significant primarily within its own context, in relation to the univocal referents of allegory.

The interplay between allegorical certainties and ethical ambivalences also dominates the long embedded narrative in the second and third cantos. In flashback, we learn that the onset of Britomart's love for Artegall was a complex and troubling experience. Although Spenser establishes the virtue of both lovers and the rightness of their eventual union, here the conventional erotic oxymorons—living death, freezing fire, pleasing images that inflict terrible pain, and so forth—are deepened by a dramatic portrayal of love as physical, mental, and even moral affliction. Britomart sees Artegall in a magic globe that usually reveals the threats of enemies; she experiences love as sickness, enervation, and fear; she calls her passion a crime and neglects religious devotions because of it; her nurse tries to exorcise the love through witchcraft even while insisting that it is innocent and good. Britomart's love is a profoundly ambivalent, even amoral force that might better be called magical than allegorical—like an allegorical agent in being intangible and apparently autonomous, but undefined, irrational, disruptive. It is a "secret powre vnseene" (III.i.7), revealed in disturbances and represented in ambivalent periphrasis.[44]

The amoral force driving Britomart bears a crucial but complex relationship to the allegory of chastity. As is frequently pointed out,

43. K. Williams, p. 83.

44. My distinction between magical and allegorical causation is intended in part to counter Angus Fletcher's identification of the two (*Allegory*, pp. 187–90). Allegorical causation is not like the contagious magic or daemonic possession that overrides physical law and human will. It is, rather, the agency of ideas: faith combats idolatry, genius serves nature, and so forth. Only in an allegory such as *The Faerie Queene*, where human causation seems for long periods to operate autonomously, can that causation give way to magic; and even here the magical force is quite distinct from the rational agency of allegory.

Britomart alone among Spenser's heroes has no mandate from Gloriana. What motivates her is not an assigned task but a desire. Although that desire and Chastity both seem to cause her actions, so that some readers amalgamate the two into a single impulse toward virtuous love,[45] her consuming, destructive passion almost opposes what we would normally call chastity. Her desire for Artegall and her championship of chastity sometimes intersect but just as often diverge, in a counterpoint that challenges both Britomart herself and her critics.

Britomart's nurse is the first to attempt to merge eros and Virtue. Having learned that her charge does not love in violation of taboo, and having failed to dispel the love, Glauce accepts it as suprarational, not subrational: "loue can higher stye, / Then reasons reach" (III.ii.36). We may remember, however, that the nurse's name links her with blindness; her definition of love is a statement of faith.

The same kind of statement comes, ironically enough, from the seer to whom Glauce takes Britomart. Merlin assures the two women that Britomart's love is providentially directed:

> It was not, *Britomart,* thy wandring eye,
>   Glauncing vnwares in charmed looking glas,
>   But the streight course of heauenly destiny,
>   Led with eternall prouidence, that has
>   Guided thy glaunce, to bring his will to pas. . . .
>
>   [III.iii.24]

But Merlin himself was, as Spenser reminds us, "begonne / By false illusion of a guilefull Spright" (III.iii.13) and will eventually be entrapped by a deceitful lover (III.iii.10–11). And his long preview of the generations that will benefit from Britomart's love is insidiously equivocal. He begins with the successful rebellion against Saxon usurpation by Britomart, Artegall, and their immediate descendants, but the momentum of his story continues through the Saxon resurgence under Gormond. Spenser then fully exploits certain moral ambiguities that had fascinated English chroniclers since Layamon: in attempting to prolong a victory over wicked Saxon rulers, the Britons

---

45. For instance, Susannah Jane McMurphy, *Spenser's Use of Ariosto for Allegory* (Seattle: University of Washington Press, 1924), p. 41; Lewis, *Allegory of Love,* pp. 338–39.

will accept the aid of a Saxon deserter who will lead them in battle against a Saxon saint. The ensuing British defeat is not only decisive but also divinely sanctioned (III.iii.36–41). "Then woe, and woe, and euerlasting woe, / Be to the Briton babe, that shalbe borne, / To liue in thraldome of his fathers foe" (III.iii.42). Understandably, Britomart is alarmed rather than encouraged by the prophecy, and she asks if things will improve. Merlin reassures her by recounting the restoration of British power and virtue under the "royall virgin" (III.iii.44–49), but once again his vision betrays his optimistic thesis: " 'But yet the end is not,' " he proclaims, and then stops, "As ouercomen of the spirites powre, / Or other ghastly spectacle dismayd, / That secretly he saw, yet note discoure" (III.iii.50).

Merlin's chronicle serves not so much to bolster British chauvinism, as F. M. Padelford suggests, as to expound, precisely and subtly, the structure of meaning in which Britomart will move.[46] Merlin claims that the forces directing her, and thus directing history, are rational and benign. Experience that seems chaotic actually manifests providential order; Britomart's love is really a Virtue. But Merlin seeks confirmation of his grand claim in a secular, linear vision of history, thus placing the claim beyond ultimate confirmation. Allegorical order remains an optimistic hypothesis concerning ambivalent evidence.

Britomart's ensuing adventures do not support the hypothesis. As the narrative returns to the present, she parts from the Red Cross Knight and rides "without repose or rest," "Following the guidance of her blinded guest" (III.iv.6). Arriving at the coast, she sees in the stormy ocean a reflection of the internal turmoil produced by her two "bold and blind" forces: "Loue my lewd Pilot hath a restlesse mind / And fortune Boteswaine no assuraunce knowes" (III.iv.8–10). When a strange knight accosts her, her passionate sorrow becomes equally passionate anger:

> As when a foggy mist hath ouercast
>   The face of heauen, and the cleare aire engrost,
>   The world in darknesse dwels, till that at last
>   The watry Southwinde from the seabord cost
>   Vpblowing, doth disperse the vapour lo'st,

46. Padelford, pp. 372–73.

And poures it selfe forth in a stormy showre;
So the faire *Britomart* hauing disclo'st
Her clowdy care into a wrathfull stowre,
The mist of griefe dissolu'd, did into vengeance powre.

[III.iv.13]

The recurrence here of a single image, the stormy sea, produces an effect often called allegorical—the absorption of setting, dialogue, and action into one metaphoric pattern. But the pattern is not named, apart from the image of a force that transmutes one namable condition into another, as storms transform the elements.

Not surprisingly, the undefinable force issues in behavior susceptible to diverse evaluations. For overthrowing Marinell, Britomart has been called a "public menace," immature and heartless; alternatively, she has been deemed heroic and noble, especially in contrast with Marinell's unnatural inaction.[47] Both judgments are defensible: Marinell is indeed proud, ill advised, and almost bestial in his opulent isolation (III.iv.14–17, 20–24), and he threatens the hero who presumably holds our sympathies; on the other hand, hints of violence and brutality oddly darken Britomart's triumph (III.iv.16–18). Marinell's injury will ultimately bear positive results, but they cannot now be foreseen and are hardly part of Britomart's intention. Indeed, her intention seems inscrutable, even to her. Only to the eyes of faith are the turbulent forces propelling her, and her nation, identifiable with the "streight course of heauenly destiny." And while Spenser advances that kind of allegorical faith, he simultaneously undermines it, leaving us, like Britomart, to steer between absent fixities and palpable confusions.

As Britomart rides away from Marinell, leaving the episode's ambiguities where they lie, the narrative enters an interlude that is significantly irrelevant to the allegory of chastity. We learn first that Marinell's isolation was engineered by his mother, Cymoent, a sea nymph, who had been told that a "virgin strange and stout him should dismay, or kill" (III.iv.25). Then the poet describes Cymoent's own idyllic realm—her pretty games, her chariot drawn by trained

---

47. Paul J. Alpers, *The Poetry of "The Faerie Queene"* (Princeton: Princeton University Press, 1967), p. 385, and Mary Adelaide Grellner, "Britomart's Quest for Maturity," *SEL* 8 (1968):41; Iris Tillman Hill, "Britomart and *Be Bold, Be Not Too Bold*," *ELH* 38 (1971):182.

dolphins, her undersea bower (III.iv.29–43). Clearly Britomart's passion is utterly alien here, where sea storms readily abate before the nymphs' commands (III.iv.31) and where even anguish is stylized and somewhat pretty (III.iv.40–42). Equally alien is the kind of ambivalence that has troubled Britomart. Obviously decorative and sensual, the objects, words, and images of Cymoent's realm exert little pressure toward allegorical meaning and thus avoid semantic uncertainties. Certain abstract meanings do emerge, but effortlessly, borne by forms and gestures fixed in conventional codes. That is perhaps why Cymoent misinterprets the prophecy regarding Marinell: "ill" from a woman means only what it means within pastoral convention, "womens loue" (III.iv.25–27). With Marinell's injury, equivocation and mutability disrupt Cymoent's realm simultaneously, and the poet's comments identify both with the "mortall state" from which she cannot ultimately protect her son (III.iv.26–28). To live in the mortal world is to encounter "subtile sophismes" and "double senses" and thus to doubt the referents of prophecies; to reemerge from this set piece into Spenser's allegory is, similarly, to doubt once again the reference of the allegorical terms that purport to shape the narrative.

It is fitting that Marinell has entered the world of mortal uncertainties to seek Florimell, for she produces some of the book's most intriguing allegorical equivocations. Pursuit of her has already led Arthur into the same kind of ethical ambivalence that entangles Britomart, and for nearly the same reason: in pursuing a beautiful vision, each knight manifests both a Virtue and a much more ambiguous impulse. But in the fourth and fifth cantos, the ambiguity of the characters' motivation is compounded by new uncertainty, concerning their ontological status.

When John Livingston Lowes complained of a "maddening play of telescoping personalities," he meant that Spenserian figures shift from "allegorical" to "realistic," seeming to be ideas at one moment and people at the next. Changes in ontological perspective occur in all allegory, but what irritated Lowes was that Spenser's inconsistencies cannot be reconciled. Where Prudentius' syncretic agents easily subsume particular manifestations and Bunyan's allegorical metaphors slide from particular to universal, Spenser's visualizable figures act sometimes like people and sometimes like allegorical agents. On the one hand, the Red Cross Knight is not holiness but its agent; on the other hand, Gardante's wounds are not merely physical but also moral. A given agent can also move from one level of abstraction to another, and, most disturbingly, such shifts can reverse the agents' meanings. That is particularly true in Book III. In the first canto Britomart acts chastely, but she also seems to be the avatar of a larger force, eros, that arouses passion in Malecasta and perhaps in Guyon. Britomart generally acts in the first of those two perspectives, striving to control eros rather than serving as its vessel. But the ambivalence between autonomous individual and avatar appears also in other agents, particularly Florimell and those that encounter her.

Florimell bursts into the poem with the suddenness and brilliance of a supernatural sign, like a comet that alarms mortal observers (III.i.15–16). In following her unhesitatingly, Arthur and Guyon enter the "chace of beautie excellent" (III.i.19, iv.45), and we will later learn that everyone sees Florimell as "the fairest wight aliue" (III.v.5)—a puzzling phenomenon unless she is beauty itself. Many readers have so identified her.[48] Yet we see her also as a creature, a "fearefull damzell" who flees like a hare or dove from predators (III.iv.46, 49). As we follow her panicky flight through the book, we hesitate between judging her as a particular being, perhaps an excessively timid one, and reading her behavior as a philosophical proposition.

To recognize that hesitation is to suspect that Spenser's poetic vehicle redefines his philosophical tenor, that for him, Florimell's ontological instability is proper to beauty itself. She extends across the full range at which beauty can be manifested, from the essence, experienced as pure light, to the vulnerable and mutable creature. And in showing its ontological range, Florimell shows us also that beauty's nature and effects vary according to its level of being. Her "stedfast chastitie and vertue rare" (III.v.8) confirm the Neoplatonic correlation of beauty with goodness; but insofar as her beauty is sensual, it bears only an accidental connection with goodness, as will become unmistakably clear when a witch creates a copy of Florimell without her virtue. If ideal Beauty manifests the Good, in the material world the relationship between signified and signifier can be broken. To know what a lover of beauty loves is therefore difficult. Insofar as Florimell manifests virtuous beauty, Arthur's quest for her must fur-

---

48. For instance, Roche, p. 161, and William Nelson, *The Poetry of Edmund Spenser: A Study* (New York: Columbia University Press, 1963), p. 227.

ther his quest to serve Gloriana and "confound" her foes (I.ix.16–17); at the same time, Florimell the individual is an alternative to Gloriana, a fellow creature whom Arthur may find more beautiful. His pursuit of Florimell in the fourth canto is in fact a Platonic regression in which his focus shifts from the unifying and ideal nature of Beauty to the accidental individuality of beauty's incarnation.

Arthur's confusion increases with the onset of darkness, a curse to those ontologically intermediate creatures who seek spiritual good but need the sun to find it. With daylight, conversely, comes a restoration of focus. Arthur fortuitously meets a dwarf sent from the court to seek Florimell. Having asked the dwarf "what is that Lady bright," the prince learns that she is the "bountiest virgin" alive, incomparable for chastity and virtue (III.v.7–8). By imploring Arthur's aid in returning her to Gloriana's court, the dwarf redirects the pursuit of beauty toward its proper ideal objective. He thereby also reunites the quests of Florimell and of Gloriana:

> So may ye gaine to you full great renowme,
> Of all good Ladies through the world so wide,
> And haply in her hart find highest rowme,
> Of whom ye seeke to be most magnifide:
> At least eternall meede shall you abide.
>
> [III.v.11]

Even as Arthur returns to a Platonic perspective on "beauties chace," however, his squire is experiencing other versions of the play of telescoping personalities. Florimell's would-be ravisher turns out to be as ontologically unstable as she is. At first a despicable but eminently defeatable "villen" out of romance convention, the forester becomes bolder and more insidious as he flees deeper into his native terrain. He summons two brothers to help him resist Timias, and the "three / Vngratious children of one graceless sire" invite some such allegorical identification as Maclean's: "Perhaps signifying the lusts variously of eye, ear, and touch."[49] A clearer signal that Timias has encountered allegorical opposition is that in defeating the brothers he receives a deep wound in his left thigh that threatens to deprive him of honor (III.v.20, 26). What has happened to him happens often in *The Faerie Queene*, particularly in Book III, and exemplifies strikingly the

---

49. Maclean, note to III.v.15, in *Poetry of Edmund Spenser*, ed. Maclean, p. 256.

peculiarities and the power of Spenserian allegory. Initially a lustful churl out of a pseudomedieval romance, the forester swells night-marishly into lust itself. The shift overthrows semantic and ethical relationships, for the vice that Timias battles can no longer be confined within an opponent's psyche: lust invades our conception of Timias even before the forester pierces his fictional body. Both knight and squire lose their way in ontological boundary changes—the one excluded from his ideal by its particularization, the other subsumed in what he set out to destroy.

Timias' experience repeats itself after he is wounded. Under Belphoebe's compassionate treatment, the wound looks like a specific, curable injury, but the particular cure actually deepens the universal affliction by providing an object for the generalized erotic desire to which Timias has become vulnerable. To make matters worse, the agent who heals Timias is no less ambiguous than the one who wounded him, though she is considerably more benevolent. In the letter to Raleigh, Spenser identifies Belphoebe as a type both of Chastity and of Queen Elizabeth I, but she first appears in one of his most heavily sensual passages as a "mortall wight" capable of great tenderness, even of embarrassment (III.v.28–36). To love such a figure is to be caught in paradox. The exemplar of goodness and chastity properly arouses love, which Timias yields as a tribute of honor (III.v.43, 47); yet his love seeks a kind of possession that would shame both lover and beloved (III.v.44–45). Apparently Chastity has two bodies, just as does the queen. In asking whether Belphoebe is a goddess or a woman (III.v.35), Timias expresses no mere romantic hyperbole, but an urgent dilemma: how can anyone love a personified and regal Chastity without violating what he seeks to wed? The only solution, he feels, is to die (III.v.45–47).

The existence of which Timias despairs seems at this point to be a series of unbearable but unresolvable equivocations. That is, the objects of desire and of aversion are all embodied universals whose nature as embodiments differs from their nature as universals: to combat a ravisher is to incur lust; a physical cure exacerbates a spiritual malady; love for embodied chastity conflicts with chastity. At the end of the fifth canto Timias' dilemma imposes itself explicitly on the reader. The narrator, who in describing Timias' pain sympathetically has deprecated Belphoebe's coldness (III.v.43, 50), suddenly exhorts all women to emulate Belphoebe's purity (III.v.53–55).

The poem thus gives contradictory signals on the concrete and abstract levels, urging us simultaneously toward empathy with human suffering and toward approbation of the absolute virtue that withholds "that soueraigne salue" from all the world (III.v.50). The flower of Belphoebe's chastity was planted in Paradise and transferred to "stocke of earthly flesh" (III.v.52); we may suspect that the engrafting did not take. Ideals and universals oppose their own embodiments, producing a dissociation of meanings which paralyzes Timias and the narrative.

Like the ethical ambivalence in which Britomart leaves Marinell, the impasse at the end of the fifth canto is evaded by a shift in narrative mode. Once again the poem digresses into something like pastoral, and once again the digression begins with the impregnation of a sleeping nymph. This time, however, the interlude is no mere definition by contrast of the arena of serious meaning. What begins as pastoral digression ends as a myth embodying the central themes of the Legend of Chastity.

To explain Belphoebe's unnatural perfection, the narrator describes her miraculous birth: her mother, Chrysogone, was impregnated by the sun, "withouten pleasure," while she slept, and then was delivered, again asleep, "withouten paine" (III.vi.5–9, 26–27). Belphoebe is the product of a perfectly chaste sexuality. That she has a twin called Amoret seems to express in different form a reconciliation of chastity with erotic love. The discovery of the twins by Diana and Venus multiply mirrors the same theme: after quarreling over Venus' accusation that Diana has given refuge to Cupid, the goddesses make their peace; seeking Cupid together, they find instead avatars of themselves—infants who will manifest eros and its restraint—who are also doubles of each other.

The Garden of Adonis, where Venus takes Amoret to be nurtured, enshrines ideal sexuality—ideal in that eros flows freely but "[w]ithout fell rancor, or fond gealosie" (III.vi.41), ideal also in that philosophical ideals merge with erotic and generative images. If "the substratum revealed in the Garden is the inarticulate life-force," it is a life-force miraculously tempered, rationalized, purged of sin.[50] Outside the Garden, Cupid leaves disturbance and discord in his wake (III.vi.13–14), but inside, he settles down in peaceful monogamy with

50. MacCaffrey, p. 260.

Psyche (III.vi.49–50). In thus exorcising the tension between eros and
virtue, Spenser's myth implicitly resolves the conflicting demands on
Timias in the previous canto. On the one hand, Diana's relaxed and
human mood here resembles Belphoebe's when she seduced Timias,
and the Garden of Adonis recalls the "earthly Paradize" in which the
squire received his invisible erotic wound (III.v.40); on the other
hand, no one in this garden is torn as Timias was between erotic and
Platonic imperatives.

   Indeed, to say that eros and chastity are here reconciled is to stop
short of the truth. Reconciliation implies some residual difference,
but this eros and this chastity are interchangeable. Early in the canto
Diana appears in uncharacteristic dishabille, while Venus must hunt
through the wild forests for her son (III.vi.17–20). Despite some
initial embarrassment, the goddesses accept their transposition with a
good grace and pursue Cupid together. After adopting one of Chrysogone's daughters, each goddess attempts to isolate the child within
her own condition, but the twins turn out to mirror each other—the
one lovingly chaste, the other chastely loving (III.v.54–55, vi.52).
More broadly, the canto proceeds as a large interchange of opposites.
It begins presumably with the genesis of Chastity—that is,
Belphoebe's birth—but the narrative of Chrysogone's impregnation
turns out to be richly sensual. From there, the "thread unwound half-
wittingly by the poet," to use MacCaffrey's phrase, takes us into the
search for Cupid, the discovery of Chrysogone's daughters, and the
nurturing of one of them—not Belphoebe after all, but Amoret.[51] In
the end, more than half the canto concerns the locus and the lessons
not of Diana but of Venus. It is striking that the Garden of Adonis, a
sexual *plaisance* and universal nursery, should be widely regarded as
the Legend of Chastity's allegorical core. Those who so regard it are
not mistaken. What makes the Garden so attractive is precisely that
without discontinuity or impropriety it substitutes a myth of fecundity for the vision of chastity toward which we and the characters
have been struggling.

   In doing so, the Garden ends another kind of struggle as well. For
most of the sixth canto, meanings emerge from the text without the
hesitations and equivocations that have thus far separated images
from concepts. They do so largely because of the conventional and

51. Ibid., p. 257.

thus automatic identifications of such mythic figures as Venus and Diana, identifications that the narrative sustains. The canto becomes slightly more opaque where Spenser turns to philosophical myth, but there too his meanings are decipherable allusions: the modern reader rightly expects clear explanatory footnotes for the iron and golden walls, the wheel of regeneration, the derivation of substance from Chaos, and so forth. The one apparent exception illuminates the rule. The "naked babes" that grow in the Garden, repeatedly called "shapes" or "formes" of creatures, have been diversely identified, and with good reason: while suggesting abstract, unchanging Platonic forms, they also "are variable and decay," like an "outward fashion" and unlike the changeless substance that temporarily clothes them (III.vi.38).[52] But the ambiguity is not an equivocation but a *discordia concors*. The naked babes are mutable compounds of eternal pattern and everlasting substance, somewhat like earthly creatures. They differ from earthly creatures in being eternally recurrent, counteracting the ravages of time through the cycles of time. More fundamentally, they differ from creatures in embodying their ideals perfectly: growing without corruption, loving without discord, and reproducing by direct action of "the mightie word, / Which first was spoken by th'Almightie lord" (III.vi.34), they avoid the conflict between change and stability which has plagued fleshly life since the Fall. Their mutable physical forms are not essentially opposed to their Platonic forms. Thus we can respond to them simply as "forms," without interpretation, just as we can read the rest of the canto without hesitating between incompatible meanings. The Garden of Adonis is a semiotic idyll, equating what is elsewhere opposed—concept and image, essence and manifestation, and the double senses of single signs.

One might therefore accept Spenser's myth as a definitive solution of the aesthetic, philosophical, and sexual problems that Book III explores—if one could ignore the mode that makes the solutions possible. Granted that myth can convey truths that lie deeper than fact, justifying a suspension of disbelief in its improbabilities, in this

---

52. Among the most useful discussions of the naked babes are Judith C. Ramsay, "The Garden of Adonis and the Garden of Forms," *UTQ* 35 (1965–66):188–206; John E. Hankins, *Source and Meaning in Spenser's Allegory: A Study of "The Faerie Queene"* (Oxford: Clarendon Press, 1971), pp. 264–77; Fred L. Milne, "The Doctrine of Act and Potency: A Metaphysical Ground for Interpretation of Spenser's Garden of Adonis Passages," *SP* 70 (1973):279–87; MacCaffrey, pp. 259–67.

case to suspend disbelief is to read deficiently. From the beginning of the sixth canto, Spenser calls attention to the artificiality of his myth.

He does so partly by making extravagant claims for the myth's reality. His distancing of the Garden of Adonis from his narrative and his claims to have experienced it himself might have released it from fiction into general psychic or philosophical reality. But he undoes that effect by claiming for the Garden an empirical reality that it clearly does not possess. Though he has been there, the narrator does not know whether the Garden is at Paphos, on Cyprus, or at Cnidus; in any case, it is "farre renowmed by fame" (III.vi.29). The survival of Adonis is not a mystical truth but a widespread report: "some say," "they say," "they call" (III.vi.46–48). The miraculous impregnation of Chrysogone by the sun is recorded in "antique books," and besides, "reason teacheth" that sunbeams engender living things (III.vi.6–8). Through such pseudoverification, Spenser's myths take on the character of tall tales.

They further outstrip credulity by speciously appropriating existing systems of belief, as when Spenser invites us to see the conception of Belphoebe and Amoret as a new Immaculate Conception:

> For not as other wemens commune brood,
> They were enwombed in the sacred throne
> Of her chaste bodie. . . .
> . . .
> But wondrously they were begot, and bred
> Through influence of th'heauens fruitfull ray. . . .
>
> [III.vi.5–6]

The lovely story trembles on the edge of blasphemy. Later episodes commit a pagan version of blasphemy: the reconciliation of Venus and Diana, the survival of Adonis, and the daughter born to Cupid and Psyche are all apocryphal with regard to classical mythology. The Garden itself might be called apocryphal with regard to cosmology. If it recalls the realm of Platonic ideas or Augustinian *rationes seminales,* Spenser claims also that it exists within the universe and that its inhabitants periodically pass through a gate to the earth that we know. Thus the Garden claims to be both a fictional model for reality and a part of nonfictional reality.

All myth makes that claim, according to Roland Barthes: it shows us fabricated signs that are also, it would have us believe, natural ones.[53] But Spenser exposes the claim even while making it. Granted that his myths are poetically true, bearing wide significance for the rest of the poem and even for extratextual reality, they bear as well palpable signs of their own fabrication. The meaning of the Garden of Adonis is not so much that oppositions unite in love as that such unity is the product of the ardent imagination.

Taken together, the first six cantos of the Legend of Chastity imply that allegorical certainty exists only in an artificial world: where the narrative points clearly to Reality, it undermines its references to material reality, and where it imitates human experience most closely, its allegorical referents are unusually distant. The second half of the book confirms and extends that pattern.

Not surprisingly, allegorical certainty again withdraws from the world of the poem after the Garden of Adonis. At the end of the seventh canto the Squire of Dames flatly denies that ideals govern erotic behavior, having induced innumerable women to provide proof (III.vii.53–61). His claim is heinous but difficult to refute. Where ideal chastity does govern sexual attractiveness, in Florimell, it depends for survival on such contingencies as exhaustible palfreys and untrustworthy hosts. For two cantos the Knight of Chastity herself must play a walk-on role in a grotesque drama of possessiveness and lust (III.ix–x). And if Virtue loses its sovereignty over the narrative, the dominance of Vice remains covert. The most frightening thing about the later portions of Book III is that the allegorical hypotheses now center around evil but still defy formulation, so that they induce a kind of paranoia. When Florimell flees one ravisher only to be nearly caught by another, or when successive lustful monsters behave with nightmarish similarity, we dimly sense some terrible elemental agent capable of infinite metamorphosis and more real than the overtly discrete episodes. The possibility of a comprehensive diabolical referent haunts the text.

The last two cantos make the diabolical agent explicit, in a countermyth to the Garden of Adonis. Instead of a *discordia concors*, the House of Busyrane proposes universal anarchy: here social bonds are transgressed, pleasure and pain interchange, love is indistinguishable from hate, and the gods shift shapes and change their natures. But this

53. Roland Barthes, *Mythologies* (1957), trans. Annette Lavers (New York: Hill & Wang, 1972), pp. 129–31.

time the claims of the myth to be real cannot be dismissed as ironic, for the most terrible aspect of Busyrane's unprincipledness is that it confounds the distinction between construct and reality. Beginning as a mere tapestry and a masque led by poets, his myth swells into allegory and finally assumes unmistakable power over a victim. Busyrane's ontologically ambivalent metaphors have been variously identified as Petrarchan conceits and as projections from one or another character's psyche;[54] their ultimate claim is to be at once artificial, psychologically real, and cosmically Real, a vision of Love itself. Busyrane proposes that the one comprehensive certainty is a magical force that annihilates certainties.

Against Busyrane's vision, the last part of the Legend of Chastity does propose a force for moral and ontological stability: the individual will. The two great victories of the book, Florimell's over Proteus and Britomart's over Busyrane, are neither mythic nor strictly allegorical, but personal. Thomas Roche violates his own proscription on "the 'predicate nominative' stage of criticism" when he writes of Florimell's resistance, "Spenser is telling the reader that beauty and love are above the physical, mutable realm of Proteus."[55] On the contrary, if Florimell were beauty and love, then her harrowing experiences throughout Book III would mean that beauty and love can indeed be defiled by the physical, mutable realm, and the present episode would demonstrate their vulnerability to Proteus: he imprisons Florimell forcibly and will later release her only by special favor to Cymodoce. But in fact, we are shown not that beauty, love, or chastity transcends mutability, but that Florimell decides to remain chaste at any cost:

54. Felicity A. Hughes, for instance, asserts that Busyrane's house "represents a psyche (Amoret's) disturbed by passion"; A. Kent Hieatt calls Busyrane "an element in Scudamour himself"; and William Nelson suggests that Britomart is here fighting an internal battle. See Hughes, "Psychological Allegory in *The Faerie Queene* III.xi–xii," *RES* n.s. 29 (1978):129; Hieatt, *Chaucer, Spenser, Milton* (Montreal: McGill/Queens University Press, 1975), p. 130; Nelson, *Poetry of Edmund Spenser*, pp. 230–32. The observation that Busyrane's tapestry and pageant originate in courtly conceits has become common since its statement by Roche in *Kindly Flame*, pp. 76–88. My conclusion about Busyrane was suggested in part by a remark of Berger's about Acrasia: he calls her a "demonic allegorist" who presents false images as if they were real (*Allegorical Temper*, pp. 224–26).

55. Roche, pp. 5, 162.

> Downe in a Dongeon deepe he let her fall,
> And threatned there to make her his eternall thrall.
>
> Eternall thraldome was to her more liefe,
>   Then losse of chastitie, or chaunge of loue:
>   Die had she rather in tormenting griefe,
>   Then any should of falsenesse her reproue,
>   Or looseness, that she lightly did remoue.
>
> [III.viii.41–42]

Having wavered for so long between fugitive essence and timid creature, Florimell here looks very much like a human being. What preserves her virtue is the same thing that endangered it: its incarnation in a particular creature who can accept or resist defilement.

Similarly, Amoret escapes Busyrane not because Chastity is stronger than Incontinence—chaste Amoret cannot escape by herself—but because Britomart alleges chastity to be stronger and makes good on her claim. Like Scudamour, Britomart suspects that Busyrane may be an unopposable "god" (III.xi.22); like Amoret, she is horrified and bewildered at the apparent reality of his pageantry (III.xi.49–54, xii.36–37); but she treats the masque as "idle shewes" (III.xii.29) and the enchanter as an ordinary mortal enemy. Whatever equivocal messages she receives, she "still with stedfast eye and courage stout / [Abides], to weet what end [will] come of all" (III.xii.37). We attribute her victory not to the force of chastity but to her own strength of character. The terrifying ambivalence of the Legend of Chastity can be resolved only by what we might call an existential decision and what Spenser would probably have called an act of faith.

In a text that is still to some degree allegorical, to some degree shaped by intelligibles that transcend the individual, such a resolution must be tentative. After recounting Florimell's heroic decision, the narrator asserts that her "famous deed" even now earns praise in heaven (III.viii.42): as before, an extravagant claim to empirical reality undermines itself, reminding us that Spenser has invented deeds that ought to have been done. Ironic assertion gives way to plain exhortation when the narrator adds that he has praised Florimell in order "to enroll [her] memorable name, / In th'heart of euery honourable Dame, / That they [her] vertuous deedes may imitate, / And be partakers of [her] endless fame" (III.viii.43). The reality of Florimell's

act is its possibility: it must be realized by Spenser's readers. Harry
Berger, Jr., makes a similar point about Britomart's victory when he
calls it premature and argues that in subsequent books the principle
represented by Busyrane will be "*introjected* into the souls of true
lovers."[56] In the poem and outside it, Proteus and Busyrane survive.
Where Reality itself remains ambivalent, a resolution in favor of
Virtue depends perpetually on innumerable potential heroes.

Both as a whole and in its parts, *The Faerie Queene* is notoriously
inconclusive. The end of the third book leaves us "in the middest" of
plot and meaning alike. Perhaps Books III and IV together convey a
vision of the relationship between human sexuality and the ideal
order whose sexual aspect we call chastity, but that vision would be
difficult to articulate. Even to set forth its terms as I have done is to
delimit it unduly, since Spenser does not name the referents of his
allegory. With the qualified exception of Malbecco, whose obsessive
approach to Jealousy constitutes a grotesque deformation (III.ix–x),
the book's agents are not abstractions or intelligibles. On the other
hand, neither are they people; so to regard them is, as Jonathan
Goldberg points out, to accept the "lure of the proper name," which,
like the complementary invitation to translate characters into abstractions, tempts us "to take one figure for another."[57] Either Elfins or
legends, Spenser's agents betray their inventedness as clearly as do
their names. Pure abstraction and recognizable humanity are the opposing limits of their condition, repeatedly approached but, like the
pillar on Olympus, zealously avoided (III.vii.41). Without violating
that avoidance, we cannot summarize the story in either psychological or allegorical terms.

Movement toward an unattainable referent is fundamental to *The
Faerie Queene*. Although this study has emphasized Spenser's perpetual deferral of allegorical Reality, Book III also regularly invokes
but disclaims empirical truthfulness. In asserting that one can still hear
Merlin's "sprights" working underground near Carmarthen (III.iii.8–
9), that Queen Elizabeth descends from Britomart (III.iii.49), and that
Faeryland is credible in the same way as were Virginia and South

56. Berger, "Busirane and the War between the Sexes: An Interpretation of *The
Faerie Queene* III.xi–xii," *ELR* 1 (1971):115.
57. Goldberg, p. 76n.

America before their European discovery (II, Proem, 1–3), Spenser subverts the serious claims to factual authenticity that he makes elsewhere. His exaggerated appeals to history and geography defeat themselves in the same way as do the overly neat allegorical hypotheses in the opening cantos. James Nohrnberg speaks of the *"worldization* of presence" in *The Faerie Queene* and other Renaissance literature—that is, "the transposition of its sphere from an eternal to a temporal context." If "presence" is the reality attributed to some extratextual referent, *The Faerie Queene* does not so much transpose presence as multiply it. Deferred reality surrounds the text on all sides—in the "sempiternal or transcendent sphere," in history, in myth, in individual subjectivity.[58] The poem is in fact named for a determining referent who never appears.

Perhaps its ultimate subject is therefore the absence of all its referents. Its allusions, more numerous and broader than those of other allegories, are also remarkably, self-consciously artificial; as Berger notes, "Spenser's Faery is not merely a projection of his romantic imagination; it is an image which he has labeled for all to see, 'Projection of Man's Imagination.'"[59] The poem's patent improbabilities, its stylization and decorative anachronism, its blatant invocations of literary convention, and its absurd claims to veracity all emphasize its status as a fabrication. Thus it both magnifies and subverts the potential connections between poetic language and various realities.

But to regard *The Faerie Queene* as primarily a deconstruction of linguistic reference would be to impoverish it. The poem asserts connections as energetically as it undoes them—connections not just between text and external reality, but also among levels of reality and among kinds of text. Michael Murrin rightly sees in Faeryland not the "true imaginative absence of all particular space or time" which Coleridge noted, but a "euhemeristic amalgam" of many inconsistent times and places.[60] As is well known, Spenser also invokes the ontological hierarchies of Neoplatonism by, for instance, "shadowing" ideas with agents, or by nominally unifying various levels of abstraction in such a character as Florimell; that he simultaneously denies

58. James Nohrnberg, *The Analogy of "The Faerie Queene"* (Princeton: Princeton University Press, 1976), p. 53.

59. Berger, *Allegorical Temper,* p. 171.

60. Michael Murrin, *The Allegorical Epic: Essays in Its Rise and Decline* (Chicago: University of Chicago Press, 1980), chap. 5, especially p. 131.

the correspondences merely sends us in search of more. He both affirms and denies still other kinds of correlation in his poem's literary structure, for the principle of composition of *The Faerie Queene* seems to be the assimilation of the dissimilar: classical myths merge with traditional episodes from romance and with biblical stories, while disparate genres—epic and romance, Chaucerian burlesque and Platonic myth, rustic fantasy and ethical discourse—form uneasy unions. Conversely, Spenser often defracts a single plot motif through episodes with divergent or even opposing meanings. "Elements spiral through our consciousness, altered each time they appear to us but always recognizable in their new contexts, always enhanced in significance by their old."[61] In an atmosphere so charged with fusion, many readers come to regard successive episodes and agents as parts of larger units or versions of each other. Such connections turn out to be unstable but irresistible; analogy is the poem's universal mirage.

Susanne Murphy tells us that the tradition of Neoplatonic theory, in which she places Spenser's thought, maintained, "first, that proper contemplation of the world below leads the contemplator to the truth which lies beyond it; and second, that each discernible lack in this world guarantees the existence of the ideal form in which that lack will be fulfilled."[62] If that is true, Neoplatonists sought ontological correspondences but observed discontinuities and absences. It seems to me that Renaissance writers' assertions of correspondence do in fact accompany a new awareness of disjunctions: earlier versions of the Elizabethan world picture had not needed drawing. A defensive tone certainly pervades the allegorizations that the analogical premise produced in Renaissance literary criticism. Thus the duplicity of Spenserian allegory is one reflex of a vast urge to harmonize claims to reality whose incompatibility must nonetheless be acknowledged. Idea and image, sign and referent, history and vision, Britain and Faeryland, whimsy and philosophy, poem and world are simultaneously identified and opposed, producing what A. Bartlett Giamatti has called a "dialectic" between synthesis and dissolution. On the one hand the poet's mind can hold various worlds "in a loose synthesis together,

61. Susan C. Fox, "Eterne in Mutabilitie: Spenser's Darkening Vision," in *Eterne in Mutabilitie*, ed. Atchity, p. 29.

62. Susanne Murphy, "Love and War in Spenser's *The Faerie Queene*," in *Eterne in Mutabilitie*, p. 128.

yielding itself . . . to the passion of detecting analogies and correspondences between them." On the other hand, that passion is a kind of "artistic greediness" which inevitably pushes beyond feasible coherences to the brink "of anarchism, of dissolution, of decay."[63]

We associate that kind of dialectic more often with some of Spenser's contemporaries and immediate successors than with Spenser himself. The quotations in my last two sentences come in fact from discussions of Elizabethan dramatists and Metaphysical poets, commonly regarded as essentially unlike Spenser. But they fit Spenser, just as certain remarks by recent Spenserians might be appropriated to describe Metaphysical wit: "In any analogical relation such as that between Image A and Idea B, Spenser is likely to exploit the differences between the two"; Spenser "found nothing incompatible in the association of an absurd tale and a deeply moral significance. . . . Such disparity between story and meaning goes against the modern grain." In a brief but suggestive article, Judith Dundas associates allegory with certain forms of seventeenth-century wit: "the bringing together of unlike things may be contained in one of Donne's figures—the flea or the canonization—or it may furnish the figural structure for a more ambitious effort like *The Faerie Queene*." "Why," she asks, "are we willing to accept the judgment of Donne's contemporaries that he was a witty poet but not the judgment of Spenser's contemporaries that he too was witty?"[64]

In concurring with Dundas that Spenserian allegory is a form of wit, I do not mean to enter the debate over schools of seventeenth-century imagery. To determine once and for all the degrees of resemblance between "Elizabethan" and "Metaphysical" probably would not teach us much, even if it could be done. But the distinctions commonly drawn have curtailed our understanding of *The Faerie Queene*. Even in proposing similarities between allegory and the con-

---

63. A. Bartlett Giamatti, *Play of Double Senses: Spenser's "Faerie Queene"* (Englewood Cliffs, N.J.: Prentice-Hall, 1975), pp. 68–70; Basil Willey, *The Seventeenth-Century Background* (1934; rpt. Garden City, N.Y.: Doubleday Anchor Books, 1953), p. 50; T. S. Eliot, "Four Elizabethan Dramatists" (1924), in *Selected Essays, 1917–1932* (1932; rpt. New York: Harcourt, Brace, 1950), p. 98.

64. Berger, *Allegorical Temper*, pp. 122–23; Nelson, "Spenser *ludens*," in *A Theatre for Spenserians*, ed. Judith M. Kennedy and James A. Reither (Toronto: University of Toronto Press, 1973), pp. 96–97; Judith Dundas, "Allegory as a Form of Wit," *Studies in the Renaissance* 11 (1964):223, 233.

ceit, Dundas calls the latter "an uncommitted or ironical seeing of resemblances" which "instead of asserting a world order, . . . reflects the breaking up of one," in contrast to allegory, "a mode of expression using a coherent set of symbols" which "asserts too much for our doubtful minds."[65] Dundas here misses the implications of her own reclassification of Spenser. A poem that borrows its plot from a parody, recasts it as the soul's ascent to Glory, and presents • the result as both a satire and a political compliment is a most peculiar "mode of expression" with a most precarious kind of coherence. Only if we approach it with a priori ideas about its meaning can we regard its assertions of order as incompatible with doubt and irony.

Such mistaken distinctions rest on the received definition of allegory as the mode that disallows uncertainty and open-endedness. Thus Cleanth Brooks sets the Cavalier and Metaphysical poets apart from the Spenserians because the latter "tended to approach the poem as an allegorical construct, that is, as an abstract framework of statement which was to be illustrated and ornamented by overlaying the framework with concrete detail."[66] But the dismissive category "ornament" is no more legitimate for allegory than for other texts, and *The Faerie Queene* uses abstract statement not as a framework but as one component of meaning in problematic juxtaposition with others. Admittedly the Metaphysical conceit differs significantly from allegory in what Earl Miner calls its private mode;[67] admittedly, too, allegory's universal scope and its incorporation of various doctrines decompress its ironies, so that dissimilarities are not exactly yoked together, certainly not with violence. But even those differences may be referred to scale rather than to the structure of meanings. Spenser's allegorical vision does have a subjective basis, if we can believe the humble and even anxious poet-narrator.[68] In the allegorical core of Book VI, Calidore will see concentric rings of allegory and myth dance around Colin Clout's lass and finally vanish to leave only the singer himself. And if Spenser elsewhere presents the heterogeneous

65. Dundas, p. 233.
66. Cleanth Brooks, *Modern Poetry and the Tradition* (1939; rpt. New York: Oxford University Press, Galaxy Books, 1965), p. 220.
67. Earl Miner, *The Metaphysical Mode from Donne to Cowley* (Princeton: Princeton University Press, 1969), chap. 1.
68. On the subjectivity of Spenserian allegory, see Judith H. Anderson, *The Growth of a Personal Voice* (New Haven: Yale University Press, 1976).

elements of his vision as variant realities, wider than the poet's psyche, their ironic juxtaposition gains in resonance what it loses in intensity.

Our two greatest allegories establish what has been traditionally called an integument between Truth and its perceivers. Because the integument is a network of signs, to attempt to rend it is to destroy the means of perception. Humbly following those signs, Dante's pilgrim grasps at last the fusion of Truth and veil, form and image, Word and flesh. Spenser's poem, in contrast, ends not with a vision but with a prayer for one (VII.viii.2). Like John Donne, Spenser inhabits a world "runne quite out of square," where not even the stars manifest God's order perfectly:

> for the heauens reuolution
> Is wandred farre from, where it first was pight,
> And so doe make contrarie constitution
> Of all this lower world, toward his dissolution.
>
> [V, Proem, 4]

Rather than dramatizing the dialectic of dissolution and synthesis in the individual mind, like Donne, Spenser assigns his imagination the admittedly impossible task of realigning heaven and earth. His achievement can be regarded as both the pinnacle of allegory and its undoing. Where the traditional allegorist subsumed reality at the most syncretic level, where Bunyan posited the interconvertibility of universals with individual experience, *The Faerie Queene* acknowledges alternative realities—intelligible, sensible, and artificial—and embraces them all. But where other allegories resolve themselves into intelligibles, or into irony, or into novelistic reality, there is no place for the weary Spenserian navigator to rest. His world continually needs allegorizing, his allegory calls out for substantiation, and his fiction asserts its independence of both. *The Faerie Queene* redefines allegory as the speech whose reference will remain in doubt, at least until the promised "Saboaths sight."

Epilogue:
Allegory's Aftermath

Midway through her journey toward self-integration, the protagonist of Charlotte Brontë's *Villette* finds herself in a kind of *psychomachia*. A question that she has asked herself is answered by "Reason, coming stealthily up to me through the twilight of [a] long, dim chamber." Reason utters an eloquent but absolutely cheerless analysis of Lucy Snowe's situation. Then, drifting toward sleep, Lucy encounters Reason's "soft, bright foe, *our* sweet Help, our divine Hope," a "Deity unquestioned . . . [whose] essence foils decay." But if this "daughter of Heaven" holds sway through the night, Reason returns at dawn, with the rain, the wind, and the icy water of Lucy's bedside carafe. She is displaced again some twenty-five pages later by her enemy, now called Feeling, but she soon forcefully reenters Lucy's heart and acts through her body.[1]

That Charlotte Brontë should thus evoke a mode as embarrassingly implausible in her day as allegory may be attributed to what Tony Tanner calls her "new 'readings' of reality, which slip away from the constraining bourgeois house of consciousness."[2] That is, the passage may be seen as a resurrection of allegory effected by a writer who felt

1. Charlotte Brontë, *Villette*, ed. Mark Lilly, introd. Tony Tanner (New York: Penguin, 1979), pp. 307–9, 334–35.
2. Tanner, Introduction to *Villette*, p. 27.

claustrophobic amidst empirical realism. Yet from another point of view, Brontë's venture into personification shows how far she is from the tradition of narrative allegory. What she here explores is, as Tanner says, consciousness—mental states, not the organizing principles of the universe. If the antirational force variously called Hope, Feeling, and Imagination constitutes a "Deity" potentially transcending social reality, it remains essentially a personal goddess, numinously maternal, appearing in Lucy Snowe's most deeply private moments. As for Reason, the proof of her superior claim to Lucy's obedience is her dissolution into cold fact and socially presentable action.

Writers of the eighteenth and nineteenth centuries transplant allegory into a new context that changes it utterly. Locally, intelligibles and abstractions act and receive action, but only as brief variations on a narrative code whose substantives are concrete. Empress Fame may publicize his coronation, but we have no doubt that the blanks in Sh____'s name are to be filled with deictic syllables. Time and Steel, Megrim and Affectation appear in Belinda's world as rhetorical correlatives to the real agents' self-inflation. Where they do not satirize by ontological hyperbole, as in the examples from Dryden and Pope, the abstract agents of eighteenth-century poetry bear a slightly mannered air, summoning up—with, in the best literature, a fine, self-aware irony—the grand stabilities of a golden age. The Romantics take the allegorical realm more seriously, as do those novelists such as Brontë whom they influenced, but they ground it in their own kind of particularity: the self. Wordsworth promises to sing "of Truth, of Grandeur, Beauty, Love, and Hope, / And melancholy Fear subdued by Faith," among other capitalized abstractions; but "I sing," the main clause of his Miltonic sentence, receives maximum prominence. And while he asserts for Beauty a reality surpassing that of "the most fair ideal Forms," Wordsworth suggests that such transcendent presences originate in a marriage between human intellect and the observable universe.[3] Not their actions and relations but his own reaching out (or reaching in) toward them shapes his narrative poetry. Wordsworth thus continues, albeit in a different spirit, Bunyan's insistence

---

3. William Wordsworth, Preface to the 1814 edition of *The Recluse,* in *The Poetical Works of William Wordsworth,* ed. Ernest de Selincourt and Helen Darbishire, vol. 5 (Oxford: Clarendon Press, 1949), ll. 10–23, 42–55.

on the intuitive validation of universals and Locke's relocation of the study of ideas from ontology to epistemology.

The history of allegory since Wordsworth and Brontë is more complex. If those writers transmit a heritage of Lockeian empiricism, they stand also at the beginning of a new intellectual era, one in which empiricism and its literary reflexes would come to seem naive and impoverished. Many recent writers seem to share the conviction of Louis MacNeice that "realism in the photographic sense is almost played out and no longer satisfies our needs."[4] That conviction may have led to the current resurgence of interest in allegory among critics and scholars. If those scholars are to be believed, it has led also to a resurgence of allegory itself. In the work of Emerson, Hawthorne, Melville, Kafka, and others, many students of allegory see evidence that we have entered a new allegorical age.[5]

Having motivated some excellent rereadings, that claim carries a certain weight. But it seems to me that the best of the rereadings either proceed without significant reference to the modern works' status as "allegory" or use allegory primarily as a point of contrast. And in fact any definition of allegory that applies equally to the *Psychomachia* and *Gravity's Rainbow*, or even to *The Faerie Queene* and "Rappaccini's Daughter," cannot be particularly useful or credible. Such definitions either focus on criteria that are important but not definitive for allegory, such as the use of wordplay to generate narrative structure, or seem "ultimately to amount," in Humphrey Tonkin's words, "to 'all kinds of literature and literary elements which are not mimetic.' "[6] A more precise definition of allegory—for instance, "narrative whose agents and objects are Realistic"—must, it seems to me, exclude virtually everything after Bunyan. Generic boundaries are seldom absolute, of course; even Dante and Spenser vary the classic form significantly by postponing or deferring their Real referents. But the writing of the past century preserves the allegorical tradition in so radically changed a form that it should be called not allegorical but postallegorical.

4. MacNeice, *Varieties of Parable,* p. 26.
5. I refer particularly to the studies by Edwin Honig, Angus Fletcher, Stephen Barney, and Maureen Quilligan. Louis MacNeice takes a similar approach, but his loose term "parable" seems to me less misleading for modern literature than "allegory," and he explores divergences within the parabolic tradition.
6. Humphrey Tonkin, "Some Notes on Myth and Allegory in the *Faerie Queene,*" *MP* 70 (1972–73):292.

Postallegorical literature takes two general forms. The one that looks most like classical allegory, although most of its texts are not intended as fiction, can be called social and psychological dialectics. Hardly a single movement or set of beliefs, it is loosely unified by the explanation of human history and behavior as the conflicts among abstractions—for instance, Marx's economic forces and Freud's components of the psyche. The writings of Marx and Freud have become increasingly important to literary criticism, not only as heuristics but also as complex readings of reality which in some ways resemble narrative and drama. Moreover, from Marxian ideas have arisen plays that seem to revive morality drama, with *dramatis personae* named Man, Woman, Billionaire, Doctor, and so forth.[7] What distinguishes such confrontations among abstractions from allegory is twofold. First, the ideas in such texts are irrevocably linked with their authors, regularly spoken of as *someone*'s ideas; with good reason Marxian drama is generally called not allegory but expressionism. We are back to Locke. Second, and complementarily, those authors base their ideas on observable reality. "Economic categories are only the theoretical expressions, the abstractions of the social relations of production," declares Marx.[8] In Marxian drama, ideas are subject not only to individual authors' changing visions but also to individual characters' wills: the Billionaire is particularized through four highly diverse generations. For Freud, too, ideas are not Realities but hypotheses, embedded in sentences whose main subjects are concrete: "As we are now prepared to find . . . ," "Here we may add that . . . ," "I ascribe this to . . ." To read such texts as allegories is to allegorize them—to suppress meaning.

Allegory's other vestige is the postrealistic narrative usually cited by those who claim that the genre lives on. To a certain point the claim holds, for the work of such writers as Hawthorne, Kafka, Mann, Beckett, and Pynchon is haunted by allegory. Through names or plot motifs, many of those writers evoke archetypal stories, including allegories: a young man looks into a paradisal garden and sees a supremely beautiful Beatrice; a stranger arrives in a snowy village and

7. Louis Broussard, *American Drama: Contemporary Allegory from Eugene O'Neill to Tennessee Williams* (Norman: University of Oklahoma Press, 1962), pp. 5–6. Broussard cites the plays of Kaiser, Toller, and Capek.

8. Karl Marx, *The Poverty of Philosophy* (1847), in *Karl Marx: Selected Writings*, ed. David McLellan (Oxford: Oxford University Press, 1977), p. 202.

finds no room at the inn; a protagonist living near a vacant lot is named Oedipa Maas. In a more general way, elements of the plots—an ethical conflict, a confrontation or anticipated confrontation with some supreme authority, a journey that turns into an obsessive and portentous quest—initiate, in Stephen Barney's words,

> the process of drawing the reader's mind away from the flow of the text, as he ceases to respond to what he reads in the way that he responds to actual history. When we stop saying, "I have seen that," or "I know how he feels," and start saying, "I have read this sort of thing before," we begin to penetrate to the Other (we are alienated) and to sense the presence of allegory—we become distracted, "drawn aside."[9]

A precondition for such "distracted" reading is some rhetorical sign that subverts the realistic premises on which we read modern narrative. It may be a signal that some supernatural phenomenon is not merely the hallucination of the character who perceives it. It may be a preternatural congruence among apparently disparate parts of the narrative, as in Nabokov and Pynchon. It may be the apparent generation of narrative action by the words that ought, if realism holds, merely to reflect action—an effect astutely explored by Maureen Quilligan. In Kafka and Beckett, it is often an opaque particularity, a stark and extreme deictic reference that promises, by a brilliant paradox, to turn into symbolism of tremendous scope and significance: "It was late in the evening when K. arrived. The village was deep in snow. The Castle hill was hidden. . . ." "[A country road. A tree. Evening.] ESTRAGON. Nothing to be done."[10]

But the promise is never quite fulfilled. What Helen Adolf writes of *The Trial*—that it "is an Everyman story that never gets beyond the first line of the old parable"—might be applied to many of the post-allegorical texts.[11] Or, as Yvor Winters writes of Hawthorne's four unfinished romances,

---

9. Barney, *Allegories of History,* p. 16.

10. Franz Kafka, *The Castle,* trans. Willa and Edwin Muir (New York: Knopf, 1959), p. 3; Samuel Beckett, *Waiting for Godot* (New York: Grove, 1954), pp. 6–7.

11. Helen Adolf, "From *Everyman* and *Elckerlijc* to Hofmannsthal and Kafka," *Comparative Literature* 9 (1957):212.

> We have . . . all of the machinery and all of the mannerisms of the
> allegorist, but we cannot discover the substance of his communica-
> tion, nor is he himself aware of it so far as we can judge. We have the
> symbolic footprint, the symbolic spider, the symbolic elixirs and poi-
> sons, but we have not that of which they are symbolic; we have the
> hushed, the tense and confidential manner, on the part of the nar-
> rator, of one who imparts a grave secret, but the words are inaudi-
> ble.[12]

Winters might have said that the inaudible voice *should* not be heard,
although it cannot be stifled; Hawthorne overgoes Spenser in that his
allegorical hypotheses are not merely elusive but also dangerous. In
Hawthorne's successors, the Realistic referent is a perpetual chimera,
the seeking of which exhausts both characters and readers.

Allegory in the broadest sense probably cannot die as long as language endures, for it is the reflex of linguistic reference itself. Once we
postulate, as we must, that any statement has a limited range of
reference, the possibility arises of doubling or extending that range, of
meaning something else. Under that very broad definition, ours is
certainly an age fascinated by allegory. But such a linguistic tendency
hardly constitutes a genre, as the variety of its current manifestations
can attest. Allegory as genre derives from one manifestation of that
tendency: syncretic statement, bearing simultaneous and equally priv-
ileged reference to concrete particulars and to universals or intelligibles. The genre has been, if not dead, changed past recognition for
centuries. The reason is not that we no longer hold to a central
dogma, as is sometimes asserted, for the "dogma" informing the
Romance of the Rose and *The Faerie Queene* is not in any significant
sense uniform. Rather, what we have lost, losing thereby the ability to
write allegory, is a certain perspective on reality—a readiness to seek
the objects of mimesis in a realm irreducible to the sensible and the
subjective.

Rosemary Freeman tells us that in 1713 Lord Shaftesbury advised
painters to place Virtue in realistic perspective. They might portray
her strength, for instance, by "designing her to stand firmly on one

---

12. Yvor Winters, "Maule's Curse, or Hawthorne and the Problem of Allegory," in
Maule's Curse: Seven Studies in the History of American Obscurantism (Norfolk,
Conn.: New Directions, 1938), pp. 19–20.

foot, the other raised upon a piece of rocky ground; there is no need
for her to be poised triumphant upon a globe."[13] That expectation of
firm empirical ground, once established, could not be waived by any
author or text, and the generations that have inherited it have approached the allegorical premise as hypothesis, private vision, or
something clutched in free-fall. Truth has withdrawn from narrative
and dramatic time, leaving fiction in its shadow.

13. Rosemary Freeman, *English Emblem Books* (London: Chatto & Windus,
1948), p. 17.

Works Cited

ADENEY, ELIZABETH. "Bunyan: A Unified Vision?" *Critical Review* 17 (1974):97–109.

ADOLF, HELEN. "From *Everyman* and *Elckerlijc* to Hofmannsthal and Kafka." *Comparative Literature* 9 (1957):204–14.

ALANUS DE INSULIS. *The Complaint of Nature by Alain de Lille*. Trans. Douglas M. Moffat. Yale Studies in English 36. New York: Holt, 1908.

ALLEN, DON CAMERON. *Mysteriously Meant: The Rediscovery of Pagan Symbolism and Allegorical Interpretation in the Renaissance*. Baltimore: Johns Hopkins University Press, 1970.

ALPAUGH, DAVID M. "Emblem and Interpretation in *The Pilgrim's Progress*." *ELH* 33 (1966):299–314.

ALPERS, PAUL J. *The Poetry of "The Faerie Queene."* Princeton: Princeton University Press, 1967.

ANDERSON, JUDITH H. *The Growth of a Personal Voice: "Piers Plowman" and "The Faerie Queene."* New Haven: Yale University Press, 1976.

ATCHITY, KENNETH JOHN. "Dante's *Purgatorio*: The Poem Reveals Itself." In *Italian Literature: Roots and Branches: Essays in Honor of Thomas Goddard Bergin*, ed. Giose Rimanelli and Kenneth John Atchity. New Haven: Yale University Press, 1976.

——, ed. *Eterne in Mutabilitie: The Unity of "The Faerie Queene": Essays Published in Memory of Davis Philoon Harding, 1914–1970*. Hamden, Conn.: Shoe String Press, Archon Books, 1972.

AUERBACH, ERICH. *Dante: Poet of the Secular World*. Trans. Ralph Manheim. Chicago: University of Chicago Press, 1961.

——. "Figura." 1944. Trans. Ralph Manheim. Reprinted in *Scenes from the Drama of Western Literature*. New York: Meridian Books, 1959.

———. "Figurative Texts Illustrating Certain Passages of Dante's *Commedia.*" *Speculum* 21 (1946):474–89.

BAIRD, CHARLES W. *John Bunyan: A Study in Narrative Technique.* Port Washington, N.Y.: Kennikat Press, National University Publications, 1977.

BARBI, MICHELE. "The Divine Comedy." In *Life of Dante,* trans. and ed. Paul G. Ruggiers. Reprinted in *Essays on Dante,* ed. Mark Musa. Bloomington: Indiana University Press, 1964.

BARDSLEY, CHARLES W. *Curiosities of Puritan Nomenclature.* London: Chatto & Windus, 1897.

BARFIELD, OWEN. "The Meaning of the Word 'Literal.'" In *Metaphor and Symbol,* ed. Lionel C. Knights and Basil Cottle. London: Butterworth, 1960.

———. *Poetic Diction: A Study in Meaning.* 3d ed. Middletown, Conn.: Wesleyan University Press, 1973.

BARNEY, STEPHEN A. *Allegories of History, Allegories of Love.* Hamden, Conn.: Shoe String Press, Archon Books, 1979.

BARTHES, ROLAND. *Mythologies.* 1957. Trans. Annette Lavers. New York: Hill & Wang, 1972.

———. *S/Z.* Trans. Richard Miller. New York: Hill & Wang, 1974.

BATANY, JEAN. *Approches du "Roman de la Rose."* Bordas Etudes 363. Paris: Bordas, 1973.

BATES, KATHERINE LEE. *The English Religious Drama.* New York: Macmillan, 1893.

BECKETT, SAMUEL. *Waiting for Godot.* New York: Grove Press, 1954.

BENDER, JOHN B. *Spenser and Literary Pictorialism.* Princeton: Princeton University Press, 1972.

BERGER, HARRY, JR. *The Allegorical Temper: Vision and Reality in Book II of Spenser's "Faerie Queene."* Yale Studies in English 137. New Haven: Yale University Press, 1957.

———. "Busirane and the War between the Sexes: An Interpretation of *The Faerie Queene* III.xi–xii." *ELR* 1 (1971):99–121.

———. Introduction. In *Spenser: A Collection of Critical Essays,* ed. Harry Berger, Jr. Twentieth Century Views. Englewood Cliffs, N.J.: Prentice-Hall, 1968.

BEVINGTON, DAVID M. *From Mankind to Marlowe: Growth of Structure in the Popular Drama of Tudor England.* Cambridge: Harvard University Press, 1962.

———, ed. *Medieval Drama.* Boston: Houghton Mifflin, 1975.

BLACK, MAX. "Metaphor." In *Models and Metaphors: Studies in Language and Philosophy.* Ithaca: Cornell University Press, 1962.

BLONDEL, JACQUES. *Allégorie et réalisme dans "The Pilgrim's Progress" de John Bunyan.* Archives des lettres modernes 28 (1959).

BLOOMFIELD, MORTON W. "Allegory as Interpretation." *NLH* 3 (1972):301–17.

———, ed. *Allegory, Myth, and Symbol.* Harvard English Series 9. Cambridge: Harvard University Press, 1981.

BRIDGES, ROBERT. "Bunyan's *Pilgrim's Progress.*" *Speaker,* April 1905. Reprinted in *Bunyan: "The Pilgrim's Progress": A Casebook,* ed. Roger Sharrock. London: Macmillan, 1976.

BRILL, LESLEY W. "Battles That Need Not Be Fought: *The Faerie Queene,* III.i." *ELR* 5 (1975):198–211.

BRONTË, CHARLOTTE. *Villette.* Ed. Mark Lilly. New York: Penguin, 1979.

BROOKS, CLEANTH. *Modern Poetry and the Tradition.* 1939. Reprint. New York: Oxford University Press, Galaxy Books, 1965.

BROUSSARD, LOUIS. *American Drama: Contemporary Allegory from Eugene O'Neill to Tennessee Williams.* Norman: University of Oklahoma Press, 1962.

BRUSS, ELIZABETH W. *Autobiographical Acts: The Changing Situation of a Literary Genre.* Baltimore: Johns Hopkins University Press, 1976.

BUNYAN, JOHN. *"Grace Abounding to the Chief of Sinners" and "The Pilgrim's Progress from This World to That Which Is to Come."* Ed. Roger Sharrock. Oxford Standard Authors. London: Oxford University Press, 1966.

———. *"Life and Death of Mr. Badman" and "The Holy War."* Ed. John Brown. Cambridge: The University Press, 1905.

———. *The Pilgrim's Progress from This World to That Which Is to Come.* Ed. James Blanton Wharey. 2d ed., ed. Roger Sharrock. Oxford: Clarendon Press, 1960.

CAMBON, GLAUCO. "Synaesthesia in the *Divine Comedy.*" *Dante Studies* 88 (1970): 1–16.

Castle of Perseverance, The. In *Medieval Drama,* ed. David M. Bevington. Boston: Houghton Mifflin, 1975.

CAWLEY, A. C., ed. *Everyman.* Manchester: Manchester University Press, 1961.

CHAMBERS, EDMUND KERCHEVER. *English Literature at the Close of the Middle Ages.* Oxford: Clarendon Press, 1957.

CHANDLER, S. BERNARD, AND J. A. MOLINARO, eds. *The World of Dante: Six Studies in Language and Thought.* Toronto: University of Toronto Press, 1966.

CHARITY, A. C. *Events and Their Afterlife: The Dialectics of Christian Typology in the Bible and Dante.* Cambridge: Cambridge University Press, 1966.

CHIARENZA, MARGUERITE MILLS. "The Imageless Vision and Dante's *Paradiso.*" *Dante Studies* 90 (1972):77–91.

CLIFFORD, GAY. *The Transformations of Allegory.* London: Routledge & Kegan Paul, 1974.

COLERIDGE, SAMUEL TAYLOR. *Literary Remains.* Ed. Henry Nelson Coleridge. 4 vols. London: William Pickering, 1836–39.

———. *Miscellaneous Criticism.* Ed. Thomas Middleton Raysor. Cambridge: Harvard University Press, 1936.

CULLER, JONATHAN. *The Pursuit of Signs: Semiotics, Literature, Deconstruction.* Ithaca: Cornell University Press, 1981.

——. *Structuralist Poetics: Structuralism, Linguistics, and the Study of Literature.* Ithaca: Cornell University Press, 1975.

DAHLBERG, CHARLES R. Introduction. In *The Romance of the Rose by Guillaume de Lorris and Jean de Meun,* trans. Charles R. Dahlberg. Princeton: Princeton University Press, 1971.

DAMON, PHILLIP. "The Two Modes of Allegory in Dante's *Convivio.*" *Philological Quarterly* 40 (1961):144–49.

DANTE ALIGHIERI. *Convivio.* Trans. Philip H. Wicksteed. London: J. M. Dent, 1940.

——. *Dantis Alagherii Epistolae; The Letters of Dante.* Ed. and trans. Paget Toynbee. 2d ed. Oxford: Clarendon Press, 1966.

——. *The Divine Comedy.* Trans. Charles S. Singleton. 3 vols. in 6. Bollingen Series LXXX. Princeton: Princeton University Press, 1970.

——. *The Divine Comedy of Dante Alighieri.* Ed. and trans. John D. Sinclair. Rev. ed. 3 vols. 1939. New York: Oxford University Press, 1946.

——. *La Vita Nuova.* Trans. Barbara Reynolds. Baltimore: Penguin, 1969.

DEES, JEROME S. "The Narrator of *The Faerie Queene:* Patterns of Response." *TSLL* 12 (1970–71):537–68.

DE MAN, PAUL. *Allegories of Reading: Figural Language in Rousseau, Nietzsche, Rilke, and Proust.* New Haven: Yale University Press, 1979.

——. "The Rhetoric of Temporality." In *Interpretation: Theory and Practice,* ed. Charles S. Singleton. Baltimore: Johns Hopkins University Press, 1969.

DEMARAY, JOHN G. *The Invention of Dante's "Commedia."* New Haven: Yale University Press, 1974.

DERRIDA, JACQUES. *Of Grammatology.* Trans. Gayatri Chakravorty Spivak. Baltimore: Johns Hopkins University Press, 1976.

DONALDSON, E. TALBOT. "Patristic Exegesis in the Criticism of Medieval Literature: The Opposition." In *Critical Approaches to Medieval Literature,* ed. Dorothy Bethurum. Selected Papers from the English Institute, 1958–59. New York: Columbia University Press, 1960.

DOWDEN, EDWARD. "Spenser, the Poet and Teacher." 1882. Reprinted in *Spenser: The Faerie Queene; A Casebook,* ed. Peter Bayley. New York: Macmillan, 1977.

DUNBAR, H. FLANDERS. *Symbolism in Medieval Thought and Its Consummation in the Divine Comedy.* New Haven: Yale University Press, 1929.

DUNDAS, JUDITH. "Allegory as a Form of Wit." *Studies in the Renaissance* 11 (1964):223–33.

EAGAN, SISTER M. CLEMENT, trans. "The Spiritual Combat." In *The Poems of Prudentius,* vol. 2. Fathers of the Church 52. Washington, D.C.: Catholic University of America Press, 1965.

ECCLES, MARK, ed. *The Macro Plays.* E.E.T.S. 262. London: Oxford University Press, 1969.

ECONOMOU, GEORGE D. *The Goddess Natura in Medieval Literature.* Cambridge: Harvard University Press, 1972.

——. "The Two Venuses and Courtly Love." In *In Pursuit of Perfection:*

Courtly Love in Medieval Literature, ed. Joan M. Ferrante and George D. Economou. Port Washington, N.Y.: Kennikat Press, 1975.

ELIOT, T. S. "Four Elizabethan Dramatists" (1924). In *Selected Essays, 1917–1932.* 1932. Reprint. New York: Harcourt, Brace, 1950.

EMERSON, RALPH WALDO. "Nature." In *The Complete Works of Ralph Waldo Emerson,* vol. 1. Boston: Houghton Mifflin, 1903.

Everyman. In *Medieval Drama,* ed. David M. Bevington. Boston: Houghton Mifflin, 1975.

FERGUSSON, FRANCIS. *Dante's Drama of the Mind: A Modern Reading of the "Purgatorio."* Princeton: Princeton University Press, 1953.

FIFIELD, MERLE. *The Rhetoric of Free Will: The Five-Act Structure of the English Morality Play.* Leeds Texts and Monographs, n.s. 5. Ilkley, Yorkshire: Scolar Press, 1974.

FINEMAN, JOEL. "The Structure of Allegorical Desire." In *Allegory and Representation,* ed. Stephen J. Greenblatt. Baltimore: Johns Hopkins University Press, 1981.

FISH, STANLEY E. "Progress in *The Pilgrim's Progress.*" In *Self-Consuming Artifacts: The Experience of Seventeenth-Century Literature.* Berkeley: University of California Press, 1972.

FLETCHER, ANGUS. *Allegory: The Theory of a Symbolic Mode.* Ithaca: Cornell University Press, 1964.

———. *The Prophetic Moment: An Essay on Spenser.* Chicago: University of Chicago Press, 1971.

FORREST, JAMES F. "Bunyan's Ignorance and the Flatterer: A Study in the Literary Art of Damnation." *Studies in Philology* 60 (1963):12–22.

FOX, SUSAN C. "Eterne in Mutabilitie: Spenser's Darkening Vision." In *Eterne in Mutabilitie: The Unity of "The Faerie Queene,"* ed. Kenneth John Atchity. Hamden, Conn.: Shoe String Press, Archon Books, 1972.

FRANK, ROBERT WORTH, JR. "The Art of Reading Medieval Personification-Allegory." *ELH* 20 (1953):237–50.

FRECCERO, JOHN. "The River of Death: *Inferno* II, 108." In *The World of Dante: Six Studies in Language and Thought,* ed. S. Bernard Chandler and J. A. Molinaro. Toronto: University of Toronto Press, 1966.

———, ed. *Dante: A Collection of Critical Essays.* Twentieth Century Views. Englewood Cliffs, N.J.: Prentice-Hall, 1965.

FREEMAN, ROSEMARY. *English Emblem Books.* London: Chatto & Windus, 1948.

FRIEDMAN, LIONEL. " 'Jean de Meung,' Antifeminism, and 'Bourgeois Realism.' " *Modern Philology* 57 (1959–60):13–23.

FRYE, NORTHROP. "Allegory." In *Princeton Encyclopedia of Poetry and Poetics,* ed. Alex Preminger. Enl. ed. Princeton: Princeton University Press, 1974.

———. *Anatomy of Criticism: Four Essays.* Princeton: Princeton University Press, 1957.

———. "Literary History." *NLH* 12 (1981):219–25.

———. "The Structure of Imagery in *The Faerie Queene.*" *UTQ* 30 (1960–61):109–27.

GIAMATTI, A. BARTLETT. *Play of Double Senses: Spenser's "Faerie Queene."* Landmarks in Literature Series. Englewood Cliffs, N.J.: Prentice-Hall, 1975.

GILSON, ETIENNE. *Dante the Philosopher.* Trans. David Moore. New York: Sheed & Ward, 1949.

GOETHE, JOHANN WOLFGANG VON. *Maximen und Reflexionen.* In *Goethes Werke: Hamburger Ausgabe,* vol. 12. Hamburg: Christian Wegner, 1953.

GOLDBERG, JONATHAN. *Endlesse Worke: Spenser and the Structures of Discourse.* Baltimore: Johns Hopkins University Press, 1981.

GOLDER, HAROLD. "Bunyan's Valley of the Shadow." *MP* 27 (1929–30):55–72.

GOMBRICH, E. H. *Art and Illusion: A Study in the Psychology of Pictorial Representation.* A. W. Mellon Lectures in the Fine Arts, 1956. Bollingen Series XXXV, 5. Princeton: Princeton University Press, 1969.

GRANDGENT, C. H., ed. *La Divina Commedia di Dante Alighieri.* Rev. ed. Boston: D. C. Heath, 1933.

GREEN, RICHARD HAMILTON. "Dante's 'Allegory of Poets' and the Mediaeval Theory of Poetic Fiction." *Comparative Literature* 9 (1957):118–28.

GREENBLATT, STEPHEN J., ed. *Allegory and Representation.* Selected Papers from the English Institute, 1979–80, n.s. 5. Baltimore: Johns Hopkins University Press, 1981.

GREENE, HERBERT EVELETH. "The Allegory as Employed by Spenser, Bunyan, and Swift." *PMLA* 4 (1889):145–93.

GREENE, THOMAS. *The Descent from Heaven: A Study in Epic Continuity.* New Haven: Yale University Press, 1963.

GRELLNER, MARY ADELAIDE. "Britomart's Quest for Maturity." *SEL* 8 (1968):35–43.

GUILLAUME DE LORRIS AND JEAN DE MEUN. *Le Roman de la Rose par Guillaume de Lorris et Jean de Meun.* Ed. Ernest Langlois. Société des anciens textes français. 5 vols. Paris: Didot (vols. 1–2), Champion (vols. 3–5), 1914–24.

——. *The Romance of the Rose.* Trans. Harry Robbins. Ed. Charles W. Dunn. New York: E. P. Dutton Paperbacks, 1962.

——. *The Romance of the Rose by Guillaume de Lorris and Jean de Meun.* Trans. Charles Dahlberg. Princeton: Princeton University Press, 1971.

GUNN, ALAN M. F. *The Mirror of Love: A Reinterpretation of "The Romance of the Rose."* Lubbock: Texas Tech Press, 1952.

HAMILTON, A. C. *The Structure of Allegory in "The Faerie Queene."* Oxford: Clarendon Press, 1961.

——, ed. *The Faerie Queene.* London: Longmans, 1977.

HANKINS, JOHN ERSKINE. *Source and Meaning in Spenser's Allegory: A Study of "The Faerie Queene."* Oxford: Clarendon Press, 1971.

HANSON, RICHARD PATRICK CROSLAND. *Allegory and Event: A Study of the Sources and Significance of Origen's Interpretation of Scripture.* London: SCM Press, 1959.

HAZLITT, WILLIAM. "Chaucer and Spenser." *Lectures on the English Poets* (1818). In *The Collected Works of William Hazlitt,* ed. A. R. Waller and Arnold Glover, vol. 5. London: J. M. Dent, 1902.

HIEATT, A. KENT. *Chaucer, Spenser, Milton: Mythopoeic Continuities and Transformations.* Montreal: McGill/Queen's University Press, 1975.

HILL, IRIS TILLMAN. "Britomart and *Be Bold, Be Not Too Bold,*" *ELH* 38 (1971):173–87.

HINKS, ROGER. *Myth and Allegory in Ancient Art.* Studies of the Warburg Institute 6. 1939. Reprint. Nendeln, Liechtenstein: Kraus, 1968.

HINTON, STAN. "The Poet and His Narrator: Spenser's Epic Voice." *ELH* 41 (1974):165–81.

HOLLANDER, ROBERT. *Allegory in Dante's "Commedia."* Princeton: Princeton University Press, 1969.

HONIG, EDWIN. *Dark Conceit: The Making of Allegory.* 1959. Reprint. Cambridge: Walker-DeBerry, Boar's Head, 1960.

HOUGH, GRAHAM. *A Preface to "The Faerie Queene."* 1962. Reprint. New York: W. W. Norton, 1963.

HOWARD, RICHARD. "A Note on *S/Z.*" Prefatory to Roland Barthes, *S/Z,* trans. Richard Miller. New York: Hill & Wang, 1974.

HUGHES, FELICITY A. "Psychological Allegory in *The Faerie Queene* III.xi–xii." *RES* n.s. 29 (1978):129–46.

HUSSEY, MAURICE. "The Humanism of John Bunyan." In *The Pelican Guide to English Literature,* vol. 3. Rev. ed. Baltimore: Penguin, 1960.

IRVINE, MARTIN. "Cynewulf's Use of Psychomachic Allegory: The Latin Sources of Some 'Interpolated' Passages." In *Allegory, Myth, and Symbol,* ed. Martin W. Bloomfield. Cambridge: Harvard University Press, 1981.

JACKSON, W. T. H. "Allegory and Allegorization." *Research Studies* 32 (1964):161–75.

——. "The Nature of Romance." *Yale French Studies* 51 (1974):12–25.

JAUSS, HANS ROBERT. "La Transformation de la formé allégorique entre 1180 et 1240: D'Alain de Lille à Guillaume de Lorris." In *L'Humanisme médiéval dans les littératures romanes du XIIe au XIVe siècle,* ed. Anthime Fourrier. Paris: Klincksieck, 1964.

JUNG, CARL. *The Archetypes and the Collective Unconscious.* Trans. R. F. C. Hull. 2d ed. Bollingen Series XX. Princeton: Princeton University Press, 1969.

JUNG, MARC-RENÉ. *Etudes sur le poème allégorique en France au moyen age.* Romanica Helvetica 82. Berne: Francke, 1971.

KAFKA, FRANZ. *The Castle.* Trans. Willa Muir and Edwin Muir. New York: Knopf, 1959.

KASKE, R. E. "Dante's *DXV.*" In *Dante: A Collection of Critical Essays,* ed. John Freccero. Twentieth Century Views. Englewood Cliffs, N.J.: Prentice-Hall, 1965.

KAUFMANN, U. MILO. *"The Pilgrim's Progress" and Traditions in Puritan Meditation.* New Haven: Yale University Press, 1966.

KELMAN, JOHN. *The Road of Life: A Study of John Bunyan's "Pilgrim's Progress."* 2 vols. New York: Hodder & Stoughton, n.d.

KENNEDY, WILLIAM J. "Irony, Allegoresis, and Allegory in Virgil, Ovid, and Dante." *Arcadia* 7 (1972):115–34.

———. "Rhetoric, Allegory, and Dramatic Modality in Spenser's Fradubio Episode." *ELR* 3 (1973):351–68.

KNIGHT, G. WILSON. "The Spenserian Fluidity." In *The Burning Oracle: Studies in the Poetry of Action.* London: Oxford University Press, 1939.

KNOTT, JOHN R., JR. "Bunyan's Gospel Day: A Reading of *The Pilgrim's Progress.*" *ELR* 3 (1973):443–61.

KNOWLTON, E. C. "The Allegorical Figure Genius." *Classical Philology* 15 (1920):380–84.

———. "Genius as an Allegorical Figure." *MLN* 39 (1924):89–95.

KOLVE, V. A. "*Everyman* and the Parable of the Talents." In *The Medieval Drama,* ed. Sandro Sticca. Papers of the Third Annual Conference of the Center for Medieval and Early Renaissance Studies. Albany: State University of New York Press, 1972.

KRIEGER, MURRAY. "'A Waking Dream': The Symbolic Alternative to Allegory." In *Allegory, Myth, and Symbol,* ed. Morton W. Bloomfield. Cambridge: Harvard University Press, 1981.

LAVARENNE, M., ed. and trans. *Prudence.* 3 vols. Paris: Belles Lettres, 1948.

LEAVIS, F. R. Afterword. In *The Pilgrim's Progress,* ed. Catharine Stimpson. New York: Signet, New American Library, 1964.

LEWALSKI, BARBARA KIEFER. "Typological Symbolism and the 'Progress of the Soul' in Seventeenth-Century Literature." In *Literary Uses of Typology from the Late Middle Ages to the Present,* ed. Earl Miner. Princeton: Princeton University Press, 1977.

LEWIS, C. S. *The Allegory of Love: A Study in Medieval Tradition.* Oxford: Clarendon Press, 1936.

———. *Spenser's Images of Life.* Ed. Alastair Fowler. Cambridge: Cambridge University Press, 1967.

———. "The Vision of John Bunyan." In *Selected Literary Essays,* ed. Walter Hooper. Cambridge: Cambridge University Press, 1969.

LEYBURN, ELLEN DOUGLASS. *Satiric Allegory: Mirror of Man.* Yale Studies in English 130. New Haven: Yale University Press, 1956.

LIBERMAN, M. M., AND EDWARD E. FOSTER. *A Modern Lexicon of Literary Terms.* Glenview, Ill.: Scott, Foresman, 1968.

LIMENTANI, U., ed. *The Mind of Dante.* Cambridge: Cambridge University Press, 1965.

LOUIS, RENÉ. *"Le Roman de la Rose": Essai d'interprétation de l'allégorisme érotique.* Nouvelle Bibliothèque du Moyen Age. Paris: Champion, 1974.

LOWES, JOHN LIVINGSTON. "The Pilgrim's Progress." In *Essays in Appreciation.* Boston: Houghton Mifflin, 1936.

MACCAFFREY, ISABEL G. *Spenser's Allegory: The Anatomy of Imagination.* Princeton: Princeton University Press, 1976.

MACLEAN, HUGH, ed. *Spenser's Poetry: Authoritative Texts and Criticism.* New York: W. W. Norton, 1968.

McMURPHY, SUSANNAH JANE. *Spenser's Use of Ariosto for Allegory.* University of Washington Publications in Language and Literature, vol. 2, no. 1. Seattle: University of Washington Press, 1924.

MacNEICE, LOUIS. *Varieties of Parable.* Clark Lectures, 1963. Cambridge: Cambridge University Press, 1965.

McNULTY, ROBERT. Introduction to Lodovico Ariosto, *Orlando Furioso as Translated into English Heroical Verse by Sir John Harington.* Oxford: Clarendon Press, 1972.

Mankind. In *Medieval Drama,* ed. David M. Bevington. Boston: Houghton Mifflin, 1975.

MARSHALL, MARY H. "Aesthetic Values of the Liturgical Drama." In *Medieval English Drama: Essays Critical and Contextual,* ed. Jerome Taylor and Alan H. Nelson. Chicago: University of Chicago Press, 1972.

MARX, KARL. *The Poverty of Philosophy.* 1847. In *Karl Marx: Selected Writings,* ed. David McLellan. Oxford: Oxford University Press, 1977.

MAZZEO, JOSEPH ANTHONY. "Dante's Three Communities: Mediation and Order." In *The World of Dante,* ed. S. Bernard Chandler and J. A. Molinaro. Toronto: University of Toronto Press, 1966.

———. *Medieval Cultural Tradition in Dante's "Comedy."* Ithaca: Cornell University Press, 1960.

———. *Structure and Thought in the "Paradiso."* Ithaca: Cornell University Press, 1958.

MILLER, J. HILLIS. "The Two Allegories." In *Allegory, Myth, and Symbol,* ed. Morton W. Bloomfield. Cambridge: Harvard University Press, 1981.

MILNE, FRED L. "The Doctrine of Act and Potency: A Metaphysical Ground for Interpretation of Spenser's Garden of Adonis Passages." *Studies in Philology* 70 (1973):279–87.

MINER, EARL. *The Metaphysical Mode from Donne to Cowley.* Princeton: Princeton University Press, 1969.

MURPHY, SUSANNE. "Love and War in Spenser's *The Faerie Queene.*" In *Eterne in Mutabilitie,* ed. Kenneth John Atchity. Hamden, Conn.: Shoe String Press, Archon Books, 1972.

MURRIN, MICHAEL. *The Allegorical Epic: Notes on Its Rise and Decline.* Chicago: University of Chicago Press, 1980.

———. *The Veil of Allegory: Some Notes toward a Theory of Allegorical Rhetoric in the English Renaissance.* Chicago: University of Chicago Press, 1969.

MURTAUGH, DANIEL M. "'Figurando il paradiso': The Signs That Render Dante's Heaven." *PMLA* 90 (1975):277–84.

MUSA, MARK. *Advent at the Gates: Dante's "Comedy."* Bloomington: Indiana University Press, 1974.

———, ed. *Essays in Dante.* Bloomington: Indiana University Press, 1964.

MUSCATINE, CHARLES. *Chaucer and the French Tradition: A Study in Style and Meaning.* Berkeley: University of California Press, 1957.

NELSON, WILLIAM. *The Poetry of Edmund Spenser: A Study*. New York: Columbia University Press, 1963.

——. "Spenser *ludens*." In *A Theatre for Spenserians*, ed. Judith M. Kennedy and James A. Reither. Papers of the International Spenser Colloquium. Toronto: University of Toronto Press, 1973.

NEUSS, PAULA. "Active and Idle Language: Dramatic Images in *Mankind*." In *Medieval Drama*, ed. Neville Denny. Stratford-upon-Avon Studies 16. London: Edward Arnold, 1973.

NOHRNBERG, JAMES. *The Analogy of "The Faerie Queene."* Princeton: Princeton University Press, 1976.

NORTON, GLYN P. "Retrospection and Prefiguration in the Dreams of *Purgatorio*." *Italica* 47 (1970):351–65.

NUTTALL, A. D. *Two Concepts of Allegory: A Study of Shakespeare's "The Tempest" and the Logic of Allegorical Expression*. London: Routledge & Kegan Paul, 1967.

PADELFORD, FREDERICK M. "The Allegory of Chastity in *The Faerie Queene*." *Studies in Philology* 21 (1924):367–81.

PIEHLER, PAUL. *The Visionary Landscape: A Study in Medieval Allegory*. Montreal: McGill/Queen's University Press, 1971.

PINDELL, RICHARD. "The Mutable Image: Man-in-Creation." In *Eterne in Mutabilitie*, ed. Kenneth John Atchity. Hamden, Conn.: Shoe String Press, Archon Books, 1972.

POPE, ALEXANDER. *Martinus Scriblerius' "Peri Bathous: The Art of Sinking in Poetry."* Ed. Edna Leake Steeves. New York: King's Crown Press, 1952.

POTTER, ROBERT. *The English Morality Play: Origins, History, and Influence of a Dramatic Tradition*. London: Routledge & Kegan Paul, 1975.

PROVOST, FOSTER. "Treatments of Theme and Allegory in Twentieth-Century Criticism of *The Faerie Queene*." In *Contemporary Thought on Edmund Spenser*, ed. Richard C. Frushnell and Bernard J. Vondersmith. Carbondale: Southern Illinois University Press, 1975.

PRUDENTIUS, AURELIUS CLEMENS. *Psychomachia*. In *Prudentius*, trans. H. J. Thomson, vol. 1. Loeb Classical Library. Cambridge: Harvard University Press, 1949.

QUILLIGAN, MAUREEN. "Allegory, Allegoresis, and the Deallegorization of Language: The *Roman de la Rose*, the *De planctu naturae*, and the *Parlement of Foules*." In *Allegory, Myth, and Symbol*, ed. Morton W. Bloomfield. Cambridge: Harvard University Press, 1981.

——. *The Language of Allegory: Defining the Genre*. Ithaca: Cornell University Press, 1979.

QUINTILIANUS, MARCUS FABIUS. *The Institutio Oratoria of Quintilian*. Ed. and trans. H. E. Butler. 4 vols. Loeb Classical Library. New York: Putnam, 1922.

RAMSAY, JUDITH C. "The Garden of Adonis and the Garden of Forms." *UTQ* 35 (1965–66):188–206.

RIFFATERRE, MICHAEL. *Semiotics of Poetry*. Bloomington: Indiana University Press, 1978.

ROBERTSON, D. W., JR. "The Doctrine of Charity in Mediaeval Literary Gardens: A Topical Approach through Symbolism and Allegory." *Speculum* 26 (1951):24–49.

ROCHE, THOMAS P., JR. *The Kindly Flame: A Study of the Third and Fourth Books of Spenser's "Faerie Queene."* Princeton: Princeton University Press, 1964.

ROSSMAN, VLADIMIR R. *Perspectives of Irony in Medieval French Literature.* De Proprietatibus Litterarum, Series Maior, 35. The Hague: Mouton, 1975.

RUSKIN, JOHN. *The Stones of Venice.* 3 vols. New York: John Wiley, 1872.

RYAN, LAWRENCE V. "Doctrine and Dramatic Structure in *Everyman.*" *Speculum* 32 (1957):722–35.

SAPEGNO, NATALINO. "Genesis and Structure: Two Approaches to the Poetry of the 'Comedy.'" Trans. P. Boyde. In *The Mind of Dante,* ed. U. Limentani. Cambridge: Cambridge University Press, 1965.

SAYERS, DOROTHY, trans. *Purgatory.* London: Penguin, 1962.

SCOTT, JOHN A. "Dante's Allegory." *Romance Philology* 26 (1972–73):558–91.

SEUNG, T. K. *Cultural Thematics: The Formation of the Faustian Ethos.* New Haven: Yale University Press, 1976.

SHARROCK, ROGER. *John Bunyan.* London: Hutchinson's University Press, 1954.

——. "Women and Children." In *Bunyan: "The Pilgrim's Progress": A Casebook,* ed. Roger Sharrock. London: Macmillan, 1976.

——, ed. *Bunyan: "The Pilgrim's Progress": A Casebook.* London: Macmillan, 1976.

SHERRY, RICHARD. *A Treatise of Schemes and Tropes.* 1550. Reprint. Gainesville, Fla.: Scholars' Facsimiles and Reprints, 1961.

SILVESTRIS, BERNARD. *Commentary on the First Six Books of Virgil's "Aeneid."* Trans. Earl G. Schreiber and Thomas E. Maresca. Lincoln: University of Nebraska Press, 1979.

SINGLETON, CHARLES S. *Dante Studies 1. Commedia: Elements of Structure.* Cambridge: Harvard University Press, 1954.

——. *Dante Studies 2. Journey to Beatrice.* Cambridge: Harvard University Press, 1958.

——. "In Exitu Israel de Aegypto." *Dante Studies* 78 [*78th Annual Report of the Dante Society of America*] (1960):1–24.

——. "The Irreducible Dove." *Comparative Literature* 9 (1957):129–35.

——. "The Irreducible Vision." In *Illuminated Manuscripts of the Divine Comedy,* ed. Peter Brieger, Millard Meiss, and Charles S. Singleton, vol. 1. Bollingen Series LXXXI. Princeton: Princeton University Press, 1969.

SMALLEY, BERYL. *The Study of the Bible in the Middle Ages.* 2d ed. Oxford: Basil Blackwell, 1952.

SMITH, MACKLIN. *Prudentius' "Psychomachia": A Reexamination.* Princeton: Princeton University Press, 1976.

SPENSER, EDMUND. *The Faerie Queene.* Ed. Edwin Greenlaw et al. Vols. 1–6 of *The Works of Edmund Spenser: A Variorum Edition.* Baltimore: Johns Hopkins University Press, 1932–39.

SPIVACK, BERNARD. *Shakespeare and the Allegory of Evil: The History of a Metaphor in Relation to His Major Villains.* New York: Columbia University Press, 1958.

STEADMAN, JOHN M. "The Arming of an Archetype: Heroic Virtue and the Conventions of Literary Epic." In *Concepts of the Hero in the Middle Ages and the Renaissance,* ed. Norman T. Burns and Christopher J. Reagan. Papers of the Fourth and Fifth Annual Conferences of the Center for Medieval and Early Renaissance Studies. Albany: State University of New York Press, 1975.

STEELE, OLIVER LEE, JR. "The Rhetorical Functions of the Narrator in *The Faerie Queene.*" Ph.D. diss., University of Virginia, 1965.

STONE, DONALD, JR. "C. S. Lewis and Lorris' Lady." *Romance Notes* 6 (1965):196–99.

STROHM, PAUL. "Guillaume as Narrator and Lover in the *Roman de la Rose.*" *Romanic Review* 59 (1968):3–9.

SUTHERLAND, JAMES. *English Literature of the Late Seventeenth Century.* Oxford: Clarendon Press, 1969.

TALON, HENRI. *John Bunyan: The Man and His Works.* Trans. Barbara Wall. Cambridge: Harvard University Press, 1951.

——. "Space and the Hero in *The Pilgrim's Progress:* A Study of the Meaning of the Allegorical Universe." *Etudes anglaises* 14 (1961):124–30.

TANNER, TONY. Introduction to Charlotte Brontë, *Villette,* ed. Mark Lilly. New York: Penguin, 1979.

TATE, J. "On the History of Allegorism." *Classical Quarterly* 28 (1934):105–14.

THOMPSON, DAVID. "Figure and Allegory in the *Commedia.*" *Dante Studies* 90 (1972):1–11.

THOMPSON, ELBERT N. S. "The English Moral Plays." *Transactions of the Connecticut Academy of Arts and Sciences* 14 (1910):293–414.

TINDALL, WILLIAM YORK. *The Literary Symbol.* New York: Columbia University Press, 1955.

TODOROV, TZVETAN. *The Poetics of Prose.* Trans. Richard Howard. Ithaca: Cornell University Press, 1977.

TONKIN, HUMPHREY. "Some Notes on Myth and Allegory in the *Faerie Queene.*" *MP* 70 (1972–73):291–301.

TUVE, ROSEMOND. *Allegorical Imagery: Some Mediaeval Books and Their Posterity.* Princeton: Princeton University Press, 1966.

WARREN, MICHAEL J. "*Everyman:* Knowledge Once More." *Dalhousie Review* 54 (1974):136–46.

WASSON, JOHN. "Interpolation in the Text of *Everyman.*" *Theatre Notebook* 27 (1972):14–20.

WEBSTER, JOHN C. "The Allegory of Contradiction in *Everyman* and *The Faerie Queene*." In *Spenser and the Middle Ages (1976)*, ed. David A. Richardson. Cleveland: Cleveland State University Press, 1976. Microfiche.

WEIDHORN, MANFRED. *Dreams in Seventeenth-Century Literature*. Studies in English Literature 57. The Hague: Mouton, 1970.

WETHERBEE, WINTHROP. *Platonism and Poetry in the Twelfth Century: The Literary Influence of the School of Chartres*. Princeton: Princeton University Press, 1972.

WHEELWRIGHT, PHILIP. *The Burning Fountain: A Study in the Language of Symbolism*. Bloomington: Indiana University Press, 1954.

WICKHAM, GLYNNE. *Shakespeare's Dramatic Heritage: Collected Studies in Mediaeval, Tudor, and Shakespearean Drama*. New York: Barnes & Noble, 1969.

WILLEY, BASIL. *The Seventeenth Century Background: Studies in the Thought of the Age in Relation to Poetry and Religion*. 1934. Reprint. Garden City, N.Y.: Doubleday Anchor Books, 1953.

WILLIAMS, ARNOLD. *The Drama of Medieval England*. East Lansing: Michigan State University Press, 1961.

——. "The English Moral Play before 1500." *Annuale Mediaevale* 4 (1963):5–22.

WILLIAMS, CHARLES. *The Figure of Beatrice: A Study in Dante*. London: Faber & Faber, 1943.

WILLIAMS, KATHLEEN. *Spenser's World of Glass: A Reading of "The Faerie Queene."* Berkeley: University of California Press, 1966.

WILSON, THOMAS. *The Arte of Rhetorique*. 1553. Reprint. Gainesville, Fla.: Scholars' Facsimiles and Reprints, 1962.

WINTERS, YVOR. *The Function of Criticism: Problems and Exercises*. Denver: Alan Swallow, 1957.

——. "Maule's Curse, or Hawthorne and the Problem of Allegory." In *Maule's Curse: Seven Studies in the History of American Obscurantism*. Norfolk, Conn.: New Directions, 1938.

Wisdom. In *Medieval Drama*, ed. David M. Bevington. Boston: Houghton Mifflin, 1975.

WOOD, ROBERT E. "Britomart at the House of Busyrane." *South Atlantic Bulletin* 43 (May 1978):5–11.

WORDSWORTH, WILLIAM. Preface to the 1814 edition of *The Recluse*. In *The Poetical Works of William Wordsworth*, ed. Ernest de Selincourt and Helen Darbishire, vol. 5. Oxford: Clarendon Press, 1949.

YEATS, WILLIAM BUTLER. *Essays and Introductions*. London: Macmillan, 1961.

ZUMTHOR, PAUL. "Narrative and Anti-Narrative: *Le Roman de la Rose*." Trans. Frank Yeomans. *Yale French Studies* 51 (1974):185–204.

Index

Library of Congress Cataloging in Publication Data

Van Dyke, Carolynn, 1947–
    The fiction of truth.

    Bibliography: p.
    Includes index.
    1. Allegory. I. Title.
PN56.A5V3 1985   809′.915   84-15607
ISBN–0–8014–1760–0 (alk. paper)